Contemporary Canadian Marketing Cases

FIFTH EDITION

H. F. (Herb) MacKenzie

Goodman School of Business
Brock University

Toronto

Library and Archives Canada Cataloguing in Publication

Contemporary Canadian marketing cases/[compiled by] H.F. (Herb) MacKenzie.—Fifth edition
Includes bibliographical references and index. ISBN 978-0-13-282790-4 (pbk.)
   1. Marketing—Canada—Case studies.   2. Marketing—Canada—Textbooks. I. MacKenzie,
H. F., editor of compilation
HF5415.12.C3C65 2013   658.800971   C2013-902124-8

Vice-President, Editorial Director: Gary Bennett
 Managing Editor: Claudine O'Donnell
Acquisitions Editor: Deana Sigut
Senior Marketing Manager: Leigh-Anne Graham
Team Leader, Development: Madhu Ranadive
Developmental Editor: Louise MacKenzie
Lead Project Manager: Susan Johnson
Production Editor: Niraj Bhatt/Aptara®, Inc.
Copy Editor: Karen Alliston
Proofreader: Cat Haggert
Compositor: Aptara®, Inc.
Art Director: Zena Denchik
Cover Designer: Anthony Leung
Cover Image: ShutterStock

If you purchased this book outside the United States or Canada, you should be aware that it has
been imported without the approval of the publisher or the author.

10 9 8 7 6 5 4 3 2 1 [WC]

Contents

Preface   x
Introduction for Students   xiv

Case 1:   **Cott Corporation   1**
H. F. (Herb) MacKenzie

Cott Corporation manufactures branded products for many types of customers in many markets. Students should consider what factors the company must take into account when operating in international markets, and what changes in the marketing mix may be required.

Case 2:   **Marketing Metrics   3**
H. F. (Herb) MacKenzie and Massine Bouzerar

A number of exercises are included that give students the opportunity to practise sales, markup, and breakeven analyses, and analyses related to elements of the marketing mix.

Case 3:   **Prairie Home Appliance Service   10**
Eric Dolansky

Customer service complaints are increasing, and the director of customer service must find the root of the problem and develop a strategy to create effective change.

Case 4:   **Green Village Grocer   15**
H. F. (Herb) MacKenzie

A dissatisfied customer has written a letter to the president of Green Village Grocer following a series of service failures at one of its store locations.

Case 5:   **The Writers at Woody Point Festival   18**
Jose Lam

A not-for-profit organization in a small community must develop a marketing plan for an annual festival that is important to its economic sustainability.

Case 6:   **Centre for the Arts   28**
H. F. (Herb) MacKenzie

The Centre for the Arts' managing director is worried that, with only two days to go before the first theatrical performance of the season, ticket sales are disappointingly low. She's wondering how to increase sales in the short term, but also what to do in the long term.

Case 7: **Ethical Issues in Marketing Management 37**
Massine Bouzerar and H. F. (Herb) MacKenzie

A number of ethical dilemmas in marketing management are presented here, with each dilemma requiring analysis and action.

Case 8: **Massine Bouzerar's First Car 43**
Massine Bouzerar and H. F. (Herb) MacKenzie

A university student embarks on his first major consumer purchase, a car. After considering several alternatives, he must make a choice.

Case 9: **Continue, Modify, or Abandon: The Marketing Research Project 48**
Donna Stapleton and Colleen Sharen

A commercial research firm has just conducted survey research on behalf of a church organization. Given some issues experienced in the design and collection of data, the manager must decide whether to continue with the analysis, notify the client of his data concerns, abandon the project, conduct additional research, or start all over.

Case 10: **Riverside Credit Union 58**
Jeff Schulz and Peggy Cunningham

The credit union's vice-president of marketing has led an initiative to segment the membership base. He now must consider new marketing strategies to better target appropriate financial products to members so that company profitability will improve.

Case 11: **Fork and Dagger 63**
Massine Bouzerar and H. F. (Herb) MacKenzie

The owner of a small pub is considering turning over the business to his two sons, who have very different ideas about how to improve revenue. The owner has asked each son to present him with a plan so that he can make the final decision before his retirement.

Case 12: **Academic-Zone 70**
Massine Bouzerar and H. F. (Herb) MacKenzie

A university has developed an in-house learning resource and wishes to commercialize it. A co-op student has been hired to prepare a marketing plan, complicated by the fact that the product strategy is still evolving.

Case 13:   **"Greener Pastures": The Launch**
of StaGreen by HydroCan 79
Anne T. Hale

HydroCan, a new venture with a potentially profitable product called
StaGreen, has hired a consulting firm to develop a comprehensive marketing
strategy for StaGreen's launch.

Case 14:   **Dillon Controls Ltd. 86**
James E. Nelson and Mark S. Johnson

Dillon Controls, a Canadian manufacturer of high-tech equipment for the
monitoring and control of pressurized water flows, has commissioned
some market research on the U.S. market, and Jac Dillon is now deciding
whether to expand operations in that market.

Case 15:   **Barry Davis: Back on Board? 93**
Barb Gardner

Barry Davis is considering whether to continue with his accounting studies
or to resurrect his dream of owning and operating his skateboard business.
There are many other decisions that must be made if he is to revive his
business.

Case 16:   **Tools n' Rules 99**
H. F. (Herb) MacKenzie

An entrepreneur has developed a superior measuring device for bricklayers.
After bringing it to market, he's faced with a number of opportunities to
consider, and he's wondering whether and how he might change his
marketing strategy.

Case 17:   **Heat-eze 106**
William A. Preshing and Denise Walters

A successful Canadian entrepreneur has purchased the rights to an
innovative new product that might be sold in consumer or institutional
markets. A marketing plan is needed that focuses on one or both markets.

Case 18:   **MetroPaint 113**
Monique Finley, Cosimo Girolamo, Allison Carryer,
and H. F. (Herb) MacKenzie

Mary Anderson has just joined MetroPaint, a business venture that wants
to franchise its operations. She's under pressure to recommend a structure
for franchisee payments to her two co-managers, who have very different
views about how fees and royalties should be determined.

Case 19: **Harrison Measurement Devices Ltd. 123**
Philip Rosson

A U.K. distributor that represents a Canadian manufacturer of precision instruments is questioning the relationship between the two companies—specifically, what appears to be a growing indifference to the distributor's needs. The owner must decide which course of action he should take.

Case 20: **Kingston Frontenacs 127**
H. F. (Herb) MacKenzie

The director of marketing and communications for a junior hockey team must make recommendations on how to increase revenue, particularly from ticket sales. While increasing short-term revenue is important, he must also consider long-term fan support.

Case 21: **SPARK Marketing: Responding to Market Opportunities and an Industry Shakeup 134**
Susan Myrden and Donna Stapleton

One of the co-founders of a small, full-service advertising agency must decide on a growth strategy, precipitated in part by the exit of one of its major competitors in the communications industry. The question is whether he should expand online capabilities, focus on new market segments, or attempt to win clients from competitors.

Case 22: **The Road to the Beaches 142**
Megan Denty and Donna Stapleton

With the peak season for tourism already in full gear, a tourism association's newly appointed marketing coordinator is faced with limited resources and pressure to decide on a marketing plan.

Case 23: **Wilderness Newfoundland Adventures 157**
Cori-Jane Radford and H. F. (Herb) MacKenzie

Stan Cook, Jr., who is reviewing the previous year's promotional expenditures for his family's ecotourism business, needs to decide on the budget for the current year, and how it should be allocated.

Case 24: **Wilson's Family Restaurant 172**
Massine Bouzerar and H. F. (Herb) MacKenzie

The owner of a small, family-owned restaurant is faced with impending competition from a major restaurant chain. He must decide how he can best mitigate the impact this new competitor will have on his business.

Case 25:   ECCO Shoes   178
Sherry Finney and Kyle Gillis

The company has just established new communication objectives, and the project manager of interactive marketing must help develop the most effective online strategy to reach the company's target audience.

Case 26:   Tyndale Treasures Community Store   185
Dave McKenzie and Christopher A. Ross

A small used-goods store is facing strong competition, and is considering how it can increase sales at its location so that it can make a better financial contribution to the not-for-profit organization that owns it. It's constrained by a lack of resources, and needs to consider its obligation to serve the underprivileged population in its surrounding community.

Case 27:   The Medicine Chest   199
Tashia Batstone and Donna Stapleton

The owner of a small pharmacy is considering purchasing a computerized prescription ordering process and packaging system. While this would improve the pharmacy's efficiency and customer service, there are cost implications, and so the owner must decide whether to charge for the service, and if so, how much.

Case 28:   Scheff Rotary Cutting Tools   207
H. F. (Herb) MacKenzie

The president of a cutting tool distributor has just been informed that one of his salespeople has resigned. The president is wondering whether he should make a tactical decision and replace the salesperson, or if this is the time to make a more strategic channel decision.

Case 29:   Homes of Distinction   213
Massine Bouzerar and H. F. (Herb) MacKenzie

The new chair of the organizing committee for an annual home tour fundraiser has been assigned the task of increasing revenue from the upcoming event. She has several ideas, but is unsure which of these are viable and which she must implement.

Case 30:   Trinity University: The Annual Fund Campaign   221
H. F. (Herb) MacKenzie and Mariya Yurukova

The manager of a university's annual fundraising campaign has been asked to review who the campaign has been targeting, and whether there are better communications channels for reaching potential donors. With limited resources, there is also an increased need to grow donations.

Case 31: Canadian Defence Production Ltd. 229
H. F. (Herb) MacKenzie

A salesperson has been asked to accept a new order at the previous year's price. He must consider the previous price, the customer's wishes, and a change to the cost of the product since the previous sale. Ethics is also a factor.

Case 32: Seeing Clearly: Lucentis and Avastin 231
Eric Dolansky

An anesthesiologist is considering alternative treatments for his mother's condition. Two very similar drugs are available at very different prices. Only one is approved in Canada to treat her condition, but a recent U.S. report concluded that both drugs were equally effective for treating the condition.

Case 33: Bridge View Custom Cabinets 238
Michael Madore

The co-owner of a small cabinet manufacturer, concerned about his company's slow growth, has approached a marketing consultant for advice about whether there might be more opportunities to pursue.

Case 34: Caribou Mathematics Competition 245
Massine Bouzerar and H. F. (Herb) MacKenzie

A mathematics professor has developed a mathematics contest for elementary students. His main sponsor has withdrawn its support, just when he was considering expanding his contest to include students in high school. He must consider how to raise money, particularly if he decides to expand his competition.

Case 35: Bovine Booties 253
H. F. (Herb) MacKenzie

The owner of a successful boot-import venture is discussing opportunities with a friend when they focus on a business case they studied during their undergraduate program. Wondering whether the failed product might have been a success if a different marketing strategy had been used, they agree to give it some consideration before deciding whether they should proceed with a similar product.

Case 36: Enviro-Plumber 259
Carman Cullen

An entrepreneur has the North American distribution rights for what he calls "the best product in the world." He has approached a small business consulting group for recommendations on a marketing strategy.

Case 37:   Page Two   263

H. F. (Herb) MacKenzie

The owner of a used-book business has an opportunity to change locations. While considering this decision, he recognizes that he needs to make several other decisions relating to promotion, distribution, pricing, and product mix.

Case 38:   W. H. Plastics Inc.   270

Christopher A. Ross

A successful, family-owned business that manufactures plastic parts and products is faced with a number of challenges: the rising value of the Canadian dollar, potential competition from China, and a dependence on one customer that accounts for most of its revenue. The owner must develop a plan of action for the future.

Case 39:   Spriware Canada Inc.   284

Mark Parker

The CEO of an appliance manufacturer is considering two strategic options for his company: cutting prices to drive an increase in market share (a market penetration strategy) or entering a new international market where there appears to be considerable potential (a market development strategy).

Case 40:   Petridis Vineyard: To Wine or Not to Wine   288

Mark Parker

An entrepreneur is considering how to get involved in the wine industry: whether to be a grape grower or a wine producer through outsourcing his production, and if the latter, whether he should enter the Chinese market and what marketing strategy he should implement.

Case 41:   The Investment Proposal   292

Kenneth Harling

A Canadian venture capitalist has just listened to a presentation on an opportunity to invest in a service-related business in India, and is now in a position to ask questions of the presenters prior to giving them a decision.

Preface

Contemporary Canadian Marketing Cases, Fifth Edition, is a collection of 41 marketing cases by some of Canada's best case writers. I believe that the selection continues to grow stronger, and I hope you'll agree that it offers the flexibility to personalize a course that will provide enjoyment and learning for you and your students.

Two considerations helped focus my case selection. First, I believe that cases should act as a basis for building rapport among everyone involved in the learning environment; they should be fun and interesting for students and instructors alike. And so this collection addresses current marketing issues in the context of a variety of Canadian industries— there are cases that involve both business and consumer markets; for-profit and not-for-profit businesses; services marketing; sports, tourism, and the arts; entrepreneurship and franchising; online and social-network marketing; service failure and recovery; and international marketing.

Second, I believe that the best cases offer a rich environment for student learning. You'll find lots of suggestions in the Teaching Notes to help you decide on particular strategies. And since feedback from some instructors suggested that more cases engendering creative thinking would be welcome, I've provided many. Review the large number of cases that have strategy planning and implementation as a focus—a number of these are excellent for classroom instruction, for examinations, or for hand-in assignments. Finally, you'll find numerous cases in the fifth edition that allow for increased flexibility in teaching and learning. (The last case, for example, involves playing the role of venture capitalist. Is there a budding "dragon" in your class?)

Exhibit 1 lists the 41 cases in this edition. While many have breadth well beyond what's shown in this table, I've indicated the bases on which I chose them.

—H. F. (Herb) MacKenzie
Goodman School of Business
Brock University, St. Catharines, Ontario

EXHIBIT 1	Primary (P) and Secondary (S) Focus of Cases											
		Introduction to Marketing	Marketing Environment	Strategy Planning and Implementation	Customer Buying Behaviour	Marketing Research and Sales Forecasting	Segmentation, Targeting, and Positioning	Product and Services Marketing	Retailers, Wholesalers, and Channels	Advertising, Selling, and Communications	Pricing Strategy	Ethics, Social Responsibility, and Not-for-Profit	International and Global Marketing
1	Cott Corporation	P											S
2	Marketing Metrics	P											
3	Prairie Home Appliance Service			P	S			S					
4	Green Village Grocer			P	S			S	S				
5	The Writers at Woody Point Festival			P								S	
6	Centre for the Arts			P				S		S	S		
7	Ethical Issues in Marketing Management											P	
8	Massine Bouzerar's First Car				P								
9	The Marketing Research Project					P							
10	Riverside Credit Union							P	S				
11	Fork and Dagger			P				S	S	S			
12	Academic-Zone			P				S	S		S	S	
13	The Launch of StaGreen by HydroCan			S	S			P	S	S			
14	Dillon Controls Ltd.				P	S	S	S					S
15	Barry Davis: Back on Board?		S	S				S	P				
16	Tools n' Rules			S				P	S	S	S		
17	Heat-eze			S	S	S	S	P	S				
18	MetroPaint								P		S		
19	Harrison Measurement Devices Ltd.							S	P				S
20	Kingston Frontenacs			P				S	S		S	S	

EXHIBIT 1	Primary (P) and Secondary (S) Focus of Cases (continued)											
		Introduction to Marketing	Marketing Environment	Strategy Planning and Implementation	Customer Buying Behaviour	Marketing Research and Sales Forecasting	Segmentation, Targeting, and Positioning	Product and Services Marketing	Retailers, Wholesalers, and Channels	Advertising, Selling, and Communications	Pricing Strategy	Ethics, Social Responsibility, and Not-for-Profit	International and Global Marketing
21	SPARK Marketing			P				S		S			
22	The Road to the Beaches			P				S		S		S	
23	Wilderness Newfoundland Adventures						P			S			S
24	Wilson's Family Restaurant			P				S	S	S	S		
25	ECCO Shoes							S		P			
26	Tyndale Treasures Community Store		S	S								P	
27	The Medicine Chest			S			S	P		S			
28	Scheff Rotary Cutting Tools			S					S	P			
29	Homes of Distinction			P								S	
30	Trinity University: The Annual Fund Campaign			S			S			P		S	
31	Canadian Defence Production Ltd.										S	P	
32	Seeing Clearly: Lucentis and Avastin		S									P	
33	Bridge View Custom Cabinets			P				S	S	S	S		
34	Caribou Mathematics Competition			S				P		S	S	S	
35	Bovine Booties			P				S	S	S	S		
36	Enviro-Plumber			P	S			S	S	S	S		
37	Page Two			P				S	S	S	S		
38	W. H. Plastics Inc.			P	S					P			
39	Spriware Canada Inc.			S							S		P
40	Petridis Vineyard			S			S	S		S	S		P
41	The Investment Proposal		S	P									S

Supplements

Teaching Notes (ISBN 978-0-13-341921-4)

The Teaching Notes include valuable and detailed information about each case. Each set of notes includes a synopsis with clear teaching objectives, suggested teaching strategies, questions for discussion, and an analysis with comprehensive answers. The Instructor's Manual is available for downloading from a password-protected section of Pearson Education Canada's online catalogue (www.pearsoned.ca/highered). Navigate to your book's catalogue page to view a list of available supplements. See your local sales representative for details and access.

CourseSmart for Instructors (ISBN 978-0-13-283949-5)

CourseSmart goes beyond traditional expectations—providing instant online access to the textbooks and course materials you need at a lower cost for students. And even as students save money, you can save time and hassle with a digital eTextbook that allows you to search for the most relevant content at the very moment you need it. Whether it's evaluating textbooks or creating lecture notes to help students with difficult concepts, Course-Smart can make life a little easier. See how when you visit www.coursesmart.com /instructors.

Pearson Custom Library

You can create your own textbook by choosing the chapters that best suit your own course needs. To begin building your custom text, visit www.pearsoncustomlibrary.com. You may also work with a dedicated Pearson Custom editor to create your ideal text—publishing your own original content or mixing and matching Pearson content. Contact your local Pearson Representative to get started.

Introduction for Students

LEARNING FROM CASES

One of the most valuable experiences for marketing students is the opportunity to participate in marketing case analyses and discussions. However, if you are to benefit most from this experience, it's important to be an active rather than passive participant. Many students, particularly if their educational experiences have been focused on readings and lectures, find it difficult to do case analyses, and even more difficult to express themselves in case discussions. This is unfortunate because case analyses and discussions can add a whole new dimension to your marketing education and to your personal growth.

While lectures may be the most efficient method of transferring knowledge, case analyses and discussions foster learning through the development of independent thought and creativity, interpersonal communication, and decision-making skills. The focus changes from simple content to both content and process. This means that students must share responsibility for their learning while instructors must be confident in sharing power in the classroom, encouraging student views and participation. Such collaboration provides a positive learning environment for everyone. Learning from case analyses and discussions, then, should begin with the initial reading of the case and individual case preparation, and continue through small and large group discussions.

INDIVIDUAL CASE PREPARATION

Cases vary in scope. Some are comprehensive cases that require a complete analysis, including consideration of the marketing environment; buyer behaviour; segmentation, targeting, and positioning strategies; and product, price, promotion, and distribution strategies. Other cases are more narrowly focused. So you should begin by quickly reading through a case, paying particular attention to the opening and closing sections to gain some idea of what the case involves and what decisions you're required to make.

Then you should read the case more carefully. This is when you should underline important facts and make notes in the margins concerning your thoughts as you proceed through the case. Some careful thought after this reading will help you decide how to proceed: what decisions you must make, what numerical analysis is important, what alternatives may be appropriate, and what qualitative facts you must consider before making action-related recommendations. A word of caution here: avoid focusing on one alternative too early. That will constrain your analysis. In most situations there are several good alternatives, and effective managers recognize that different courses of action may enable an organization to meet its objectives.

Once you've completed your analysis, it's time to think about action—what you will do. It's sometimes easy to argue that more information is needed before you should act, but the reality is that managers are often required to make decisions with incomplete or imperfect information. You may need to make some assumptions, and you should test the robustness of those assumptions. For example, your success may depend very much on competitive reaction to your market strategy. You may need to assume that a competitor's response will be to reduce its price by 10%. What effect will this have on the success of your strategy? What if the competitor reduces its price by 15%, or even 20%? How would this affect your performance? Would these price reductions require additional changes to your marketing strategy?

A final recommendation when doing individual case preparation is to stay within the context of the case. While you may have information relating to events subsequent to the writing of the case, try to ignore this information when doing your analysis and deciding on your recommendations. Cases are written concerning problems and issues at a particular point in time, and the situations that the decision maker faced at that time. You should analyze the case with the same information that the decision maker had, since this is the information that would have determined his or her actions. After the case discussion, or at a point where the instructor requests, you may wish to contribute additional knowledge.

While you can do too little analysis on a case, you can also do too much. You need to consider what you're expected to do with your case analysis. If you are to make a formal class presentation or hand in a written analysis and action plan, more time and effort will be required than if you're preparing for a large group discussion. For most cases, you should spend two to four hours doing your individual analysis. Cases can, if you're not careful, take all the time you allow them. Beyond some point, however, there's a diminishing return from working alone on a case. You need to consider participating in a small group discussion.

SMALL GROUP DISCUSSIONS

In some classes, you may be assigned to a small discussion group or you may wish to consider forming your own group. Discussing your analysis and recommendations among a small group of peers allows you to refine and test your thinking. It provides additional learning opportunities for all participants. Many students feel more comfortable presenting and defending their recommendations, and the assumptions they've used, in this environment. To be effective, groups should consist of approximately four to six members committed to doing individual case analyses before the meetings and making contributions during the meetings. The duration of these small group discussions may vary depending on the case, but you should expect to spend 20 to 30 minutes for each meeting.

LARGE GROUP DISCUSSIONS

In an effective case course, the most significant learning takes place in large group discussions. Even if your instructor has organized the course around formal group presentations, there's usually time for questions and discussions after each presentation.

To get the most from large group discussions, you should be committed to active participation. You must be able to listen to what others are saying and to follow where the discussion is going. That means you should limit, or eliminate, note taking. After all, it's difficult to listen to what others are saying if you're focused on taking notes. That's a strategy you use when someone is transferring knowledge to you; for example, during a lecture. During large group discussions, by contrast, you should be learning from the process, not focusing simply on the content. It's important to listen in order to understand what's happening if you wish to make an appropriate contribution. At the end of an effective case discussion, you should be able to review what has happened and to summarize what you've learned from the experience.

Participation is essential when working with case analyses. Some students find this process exciting and challenging, while others are intimidated and fear speaking in a large group of their peers. Small group discussions prior to class often help. Another consideration is your seating position in class. Some students gravitate to the back of the class, as they find this seating position less threatening. You may wish to consider moving forward. Many students find it easier to participate from the front row. From that position the size of the classroom seems smaller, and the interaction with the instructor seems more personal.

Also, participation becomes easier with practice. Like most worthwhile skills, if you don't practise, you won't improve. By partaking early on in the dialogue, it's often easier to continue making contributions as the case continues. For students who are less confident during discussions, another good opportunity to participate is when the direction of the discussion changes. As your confidence increases, you can increase your involvement in large group discussions.

MARKETING STRATEGY

When developing marketing strategies, managers must consider both internal and external factors that may affect marketing decisions. A marketing strategy is a plan of action focused on developing, pricing, promoting, and distributing need-satisfying goods and services to target customers. The development of a marketing strategy requires the consideration of many aspects, so it often helps to have an outline to guide your thinking. Organized around internal and external analysis and action, Exhibit 2 provides a framework of factors to consider during this development.

EXHIBIT 2	A Framework for Case Analysis and Action
Internal Analysis:	
Objectives	Strengths/Weaknesses
Sales growth	Marketing and sales
Market share	(people and knowledge)
Increased profit	Other personnel
Product development	Financial condition
Innovation	Costs and revenues
Quality (products and service)	Marketing information systems
Reputation and image	Production capacity
Employee satisfaction	Distribution channels
	Reputation and image
	Quality (products and service)

EXHIBIT 2	A Framework for Case Analysis and Action (continued)

External Analysis:

Customers	Competitors
Size and growth	Relative size or market share
Segments (sizable, measurable, accessible, responsive)	Market leaders or followers
Purchase criteria (quality, price, service, etc.)	Strengths and weaknesses
Roles (initiator, user, influencer, decider, buyer, gatekeeper)	Reaction profile (aggressive or passive)
Relationship needs (transactional, or long-term orientation)	
Buying conditions (limited or extended problem solving; new task buy, straight rebuy, or modified rebuy)	
Search (extent and type)	

Opportunities/Threats	Distribution Channels/Suppliers
Competition	Relationships (power, dependence, interdependence, cooperation)
Buyer needs (unmet, changing)	Availability, development, capacity
Channels (availability, development capacity)	Technological capabilities
Resources (human, financial, material)	Financial condition
Technology	Cost
Market (size, growth, share)	
Economic conditions	
Political and legal changes	

Action:

Product	Price
Quality (higher, competitive, lower)	Level (premium, competitive, low)
Service (superior, competitive, inferior)	Discounts (cumulative, noncumulative, trade, cash, seasonal)
Branding (generic, family vs. independent, manufacturer vs. distributor)	
Warranty or guarantee	
Line (depth and breadth)	
Packaging	

Promotion	Distribution
Objectives (inform, persuade, remind)	Intensity (intensive, selective, exclusive)
Budget	Motivation (margin, support)
Mix (advertising, personal selling, sales promotion, publicity)	
Push vs. pull (or both)	

As you can see from this exhibit, there are many things to consider at the analysis stage, and many more to consider before deciding a course of action. A framework helps reduce confusion by providing a basis for beginning your analysis and for deciding action. Hopefully you'll find this framework useful, and the case process enjoyable and rewarding.

Cott Corporation

H. F. (Herb) MacKenzie

Cott Corporation is the world's largest supplier of retailer-branded, carbonated soft drinks, producing and distributing products to mass-merchandise, grocery, drugstore, and convenience-store chains from its 15 beverage manufacturing facilities in Canada, the United States, and the United Kingdom. For example, Cott produces private-label brands for Walmart in the United States, and President's Choice drinks for Loblaw Companies Limited in Canada.

Cott began operations in Quebec in 1952, importing carbonated beverages from the United States. Eventually the company started producing its own product in Canada. Expansion followed to Ontario, western Canada, and the Atlantic provinces, and to both the United States and Europe. Cott has differentiated itself through innovation and by producing quality products, providing superior service, and achieving cost efficiency. Cott's growth can be largely attributed to these factors and to its strategic retail branding and category management expertise, which it customizes to meet the specific needs of each retail customer.

Because Cott manufactures branded products for its customers, its products compete with manufacturer, or national, brands for shelf space and for sales in retail stores where they're sold. Its largest competitor is the U.S.-based Coca-Cola Company, the global soft-drink industry leader. Coca-Cola has approximately 21% market share of the non-alcoholic, ready-to-drink beverage market in both Canada and the United States. However, the company and its subsidiaries sell products in nearly 200 countries around the world, with approximately 70% of volume and 80% of profit coming from these global markets. And when Cott-produced products compete with Coca-Cola products outside Canada and the United States, special issues may arise owing to differences in the market environment.

In Britain, for example, the largest supermarket chain, J. Sainsbury PLC, contracted with Cott Corporation for the supply of a retailer-branded cola. At the time Coca-Cola had a 60% share of the £670-million cola market. The Sainsbury cola was packaged in red and white cans, as was Coca-Cola. Where "Coca-Cola" was written vertically down the can, Sainsbury had "Cola" written in a similar but slightly more silvery red script. The Sainsbury brand also had the word "Classic" on the can, along with "Original American Taste." Sainsbury stocked the competing products side by side, but priced its private-label brand 25% lower than the "real thing." While Coca-Cola might have sued, it's questionable whether it could have won. The cola giant would have had an easier time almost anywhere else in Europe, where many countries have a general concept of unfair competition—a concept missing from British law, which focuses on a narrow definition of trademark.

Japan has one of the world's most competitive soft-drink markets. Approximately 500 manufacturers offer more than 7000 different soft drinks, and introduce about 1000 new ones annually. Cott Corporation doesn't yet operate there; however, Coca-Cola Japan manages more than 25 brands and 60 flavours. The company and its Japanese partners maintain 930 000 vending machines, as this method of distribution accounts for more than 50% of all soft-drink sales there. In some years Japan has provided as much as 20% of the company's global profit. However, the company's most popular product in Japan isn't its flagship brand, but a milky sweet drink called Georgia Coffee.

In the future, if Cott wishes to continue its strong growth trend, it may wish to consider entry into Japan or some other Asian market.

Marketing Metrics

*H. F. (Herb) MacKenzie and
Massine Bouzerar*

Fundamental to any marketing analysis is an analysis of the financial and economic data relevant to each situation. You must understand what the numbers are telling you: where you are. This, along with more qualitative considerations, will suggest various courses of action. You must then be able to assess the effect of implementing these actions on financial performance: where you will be.

The following exercises provide the opportunity to practise market share, sales, markup and markdown, and breakeven analyses, along with analyses related to advertising, salesperson, and channel strategy effectiveness as well as product line performance.

A. MARKET SHARE

1. Five computer retailers in Vancouver and five in Halifax were surveyed to estimate the number of computers sold per quarter, as well as total sales dollars. Analyze the information below to estimate the market share of the five computer brands. What insights can you suggest from your analysis?

| | Vancouver | | | | Halifax | | | |
| | Laptops | | Desktops | | Laptops | | Desktops | |
	Units	Dollars	Units	Dollars	Units	Dollars	Units	Dollars
Dell	3194	$1 277 600	1788	$625 800	3664	$1 465 600	3174	$1 110 900
HP	2435	$1 339 250	2304	$1 152 000	2774	$1 525 700	3458	$1 729 000
Apple	1978	$1 780 200	3147	$2 674 950	2994	$2 694 600	2605	$2 214 250
LG	3954	$2 372 400	3994	$2 196 700	1983	$1 189 800	1997	$1 098 350
Lenovo	4568	$2 055 600	2709	$1 083 600	2380	$1 071 000	1699	$679 600

B. SALES ANALYSIS

Canada Controllers Inc. manufactured electric motor starters and motor control centres used in all types of industrial plants, including mines, pulp mills, and manufacturing plants. Motor starters were installed on or near individual pieces of equipment and usually operated only a single motor. They ranged in price from $50 to several thousand dollars. Motor control centres consisted of dozens or even hundreds of motor starters that were combined in a customized enclosure and were capable of starting motors in various areas of the plant from a centralized location. They ranged in price from less than $50 000 to several hundred thousand dollars.

Analyze the following sales data for Canada Controllers Inc.

Year	Company Sales	Industry Sales
1998	$10 250 970	$74 600 000
1999	$11 844 888	$92 300 000
2000	$13 384 152	$111 700 000
2001	$14 722 155	$133 500 000
2002	$16 040 063	$158 900 000

Analyze the following sales data for 2002.

Product Line	Company Forecast	Company Sales	Industry Sales
Control centres	$2 500 000	$3 233 727	$20 250 000
Motor starters	$11 500 000	$10 406 040	$122 400 000
Repair parts	$2 000 000	$2 400 296	$16 250 000
Total	$16 000 000	$16 040 063	$158 900 000

Analyze changes in the following sales data from 2001 to 2002.

Product Line	2001		2002	
	Sales (units)	Sales ($)	Sales (units)	Sales ($)
Control centres	28	$1 766 740	38	$ 3 233 727
Motor starters	16 775	$11 041 600	18 305	$10 406 040
Repair parts	*	$1 913 815	*	$ 2 400 296
Total		$14 722 155		$16 040 063

*Unit volume of repair parts not monitored.

C. MARKUP AND MARKDOWN ANALYSIS

1. Yvonne Belanger, owner of Yvonne's European Deli, has decided that she wants to add a new item to the current selection of baked goods she sells in her upscale deli. Currently, she sells cookies and brownies for $2 each, and muffins for $3 each. She makes a standard 30% margin on all sales. Yvonne wants to buy homemade apple, cherry, and lemon pies from a local supplier and sell them for $10 each.

    a. If she insists on making a 30% margin on sales, what's the highest price she can pay for these pies and still achieve her target profit margin?

    b. If she does make exactly 30% margin on sales, what markup on cost does this represent?

    c. If Yvonne wanted to have an introductory promotional sale at her deli, but still wanted to make a markup of 10% on cost, what would be her selling price?

    d. At this new selling price, what would be her margin on sales?

2. Stephen O'Connor has just graduated from a post-secondary institution in British Columbia and is about to move to Belleville, Ontario. To make some extra cash, Stephen has decided to bring along a truck full of canned tuna that he bought from a local B.C. cannery. He paid $0.50 per can, based on purchasing an entire truck-load of product. He now hopes to sell these cans of tuna through grocery wholesalers around the Toronto area. According to his old schoolmate Ted Phillips, wholesalers generally expect to make 15% markup on their cost, and retailers won't generally sell items like this unless they make 40% margin on their selling price. Stephen thinks he should make $0.35 profit on each can of tuna. What is Stephen's markup on his cost? What is Stephen's margin on his selling price? What price will the consumer have to pay in order for all channel members to achieve their desired markups/margins?

3. Fashion Forward operates three retail locations across Canada: in Halifax, Toronto, and Vancouver. It recently purchased a limited-edition collection of 300 designer dresses and sent 100 to each city. The dresses were all suggested to sell for $1200

each; all dresses had a net cost to Fashion Forward of $400. Sales results from the three locations varied:

	Halifax	Toronto	Vancouver
Price: $1200	50	72	90
Price: $1000	28	18	10
Price: $ 800	22	10	0
Total	100	100	100

a. What is the markdown percentage on this line at each location?

b. Why would management be interested in calculating markdown percentages?

c. What is Fashion Forward's markup on this line at each location?

d. What is Fashion Forward's margin on this line at each location?

D. BREAKEVEN ANALYSIS

1. Ontario Steel Manufacturing (OSM) manufactures steel components for other manufacturers. It has the opportunity to make stainless steel taps and faucets for a Canadian hardware company that will then package the products and sell them under its own brand name. The customer expects to pay $149.99, and the variable cost for manufacturing the taps and faucets is $130. The total fixed cost that OSM will allocate to this product is $56 900. OSM has an opportunity to purchase a more modern steel-moulding machine at a cost of $25 000. If it does, its variable cost will be reduced by $13 per unit. Do a breakeven analysis for each scenario. Which is the better choice if OSM can sell 2750 sets of taps and faucets?

2. Owing to greater consumer concern about sugar in prepared foods, a Canadian syrup manufacturer formulated a new product: Slim Maple Syrup. The product was basically regular maple syrup with less than half the sugar, but with added cinnamon and brown sugar flavouring. Focus groups indicated that the product would be very popular once people tried it. The manufacturer planned on selling the maple syrup in a 250-millilitre squeezable plastic bottle. Test marketing indicated that consumers would be willing to pay somewhere between $4.29 and $5.29 per bottle. Recognizing that it had to allow reasonable margins for wholesalers and retailers, the manufacturer finally decided on a suggested price to consumers of $4.89 per bottle and trade discounts of 20/15%, with the expectation that wholesalers would pass along the 20% to retailers and keep the 15% discount for themselves. The variable cost of producing Slim Maple Syrup was $2.96 per bottle, and it was packaged 24 bottles per case. Fixed costs that the manufacturer allocated for this product totalled $55 000.

a. What is the manufacturer's breakeven volume in cases?

b. What is the manufacturer's breakeven volume in dollars?

c. For wholesalers, what is the contribution margin as a percentage of cost?

d. For retailers, what is the contribution margin as a percentage of cost?

e. The brand assistant for this product suggested that the manufacturer might be better off lowering the price to $4.69. Her research indicated that at this price, sales volume would increase by 4%. However, the brand manager was adamant that $4.89 would be the suggested retail price. Do you agree with the brand assistant or the brand manager? Explain your reasoning by calculating the new breakeven volume for the manufacturer.

3. Luigi Rossi operates a small pizzeria just outside of Cambridge, Ontario. He sells his items mostly to dine-in customers and through delivery orders and catering for local events. Luigi reviewed his sales for 2012:

	Dine-In	Delivery	Catering
Sales	$487 908	$398 645	$569 394
Cost of goods	$188 589	$214 598	$259 698
Contribution	$299 319	$184 047	$309 696

Luigi's major problem is that his pizzeria has limited space. He has only 10 tables in his dining room, and his back kitchen is also very limited. Luigi now has an opportunity to rent the retail space next door to expand the dining room, as the current owner has left. This would increase his yearly rent by $67 000, and he estimates that he'd have to spend $45 000 in renovations to make the new area presentable.

How much additional business does Luigi need to make to cover his increased costs?

E. EVALUATING ADVERTISING EFFECTIVENESS

You are the advertising manager for a firm that manufactures piping products for the pulp-and-paper and petrochemical industries. You've been working with a national advertising firm to develop an advertisement. You've decided to place the ad in trade magazines targeted at purchasing agents in these industries, and also to send it out in a direct mailing targeted to a list of 500 purchasing professionals who work in these industries. To control advertising expenses, you will use exactly the same ad for both advertising campaigns. The results of the two campaigns follow:

- *Campaign A:* You have placed the ad in two trade magazines: *Pulp & Paper Canada* and *Canadian Oil & Chemical.* The cost to advertise in the first magazine was $4745 and to advertise in the second magazine was $4350. It was expected that the ad would be read by 700 purchasing agents in the target industries. The ad generated 206 inquiries, 105 of which were later qualified by telemarketing (an average of four calls per hour, and they were paid $16.50 per hour) as worthy of follow-up by a sales representative. The ad was believed responsible for 28 sales, averaging $63 344 with a 21.4% gross margin.

- *Campaign B:* A copy of the ad was mailed to 1000 purchasing professionals on a mailing list that had been purchased for $1100 from a mailing list supplier. Other costs included printing, $1285; cover letters and envelopes, $115; and postage, $990. The ad resulted in 310 inquiries, 164 of which were later qualified by telemarketing (an average of four calls per hour, and they were paid $16.50 per hour) as worthy of follow-up by a sales representative. The ad was believed responsible for 44 sales, averaging $41 445 with a 22.2% gross margin.

F. EVALUATING SALESPERSON EFFECTIVENESS

You are the sales manager for a large Canadian manufacturer of household and industrial tools, and you're evaluating the salespeople at the Calgary branch. Analyze the sales performance data below. What insights can you suggest from your analysis? What other information would you like to have?

Salesperson	Sales	Gross Margin %
Harry	$2 305 222	23.5
Syed	$2 678 903	24.4
Brenda	$1 980 092	25.8
Sam	$2 983 233	24.1
John	$1 687 454	26.4
Brewster	$3 219 117	26.0
Navpreet	$2 785 786	25.1
Connie	$3 091 001	24.8
Dan	$1 782 309	25.3
Stan	$3 504 600	23.3
Henry	$2 104 502	25.0
Victor	$1 877 782	26.3

What are some additional factors that can be considered when evaluating salespeople? Provide examples.

G. EVALUATING DISTRIBUTION CHANNELS

Upper Canada Clothing Company has been selling its industrial clothing across Canada for over 20 years. It has a four-member sales force, with three in Ontario and one in Quebec. Total sales by this sales force in 2012 were $3.9 million. Total industry sales for competing products in Ontario and Quebec were $15.8 million. The company also has nine manufacturer's agents, who are paid an 8% commission on sales. Their 2012 performance follows:

Territory	Number of Agents	Sales	Market Share
British Columbia	2	$886 458	17.5%
Alberta	2	$742 458	13.4%
Saskatchewan and Manitoba	2	$1 244 553	19.5%
Atlantic provinces	3	$937 887	26.3%
Total		$3 811 356	

The agents that sell your clothing sell between three and eight other non-competing product lines. One of the agents in British Columbia has recently complained about the commission she's being paid, and has informed you that your major competitor is paying its agents a 10% commission. You've decided that it's time to reassess your channel strategy. You're wondering whether you should continue with your current strategy or replace all manufacturer's agents with company salespeople. The direct selling costs (salaries and selling-related expenses) for each salesperson you hire would be $90 000. You'd need one salesperson for each territory. After an analysis of the situation, what would you recommend?

H. EVALUATING PRODUCT LINES

Select Floorings Inc. is a British Columbia–based home hardware manufacturing company that sells its products to retailers across Canada. With the company growing year after year, new products have been developed to replace obsolete ones. As the product manager for the hardwood flooring division, you've been asked to cut one of the current flooring selections, as a new hardwood type is being developed. Taking into account the profitability of each product in your product line, which hardwood type would you recommend that the chief marketing officer eliminate?

Product	Suggested Retail Price per Square Foot*	Projected 2013 Square Footage Sold	Estimated Average Growth Rate, 2014–2018
Maple & Birch	$4.79	44 000	9%
Bamboo	$3.29	28 000	7%
Pine, Hemlock, & Fir	$4.29	39 000	5%
Ash	$5.29	47 000	3%
Oak	$4.59	54 000	4%
Walnut & Cherry	$6.29	14 000	2%
Production overhead costs		$157 500	
Plant administrative expenses		$ 27 585	
Allocation of corporate overhead		$ 32 556	
Direct Variable Cost as a Percentage of Manufacturer's Selling Price			
Maple & Birch		50%	
Bamboo		60%	
Pine, Hemlock, & Fir		60%	
Ash		63%	
Oak		68%	
Walnut & Cherry		70%	

*All sales were through retailers who insisted on a markup of 50% on sales, and who expected shipments F.O.B. destination. The average cost of shipping hardwood was 1.25% of the retail price.

The company doesn't have a sales force, but sells through manufacturer's agents who receive a 7% commission on sales.

Prairie Home Appliance Service

Eric Dolansky

Becky Freeman, director of customer service at the Canadian central customer service centre for Prairie Home Appliance Service, was at a loss for what to do. Prairie Home Appliance Service had once been synonymous with reliability and excellent customer service, but now it seemed that all Becky dealt with were complaints. She looked over the customer file of the most recent thorn in her side, Roger Blahut. Mr. Blahut had called in numerous times and, as trained, her team of customer service representatives had made detailed notes about the problems he'd had with Prairie Home Appliance Service.

Becky had to wonder if there were bigger problems that she had to deal with. She recalled from her business courses that urgent, immediate problems often popped up because of underlying issues, and she wanted to get to the bottom of what those were.

PRAIRIE HOME APPLIANCE SERVICE

Prairie Home Appliance Service (PHAS) was a fully owned subsidiary of Prairie Co-op, most famous for its co-op retail stores and catalogue. The retail operations of Prairie Co-op had been a fixture in western Canada for a century, and had come to represent reliable, quality products at reasonable prices. Capitalizing on this reputation, Prairie Co-op had branched out and begun other businesses, including PHAS. PHAS's stated mission was to service any appliances and fixtures in the home, such as those in the kitchen and bathroom, as well as heating and cooling systems. It promised fast, efficient service, reasonable prices, and friendly personnel. To date, PHAS had been a big success—it had clients all across western Canada and even some in the nearby American states; enjoyed high initial satisfaction rates; and tended to be the home-repair brand with the highest brand recognition and reputation scores. It was common for customers to call PHAS even when the product they wished repaired hadn't been purchased through Prairie Co-op's retail arm.

Given western Canada's sheer geographic size, it was impossible to centralize all of PHAS's operations. The central customer service (CCS) operations were structured so that when a customer called, he or she would be routed to a CCS call centre.[1] Once the request was taken, it would be sent to the regional service centre (RSC), which would handle the scheduling of visits, ordering of parts, and so on. Following successful completion of the request, details would be sent back to the CCS centre and the file would be closed.

BECKY FREEMAN

A graduate of a large Canadian university, Becky Freeman took a job as a department manager in one of Prairie Co-op's retail stores. This job included managing inventory, sales promotions, sales staff, scheduling, and customer service within the department as well as meetings with the store's general manager about profit and loss statements and other ongoing store issues. Becky found that she enjoyed coaching the sales staff, particularly with regard to customer service. Because of her interest in the topic, she applied to become a manager in Prairie Co-op's retail arm's central customer service division. She got the job, based on a strong recommendation from her store's general manager and her positive track record.

While at the customer service centre, Becky had the opportunity to take courses and seminars in customer service, customer orientation, consumer behaviour, and branding, all paid for by Prairie Co-op. She enjoyed her work and wanted to stay at the central customer service centre, but opportunities for advancement were slim—both her supervisor and her supervisor's supervisor were far from retirement and weren't looking to advance beyond their current positions. Because of this, Becky applied for the director role at PHAS's CCS centre, and got the job.

In her new job, Becky stressed customer contact as a key driver of satisfaction. She wanted to make sure that customer service managers examined all open files on a regular basis, and that they contacted those customers whose repairs were pending to make appointments and complete the request quickly. She also instituted the training of customer service representatives to make detailed notes on all customer calls and to red-flag those customers who called into the CCS centre prior to their request being completed. Finally, Becky began an initiative that she believed would benefit both Prairie Co-op and its customers. She instituted the practice of service technicians taking note of other appliances in customers' homes and telling customers about common but hard-to-find products that Prairie Co-op sells, such as stainless steel cleaning supplies and oven vent filters.

---

[1]All incoming calls went to the central call centre; the regional call centres did not accept incoming calls from customers.

PHAS'S RECENT TROUBLES

It seemed as though PHAS had been running smoothly for a while when Becky started noticing an increase in customer complaints. At first she attributed it to a random spike in calls, which she knew could happen from time to time from her experience with the retail arm of Prairie Co-op. When the spike didn't end, Becky started to become concerned. The company hadn't made any important procedural or human resource decisions of late. The changes Becky had made resulted in greater efficiency and reporting, so she didn't think they were the cause of the increased dissatisfaction. If anything, PHAS was doing better than ever, with revenue growing from quarter to quarter and more and more calls coming in.

Becky tried to coach the managers under her to process the requests quickly and efficiently, and to examine all completed-request notices coming in from the RSC. Special attention was paid to those customer files that were red-flagged. Some of these calls were simply to get information, but others were complaints. A typical complaint file was one like Mr. Blahut's, where there had been repeated visits to his home, numerous outgoing and incoming calls, and in the end, a very dissatisfied customer.

Becky wanted to get to the bottom of the problem. She looked over the timeline she'd constructed based on the information in Mr. Blahut's file (see Exhibit 1), both from PHAS's files and from information Mr. Blahut had given the customer service representatives. Becky sighed and wondered how problems like this could be avoided in the future.

EXHIBIT 1	Timeline of Mr. Blahut's Service

January 23-Blahut's oven stops working.

January 28-Blahut calls PHAS to book an appointment. File is created and sent to Regina regional service centre (Regina).

January 30-Regina calls Blahut to inform him he has an appointment on Tuesday, February 3. Blahut changes it to Wednesday, February 4, saying he is unavailable on Tuesdays.

February 3-Regina calls Blahut with a reminder, telling him that the service technician will be there between 8:30 a.m. and 12:30 p.m.

February 4-Technician arrives at 1:30 p.m., one hour late. Assesses problem to be a malfunctioning timer/clock mechanism. Part is ordered from Vancouver, and technician makes appointment for Wednesday, February 18. Blahut pays for initial service call ($90.48).

Technician notes that Blahut has a water-dispensing refrigerator and lets him know that Prairie Co-op sells filters for that type of refrigerator. Blahut declines.

February 17-Regina calls Blahut (no one home—voice mail left) with a reminder, telling him that the technician will be there between 12:30 and 4:30 p.m.

February 18-Technician calls Blahut at 4:00 p.m. to tell him that he won't be there until after 5:00 p.m. Blahut tells him not to come as he won't be home at that time. New appointment is made for the morning of February 19.

February 19-Technician arrives at 11:00 a.m. and replaces timer/clock mechanism. New mechanism is defective and unusable. New part is ordered from Vancouver, and technician makes appointment for Wednesday, February 25, between 10:00 a.m. and 2:00 p.m. Blahut pays nothing for the call, as no repair was made.

EXHIBIT 1	Timeline of Mr. Blahut's Service (continued)

Technician notes that Blahut has an odd-shaped window above his fireplace, and informs him that Prairie Co-op sells a film that will block out UV rays that can be cut to order. Blahut declines.

February 25-Blahut calls CCS at 1:30 p.m. as he hasn't heard from the technician. He's informed that the appointment was cancelled as no part was received. Blahut expresses dissatisfaction at the lack of a call informing him that the appointment was cancelled. The customer service representative says he'll contact Regina to make a new appointment. Regina is contacted and instructed to phone Blahut.

At 3:00 on the same day, Regina calls Blahut to inform him that an appointment has been made for the following day, Thursday, February 26. While Blahut is on the phone with Regina, a different customer service representative from Regina calls and leaves a message that his appointment on February 26 is cancelled because the part hasn't arrived from Vancouver.

Blahut calls back CCS to express his displeasure. He recounts his experience with PHAS thus far. Customer service representative records information in file and promises compensation when the oven is finally repaired. Blahut is told to call back within a few days if he doesn't hear from PHAS (Regina).

March 2-At 10:00 a.m., Blahut calls CCS to inquire about the status of his repair. He's told that a message will be sent to the regional office to call him. Regina is contacted and instructed to phone Blahut.

At 4:00 p.m., Regina calls Blahut to inform him that an appointment has been booked for the following day, Tuesday, March 3. Blahut changes it to March 4 because he's not available on Tuesday.

March 3-At 2:30 p.m., Regina calls Blahut (no one home—voice mail left) with a reminder, telling him that the technician will be there between 12:30 and 4:30 p.m.

At 3:00 p.m., Regina calls and leaves a message that his appointment on March 4 is cancelled because the part hasn't arrived from Vancouver.

At 5:30 p.m., Blahut calls CCS to express dissatisfaction with the cancellation. He refers to his previous calls and the offer of compensation. He instructs the customer service representative that PHAS is not to call him to book an appointment unless they have the part in hand, and that he's willing to go to Vancouver to pick it up himself if PHAS would cover his cost. Note is made on file not to contact Blahut until the part is in hand.

March 5-Regina calls Blahut (no one home—message left) to tell him that an appointment is booked for Tuesday, March 10.

Later that day Blahut calls CCS to inquire if the part has arrived. The part hasn't arrived, but is due to arrive on March 10, and PHAS wanted to book the appointment in advance. Blahut cancels appointment for March 10 and reiterates instruction not to call unless the part is in hand. New note is made on file to this effect. Blahut is told to call back in a week if he hasn't heard anything.

March 9-Regina calls and tells Blahut that he has an appointment booked for the following day, Tuesday, March 10. Blahut inquires about the part and is told it has arrived and that it's functioning. Blahut changes the appointment to Thursday, March 12, between 9:30 a.m. and 12:30 p.m., because he can't be available on Tuesday.

Blahut then calls CCS to again inquire about the part and is told that it has arrived and is functioning.

EXHIBIT 1 | **Timeline of Mr. Blahut's Service** (continued)

March 11–Regina calls with a reminder, telling Blahut that the technician will be there between 10:00 a.m. and 2:00 p.m.

March 12–Technician arrives at 11:00 a.m., replaces part, oven functioning. Blahut pays total amount owing ($463.72).

Technician notes that Blahut has stainless steel appliances, and offers to sell him stainless steel cleaning supplies. Blahut declines.

At 11:45 a.m., Blahut calls CCS to inform them that his oven is functioning and that he wants to discuss compensation. Customer service representative asks if he would rather call in 24 or 48 hours, in case there are further problems with the oven. Blahut says he wants to discuss the issue right then. Blahut is informed that he'll receive a $75 Prairie Co-op retail gift card and a standard apology letter from Prairie Co-op.

Letter and gift card are mailed out that day. File closed.

Green Village Grocer

H. F. (Herb) MacKenzie

Amanda Porter was a marketing consultant in Struan, Ontario. She and her husband, Johnson Carruthers, a prominent corporate tax lawyer, earned a combined income of over $575 000 (before taxes). They had three small children, all under six years of age.

Amanda enjoyed grocery shopping as it gave her a break from her professional and family obligations. She referred to it as "mindless" work, but she prided herself on being good at it. Amanda usually alternated between two major grocery chains in her town, Green Village Grocer and Sobeys.

Following a series of dissatisfying experiences at one of her regular grocery stores, she decided to write to the company president. Her letter follows.

EXHIBIT 1	Letter to Green Village Grocer

October 23, 2012
16 Eden Loch Road
Struan, ON
L6A 4R7

President
Green Village Grocer
476 Golden Pheasant Drive
Oshawa, ON
L9Q 8Y8

Dear Sir or Madam:

I write you today because I've been a customer of Green Village Grocer for over 30 years, but I'm increasingly disturbed by a series of experiences I've had at the Cambridge Street location in our town.

Over the past year, I've been charged incorrect prices at the checkouts seven times—three times at your competitor, Sobeys, and four times at Green Village Grocer. I must say, I admire the response I received each time at Sobeys, and I've left your store dissatisfied each time. Let me recount some of my experiences for you so that you might appreciate the difference between what I've experienced at both stores.

My first experience was at Sobeys. I'd purchased a two-litre container of ice cream. When I went through the checkout, I was overcharged $0.50. The ice cream was supposed to be on sale for $3.59, but the scanner read the regular price of $4.09. I complained to the woman at the service desk, and she insisted that I accept a full refund of $4.09. I told her I'd be happy to simply get my $0.50, but she insisted that it was store policy that when customers get charged the wrong price at the checkout, they get a full refund and get the item free of charge. She refunded my money, apologized for the mistake, and asked me to please return to the store for my future grocery needs. Since then, I've had two similar experiences at Sobeys.

Now I'll recount four experiences at your store. My first experience was about a year ago. I was overcharged $1 on a bottle of olive oil. I took it to the service desk and advised the woman there that I'd been overcharged for the item. At that point I didn't know that you had a similar policy to Sobeys, and I didn't care, as I was perfectly willing to settle for a $1 refund. However, the woman on the service desk asked another employee standing nearby to check the price. The second woman seemed visibly displeased that someone should ask her to do a price check, and that may explain her subsequent behaviour. I watched her stop to talk to one of the cashiers on her way to the grocery aisle, and when she finally disappeared down the aisle and failed to return after about 10 minutes, I went to see if she was still there. She was having a personal conversation with another shopper, so I returned to wait at the service desk to see how long the whole process would take. During this period I read your sign that explained store policy with respect to overcharged prices. Eventually, when the woman returned from doing her price check, she didn't address me at all, but simply said to the woman at the service desk, "She's right. Give missus a buck." As you might expect, I was quite upset with the process at this point, and I took further exception to being called "missus." I immediately informed her that I recognized her as a long-time employee of Green Village Grocer, and that I would have expected her to know her store policy better than I did. I told her I'd be pleased to explain it to her if she hadn't had the opportunity to read it. I grudgingly got a refund on the item.

With respect to my second experience, I admit the error was partly mine. I saw a sign that advertised white onions on special, and I decided to buy one. When I got to the checkout, I was charged a higher price than the advertised special. I asked that the price be checked, and the cashier held it in the air and asked one of the male employees who was nearby to check the price.

| EXHIBIT 1 | Letter to Green Village Grocer   (continued) |

His comment was "One onion! &$*%#!" I mentioned to the cashier that he appeared to be having a bad day, and her comment was "Oh. That's just Andrew. He's always having a bad day." The result after the price check was that the price charged was correct. Apparently, I'd taken a large white onion from under the sign that advertised white onions, but I really had a Spanish onion (as were all the others under the sign). I simply paid the price and left.

On the third occasion, which occurred less than two months ago, I noticed the service desk was very busy and, to save time, I remarked to the cashier that I should get an item free as it was scanned at the checkout at a price higher than advertised. She tried to tell me that as I hadn't paid for the item, she could simply adjust the price. When I insisted that this was unacceptable as she hadn't caught the error, she called over a supervisor who asked the same question, "Did she pay for it yet?" When told no, the supervisor instructed the cashier to adjust the price. I objected again, and the store manager was called for a third opinion. He agreed with me that the store policy stated that the customer would receive any item free if it scanned at a price higher than advertised at the checkout, and he instructed the cashier to deduct the item from the sale. He remarked to the two women, "Remember, we talked about this last week." I left the store thinking that customer service improvements were about to be made.

Unfortunately, late one evening last week, I had my most dissatisfying experience. When overcharged by a young man at the cash register, he asked another cashier (who happened to be the same one I had my previous experience with) what he should do. She told him to give me $0.50 and to put a note in the cash register and someone would fix it in the morning. I informed her that I was more knowledgeable with respect to store policy than she was, and that she should get some additional training as we'd already been through this about a month previously. Her remark, in front of a dozen customers, was "We were told by the manager not to mention this policy unless the customer mentions it first."

That was very unsettling. First, it indicates that this store grudgingly implements store policy, and only for those customers who know what it is and who insist on it. It further implies that employees at this store are willing to take advantage of less knowledgeable customers, or those customers who are less likely or unwilling to complain. In my view, this is very unethical marketing behaviour. It's also disturbing that someone in a management position in your company supports that employees will, unknowingly or, worse, knowingly, act in an unethical manner with respect to your customers. Those employees who realize that they're being asked to behave unethically may be uncomfortable doing so and, in a better economic climate, may seek employment elsewhere.

I apologize for the length of my discourse, but I want you to be aware that the problem you have at this location is not an acute one. When I talked last year to the president of one of Canada's largest hotel chains, he explained his philosophy of customer guarantees to me. I recall he commented that, for such guarantees to be effective, customers must know what the guarantees are, they must receive compensation when the company fails with respect to its promises, and employees must see that the company pays when they fail. I would suggest that you either scrap this store policy, or that you train your managers as to why it's important and why it should be implemented properly.

Sincerely,

Amanda Porter

c.c.   Manager, Green Village Grocer
Struan, ON

When she finished writing her letter, Amanda mailed a copy to the president. She then decided to visit Green Village Grocer for one of her regular shopping trips, and she took a copy of the letter, intending to personally deliver it to the store manager.

The Writers at Woody Point Festival

Jose Lam

On the first day of February, 2011, Stephen Brunt started to review his notes from the previous week's board of directors meeting of Friends of Writers at Woody Point Inc., a nonprofit organization that governs and manages the Writers at Woody Point Festival. This literary festival is celebrated every August in Woody Point, Newfoundland, a small community of 350 people.

The discussions that flowed among the members of the board highlighted the need for developing a marketing strategy and a marketing plan that would guide the event for the next three to five years. The event had grown in size, and the board felt it was time for the festival to adopt a formal marketing strategy that could provide long-term economic sustainability for Woody Point and the other nearby communities. This strategy had to consider the festival's customer base and recommend new revenue streams and customer segments. As for the marketing plan, apart from its brochures, community announcements, website, and word-of-mouth advertising, the Writers at Woody Point Festival didn't have one. The plan they needed to establish had to re-evaluate current product, pricing, distribution, and promotion strategies.

The board had already approved the program guide for the 2011 Writers at Woody Point Festival that was to be released to the public in early May; however, Stephen and other board directors looked forward to reviewing suggestions for the marketing plan and strategy at the next board meeting in mid-April, and to deciding whether changes should be made to the official program.

GROS MORNE NATIONAL PARK, NEWFOUNDLAND AND LABRADOR

Gros Morne National Park of Canada was established in 1973, and in 1987 it was designated as a UNESCO World Heritage Site. The Tablelands, a flat-topped rock mountain located near Woody Point, was formed over 100 million years ago as a result of continental collisions. The complex geology of the site, whose rocks are usually found deep in the earth's mantle, holds great interest for the international scientific community, as it was here that geologists proved the theory of plate tectonics. With its natural beauty—fjords carved out by glaciers, waterfalls, marine inlets, and sandy beaches—along with its fishing villages and its cultural history, Gros Morne offers tourists and travellers a unique experience.

Another unique feature of Gros Morne National Park (GMNP) is the presence of communities embedded within it: the towns of Rocky Harbour, Norris Point, Glenburnie-Birchy-Head-Shoal-Brook, Woody Point, Trout River, Wiltondale, Sally's Cove, St. Paul's, and Cow Head. In May, Norris Point holds the Trails, Tales & Tunes Festival; and the summer months feature the increasingly popular Gros Morne Theatre Festival, based in Cow Head, and the Gros Morne Summer Music Festival in Norris Point, Woody Point, and Corner Brook. These festivals have helped bolster economic development in the GMNP area. In 2009 an estimated 72% of the 174 000 visitors who came to GMNP were from outside the province, with resident and non-resident visitors spending an estimated $107.5 million.

THE WRITERS AT WOODY POINT FESTIVAL

In the past decade, Canadian writers' festivals have experienced growth and success as they've provided an opportunity for authors and fans to fully experience the art of the written word. In 2004 the Writers at Woody Point Festival brought this experience to Newfoundland's west coast. The festival takes place within GMNP, known for its breathtaking scenery and extraordinary landscapes. This event attracts residents from the local GMNP communities and from elsewhere in the province, as well as out-of-province tourists. For the past three years, daily attendance at the festival has been estimated at about 150 to 200 visitors. Visitors from outside the GMNP area often remain in the community for the duration of the event, while visitors from nearby communities stay for daily shows.

Stephen Brunt, a sports columnist at *The Globe and Mail,* Alison Gzowski, editor and copy editor at *The Globe and Mail,* and Shelagh Rogers, a CBC program host, founded the Writers at Woody Point Festival in 2004. Stephen, who sits on the board, is also the artistic director of the event. Other board directors include community members from Woody Point, Corner Brook, and St. John's.

The festival showcases local artists as well as artists from abroad, who perform through assorted media. The musical performances have been known to sell out quickly, and include such popular artists as Figgy Duff, Sarah Harmer, Sylvia Tyson, and Hey Rosetta!

Aside from its musical performances and readings, the festival allows local craftspeople to display and sell their handiwork.

The event incorporates youth programs such as Theatre Newfoundland and Labrador (TNL), acting as a launch pad for young actors and actresses. It also collaborates with other Gros Morne festivals, including the Gros Morne Summer Music Program (which offers no-frills jazz and folk performances aimed at introducing people to classical-style music) and the Trails, Tales & Tunes Festival in Norris Point (which combines traditional music with storytelling, walks in the park, and culinary events). In addition, the Writers at Woody Point Festival brings intangible benefits to the communities in Gros Morne by reaching out to local schools. For example, in 2010, Newfoundland author Kevin Major—who wrote a successful novel called *No Man's Land* that has been used as a teaching tool in all Newfoundland and Labrador English high school programs—visited schools in the Gros Morne area as part of an outreach activity initiated by the Writers at Woody Point Festival.

The festival has been successful in its sponsorship and fundraising activities. Its major private donors have included Scotiabank, *The Globe and Mail,* and Random House, and many small businesses in the GMNP communities have donated as well. In 2010, $22 050 was raised, which represented twice the amount raised in the previous year. The festival also received $17 800 in grants from the Governments of Canada and Newfoundland & Labrador as well as from the Newfoundland & Labrador Arts Council.

Since its inception, the Writers at Woody Point Festival has grown significantly in terms of box office sales and memberships (see Exhibit 1). Readings and musical events sell out within hours after tickets go on sale in May, almost 15 weeks before the start of the festival. As a result, in 2010 the festival expanded from a four-day to a five-day event. Although additional readings were scheduled, the demand was still higher than the supply, as the additional shows also sold out quickly, leaving a large number of potential festival visitors without tickets. For the communities around Woody Point the festival also generated tourist-related spending on such things as motels, bed and breakfasts, restaurants, and transportation.

EXHIBIT 1	Box Office and Membership Sales, 2004-2010						
	2004	2005	2006	2007	2008	2009	2010
Box office	$7 524	$12 786	$17 428	$17 885	$24 830	$22 555	$27 525
Membership	$845	$5 471	$5 470	$4 427	$5 804	$5 733	$8 060

As the festival's attendance grew, the board noticed that the availability of accommodations in the Woody Point area was a particular problem, as many visitors had trouble finding lodging. They often had to stay in motels and/or bed and breakfasts as far as 60 kilometres away, which impacted some of the late-night shows.

MANAGEMENT

The board has been fully committed to the continuing role and sustainable growth of the Writers at Woody Point Festival, as well as to the introduction of new community and tourism-related ventures. It aims to further invest in the community, ensure financial stability, and further celebrate the talent of local writers and artists. The organization has relied mostly on external funding (government funds, grants from charitable foundations, direct donations) to maintain its operations. Nevertheless, the board has been concerned that overdependence on external revenue sources could influence the reliability and predictability of the festival as a whole.

Gary Noel, a consultant in cultural tourism and a retired high school teacher-librarian, is the festival's part-time event coordinator. Working under the direction of the board—whose directors contribute volunteer hours to planning—Gary has prepared, planned, and coordinated the event, and has ensured the day-to-day management of the festival's operations prior to, during, and after the festival's run in August.

PEOPLE

A network of volunteers from the nearby communities come together to make the festival successful. As the festival grows, it continues to help build bridges between the community, writers, and local businesses, and to contribute to the economic, artistic, and cultural vitality of the area. The Friends of Writers at Woody Point and other volunteer groups are dedicated to strengthening, promoting, and celebrating the talent of featured local and national writers, and to providing an avenue for an exchange of artistry between these writers and the community.

Community volunteers have also enabled the festival's success. Through volunteer contributions, the festival has been able to sustain itself and to continue as the pride of Woody Point. The passion and hospitality of volunteers have provided a welcoming experience for both writers and visitors to the festival, and have encouraged them to revisit the area.

CUSTOMERS

Customers attending the Writers at Woody Point Festival tend to be adults over the age of 40. They are educated and have an interest in literature, culture, and the arts; they enjoy reading books and could be literary fans of particular authors. Over the years, Gary has noticed that many of the attendees are couples or pairs of couples who have come to the festival together. For many attendees, the chance to see writers in a small and sometimes intimate setting is a unique experience. Gary has estimated that about 80% of attendees come from such nearby communities as Norris Point, Rocky Harbour, Deer Lake, and Corner Brook, while the remaining 20% come from elsewhere in Newfoundland or from other provinces, and travel to Woody Point specifically for the festival.

Since its inception the festival has continually sold out its individual events, and without doing much publicity; people simply wait for the first week of May when tickets go on sale. Tickets are sold only through telephone calls, and customers can buy a maximum of four tickets per show. According to Gary, the festival has "grown in popularity, and this year [2009], I mean, we sold out in minutes. As fast as the calls were coming in, as fast as we could handle them, we sold every ticket on that morning in May."

Although members may have a better chance to secure tickets, membership doesn't guarantee getting tickets to a specific show. As a result, the festival has acquired a reputation as an event for which it's very difficult to get tickets. People who aren't able to get tickets are put on a waiting list for any shows that can be added to the program at a later time. According to Stephen, the organizers "look after most people on our waiting list, so it's not as impossible as people have occasionally said it was [to get in]."

In the past three years, Stephen and Gary have started experimenting with new shows to attract a different customer base. For example, they've tried holding readings outdoors where people can also enjoy the scenery or partake in other activities such as hiking. The inclusion of folk, jazz, and traditional Newfoundland music concerts in the program has also proved popular. The success of the opening music concert and additional music events has generated extra revenue. The music concerts have attracted younger customers aged 18 to 35, who are less interested in the readings and come specifically for the concerts. Concerts have been held indoors at the Heritage Theatre, but in 2010 the festival experimented with an evening reading and music concert on a tour boat, which went well. The event, with a capacity of about 100, sold out in a few minutes at $40 per person and was targeted to customers over age 18.

In 2010 the festival generated a total revenue of $78 020, representing a 19.1% increase from the 2009 revenue of $65 488. (This 2009 revenue represented a 5.2% decrease from the 2008 revenue of $69 101.) Revenue increased in each of the four prior years, indicating that programming of the event was growing.

MARKETING MIX

Product

The festival has attracted many emerging writers and high-profile authors, including Joan Clark, Bernice Morgan, Des Walsh, Alexander McCall Smith, Lawrence Hill, Amanda Boyden, Kevin Major, and J. A. Ricketts, among others. As Stephen put it, "They're also really taken with the community and the integration of the festival in the community and the local culture, local music, and local art which is all part of it. . . . This is a very intimate festival. You can be here and your favourite author will be sitting beside you at the legion having a beer. You can meet people in a different way and they get to meet and interact with the community." Noah Richler, a freelance journalist, rated the Writers at Woody Point Festival as one of Canada's top literary festivals in 2010.

Distribution

Readings and concerts have been held at the Woody Point Heritage Theatre (see www .heritagetheatre.nf.ca). This building, with a capacity of 170 people, is privately owned, and the festival rents the facility during the week of the event. The board has been considering making an offer to buy the building and use the facility to generate additional revenue streams from increased market penetration of such existing events as readings and concerts.

Since the festival has been running at capacity at the theatre, additional shows have been held at Woody Point's Royal Canadian Legion building. At the 2009 event, an extra show for the music group Hey Rosetta! was added because of popular demand. In that same year the festival expanded from four to five days, and in 2010 to six days (Tuesday to Sunday); however, readings were held only from Thursday to Sunday, with two daily shows on Thursday and Friday, and three daily shows on Saturday and Sunday.

Pricing

The price for readings and concerts is $20 per person; the board has been uncertain about whether to raise ticket prices for these events. The possibility of creating a differential price structure for regular and new premium shows has also been debated. In 2010, box office and membership sales together accounted for 46% of total revenue. The third largest sales stream was from poster sales, which in 2010 totalled about $1200.

The festival currently has three levels of annual memberships: Supporters ($10), Sustaining ($100), and Patrons ($500). The Supporters membership provides information about upcoming events and pre-notification of ticket sale dates. The Sustaining membership includes, for the first 30 members, an autographed poster of festival writers and musicians. The Patrons membership includes updates and pre-notifications as well as a painting by a different local artist each year. These memberships do not offer advance ticket sales. Local residents of Woody Point and nearby communities, as well as volunteers, usually buy Supporters memberships. Sustaining and Patrons memberships attract small- and medium-sized business owners.

In 2004 the festival sold $3000 worth of books during the event, but it stopped doing so after that initial year because it lacked the ability to take credit card sales and sometimes found it difficult to recruit volunteers to supervise sales. Since 2005 independent booksellers have set up tables during the event to sell their books; the festival has not charged for this service. Also, over the years Gary Noel has considered selling promotional items and festival souvenirs during the event; however, the idea hasn't been pursued owing to a lack of resources. One of Gary's goals has been to ensure that, at the very least, the festival breaks even. To date, the festival has consistently generated a surplus in its operations. For instance, in 2010, with expenses totalling $73 061, the festival generated a surplus of $4953, whereas from 2004 to 2009 it had a total surplus of $15 121.

Promotion

The festival's budget for promotion and advertising activities has been below $2000 for the past few years. Sending out information about the upcoming festival to members and word-of-mouth advertising have been very effective in generating interest. By late April of each year the website is updated with the lineup of writers, artists, and singers coming to the festival in August. In early May, official program brochures and posters are printed and distributed in tourism offices, restaurants, stores, schools, hotels, motels, and other places frequented by tourists and local residents. Ads are also placed in community and local newspapers.

COMPETITION

Canadians celebrate the written word through large and small festivals across the country. These festivals are intended to give writers an opportunity to interact with fans; reading their work in an exclusive setting also serves to showcase the significance of their books. Attendance at literary festivals has continued to increase with the popularity of these events. According to the Book and Periodical Council, about 37 literary festivals are held across Canada, offering a combination of paid and free shows. In Atlantic Canada alone, several annual literary festivals allow local authors to showcase their talent.

Board directors are aware of the popularity of other literary festivals in Canada; however, they had little information about how these festivals are run and how they generate sales revenue. In preparation for the next board meeting in April, Gary collected information on some of these other literary festivals.

Winterset in Summer Writers Festival

This three-day gathering of local and non-local writers began in 2002 and takes place every mid-August in Eastport, Newfoundland. It competes directly with the Writers at Woody Point Festival. Eastport, located on the northeast coast of the island, is a popular summer vacation destination for locals and tourists who frequent the beaches in the area. Although considered one of the smallest festivals, the event has grown to incorporate several revenue streams. One way in which the festival has obtained media attention as well as sponsorship is through presenting the BMO Winterset Award to a writer in the festival each year. The festival also relies on major sponsor and ticket sales for revenue, including tickets for a Sunday dinner where writers dine with festival participants. Tickets are $10 or $20, depending on the show.

Cabot Trail Writers Festival

Based in Cape Breton, Nova Scotia, this small, three-day event takes place in late September or early October. The festival, which began in 2009, is funded through the St. Ann's Bay Development Association. It's also sustained by three levels of corporate sponsorships, with ticket sales providing further revenue. Ticket prices are based on day passes at $20 on Fridays and Sundays and $60 on Saturdays, with dinner included. The festival's intent is to remain small, and so exploring additional revenue streams has not been a priority.

Read by the Sea

Read by the Sea is run by a volunteer committee of book lovers along the River John at the Northumberland Strait on Nova Scotia's northern shore. This small, one-day festival takes place in July, with readings held throughout the year. The festival offers a dinner with the writers, an open-microphone event, a workshop for teen writers, and an online book club. The cost of the teen writers' event is $15, including lunch. The evening reading, which includes dinner, costs $15. Other events are free. The festival depends heavily on government and corporate sponsors for funding.

Shelburne Writers Festival

This annual event in Shelburne, Nova Scotia, takes place over a weekend in late August. The festival features a dinner with the authors, in which writers display their books for sale and offer book signings, as well as an open-microphone event in which participants can attempt to impress the writers they came to see. The festival also features poetry and writing workshops. Shelburne Writers Festival relies on ticket sales, with prices ranging from $20 to $25 for readings and workshops.

Frye Festival

This bilingual event is held annually in Moncton, New Brunswick, during the last week of April. It's the largest literary festival in Atlantic Canada, with 2009 and 2010 attendance totalling 16 000 and 17 500 people, respectively. The program offers a book club, a creative writers' workshop for children, and a writing contest for local youth. Ticket prices for the festival range from $10 to $30 for readings, music, and theatre. Promotional merchandise, featuring the festival's logo on items including hats and T-shirts, is offered for sale both on site and online. This festival garners additional revenue from several levels of sponsorship as well as a "pay what you can" ticket price—allowing those who couldn't normally afford admission to contribute what they can and still enjoy the festivities.

Blue Metropolis International Literary Festival

The world's first multilingual literary festival has been held in downtown Montreal since 1999. It runs during the third week of April and features a separate children's festival that takes place in libraries, museums, and community and cultural centres around the city. Blue Metropolis relies on an extensive list of sponsors, collaborators, and friends for funding and support. Ticket sales contribute significantly to revenues; prices for events range from $7 to $20, with a $45 pass that allows unlimited access to all shows (but not workshops). Adult creative writing workshops are sold out year after year. During the festival people can visit the festival bookstore, where they can buy books as well as attend book-signing sessions. In addition to its YouTube videos, the festival offers podcasts of readings that people can access through the website.

Ottawa International Writers Festival

Launched in 1997, this week-long festival has grown each year since. It takes place twice a year, in late April and late October, and features both local writers and writers from abroad, combining science, history, poetry, politics, spoken word, and more. Although Ottawa's festival is comparatively large, its revenue streams can be projected on a smaller scale. Its organizers have established a "Festival Member Fee" in which members pay a minimum of $20 per month for several advantages, including free access to an entire year of programming, reserved seating, 10% off books purchased during the festival, special invitations, and email updates on featured artists. They also offer a "Membership Referral" program that gives participants two free tickets for referring a new member. The festival further connects with the community by offering Ottawa's Festival for Young Readers. As with most festivals, the main source of revenue comes from sponsors. Ticket prices range from $15 to $20, and several events have free admission.

Thin Air Winnipeg International Writers Festival

Thin Air takes place annually in mid-September for one week. This is a large festival and features other special events throughout the year. It also offers several options for children's workshops that generate various levels of revenue. In addition, the festival seeks corporate donations and features advertising in the "Thin Air Paperback." Corporate sponsors are a big part of this organization's funding, along with ticket sales for which individual, full-day, and full-festival passes are available. A festival pass costs $35 and offers unlimited access to all main stage events. Tickets are $12 for readings, which run from 10 a.m. to 11:30 p.m.

Saskatchewan Festival of Word

The annual Festival of Word takes place in Moose Jaw for four days in mid-July. This festival credits its success to a creative business plan, support from funding bodies and donors, and the willing work of a small, paid staff and over 140 volunteers. It has a $10 one-year membership fee, newsletters, writing programs and workshops, and a long list of corporate sponsors. The festival is heavily involved in the community, offering many corporate-sponsored workshops for teens and children. Ticket prices range from $10 to $25 for readings and workshops. An early-bird festival pass to all events costs $160. The festival offers lunch with writers, but no dinner events.

WordFest Literary Festival

For the past 15 years Calgary's WordFest has taken place from Tuesday to Sunday in early October, with supplementary events throughout the year. The festival is supported by a large number of corporate sponsors at a range of levels: bronze, silver, gold, and platinum. Festival passes grant access to all events in the area, as well as discounts at participating sponsor locations. Ticket prices for most shows range from $6 to $15, with discounts for tickets bought in advance. Special shows, including a reception, cost $25. The festival also features a dinner with the writers, which at $200 per ticket is a major fundraiser.

Sunshine Coast Festival of the Written Arts

Launched in 1983, this is Canada's longest-running summer gathering of writers. The annual festival takes place over four days in mid-August at Rockwood's heritage gardens in Sechelt, British Columbia. Revenue has grown by holding shows in multiple buildings during the festival's run. Other revenue streams come from selling promotional products and a dinner with the writers. Many of the events are corporate-sponsored. Sales revenue is generated from individual ticket sales at $15 for individual events, $250 passes that grant access to all events, and $85 day passes. The Sunshine Coast Festival also rents a large on-site tent for literary and merchandise sales.

Vancouver International Writers Festival

This annual week-long festival takes place in late October. It offers a membership fee of $35, which includes early-bird purchasing privileges, a discount on festival tickets, a personalized membership card, an invitation to a members' reception, discounts at supporting bookstores, a subscription to Book News (a weekly e-newsletter), and voting privileges at the annual general meeting. Another type of membership is offered through the Book Club Friend program, in which a minimum of five people pay $20 each and receive the same benefits as regular members along with more book discounts. The organizers also offer a unique Miles Without Borders program in which anyone can donate Aeroplan miles to help fund travel costs for writers attending the festival. Seven levels of "Festival Friends" represent various levels of sponsorship donations. Tickets are $17 for individual shows and $19 to $33 for special literary, theatre, and music performances. This festival offers a Sunday brunch that allows writers to interact with their fans. It has also established community connections with a day camp for kids.

Decisions

As Stephen reviewed the information on what other literary festivals were doing, he started thinking about how to develop a marketing strategy and marketing plan for the Writers at Woody Point Festival. As the festival's artistic director, Stephen felt strongly about not compromising on the quality of the event; he also felt that the success of literary festivals depended on the connection between authors and fans.

As a sports writer, Stephen has had several national bestsellers, including *Facing Ali: The Opposition Weighs In, Diamond Dreams: 20 Years of Blue Jays Baseball, Searching for Bobby Orr,* and *Gretzky's Tears: Hockey, Canada, and the Day Everything Changed.* From his experience following sports, he knew that strategy gave teams a competitive edge to succeed. He asked himself, "What would be the best way for the festival to remain sustainable, continue growing, and contribute to the economic development of Woody Point and nearby communities? Should the festival seek new customer segments, or offer more shows to its customer base? What other revenue streams could the festival develop? Should the festival raise its ticket prices, introduce a tiered pricing structure, or both?" Stephen knew that he had to give these issues a lot of thought. The board members would be expecting his recommendations at the upcoming meeting.

Centre for the Arts

H. F. (Herb) MacKenzie

Debbie Slade, managing director of the Centre for the Arts (www.arts.brocku.ca), was preparing for a meeting with its marketing coordinator, Erin White. Debbie had called the meeting to discuss what to do about the centre's theatrical programming. It was October 27, 2003, two days before the centre was scheduled to present *Halo*. This would be the first theatrical performance of the 2003/2004 professional entertainment season, and ticket sales were disappointingly low. Early indications were that sales for the other two performances were likely to be similar. Debbie was concerned in the short term with how to increase sales for this performance, but also for the two subsequent performances scheduled for the current season. More important, she had to decide the longer-term issue of what role live theatre should have within the centre's programming; that is, what she should do for the 2004/2005 season and beyond.

THE VENUE

The Centre for the Arts is an integral part of Brock University. The Departments of Dramatic Arts and Music are given scheduling priority, as the centre's facilities are needed for the practical components of their studies. The centre is mandated to stimulate cultural interest in the arts within the Niagara region. (See Exhibit 1 for a statement of the centre's vision, mission, and values and beliefs.) It provides hands-on experience for Brock students as well as for high school students and community users. Through its live performances and educational programs, the centre has been successful in attracting thousands of visitors annually to Brock University.

The Centre for the Arts is intended primarily as an educational and cultural resource for Brock University. Therefore, there are clear priorities when it comes to determining usage for its facilities:

1. Department of Dramatic Arts, for rehearsals, performances, and exhibitions (required 700 hours over 18 weeks during the 2003/2004 season; expected to increase needs by 30% beginning the following year)
2. Department of Music, for performance classes and concerts (required 300 hours during the 2003/2004 season for lunch-hour concerts, the Encore Concert Series, and pedagogical examinations)
3. Niagara Symphony Orchestra
4. Faculty of Education
5. University departments/groups for performances, lectures, speakers, etc.
6. Community groups
7. Centre for the Arts professional entertainment events

EXHIBIT 1	Vision, Mission, and Values and Beliefs of the Centre for the Arts

VISION

To be Niagara's *best* cultural centre, to foster excellence in the performing arts, and to be a leader in the arts community by providing access to all citizens to the live performing arts.

MISSION

To stimulate cultural interest in the performing arts within the university and the Niagara community.

VALUES and BELIEFS

1. To provide leadership for the arts and live entertainment in the community.
2. To program local, national, and international artists to reflect community needs by offering a balanced performing arts program that is shared by educational, community, and professional use on an equitable and flexible basis.
3. To provide a facility that is accessible to all citizens through a variety of programming and culturally diverse programs based on availability, market demand, and fair pricing.
4. To maintain and enhance the centre's facilities and operations at the highest possible standard in order for the Centre for the Arts to continue to be a valuable community and national asset.

The Centre for the Arts employs 10 full-time staff members. Debbie Slade is responsible for directly managing the other nine employees, and for indirectly managing 60 part-time student workers and 25 volunteers. Erin White is responsible for managing the advertising and promotion budget; media releases; magazine, radio, and newspaper advertising; and hospitality for guest artists. She's also responsible for selling advertising space in promotional programs distributed by the centre and through media and other kinds of sponsorship and in-kind gifts. A production manager is responsible for all the technical operations of the centre; for directly managing three technicians responsible for sound equipment, lighting, and computers; for enforcing fire regulations; and for acting as assistant managing director when Debbie Slade is absent. An audience services supervisor is responsible for selecting, training, and supervising part-time staff, and for managing concession inventory and bar supplies. There's also an administrative assistant, a box office manager, and a box office assistant. The number of staff hasn't increased since 1987, although the scope of operations has more than doubled. See Table 1 for a list of scheduled performances for the 2003/2004 professional entertainment season.

Table 1	Season Schedule, 2003/2004
Tower of Power	October 4
Remy Shand	October 9
Zucchero	October 22
Two Planks and a Passion Theatre: *Halo*	October 29
Chantal Kreviazuk	October 30
Harlem Gospel Choir	October 31
The Royal Winnipeg Ballet: *The Magic Flute*	November 15
The Second City National Touring Company: *The Puck Stops Here!*	November 26
Brass Rings: *A Time for Christmas*	December 4
Natalie MacMaster	December 5
Cantabile	December 10
Ron Rexsmith with Madison Violet	December 16
Holly McNarland with Shaye	January 15
The Heillig Manoeuvre	January 17
The Flaming Idiots	January 18
Motus O: *A Midsummer Night's Dream*	January 24
The Musical Box: *Genesis: Selling England by the Pound*	January 28
Dave Coulier	January 29
Smythe and Saucier	February 8
Kiran Ahluwalia	February 19
Nearly Neil and the Solitary Band	February 21
Sampradaya Dance: *Revealed by Fire*	February 28
Gregg Lawless and the Acoustic Orchestra	March 3

Table 1	Season Schedule, 2003/2004 (continued)	
Jory Nash and Aengus Finnan		March 6
One Acre Productions: *Fingers and Toes*		March 11
John McDermott		March 12 & 13
Roger Whittaker		March 14
The Cottars		March 19
Jane Bunnett and the Spirits of Havana		March 25
Sinha Danse: *Loha / Thok*		March 27
Cleo Laine & the John Dankworth Group		April 1
Catalyst Theatre: *The Blue Orphan*		April 7
Nnenna Freelon		April 16
David Usher		April 17
Shona Reppe Puppets: *Cinderella*		April 18
Rik Emmett		April 21
Buddy Wasisname and the Other Fellers		April 28
The Big Band Broadcast		April 30

THE ACT

Halo, a funny, compassionate play written by actor and playwright Josh MacDonald, concerns the sighting of an image of Jesus in small-town Nova Scotia. The play is based on a true story, the Christlike apparition having appeared under the floodlights on the outside wall of a Tim Hortons in Bras d'Or, Cape Breton, and first noticed by staff at the Lick-A-Chick restaurant across the road. The apparition appeared for several days, resulting in nightly traffic jams around the doughnut shop when as many as 4000 people came to view it.

The main character in the play is Casey Quinn, a high school dropout who's taken a full-time job at the local Tim Hortons. Casey, who resents the rigidity of her local community, has become an outcast. She ridicules the faith of her boyfriend and boss while she befriends the new priest in the community. Following the appearance of the apparition, the community becomes a "faith circus" where everyone, including Casey, has something to learn. Meanwhile, a local Christmas tree farmer and devout Catholic, Donald McMullen, has been sitting at the bedside of his daughter, who's been in a coma for the past two years. Donald's faith is tested and his motivations examined when his older daughter, Lizzie, joins him at the bedside. The two stories come together to provide a powerful and hilarious look at modern faith and community.

The play was being performed by a cast of seven members of Two Planks and a Passion Theatre (www.twoplanks.ca), founded in 1992 in rural Kings County, Nova Scotia. The company's mission is "to commission, develop, and produce challenging Canadian drama with strong roles for women that is reflective of the lives of the audiences for whom they perform, and to disseminate this work to communities large and small nationwide." Other works that it has created and produced include *Westray: The Long Way Home* and *Hockey Mom, Hockey Dad.*

The touring performers had booked numerous performances across eastern Canada, beginning with the Confederation Centre in Charlottetown, PEI, on October 16 and ending on November 8 at the Markham Theatre in Markham, Ontario. The St. Catharines performance was booked for October 29 at the 538-seat Sean O'Sullivan Theatre, Centre for the Arts, Brock University. One of the centre's main advantages was its membership in the CCI Group, which meant it could procure the services of a number of performing artists through block, or "volume," booking with other members, thereby reducing its artistic fees. For *Halo* the artistic fees amounted to $4000. These fees varied depending on the venue, and the centre simply adjusted box office prices to reflect the fees it paid.

COSTING *HALO*

When Debbie reviewed the other costs associated with *Halo,* she noted that she'd have to spend $600 for hotel accommodations for the performers. The promotional costs that were either spent or committed at that time included $950 for flyers, brochures, and posters; $475 for print advertising (newspapers); and $450 for radio advertising. Projected costs also included three local crew members to unload and set up stage props and equipment for two hours each ($27 per hour); four local crew members to take down the stage props and equipment and load them for shipment for one hour each ($27 per hour); one spot operator for two and a half hours ($27 per hour); one house manager for four hours ($15 per hour); two catering staff for five hours each ($8.50 per hour), and eight ushers for three and a half hours each ($9.85 per hour). The only other actual cost was credit card administration—the small percentage credit card companies charged for a handling fee—which Debbie estimated as being between $150 and $200. She also included a cost of $915 for theatre rental, although this wasn't actually paid to the university as a rental fee; rather, it was an opportunity cost: what the theatre would receive if it were rented for another purpose. When all costs were finally known, the centre could make up to 10% profit. Any revenue above this amount was then split between the artist or artists (80%) and the promoter (20%). This arrangement had become increasingly popular over the past few years, and almost all performers now demanded it.

SALES TO OCTOBER 27, 2003

Prior to the meeting, Debbie Slade asked for an up-to-date summary of sales. With two days remaining before the performance, there were only 225 paid seats. Table 2 shows a breakdown of sales. Historically, very few, if any, seats are sold in the last few days before a theatrical performance.

Seat prices varied depending on the particular performance. Prices for musical performances ranged from $55 per single seat for John McDermott or Natalie MacMaster, to $49.50 for Chantal Kreviazuk or Remy Shand, to $32 for the Cottars or Buddy Wasisname and the Other Fellers, to $28.50 for Ron Sexsmith or Holly McNarland. Theatrical performances were priced at the lower end of the range. All three performances scheduled for the 2003/2004 season were priced at $28.50 for single seats, with a 10% discount for groups of 10 or more and for Brock University staff and faculty; $23.50 for Gold members; and $20.50 for Platinum members. Brock University had 490 faculty members and 16 librarians in its Faculty Association, and 654 staff. The centre sold approximately 600 memberships

Table 2	Sales to October 27, 2003			
Buyer Type	Seats	Revenue	GST	CRF
Advance (ticket office)	57	$1624.50	$106.02	$57.00
Advance (internet)	16	$456.00	$29.76	$16.00
Group tickets	36	$923.40	$60.48	$36.00
Brock staff/faculty	2	$51.30	$3.36	$2.00
Gold members	45	$1057.50	$69.30	$45.00
Platinum members	69	$1414.50	$92.46	$69.00
Total	225	$5527.20	$361.38	$225.00

annually, mostly outside the university. Memberships were almost equally divided between Gold and Platinum. Gold members paid $50 annually, for which they received advance notice of upcoming performances and special events, plus an opportunity to purchase tickets prior to their offer to the general public. They also got reduced prices of up to 20% and could buy as many as six discounted tickets per show. Membership further entitled them to three complimentary parking vouchers valued at $3 each, an invitation to a special "Members' Night" sneak preview, and complimentary tickets to selected shows. Platinum members paid $100 annually and received all the benefits of Gold members; they also got discounts of up to 25%, five complimentary parking vouchers, advance purchase privileges prior to Members' Night, and could buy up to 10 discounted tickets per show.

From total revenue, the centre for the Arts had to pay GST to Revenue Canada and a $1 per seat charge that went to a capital reserve fund (CRF) for repairing and renovating the facilities when needed. One of the main marketing objectives for the 2003/2004 season was an average 80% capacity paid attendance, with 50% of all tickets sold through membership. While the centre wasn't specifically focused on generating a profit, Debbie was certainly aware that generating some positive financial contribution would position the centre better within the university hierarchy, making it easier to negotiate for things that it might need in the future.

MARKETING

Erin White, the centre's marketing coordinator, received a B.A. in Media Communications from Brock University in 1998 before being hired by a small theatre company in Fort Erie. The job was very much "trial by fire." The position was supported by a grant from Human Resources Development Canada; otherwise, the company had limited resources and no understanding of business. Taking an opportunity for a more stable position, Erin joined the university's Conference Services, where she worked for two years and gained marketing and promotion experience. Then she moved to the Centre for the Arts, responsible for marketing and promotion.

The major promotional item for the centre was a full-colour, 12 × 16.5 cm glossy brochure with a page dedicated to each of the scheduled performances. The brochure was distributed at the start of the season to all Gold and Platinum members and to

17 000 people registered in the centre's database. It was also distributed throughout Brock University via its internal mail system, to local hotels and libraries, and then at the box office throughout the performing season. Direct mail was commonly used to promote a specific item or series. For example, to promote the three theatrical performances scheduled for the 2003/2004 season, the centre made a series of mailings in late September: 404 letters were sent to people in the database who'd bought theatre tickets within the previous two years, 284 letters were sent to church and seniors groups, and 24 letters were sent to "theatre educators" at local high schools. For the latter group, the centre made a special offer of $11.75 per ticket for a group of 10 or more, plus one free ticket for every 10 tickets purchased.

The centre received some free radio publicity on local radio stations that aired "A Brock Minute" each day, a short description for the local community of what was happening throughout the university. Aside from this, radio was a regular medium for promoting the centre. For *Halo,* for example, four radio ads per day were booked on each of three local radio stations—105.7 Easy Rock FM, 97.7 Hits FM, and 610 CKTB AM Talk Radio—for the six days before the scheduled performance.

Print ads were placed locally each week during the program season from early September through late April. These quarter-page ads usually featured a particular performance, and sometimes more than one if several performances were scheduled within a particular week. *The St. Catharines Standard* gave the centre a 25% discount based on its seasonal volume. *Pulse Niagara,* a paper distributed throughout the Niagara region promoting upcoming events, offered a "buy one and get one free" promotional deal. *Halo* was advertised in both papers during the two weeks prior to its scheduled performance.

Other promotional media included email newsletters to select patrons who had agreed to receive them, occasional letters to Brock University staff and faculty, and large, 28 × 43.25 cm posters. Exhibit 2 shows the promotional poster for *Halo.* Volunteers distributed several hundred of them to businesses around town and throughout Brock University. Students were encouraged to buy "walk-up" tickets on the night of performances at just $6 per seat. For popular performances, of course, walk-up seats were never available. For some comedy or musical performances a dozen or so students might decide to see if seats were available at the last minute. For theatrical performances, it was highly unlikely that any additional seats would be sold the last few days before a performance, including student walk-up purchases.

THE MEETING

Debbie Slade had asked to meet with Erin to discuss the upcoming performance of *Halo* when it became apparent that the performance wouldn't likely generate enough box-office revenue to cover its costs. Together they reviewed the show's promotion and what could possibly be done.

The two women agreed that cancelling the performance wasn't an option, and that spending any additional money at this time would most likely be ineffective. Several alternatives were discussed, however. One alternative was to contact the 300 Gold and 300 Platinum members who hadn't purchased tickets for the performance and make them a special "buy one and get one free" offer. If this was successful, it might create some interest and gain additional sales for the subsequent theatre performances as well. However, it

| EXHIBIT 2 | *Halo* Promotional Poster |

may create dissatisfaction among those who'd booked and paid for their seats early. A similar option was to make the same offer to Brock University staff and faculty, as they could be reached on short notice through the university's email system. Only two tickets (likely a single sale) had sold so far to staff and faculty, and if that staff or faculty member became aware of this and was disappointed, it would be easy to provide him or her with two additional tickets to the performance, or to another performance.

Another option was to provide local radio stations with free tickets to give away to listeners. One issue was whether single tickets or pairs of tickets should be given away. Again though, the issue was how paying patrons might feel if too many people in the audience were attending without having paid. This type of promotion wouldn't generate much revenue immediately, but it would help build awareness around the local community, and it might also encourage new potential patrons to attend and possibly purchase tickets for other performances or even purchase a membership. Some additional revenue might be received through concession sales, with the average patron spending approximately $4 for food and beverage items. Providing promotional tickets could also generate a few immediate sales if ticket winners decided to buy additional tickets for friends or family, but Debbie and Erin agreed that this wasn't likely to generate many additional sales.

As they discussed this option, Debbie suggested they could give free tickets to other people who'd recently made some contribution to the Brock University community, for example, volunteers who'd helped with the university's United Way campaign. Giving them free tickets would help recognize their volunteer work and might also encourage some of them to attend other theatrical performances. At the very least, it would help fill the theatre. For if paying patrons viewed the theatrical performances as popular, they'd be encouraged to purchase tickets to other shows in advance to ensure they were available. Whichever way they provided free tickets, filling seats was important for the performers, for other patrons, and for reviewers who often tended to write negative reviews of poorly attended performances.

As the meeting neared its end, Debbie turned to Erin. "I guess, for your part, I'd appreciate it if you could look over the revenue and cost projections and see if there's anything we can do immediately or for the other two scheduled performances. We don't have to generate a profit on every performance we book, but there'll be increasing pressure on us to boost revenue, particularly as demand increases within the university for its facilities. We may have to book fewer performances in future years and we may have to become more concerned about which ones help us generate sales. Once I have your ideas, I'll be better able to decide what to do about the larger programming issue. It could be that theatre is better left to other venues around the community."

Ethical Issues in Marketing Management

*Massine Bouzerar and
H. F. (Herb) MacKenzie*

People in various areas of marketing management frequently face ethical dilemmas. These dilemmas can arise when conducting marketing research and when making product, price, promotion, and distribution decisions. In any organization, it's important for individuals in both management and front-line positions to consider the impact of their decision making on customers and other stakeholders. Review each of the following scenarios and decide how important the ethical issue is and what you would do in each instance.

CANINE CHOW INC.

Canine Chow Inc. was a Canadian company that manufactured and sold dog food and dog treats to retailers across North America. The packages of Canine Chow were sold only in bags of 15 kilograms each, designed to target dog owners who wanted to reduce the trips they made to the pet store and to save money by buying in bulk. This business model worked well for the company at first, until it started to notice that retailers weren't ordering its product as often as it hoped. The company's inventory began to increase, and this heightened concern about product freshness.

"Customers are just not buying your dog food often enough for us to make regular orders," said one of the retailers after getting in contact with Canine Chow. Lisa Cairns, president of Canine Chow, was considering new methods to increase the company's sales, including a proposal from Andrew Carlton, one of her chemists. "What we could do," Andrew began, "is alter our dog food recipe in a way that would decrease the amount of leptin released after food intake. Leptin, a chemical produced by the body in response to food, acts as an appetite suppressant. So if a dog doesn't release as much leptin as usual, it could eat more dog food than usual. That way, dog owners would go through the bags of dog food more quickly."

"Isn't that illegal?" said Lisa, looking amazed.

"Not at all," Andrew said. "It's not like we'd be adding any special chemical that stimulates the dogs' hunger—we'd simply be moving toward ingredients that are known to reduce their leptin level. It's not uncommon for food manufacturers to include these ingredients in their products."

If you were Lisa Cairns, what would be your response?

LETTUCE FEED YOU

Lettuce Feed You, a new local sandwich shop in downtown Struan, Ontario, has been open for only three months and its manager, John Stirling, was finding it difficult to anticipate demand for his sandwiches. From time to time, Lettuce Feed You ran out of certain ingredients and sauces for the sandwiches, which would sometimes upset regular customers. Conversely, John would often miscalculate demand and over-order some of the produce, incurring considerable waste.

When Justin Ferguson, a new part-time employee, was serving his first customer of the day, he noticed that the light-mayonnaise squeeze bottle was empty when the customer requested it on her sandwich. Still unfamiliar with where all the supplies were kept, Justin went into the back room to ask Tiffany, a co-worker, for some help. "Do you know where we keep the light mayonnaise? I think we're all out in the front," he said.

"If we're all out," she replied, "just fill the bottle with some regular mayonnaise." Justin looked at Tiffany, feeling a bit confused. "What do you mean?" he asked. "Well, when we run out of light mayonnaise, we use regular mayonnaise instead so the customers don't get upset with us. Anyway, if they're going to have mayonnaise on their sandwich, they might as well get the real thing. It's not like light mayonnaise is really going to make a big difference in their diet."

Is this an appropriate behaviour for a restaurant employee? When or where would it be more acceptable? Explain.

EXCALIBUR INSURANCE BROKERS

Kylee Stubbert has just been promoted to a full-time insurance broker at Excalibur Insurance Brokers after passing her licensing examination through the Registered Insurance Brokers of Ontario (RIBO). Kylee had taken a two-week preparation course in Hamilton, which taught her insurance fundamentals and the wording of legal documents.

Kylee was paired with Tyler Newman, an experienced insurance broker at Excalibur, to begin her on-the-job training. Tyler went over different software programs the firm used to estimate quotes for customers based on the information they provided. "So all you have to do is ask them the following questions that the system needs in order to browse through the different insurance providers we represent," said Tyler, demonstrating how to use the program. "And you just quote the cheapest insurance that the system provides?" said Kylee. "Not necessarily," answered Tyler. As she was about to ask another question, Tyler's office phone rang. "Here, I'll take this call and walk you through the process," said Tyler as he put the call through on speaker so that Kylee could listen in.

Tyler went through the entire process with the potential customer, asking him all the necessary questions to develop a quote from the selection of insurance providers in the system. Kylee paid close attention to the types of questions Tyler asked and how he input the information into the system. Near the end of the conversation, the system Tyler was using to generate quotes listed the customer's 10 least-expensive options. But when Tyler gave the customer the quote, Kylee noticed that he didn't quote the least-expensive insurance option; the price he chose was actually sixth down from the top of the list.

Once Tyler closed the sale and got off the phone, Kylee asked him why he'd quoted that particular insurance provider. "When you get the top 10 results, the broker will usually offer the one that offers the greatest commission rate. This is common practice in the industry. You'll want to do it too, once you understand that it has only a marginal effect on what the customer pays but can be a major contributor to your monthly income."

CAMBRIDGE LIFE SOLUTIONS

Cambridge Life Solutions (CLS) is new to the Canadian marketplace (2010). It offers debt settlement services to its clients, promising them savings of up to 70% on unsecured debt of $10 000 or more. CLS's business model requires its clients to withhold payments from their creditors and instead grow their personal funds to eventually seek a one-sum settlement payoff, negotiated through CLS. The company charges its clients fees—as much as 15% of the original outstanding debt—before deals are reached with creditors. In many cases, customers can be left with greater debt, less money, and a poor credit rating.

Research conducted in the United States has indicated that fewer than 10% of clients typically complete debt settlement programs. This practice has been outlawed in the United States and in Alberta and Manitoba, but remains legal in most other provinces. Many consumer advice agencies in Canada have already released alerts about debt settlement companies to warn consumers about the many hidden risks associated with these types of services.

Canadian actor Alan Thicke was the company spokesperson in a television ad campaign. His commercial begins, "Hello. Alan Thicke here. We've talked about a lot of things over the years: sitcoms, health care, hockey." He positions himself as a friend you can trust, and CLS likely chose him because of his popularity and credibility with many Canadians in its target age group. Queried about his involvement, an Alan Thicke spokesperson responded, "Debt relief is a relatively new and growing product. My due diligence clearly supports Cambridge as a leader in the field."

The important question from a marketing perspective is whether Alan Thicke will add credibility to CLS, or whether CLS will tarnish the credibility of Alan Thicke.

MAYORAL ELECTIONS

Elections were coming up in a major Canadian city, and as voting day approached, competition was beginning to intensify. The two main contenders for the position were Julie Stevenson and Mario Natale, who were doing whatever they could to gain more votes from the community. Despite the fierce competition that was developing, Michael Bernard and Erica Leeson, campaign managers for Stevenson and Natale, respectively, were still good friends.

Days away from voting, the Stevenson and Natale camps were under considerable pressure, most of it being felt by the two campaign managers. Both were attempting to brainstorm last-minute ideas to gain a competitive advantage, and the stress was beginning to wear on them.

One night Michael and Erica decided to take an evening off to get their thoughts away from the campaigns, and went together to a popular local pub. A few drinks into the evening, Michael began leading the conversation toward the Stevenson campaign, revealing detailed information about a last-minute campaign activity his party would launch in two days. The details he was sharing with Erica shocked her, as they would completely change the dynamics of the election. Eventually, Michael stopped mid-sentence. He blushed as he realized what he'd been saying, and quickly asked Erica to keep this conversation confidential. Erica nodded in agreement, thoughts of the rival party's plans floating in her mind.

The next morning, Erica was still thinking about what Michael had revealed. If she shared the information with the rest of her team, the Natale party would be able to respond quickly to the Stevenson party's actions, which could be the deciding factor in who won the election. She also knew she'd be able to cover her tracks, making it unlikely that Michael would find out what she did.

As Erica Leeson, what would you do?

COFFEE SAVVY

Coffee Savvy, a major North American coffee bean supplier, imported beans from Guatemala and Indonesia and packaged them to sell at coffee shops, grocery stores, and various other retailers. For a number of years Coffee Savvy had benefited from large markups on its products, which included different flavours of Arabica, Robusta, and Kona beans. But Sarah Walker, founder and CEO of Coffee Savvy, recently noticed that its coffee's premium pricing was unable to capture the more price-sensitive segments of the market. After announcing her concerns at a board meeting, Sarah got an interesting suggestion from her marketing director, Negeen Maneshi.

"We can offer consumers a whole new product line: Coffee Sensation. It'll be essentially the same beans we're already selling, but with the new name and cheaper packaging. We can still offer our premium coffee at the same price we have in the past, but launching a new line of beans at a lower price will help us capture a part of the market we've never had access to. With the high margin we earn on our premium coffee, we can definitely afford a product line with a lower gross margin. Although our average gross margin will decline, we'll increase our market share, our sales volume, our total net profit, and our brand recognition. What do you think?"

If you were Sarah, what would be your response to Negeen's proposal?

MAPLE LEAF FOODS

Maple Leaf Foods has been a leading Canadian food-processing company for many years. In an attempt to attract more health-conscious consumers, it's introduced a line of deli meats under the name Natural Selections, promoting it heavily as having no added preservatives. Many consumers have said that if they were comparing two deli products, one having nitrites and one nitrite-free, they would choose the latter. After all, the Canadian Cancer Society has identified nitrites as an important likely contributor to colon and some other cancers.

Maple Leaf Foods had found a way to remove nitrites from the list of ingredients in its Natural Selections line: it replaced the word "nitrites" with the words "cultured celery extract." Working in conjunction with the Canadian Food Inspection Agency, Maple Leaf Foods was able to develop the new label, promoting the product as "natural." The problem is that celery is loaded with nitrites (harmless when eaten in celery and other vegetables), and while these are naturally occurring, they are, according to nutrition expert Dr. Yoni Freedhof, biologically identical to the nitrites normally found in processed meats. In fact, a 2011 study published in the *Journal of Food Protection* found that "natural" hot dogs had up to 10 times the amount of nitrites found in regular hot dogs.

Companies are often quick to promote words that are "hot" with consumers: environmentally friendly, green, cholesterol free, sodium reduced, trans-fat free, natural, healthy, fibre rich, etc. Consumers who read "sodium reduced" on a label look to see the sodium content, but those who are less careful may not discover that the low sodium content they see on the label really relates to a small portion of what's in the can, bottle, or package. Deceptive practices, particularly by well-known companies, help increase the general skepticism many consumers feel about marketing: *caveat emptor.*

What role should government, business, and even consumers themselves play in protecting consumers?

CHEM-FREE WATER TREATMENT SOLUTIONS

Chem-Free Water Treatment Solutions was a manufacturer of home water-filtration systems for filtering household tap water. The company sold its product to households across Canada through a direct, door-to-door sales force. Prospecting for sales leads was usually done through direct mail, advertising, and consumer trade shows. Meredith Lee, the company's national sales manager, was considering a new prospecting method when she approached the company president.

"We could hire someone in each territory to survey households on attitudes toward health and the environment, and on use of a variety of household products. It would be a short survey, taking no more than five minutes, and would have a lot of filler questions that we really aren't interested in. But we could get information on which households are currently filtering their tap water, what they're using, and how important safe drinking water is to them. Since it's done through door-to-door interviews, we could identify which households are most likely to consider our products, and we could then have one of our salespeople follow up with them a month or two later. I'm sure our salespeople would be more successful closing sales and would spend less time trying to sell to customers who won't likely buy. The increased cost for the market researchers would be quickly covered by the increased sales. What do you think?"

If you were the company president, what would be your response?

HI-END AUDIO

Hi-End Audio was a manufacturer of high-end speakers and amplifiers. The company approached your school and was told you were the top marketing student and might be interested in doing some survey research as a part-time job. After some negotiation, it was determined that you'd survey 600 students through face-to-face interviews at post-secondary institutions in your city. The sample was to include 400 males and 200 females. After some thought, you decided to subcontract part of the work to two of your friends—Melissa Anderson and Bob Arnold—and that each of you would arrange to collect survey responses from 200 students. When the three of you met to begin the first day of data collection, you noticed Melissa looked particularly attractive, and you couldn't help thinking that few males would refuse to let her interview them. You asked her to specifically target male respondents while you and Bob surveyed both males and females.

One of the major purposes of the research was to find out what criteria were most important in the selection of electronic sound equipment. Among the criteria that the manufacturer wanted in the list were price, quality, brand image, appearance, and distortion level. You weren't even sure what "distortion level" meant, so when the data analysis was complete, you were surprised that so many respondents actually picked this as their most important criterion. Upon further investigation, you noticed that most respondents who made this choice were male. A little additional investigation uncovered that almost all of them were from the subgroup surveyed by Melissa Anderson. You suspected strongly that there was a problem.

What, if anything, would you do? Explain your answer.

Massine Bouzerar's First Car

Massine Bouzerar and
H. F. (Herb) MacKenzie

On May 11, 2012, Massine Bouzerar sat at his desk, deep in thought. He put his work aside so that he could consider his most pressing issue. He'd been looking at several cars over recent weeks, had test-driven a few, and now it was time to make a decision.

THE BACKGROUND

In mid-April 2012, Massine bolted from class to catch the last bus that was about to leave the university. Swiping his student card as he got on the bus, he looked around for a seat. To his disappointment, the bus was absolutely full. Pressed up against the side of the bus, one hand clutching his single-strap book bag and the other gripping the overhead rail, Massine tried to keep his balance as the bus pulled away from the curb.

With every turn and twist Massine felt his body moving, every once in a while accidentally elbowing a stranger or stepping on toes. "Sorry," he said several times on the trip home. Most people merely made eye contact and nodded. Standing on the bus always made Massine think of a complex balancing act at a circus: while he tried his best not to fall over or hit someone, the bus driver, as the ringmaster, constantly let people on the bus, making the actors perform with greater difficulty every time the bus got even more crowded. If that wasn't hard enough, the "ringmaster" would accelerate quickly and stop abruptly, make sharp turns and run red lights, and otherwise attempt to make the trip more entertaining for his audience. Every time the bus would stop Massine's heart would begin to beat faster, knowing that someone would be crowd-surfing to find their way out.

"Downtown terminal," the bus's sound system called out, making Massine's eyes blink rapidly, waking him from his doze. He stepped out of the bus into the cold night air and walked toward the platform to catch his next bus. Unfortunately he had to catch three buses, taking him over 45 minutes to finally make it home. "It'd probably take me less time if I walked," he thought to himself, looking at the LED digital clock outside the terminal. "Eleven fourteen," he read. "Should be here any minute now." The clock soon read 11:15, but no bus was to be found. When 11:20 came around and there was still no bus, Massine became restless. "Where *is* that blasted bus?" he thought to himself. "It couldn't have left early, since I'm not the only one on the platform waiting. If I don't get to my transfer point on time I'm going to miss the next bus I have to catch." Finally, at 11:22, a pair of bright white headlights pulled into the terminal, remaining stationary in front of his platform. The doors opened, allowing the waiting crowd onto the bus.

Although this bus gave Massine the chance to sit down, he still felt stressed. The bus had been seven minutes late and had to make it to his transfer point by 11:30, which was unlikely. Sure enough, the bus pulled up to his stop at 11:35, and the next bus he needed— the last bus that night—had already left and was well beyond view. Now he'd have to walk about 20 minutes to his apartment. When he finally got home he dropped his bag on the kitchen table just as the oven clock buzzed, announcing that yet another hour had gone by. "An hour to get home?" he exclaimed. "I've had enough. I'm buying a car!"

ONLINE SEARCH

Over the next several days, Massine began to do some research on different brands and models of used cars available in his region. He commenced by setting a few constraints in order to obtain narrow results specific to his needs. The first thing he knew he wanted in a car was automatic transmission. Not being a very experienced driver, Massine believed that driving a manual car would take time to get used to, and he felt he had enough to learn in his business program. Next, because he knew he'd have the same car for the next four to five years, he wanted to make sure it was loaded with options, including air conditioning, power windows, power locks, and keyless entry at the very least. Finally, he wanted a smaller, compact car that would be fuel efficient. He lived quite a distance from campus.

With all these factors floating around in his mind, Massine decided to start his search on the internet, as it was much more convenient than travelling around town and stopping at various dealerships. Because Natalie, his roommate, had just gotten a car, he asked her for some advice on where to start looking. "You should try AutoTrader first," she said. "It's easy to navigate and you can narrow your search by selecting different criteria you're looking for." AutoTrader was a website where users could post their car ads for free and people could search for particular cars they wanted. For each car the site provided a list of features, a photo album, and the seller's contact information. It was extremely easy for beginners to navigate the site.

Taking Natalie's advice, Massine went on AutoTrader. He first typed his postal code and added the farthest distance he'd be willing to go to buy a car. After selecting a 25-kilometre radius, Massine began browsing. But as soon as his results appeared, he could tell his search had been too broad—the first few pages showed cars priced at over $15 000. Massine decided to set a maximum price of $5000 before taxes; he knew he wanted to spend over $4000 on the car, as he'd use it to commute to university and eventually to his co-op work placement. Massine could pay for the car with cash, and wouldn't go much beyond this amount as he'd need to borrow money, which he didn't want to do. He also wanted at least a 2004 model and an odometer that read below 160 000 kilometres. With this narrower search Massine got only 11 results, but he decided to take a look at them anyway. He didn't really have any preference for the brand of car; he was just looking for something that had all the features he was looking for.

After looking through all his results, Massine could find only a few cars he'd even consider looking at. Discouraged, he bookmarked those cars and decided to ask Natalie for more advice. "Do you think I'm being too fussy?" he asked. "When I try my search for all the features I want, I don't like any of the cars that come up." Natalie quickly interjected: "No, no, I was like that too," she said. "You just have to look in more than one place." She recommended he try using the local Kijiji website, which contained almost 5 million free local classified ads, organized by category. This site also allowed users to narrow their search by setting up restrictions on the results they'd receive.

Once his search results came up on Kijiji, Massine was immediately satisfied. Kijiji was a much more popular website than AutoTrader, which explained why there were so many more ads available to view. Although he got only 19 results, they were much better quality than the ones he'd gotten on AutoTrader. Most of the cars had all the features he was looking for and more, making it harder to pick his favourites. Out of curiosity he decided to try another search on the site by raising his maximum price to $5500: he got three additional results. Massine figured he'd look at those as well, certain that he'd be able to negotiate a price closer to $5000. Once he'd bookmarked all the cars he was interested in, he had eight cars to consider.

DEALERSHIP SEARCH

Then Massine looked for even more possibilities. Buying from a dealership would eliminate some of the risks associated with buying a used car, so he felt that looking there might be a safer bet. Notepad and pencil in hand, he visited several car lots he'd looked up online, but to his disappointment the majority of the cars were well over his price range. Walking away with one or two cars written down, he realized that although getting a car from a dealership eliminates some risk, it also comes at a price: the premium the dealership charges above and beyond what the car is actually worth. Still, Massine knew he didn't want to buy a car that would break down within the first few months, so he seriously considered the ones at the car lots.

TEST DRIVES

On May 7, with over 10 cars making it past the first stage of his search, Massine narrowed his options further based on the car's selling price, year, kilometres registered, features, and insurance cost. After this long and rigorous process, he finally settled on three alternatives he was happy with. That same day he decided to call a dealership, which had a nice compact car for sale, and the owners of two cars he'd found on Kijiji. He scheduled test drives for all of them.

His first test drive was the very next day. The car, a silver 2005 Saturn ION Coupe he'd seen on Kijiji, was slightly over his budget; the seller was asking $5499, which would include the safety test and the emissions test. Although Massine had now developed some knowledge of the features and characteristics he was looking for, he still had very little mechanical knowledge and wouldn't be able to assess whether a car was in good condition. Aware of his limitations, he asked his friend's father, Tim, to join him for the test drives, knowing he'd be able to fill in the gaps. Arriving at the seller's home, they parked on the street and headed to the house. The dusty Saturn was parked in the driveway and the seller, who appeared to be in his early twenties, awaited their arrival wearing ripped jeans, a stained shirt, and scuffed sneakers. "Are you Massine?" he said, looking at Tim. "I'm Massine," Massine answered. "I called yesterday to come see the car."

Once Massine was given the keys, he unlocked the car and looked around inside while Tim checked out the tires and the engine. After establishing that the car looked good both aesthetically—other than the dust—and mechanically, Massine was making his way to the driver's seat when he heard the seller call out, "I want to be in the car for the test drive, just in case."

With the seller in the passenger seat and Tim in the back, Massine drove the car around the neighbourhood, getting a feel for the steering, the gas pedal, and the brakes. Out of all the cars he'd driven before, the leg room was great, especially given the fact that he was fairly tall. Getting out of the car, he instantly knew he really liked the car. It had all the features he wanted and more: power windows, power locks, a sunroof, and a great sound system. Although the car was a bit dirty, it was nothing a good car wash wouldn't fix. After negotiating the price down to $5250, which was still slightly over his budget, Massine told the seller that he'd let him know by the end of the week whether or not he'd take it.

Driving back home with Tim, Massine felt extremely happy with the test drive. "I can definitely see myself driving off with it," he said. The car was sporty, and had only 110 000 kilometres on it. It wasn't too bad on gas either, with a fuel economy of 10.23 litres per 100 kilometres. As Massine went on excitedly about how much he liked the car, Tim interrupted him. "Did he ever actually introduce himself to you?" Massine realized that the seller had never given him his name or even shaken his hand.

On May 9 Massine went with Tim to test-drive the other car he'd found on Kijiji. It was selling for $4500, but that included the safety test, the emissions test, and the Ministry of Transportation's buyer's package. Massine had made arrangements to meet the seller, Joe, at his work, Smith's Flooring Inc. As he was pulling up to the parking lot, Massine saw the silver 2005 Pontiac Pursuit Sedan. It was one of the first cars he'd found on the website and he immediately took a liking to it.

Massine went into Smith's Flooring and asked for Joe, who turned out to be Joe Smith, the owner of the company. He was selling his daughter's car; she'd just moved to a big city and no longer needed a vehicle. As Massine shook his hand he could see that Joe was dressed quite nicely, a noticeable improvement over the last seller. Joe handed him the car keys and said he'd be waiting for him inside while he drove it. Massine took the keys and started the engine, with Tim sitting in the passenger seat. They took it for a drive around the block. Massine noticed that the car's leg room was average—not as spacious as the previous car he drove, but spacious enough for him to drive in reasonable comfort. The Pontiac had the same features as the Saturn, except for a sunroof, which was a bit disappointing. Its fuel economy was comparable to the previous car's: approximately 10 litres per 100 kilometres. The odometer registered 140 000 kilometres.

Getting back to the parking lot, Massine told Joe that he'd enjoyed the ride and negotiated the price down to $4250, $750 below his budget. He let Joe know that he'd decide by the end of the week, as he still had to test-drive one more car. Driving home, Tim mentioned that the seller seemed like a trusting, and probably trustworthy, person.

The next day, Massine and Tim went to test-drive the last car on the list: a silver 2006 Pontiac Wave for sale at a used-car dealership called Steve's Wheels. Massine had been told that he could come by the dealership between 9 a.m. and 6 p.m. and that someone would be glad to assist him.

After arriving at the car lot, Massine and Tim were told to wait by the car and a salesperson would be right with them. The car had all the features Massine was looking for, except for a sunroof and power windows, which, he thought, was a big negative. However, the car was newer, with only 100 000 kilometres on its odometer, and had a fuel economy of 9.4 litres per 100 kilometres. It was certainly the most fuel-efficient car in the group. After waiting for more than 10 minutes, Massine decided to approach a salesperson, Mike, who was walking across the lot. "Oh, my apologies, I didn't think you were a serious buyer," Mike said to Massine, somewhat apologetically. Raising his eyebrows, Massine asked if he could take the car on a test drive and, after Mike checked to see his licence, Massine and Tim got in the car and drove away from the lot. The car felt great on the road: the turns were made easily and the car stopped gently, making it very comfortable to drive. The only downside was that it didn't have the best leg room; it was a more compact vehicle.

The dealer's asking price for the car was $4595, including the safety test, emissions test, buyer's package, and one year of free oil changes, but Mike didn't seem flexible with the price. Massine felt he would have liked to negotiate, as he'd done with the two previous cars. He told Mike that he'd make a decision by the next day, and Mike gave Massine his business card in case he had any additional questions. On the drive home, Tim told Massine that he thought it would be a nice, fuel-efficient car for him, but he didn't like the fact that the salesperson hadn't taken them seriously at first.

THE DECISION

It was now May 11 and time for Massine to make a decision. The first car was ideal in terms of the options it offered, but the price was slightly over his budget and the seller seemed young and naive. The second car had most of the options he wanted and the lowest selling price; however, its odometer had the highest number of kilometres. The last car was the least risky, as it was from a dealership, and it was the most fuel-efficient with the least number of kilometres, but Massine was still troubled by how the salesperson had managed the meeting.

As he considered his alternatives, Massine finally narrowed his choice to two. As he considered them both for some time, he found that the third alternative kept returning to his thoughts. But now he'd had enough: since he'd already dropped that third option from his consideration set, he wasn't going to consider it any further. Eventually, Massine decided between his last two alternatives. He poured himself another coffee and reached for the phone.

Continue, Modify, or Abandon: The Marketing Research Project

Donna Stapleton and
Colleen Sharen

It was Saturday, May 19, 2007, and Cecil James, manager of the market research division at Telelink Call Centre in St. John's, was preparing to download data that had been collected through a telephone survey during the previous 10 days.

Approximately six months earlier, Cecil had begun negotiations with Immanuel United Church of Christ (IUCC) in Sedalia, Missouri, about conducting market research on behalf of the church. Its minister, Pastor Brady Abel, was interested in surveying residents of Sedalia who didn't attend church on a regular basis so that he could better guide the church's evangelism committee in how to plan for outreach. Pastor Abel had located Telelink Research through an online client-to-business matching service.

Since then Cecil had worked closely with Pastor Abel to design and fine-tune the survey questionnaire to meet IUCC's research objectives. He knew that the pastor was anxiously awaiting the results in Missouri. With the raw survey data now in front of him, Cecil's task was to analyze the data and prepare a report on the findings. He sincerely hoped that the information gathered, and the report he was about to prepare, would address the problems Pastor Abel was facing. Given some of the issues that

Telelink had experienced in the design and collection of data, Cecil wondered whether he should continue with the analysis, notify the client of his concerns about the data, abandon the project, conduct additional research, or start all over.

TELELINK INCORPORATED

Telelink was an ISO 9001:2000 certified call centre that provided both business-to-business and business-to-consumer call centre services. Outsourcing requirements could be met on a project-by-project basis or through developing a long-term, more comprehensive, partnership.

For nearly 46 years Telelink had operated as a 24-hour, 365-days-per-year, fully automated contact centre, providing inbound and outbound call and data management in French and English for nearly 500 clients all over North America. Its facility at 44 Austin Street provided staff with an environment that had the latest in call-centre technology, was climate controlled, and was ergonomically correct for their safety and comfort.

Telelink's market research division had been in operation for over eight years and had a wide range of experience in such areas as satisfaction surveys, opinion surveys, ISO-required surveys, and political polling. Its clients included utility companies, municipal and provincial governments, colleges and universities, and several news media throughout Canada and the United States. Depending on the client's needs, Telelink Research offered a full range of services, from simple data collection on paper questionnaires to computerized data collection (CATI) using a predictive dialer and data analysis in SPSS, followed, if required, by summary reports of the findings, conclusions, and recommendations for future action.

Outbound calls were made in English and French, as required, by an experienced team of results-oriented professionals supervised by call centre team leaders. In addition to general training, interviewers undertook study-specific training sessions involving role playing for anticipated scenarios in each project to familiarize them with the specific research instrument.

Calls were monitored using the real-time audio feature of the dialer. As part of quality control, Telelink Research management usually listened to approximately 10% of the calls handled by its agents. All calls were monitored digitally, with supervisors tracking the progress of individual calls as well as the cumulative results of the dialing progress. Supervisors could track the number of calls that were live answered, non-response rates, and participation rates on a continuous basis. Moreover, all calls made by the dialer were recorded. These recordings were normally stored for a period of six months and were used to randomly spot-check that the agent had indeed entered the proper answer in response to the questions posed. This feature was particularly useful in checking what might appear to be anomalous or seemingly out-of-range data in the electronic data file.

IMMANUEL UNITED CHURCH OF CHRIST

Immanuel United Church of Christ (IUCC) was located in Sedalia, a city in west central Missouri that had been founded in 1860. In 2006, according to the U.S. Census Bureau, the population was just over 20 000 people, residing in about 9000 households. Sedalia was located within the "Bible Belt" of the United States; in 2006 there were approximately 70 places of worship within its boundaries.

IUCC had its beginnings on October 29, 1876, when nine men met with Reverend Carl Kraft to organize the Immanuel Evangelical Congregation. Reverend Kraft had been sent to western Missouri by the home mission board of the Evangelical Synod of North America, a governing body of Protestant churches in the United States, to establish a church that would serve the German-speaking people in the area. At that time, approximately one-fifth of the population of Sedalia was of German descent.

The new congregation held services in various buildings and homes until the first house of worship was constructed through volunteer labour and materials. The 60-by-20-foot frame structure was dedicated in April 1878, when the congregation numbered just over 20 families. The congregation grew, and in 1882 the sanctuary was remodelled and enlarged to seat 200 people. By 1890 the congregation was well established; Sunday school was held every Sunday afternoon, the Ladies Aid Society met regularly, and the Young People's Society was organized.

The cornerstone for the church at the present location was laid in 1896. Through the years, remodelling and the addition of central air kept the more than 100-year-old house of worship beautiful and standing strong to serve the needs of the church and the community. The sanctuary was completely remodelled in 1995.

The most important aspect of the church's history had been its ongoing Christian programs, confirmation, Christian education, ecumenical participation, and concerns of the community and the world.

THE SURVEY

The decision to conduct what would be known as "The Church Growth Survey" was initiated by Pastor Brady Abel in late 2006. He approached the evangelism committee, his closest outreach advisers within the church, with the idea of doing survey research in an effort to be more effective in outreach and to increase the size of the congregation. At that time the congregation consisted of 159 members, a number that had remained constant for the three years Pastor Abel had served; although it had had deaths and transfers of members, new members had joined, keeping its numbers stable.

The evangelism committee was supportive of this idea. After much thought and discussion, Pastor Abel and the committee members determined that they wanted to understand the attitudes and beliefs of those who didn't attend church on a regular basis. They also wanted to understand why people didn't attend church, and to get a better idea of what would encourage them to attend more frequently. Pastor Abel believed that if the church was going to invite people in the city to be part of its faith community, then it needed to be as informed as possible about who the "unchurched" people in Sedalia were. For example, if they wanted a service on a Tuesday night rather than a Sunday morning, the church could look at providing this service.

From past retail experience, Pastor Abel was convinced that the appropriate research method was a telephone survey of Sedalia residents, and so he initiated a search for a marketing research firm that had expertise in this area. He used an online matching service, Respond.com, to find a qualified research company to undertake the project. Within 16 hours of the posting, he received a response from Cecil James at Telelink Research.

After several telephone conversations with Pastor Abel, Cecil determined the church's information needs and provided the pastor with a basic outline of how the project might proceed. He also provided examples of Telelink's experience and expertise in conducting telephone survey research and a list of clients in the United States that the pastor could contact for a reference. After contacting two of these clients and receiving good reports, Pastor Abel informed Cecil of the church's US$5000 budget and the likelihood of a lengthy time frame needed to conduct the project, and then asked if Telelink would be willing to carry out the study. Cecil decided that this would be an interesting research subject and that Telelink was willing to work with the church despite these challenges.

Telelink was told that all expenditures over $1500 had to be agreed to by the church council and then voted on by the congregation. The council comprised 12 members from the congregation, plus the pastor and one member from the evangelism committee. The church council membership was representative of the congregation. Pastor Abel and Cecil proceeded with negotiations and development of the questionnaire, knowing that the congregation might not approve the budget and that the project could be cancelled at any time.

The problems facing Pastor Abel and the evangelism committee were where to find the funds and how to get a final agreement from the church council and the congregation to spend that much money on research. Pastor Abel knew that there was money in the church's outreach funds. He reasoned that, since the research project was designed to help do a better job of understanding people who don't attend church, using these funds would make sense.

An initial draft of the questionnaire was prepared at Telelink, and over the next few months Pastor Abel and Cecil corresponded via email and telephone in a collaborative process to fine-tune a questionnaire that would best meet the interests of the church. Each draft was reviewed by Pastor Abel and received feedback from members of the evangelism committee. (See Exhibit 1.)

The pastor explained that, in addition to needing support from the evangelism committee in the matter, the IUCC had to "feel that God was in this and that the research was a right move for the church spiritually." In February 2007 the evangelism committee and the pastor decided to take a month to think and pray about the research in an effort to ensure that it was in the best interest of the church to continue moving forward. For Telelink, these periods of reflection were unique in their dealings with typical commercial clients.

When the questionnaire was nearly finalized, Pastor Abel met with the outreach committee to get their input and seek their support for using the outreach funds. With the funds approved by the committee, the pastor and one member from the evangelism committee made a presentation to the church council on the Church Growth Survey. The council approved going forward with the research project and sent it to the congregation for a final vote. Pastor Abel was apprehensive about the vote's outcome, as they were seeking approval to spend a significant amount of money. However, immediately after the congregation voted, he was able to email Cecil saying, "Great news! The congregation voted overwhelmingly to proceed with the survey. Thanks for your help up to this point and I look forward to exciting results. Peace, Brady."

Within a few days, all remaining details were finalized and the data collection was completed. All that remained was to analyze the data and prepare the report.

EXHIBIT 1	Survey Questionnaire

Hi, my name is . . . and I'm calling from Telelink Research. This evening we'd like to talk to people who don't attend church on a regular basis. If this applies to you, I'd like to ask you a few questions, if I may, please.

1. How frequently do you attend church? Would you say . . .

    1 _____ Once or twice a year

    2 _____ Two or three times a year

    3 _____ Four or five times a year

    4 _____ Hardly ever

    5 _____ Never

Please tell me if you agree or disagree with the following statements.

	Agree	Disagree	No Opinion
2. I was forced to attend church as a child.	_____	_____	_____
3. Churches are only after your money.	_____	_____	_____
4. I attend church only on special occasions such as Christmas and Easter.	_____	_____	_____
5. I don't see any need to attend church.	_____	_____	_____
6. People who attend church are hypocrites; they think they're better than everyone else.	_____	_____	_____
7. There are so many different churches, I can't decide which one is best.	_____	_____	_____
8. None of my friends attend church.	_____	_____	_____
9. I'll start attending when I get older and need to.	_____	_____	_____
10. I can't spare the time to attend church.	_____	_____	_____

11. Did you ever attend church more frequently than you do now?

    1 Yes _____   (Continue at Question 12)

    2 No _____   (Skip to Question 13)

    3 Refused _____   (Skip to Question 13)

Please tell me if you agree with the following:

12. I used to attend church more frequently than I do but stopped . . .

	Agree	Disagree
12.1 . . . because it got boring	_____	_____
12.2 . . . because I got mad at the church	_____	_____
12.3 . . . because I lost interest	_____	_____
12.4 . . . because of the pastor	_____	_____
12.5 . . . because I don't have the time	_____	_____
12.6 . . . because of work or other commitments	_____	_____
12.7 . . . because of health reasons	_____	_____
12.8 . . . because I don't have transportation	_____	_____

EXHIBIT 1	Survey Questionnaire (continued)

12.9 . . . because I am physically unable _____ _____

12.10 . . . because I don't see any need to attend church _____ _____

13. Is there anything that any church could do to encourage you to attend church more often?

    1 _____ Yes / Perhaps   (Continue at Question 14)

    2 _____ No / Don't know   (Skip to Question 32)

Please tell me if any of the following would encourage you to attend church more frequently.

	Yes	No	No Opinion
14. Children's Christian Education on weekday evenings	_____	_____	_____
15. Singles groups	_____	_____	_____
16. Couples groups	_____	_____	_____
17. Social activities	_____	_____	_____
18. A meal before or after worship	_____	_____	_____
19. A prayer service or healing service	_____	_____	_____
20. Volunteer service	_____	_____	_____
21. More mission or service projects	_____	_____	_____
22. Better Sunday services	_____	_____	_____
23. Better church communications, such as a newsletter	_____	_____	_____
24. More personal contact by minister or board	_____	_____	_____
25. More spiritual classes or events	_____	_____	_____
26. Hispanic worship service	_____	_____	_____
27. A new church building	_____	_____	_____
28. More contemporary music and style of worship	_____	_____	_____
29. Traditional style of worship	_____	_____	_____
30. Evening worship during the week	_____	_____	_____

    (If "Yes" for Question 30, continue at 31; otherwise, skip to Question 32)

31. What evening would be more suitable for you?

    1 _____ Monday

    2 _____ Tuesday

    3 _____ Wednesday

    4 _____ Thursday

    5 _____ Friday

    6 _____ Saturday

32. When you think of churches in the Sedalia area, which one comes to mind first?

    1 _____ Antioch Fellowship

    2 _____ Broadway Presbyterian

    3 _____ Calvary Episcopal

    4 _____ Christ and Trinity Lutheran

EXHIBIT 1	Survey Questionnaire (continued)

5 _____ Community of Christ

6 _____ Cornerstone Baptist

7 _____ First Baptist Church

8 _____ First Christian Church

9 _____ First United Methodist

10 _____ Immanuel United Church of Christ

11 _____ Parkview Christian

12 _____ Sacred Heart

13 _____ St. Paul Evangelical Lutheran

14 _____ Other

15 _____ None   (Skip to Question 34)

33. How are you aware of _____ (bring in name of church from Question 32)?

1 _____ I used to attend

2 _____ I drive by it

3 _____ Yellow pages

4 _____ Newspaper advertising

5 _____ Radio advertising

6 _____ Television advertising

7 _____ The internet

8 _____ No answer

34. Have you ever heard of a community program called "Kids Café"?

1 _____ Yes

2 _____ No

3 _____ Don't know

35. Which of the following groupings contain your age? Is it . . .

1 _____ Up to 29

2 _____ 30 to 39

3 _____ 40 to 49

4 _____ 50 to 59

5 _____ 60 to 69

6 _____ 70 and over

7 _____ Refused

36. Gender

1 _____ Male

2 _____ Female

That's all my questions. Thank you for your time.

THE RESEARCH DESIGN

Since there was no standard way to define "regular" church attendance, serious consideration was given to include in the survey anyone who would talk about his or her church attendance, or lack thereof, and to develop different streams of questions based on frequency of attendance. But this raised an issue, as shown in the following email from Cecil to Pastor Abel in early January 2007:

> We've been considering how the agents will introduce themselves when a person answers the phone, looking at it from the perspective of talking to both churchgoers and non-churchgoers. However, that seems to pose a problem. We think that an introduction that encompasses both groups will result in most non-churchgoers refusing even before we have the chance to assure them that we need their input. Generally speaking, people don't participate in surveys when they think the subject matter doesn't involve them. If your goal is to talk to people who don't go to church, and to understand why they don't and what will attract them, I suggest we attempt to talk only to people who don't go to church.
>
> If you agree with that, the introduction would be as follows: "Hi, my name is . . . and I'm calling from Telelink Research. This evening/today/etc. we're talking to residents of Sedalia who don't attend church on a regular basis, and if that applies to you, I'd like to ask you a few questions, if I may, please?"

Pastor Abel and James gave considerable thought to the issue and finally agreed that yes, the possibility of losing those they really wanted to speak with outweighed any benefit they might get from talking to those who attended church more or less regularly. The pastor also realized that surveying church attendees might become contentious with other churches in Sedalia: "I'm thinking that we might want to keep this geared for people who aren't regularly attending church. I just wouldn't want to get other churches in any kind of uproar about surveying their members. But non–church attendees should be available for questions we want to ask." After much thought and discussion, Pastor Abel and Cecil agreed that selecting appropriate respondents wasn't so much about how many times a year people attended church, but rather their attitudes and thoughts regarding their lack of attendance. Consequently, they agreed to use the "screener" introduction Cecil had suggested, allowing respondents to participate based on their own determination that they didn't attend church on a regular basis.

Having agreed on who would respond to the survey, Cecil turned his attention to the number of respondents needed to meet the objectives of the study. In the absence of any definitive statistics from which to determine the size of Sedalia's non-churchgoing population, it was assumed that the population was large. Given that Telelink wished to provide results whose margin of error was approximately +/–5% at the 95% confidence interval, it was decided to target a sample size of 400 completed interviews.

Based on past experience, and given the nature of the topic, James recognized that it would be difficult to achieve this sample size, and so deemed it prudent to acquire a large database of phone numbers to draw from. Consequently, he purchased the complete electronic phone directory of nearly 9000 phone numbers for Sedalia. In order to ensure that every subject in the database had an even chance of being included in the survey, the database was randomized prior to being loaded in the automatic dialer. The intention was to dial from the top of the randomized database until the target sample size of 400 was achieved.

Almost immediately after calling began, Cecil's concerns about achieving this sample size were realized: after calling nearly 1200 numbers, only 27 interviews had been completed. Moreover, interviewers reported that Question 12 in the questionnaire (see Exhibit 1) provided insufficient options to cover participants' responses. Interviewing was suspended for the remainder of the session until the questionnaire was appropriately modified, and calling recommenced the following day.

At the end of 10 interviewing sessions, all phone numbers in the database had been called at least once, and only 249 interviews had been completed. After all numbers in the database had been dialed once, the nearly 1200 numbers that had been busy, hadn't been answered, or where no adult was at home on the initial call were set up for redial. A recall of these numbers netted 17 completed interviews. In addition, nearly 2400 calls initially went to voice mail; a recall of 500 of these netted just three completed interviews.

An analysis of the final call data revealed that approximately 49% of all numbers dialed were answered by a live respondent. Of that number:

- Approximately 6% agreed to do the survey, with a small percentage of these quitting before reaching the end.

- Approximately 54% refused to participate, many of them even before the introduction was complete. In fact, more than 10% simply picked up and then dropped the receiver without even speaking.

- Approximately 36% said they attended church regularly and disqualified themselves. Many of them went to some pains to convince the interviewer that they were telling the truth!

- For the remainder, no adult was available or willing to participate at the time the call was placed.

On Friday, May 18, James communicated to Pastor Abel in an email, saying,

Since we last spoke, we've managed to complete just 23 or 24 interviews. We've gone through the phone database in its entirety and have recalled over 2000 of the initially non-responsive numbers. As we say, it's worse than pulling teeth. Last night I had two agents working for about an hour and got one complete survey, so I cancelled the session. It's not unusual to struggle when recalling numbers, but this was about the worst I've ever seen: phones weren't being answered, people were hanging up, etc. I really don't think there's any point in pursuing it further. We have 249 completed interviews from which we can provide a report. From what I've seen so far I think we've collected some useful information. And, as I said in our last phone conversation, there will be no further charge for you for this project.

Within a few hours, Pastor Abel responded,

Thanks for the update. I'm meeting with the council on Sunday, and I'm expecting that we'll accept the 249 responses with the understanding that there is no additional charge. If there's any change, I'll let you know.

The following morning, after contemplating Pastor Abel's upcoming meeting with the church council, Cecil decided that it would be helpful to analyze the data and prepare a preliminary report of the survey findings.

As he sat in front of his computer to conduct the analysis, Cecil reviewed his concerns about the project. Given issues with the screener, the sample size, and the design of Question 12, he worried that the results of the study weren't as reliable as he would have liked. What should he do? If the client was dissatisfied with the project, it could reflect negatively on Telelink.

Cecil considered his options. He could continue as planned, completing the analysis and writing the preliminary report. Or he could complete the analysis, noting the potential weaknesses of the data in the report. He could do further research using a different method to validate the weaker data. He could suggest to the client that the data was too compromised to provide reliable information, or he could recommend that the current data be scrapped and they start over again with a better research design. No matter what he did, he'd have to consider the church's limited financial resources.

Cecil knew he needed to figure this out quickly, as Pastor Abel was meeting with the church council the next day.

Riverside Credit Union

Jeff Schulz and
Peggy Cunningham

Frank Timmerman, vice-president of marketing at Riverside Credit Union, sat at his desk with a smile on his face. After months of effort, he felt he really had a handle on Riverside's membership. He'd been in charge of the initiative to segment the membership base to see if he could better understand how different members contributed to the profitability of the credit union. He also wanted to know which members he should concentrate on in terms of building their business to ensure future profitability. Having a better understanding of the various segment profiles, he believed, would also help the Credit Union better target appropriate financial products to members.

BACKGROUND

Riverside is a well-established credit union with just over 100 000 retail members and a small but rapidly growing business membership of about 10 000. Credit unions are similar to banks in many respects, but there are a number of key differences.

Jeff Schulz, vice-president of marketing at VanCity Credit Union, and Peggy Cunningham, Dalhousie University, wrote this case as a basis for class discussion. It is not intended to illustrate the effective or ineffective handling of a management situation. Some data have been disguised to protect confidentiality. Copyright © 2009. Reprinted with permission.

Like banks, they offer many financial services—everything from savings and chequing accounts to investment advice. Unlike banks, credit unions don't have customers—they have members. These members are the actual owners of the credit union. Furthermore, credit unions have a strong sense of social responsibility in addition to their financial responsibility.

Riverside Credit Union, for example, describes itself as a democratic, ethical, innovative provider of financial services to its members. It's committed to doing business in a way that strengthens not only its own long-term success but also contributes to the social, economic, and environmental well-being of the community in which it operates.

It has been quite successful, with assets of almost $2.5 billion under administration. Much of its success is due to its excellent member service culture, the regular introduction of new competitive products, and an aggressive pricing policy that ensures members are always getting some of the best rates available. Riverside Credit Union also has a good distribution network with which to serve its members. It has 15 branches, 30 ATMs, PC banking, a call centre mostly dedicated to serving members, and an interactive voice-response phone banking system. It also has a number of mortgage development managers. During the past two years the branch sales force had been realigned to focus more on relationship selling. The sales force has placed the greatest emphasis on members with high deposit balances.

Riverside Credit Union is located in a large urban area that, until recently, has been growing a little faster than the rest of the country. During the last year or so the economy has been slowing, resulting in much more competition between financial institutions. There's also more competition from category killers, which have been focusing on specific product areas like credit cards and mortgages. The internet has facilitated this type of banking as well as that done by other "direct" financial institutions, which are aggressively competing for savings and investment accounts, with rates approaching term-deposit levels. Continuing pressure on margin has made it impossible for Riverside Credit Union to maintain its aggressive pricing policy, and as a result it has seen some erosion of its core business.

Riverside has long prided itself on having a strong product marketing group. Frank Timmerman was a member of this group. One of the tools that has been invaluable to the marketing group is the Member Database Information System (MDIS). This database captures all the product information (except the off-balance mutual fund business). Frank knew that although there'd been a lot of member analysis and research, most of it revolved around specific products. Little was known about the full value or nature of the relationships Riverside Credit Union had with its membership.

Thus, under Frank's leadership, a new project was launched so that the marketing department could deepen its understanding of the membership. Frank thought it was critical that Riverside Credit Union be able to anticipate its members' needs and to build long-term relationships with them. The information currently available in the database was not up to this task. Therefore, a detailed segmentation analysis was conducted of the entire retail membership. The marketing team hired an expert in segmentation to assist with the work. When the project started, no one knew exactly what the results would show.

SEGMENTATION APPROACH

Frank believed that getting this type of information was a pressing need given the growing competition in his marketplace. Since he had only a short time frame within which to complete the initial study, he decided to use only the data currently available in the MDIS for the analysis. Any external data he might want, or external research he might conduct later, could be added once he had a firmer understanding of the various member segments. Frank and the team felt that some information, such as share of wallet, would be too difficult to get for the entire membership or would be too inaccurate to be useful.

Frank and the team decided there were three things they most needed to know about the membership: (1) profitability of the relationships, (2) behaviour of the members with regard to their usage of various Riverside Credit Union products and services, and (3) future potential. Details on each of these dimensions and the data used in the analysis are outlined below.

Profitability was examined by summing the margin, fee, and service-charge revenues for each member and then subtracting the expenses. With the assistance of Accounting, the total cost for each transaction type was identified and then divided by the total number of transactions in order to generate a per-transaction cost. With input from Sales and Branch Operations, setup and maintenance costs were also determined. Even though a few numbers were missing, the team agreed that the calculation would represent each member's relative profitability. To understand the dynamics of the membership, profitability would be looked at by value and by decile.

Member behaviour, or the type of financial relationship the person had with Riverside Credit Union, was the next variable analyzed. To understand this, Riverside compiled all the data it had for each member for the past year, including age, length of membership, transactional data, account information, channel information, and more. A clustering technique was used so that members who demonstrated similar behaviours were grouped together, while keeping the groups as distinct as possible.

Potential was estimated by predictive models developed for Riverside's core products (RRSPs, mortgages, term deposits, loans, credit cards, and lines of credit, etc.). These models were created using statistical techniques (such as regression) and were based on data from members who had previously purchased the product; the model could then be used to predict future sales of that particular product. Riverside had used predictive models successfully in the past to target product campaigns, and it was pretty comfortable with their use. Each member would be scored for each product. This information was then added to the analysis.

SEGMENTATION RESULTS

Profitability: Exhibit 1 summarizes the annual member profitability analysis.

Behaviour segments: Seven different member segments emerged from the analysis. They are described in Exhibit 2 in order of average profitability. Each segment profile also includes a description of average funds under administration (FUA) and average products per member.

Frank conducted some further analysis, which quickly showed that although segments 6 and 7 had the lowest average profit and cost Riverside Credit Union money to serve, the majority of members that had negative profitability were in segment 4 (with 30% of segment

EXHIBIT 1	Annual Member Profitability Analysis			
Profit Tier	Number of Members	Percentage	Cumulative Percentage	Average Annual Profit
Top 10%	300	.3	.3	$9000
10 to 20	1 000	1.0	1.3	$2700
20 to 30	1 300	1.3	2.6	$2077
30 to 40	1 900	1.9	4.5	$1421
40 to 50	2 300	2.3	6.8	$1174
50 to 60	3 000	3.0	9.8	$900
60 to 70	4 000	4.0	13.8	$675
70 to 80	6 000	6.0	19.8	$450
80 to 90	8 000	8.0	27.8	$338
90 to 100	35 000	35.0	62.8	$77
Zero profit	19 200	19.2	82.0	$0
Negative profit	18 000	18.0	100.0	($100)
Total	**100 000**			

EXHIBIT 2	Member Segment Profiles			
Segment	Number of Members	Average Profit	Average FUA	Products/Member
1	12 000	$900	$150 000	4.5
	Complex relationship with multiple products, mortgage holders, with RRSPs, high lending, all channels utilized with high transaction levels.			
2	8 000	$600	$51 000	3.5
	High-balance non-RRSP savers, average transaction levels, traditional channel usage (phone, branch, ATM), slightly older, low lending.			
3	13 000	$310	$27 000	2.3
	Older, average transactions, average balances, low lending, ATM and branch transactions.			
4	25 000	$225	$22 000	3.2
	High lending, high transactions, all channels, similar to segment 1 except with low mortgage usage, high credit card penetration.			
5	15 000	$135	$10 000	2.2
	Savers (RRSP and other), average balances, low transactions, limited channels.			
6	7 000	$20	$ 3 100	.3
	Younger, savers with lower balances and average transactions.			
7	23 000	$17	$ 1 100	1.1
	Single-product accounts, inactive, low transactions, low balances.			

4 generating approximately 60% of the total negative profit). Segment 4 members conducted a lot of transactions across all channels, but they didn't have high enough balances or revenue to offset the transaction costs.

Potential: All the behaviour segments had some members that had higher predictive scores for some products. When the overall scores were combined to give an indication of relative potential, Frank was able to create an index for each segment. Under the indexing system, a score of 100 is average; anything over 100 means higher than average potential. Exhibit 3 outlines the segment indexes.

The segmentation analysis provided the marketing department with tremendous insight, not only about the membership's current status, but also about individual segments' future potential. With more knowledge about which members were profitable, the marketing department was able to develop member-focused strategies geared to help Riverside Credit Union either retain the member or further develop the relationship through targeted cross-selling programs. Marketing used the information to help restructure their department. Frank was convinced it would help Riverside transition from being product-focused to being more member-focused.

EXHIBIT 3	Segment Indexes	
Segment	Potential Index	High-Potential Products
1	125	Mortgage, RRSP, LOC, Credit Card
2	150	Terms, RRSP
3	140	RRSP, Term
4	200	RRSP, Mortgage, Credit Card, Loans
5	100	RRSP, Mortgage, Credit Card
6	55	Term
7	40	Low on most, some Credit Card

Fork and Dagger

Massine Bouzerar and
H. F. (Herb) MacKenzie

In October 2012, Richard Lynch, owner and founder of the Fork and Dagger pub in
Struan, Ontario, was getting close to retirement and wanted to transfer the business
ownership to his two sons, Bradley and Jason. Both sons had been working in the business for quite some time: Bradley for more than 15 years, and Jason for more than 12.
Between them, they had experience with all aspects of running the pub, and Richard felt
confident that they'd be able to manage the business. But he also knew that his two sons
had very mixed views on how to grow the pub: Bradley wanted to completely change
Fork and Dagger's positioning, targeting the lesbian, gay, bisexual, and transgendered
(LGBT) community, while Jason simply wanted to focus on developing the pub's promotions and doing renovations to attract a larger crowd. Richard had asked his two sons
to present their plans for the future of the business so that he could make the final decision about what would or wouldn't happen at Fork and Dagger before his retirement.
Richard was concerned that if he retired without having resolved the issue, the struggle
that could result between Bradley and Jason could escalate, management of the business could be affected, and ultimately the business could simply continue to lose
revenue—as it had been slowly doing over the past few years.

COMPANY BACKGROUND

Fork and Dagger was founded in 1993 by Richard Lynch, who saw potential growth in Struan's food and hospitality industry, specifically its pubs and bars. Having worked as kitchen manager for a large chain restaurant, Richard felt he could provide the Struan community with a more casual dining atmosphere while still serving good-quality food at reasonable prices. That was how he came up with the pub's slogan: "Where the beer is hot, the food is cold, and the servers are delicious!"

As a way of attracting business, Fork and Dagger provided both a quiet, semi-formal dining area for those wanting a better dining experience and a bar area where many people came simply to socialize and share a few drinks, sometimes with light snacks or "pub food." Richard believed that attracting such a broad market gave the pub a competitive advantage, and that this was a sustainable strategy for his business.

In order to compete with other restaurants in the area, Richard felt that Fork and Dagger needed all the features the current market offered. Therefore, within the first year of operations, he invested in 10 wall-mounted televisions and a cable subscription. Sporting events played continuously on the screens in the bar area, while in the dining area programming varied depending on the time of day (with sporting events seldom shown). In that same year the 1994 Winter Olympics were broadcast live from Norway, with the time difference meaning that events were on late at night. A large crowd of late-night sports enthusiasts was attracted to the pub, and this quickly helped create awareness for Fork and Dagger. Sales increased rapidly and the pub gained a reputation for being a fun place to meet and socialize.

At first, Richard relied heavily on this word-of-mouth advertising to help his business get started. The sports crowd was supplemented by family friends and a large group of students from the nearby college. Students were particularly attracted on Thursday and Friday nights, with a number of faculty members also showing up on those nights. Many people from the local business community came in at the end of the workday for a beer or two, but most stayed only an hour or so, and only occasionally did they order food. Saturdays and Sundays were especially popular for food sales, with many from the local community coming in for lunch or dinner on those days. Fork and Dagger eventually grew to include 28 bar tables, each with four movable stools; 12 more-formal dining tables, each with four to six chairs; and six booths, each with seating for four to six people.

Sales Revenue, 2009-2012

Richard was concerned when it became apparent that Canada was in a recession in 2008, but his fears were unfounded. While many more expensive restaurants saw a decline in sales, Fork and Dagger seemed to be more or less immune to the changing economic climate. Sales in 2008 were higher than in 2007, and there was no indication that Fork and Dagger's revenues would suffer. However, in 2009 Richard saw sales decline for the first year since he'd started the business 17 years earlier. It was only a small decrease, but significant for being the first Fork and Dagger had ever experienced. Revenues continued to decrease in 2010 and again in 2011. Exhibit 1 shows Fork and Dagger's 2008–2011 income statements.

EXHIBIT 1	Fork and Dagger's Year-End Income Statements, April 30, 2008-2011			
	2008	**2009**	**2010**	**2011**
REVENUES				
Alcohol	$1 209 350	$1 168 001	$1 125 964	$1 056 709
Food	$1 273 000	$1 229 475	$1 185 225	$1 112 325
Merchandise	$63 650	$61 474	$59 261	$55 616
TOTAL REVENUES	$2 546 000	$2 458 950	$2 370 450	$2 224 650
EXPENSES				
Cost of Goods Sold				
Liquor	$76 380	$73 769	$71 114	$66 740
Beer	$152 760	$147 537	$142 227	$133 479
Draft	$203 680	$196 716	$189 636	$177 972
Wine	$45 828	$44 261	$42 668	$40 044
Food	$547 390	$528 674	$509 647	$478 300
Total	$1 026 038	$990 957	$955 291	$896 534
Operating Expenses				
Wages*	$611 040	$598 148	$579 908	$556 916
EI expense	$15 276	$14 954	$14 423	$14 048
Casual labour	$30 552	$29 507	$28 445	$26 696
CPP expense	$22 914	$22 131	$21 334	$20 022
WCB	$9 165	$9 165	$9 165	$9 165
Benefits	$7 638	$7 377	$7 111	$6 674
Total Payroll	$696 585	$681 282	$660 386	$633 521
Advertising	$40 736	$40 343	$40 027	$40 594
Restaurant supplies	$68 742	$66 392	$64 002	$62 066
Entertainment	$127 300	$125 948	$122 523	$123 233
Total	$933 363	$913 965	$886 938	$859 414
General & Admin				
Bookkeeping	$25 466	$25 550	$25 254	$25 330
Cleaning	$25 460	$25 170	$24 860	$24 190
Insurance	$15 276	$15 328	$15 331	$15 367
Bank charges	$25 460	$25 408	$25 479	$24 511
Sponsorships	$12 730	$13 000	$11 200	$11 600
Office supplies	$1 527	$1 611	$1 559	$1 570
Promotions	$50 920	$49 010	$47 870	$43 330
Cable	$5 092	$5 109	$5 158	$5 211
Rent	$127 300	$127 300	$127 300	$127 300

EXHIBIT 1	Fork and Dagger's Year-End Income Statements, April 30, 2008–2011 (continued)			
	2008	**2009**	**2010**	**2011**
Repairs & maintenance	$38 190	$37 000	$37 300	$38 000
Telephone	$6 365	$6 378	$6 395	$6 409
Gas	$17 822	$17 853	$17 809	$17 798
Hydro	$38 190	$38 330	$38 370	$38 280
Water	$10 184	$10 164	$10 178	$10 157
Total	$399 982	$397 211	$394 063	$389 053
TOTAL EXPENSES	$2 359 383	$2 302 133	$2 236 292	$2 145 001
NET INCOME	$186 617	$156 817	$134 158	$79 649

*Richard, Bradley, and Jason all took a salary from the business, included in the wages.

It was evident to Richard that the market for pubs and bars in Struan was slowly becoming more and more saturated. Most customers who visited Fork and Dagger on a regular basis continued to do so, but some who'd been regulars in the past simply stopped appearing at the pub. Richard believed they had moved to other venues. For example, the local golf club had recently renovated its bar area and was making a concerted effort to attract a loyal group to socialize there. Other bars and pubs in Struan were beginning to offer additional features that hadn't been offered in the past. Big Joe's Sports Bar, several blocks away from Fork and Dagger, had recently renovated its premises, providing its customers with six pool tables in addition to the flat-screen TVs it already had. The Shark Tank, another nearby pub, had recently begun to offer free karaoke nights every Saturday night, and was bringing in a live blues band every Sunday afternoon.

Richard wasn't keen to add these features to Fork and Dagger, since it would mean having to focus more on the bar area of his business, compromising his dining room customers' experience. And with limited room in the pub, he'd have to eliminate several tables to accommodate pool tables and a karaoke stage, which he really didn't want to do. He was also concerned that live music in the bar area in the afternoons would drive away his dining room crowd on Sundays. Richard believed that the atmosphere he'd established at the pub, as well as the outstanding service his staff provided, would continue to set Fork and Dagger apart from its competitors. Still, knowing he'd have to make changes or sales would continue to decline, he decided it was time to get Bradley and Jason more involved in the decision making. After all, the future of Fork and Dagger would be their concern. He'd now asked each of them for their thoughts, knowing very well that they'd have very different views of what should be done to increase sales.

BRADLEY'S PROPOSAL: TARGETING A NEW MARKET

Bradley Lynch obtained his Bachelor of Arts degree in 2005 from a prestigious Ontario university. He continued to work at Fork and Dagger during summer vacations and breaks from his studies. After graduation he returned from university with his friend, Lester

Branson, and the two got an apartment in downtown Struan. Bradley continued to work at the pub, while Lester, because he and Bradley were uncomfortable with Richard and Jason's reactions once their relationship was made public, decided to keep away from Fork and Dagger. He found a job as a salesperson at a local car dealership. After a while, though, Lester began to come to Fork and Dagger, and he and Bradley soon found acceptance by both Richard and Jason. Bradley eventually became the food and service manager, responsible for hiring, training, and managing the bar, dining room, and kitchen staff, and for ensuring that customers enjoyed their time at Fork and Dagger. He was very effective in engaging customers and finding out what they liked and what they wanted to see improved at Fork and Dagger. He was constantly considering the pub's strengths, who its customers were, and where there might be additional opportunities to increase their satisfaction.

Over the last couple of months Bradley has been entertaining the idea of changing the pub's positioning strategy. Fork and Dagger was targeting a huge but undifferentiated market: people who lived and worked in Struan and the surrounding areas. With such a broad target market Bradley felt that all advertising effort was wasted, and that it might be better aimed at one or more concentrated market segments. If Fork and Dagger could attract a large, underserved segment, it could establish greater customer loyalty and hence reverse its revenue decline.

Then, one Friday night, Bradley thought he had an insight. Lester was sitting at a table with about a dozen of their friends when it dawned on Bradley that these weren't the only gay customers in the bar; in fact, when he looked around the pub area, he realized that about 15% of the customers were LGBT. Bradley had read somewhere that about 10% of the population were members of the LGBT community, and if that were true, then Fork and Dagger was already attracting a good following within this market segment. No other pub in the Struan area was targeting the segment, and Bradley began to wonder whether there was an opportunity here. Furthermore, as a homosexual male, Bradley figured he'd be in a better position to identify with this market's wants, allowing him to better attract the LGBT community.

When developing his proposal, Bradley did some informal marketing research. He began by identifying friends he knew were homosexual and collecting information on their "per-person average expenditure" during their visits to Fork and Dagger. Over a two-week period he identified 50 tables where he knew the customers were all homosexual. Many of these customers were included several times, as they were regulars and often came to the pub with different friends each time. Among the 50 tables he included in his sample were 163 people; Bradley estimated this total as comprising about 82 unique individuals. For his comparison sample he randomly chose 50 tables of people he knew weren't homosexual. Among these 50 tables were a total of 145 people, translating to about 128 unique individuals. When he compared the cash register receipts, he found that those whom he'd identified as homosexual spent, on average, about 10% more than the other customers. Furthermore, they came in larger than average groups—3.3 people per table versus 2.9—and they seemed to be more loyal, since there were fewer unique individuals among this group compared with the comparison group. Bradley was unsure whether this last assumption was a valid one, but it did agree with what he believed to be likely.

These results were far better than Bradley had expected, and the more he thought about it, the more convinced he became that targeting the LGBT community would be a great idea. He was certain he'd get resistance from his father and brother, but he felt that now was the time to make his pitch. Fork and Dagger certainly couldn't continue to lose revenue if he and Jason were to have a long-term successful business.

JASON'S PROPOSAL: MARKET PENETRATION

After graduating from high school in 2006, Jason Lynch began working at Fork and Dagger as a bartender. Over subsequent years he worked in every area of the business, from waiter, to cook, to buyer. He eventually gravitated to internal operations, becoming responsible for purchasing food, alcohol, and supplies; for scheduling staff to ensure that adequate people were on hand to meet the pub's needs throughout the week; for organizing costing information about purchases and wages so that it was available for the pub's accountant; and for handling the accounts payable, including issuing cheques each week to staff. Over the years he gained considerable technical knowledge of how to manage the pub. He was interested in all aspects of the business, although he lacked Bradley's engaging personality and was less interested in the pub's customers.

When hearing from his father that the pub's sales were declining, Jason wasn't surprised: he'd been noticing that his purchases were getting smaller and that he'd often have to send staff home early when he miscalculated demand. In his opinion, the main reason Fork and Dagger's revenues were declining was that the customers were becoming bored with the place and starting to visit other venues. The walls had been the same colour for years, and the decorations were the same as when he first started to work in the business. The wall-mounted televisions were getting old and there were no exciting attractions to set the pub apart from its competitors.

From talking to some of his friends who were regulars, Jason concluded that renovations would improve the pub's atmosphere and make it a more enjoyable experience. He hadn't given promotions a lot of thought, but he knew there had to be many possibilities for better promoting the business. He was thinking about the traditional ones: ladies' night, happy hours, etc. He was also wondering if the pub could leverage social media somehow, since he'd heard of some restaurants that promoted specials through Twitter and others that provided online coupons. What he knew for sure was that people were no longer looking for a place to simply eat and drink; they were looking for entertainment and excitement. They wanted to be engaged, to feel part of the business where they spent their money.

Because the pub was operating well below full capacity, Jason thought it would be a good idea to replace a few tables in the bar area with pool tables—and with some creative organization, he'd need to get rid of only eight bar tables. He estimated the cost of four fully equipped pool tables to be about $5000 each. Jason also wanted to install a karaoke system, which he thought would cost about $1500, and to hire a DJ and some live music for special events throughout the year. DJs usually charged between $75 and $125 per hour. Musicians and live bands could vary from $40 per hour for a single singer or musician to as much as $200 per hour for a three- or four-person band. Of course, he'd vary the music depending on time of day and whatever group of customers might be in attendance at any particular time. Repainting the pub's interior would cost about $6000, and new seating would cost about $900 per bar table (including four chairs), $2000 per dining room table (including four chairs), and $2500 for each new booth.

THE FUTURE OF FORK AND DAGGER

After listening to both Bradley and Jason, Richard was concerned that their views for the future of Fork and Dagger were so very different. He was wondering which approach the business should take. Should the pub target the LGBT community and shift to a narrowly targeted population? Or should it change its decor, modernize its seating, and add new forms of entertainment to compete with some of the newer pubs in the area? Was there a way to accommodate the wishes of both Bradley and Jason, given that both would need to be happy with the pub's direction if they were to remain committed to its success? Richard wasn't pressed for a rush answer, but he knew he couldn't retire until the issue was resolved. He wanted to leave a sustainable, if not growing, business. He certainly didn't want to abandon the place when it was in decline.

Academic-Zone

Massine Bouzerar and
H. F. (Herb) MacKenzie

In May 2012, Aaron Gorka, a co-op B.B.A. student, was hired to assist Academic-Zone Learning Services in the Student Development Centre at Brock University. His mandate was to help commercialize Academic-Zone, a learning resource created in-house at the university. In his first week Aaron spent some time familiarizing himself with the product and understanding Academic-Zone's customers. In the second week he was approached by Jill Brindle, Academic-Zone's manager, and Margaret Groombridge, its assistant manager, and asked to prepare a preliminary marketing plan. Aaron needed to decide a targeting strategy and make recommendations, specifically with respect to price and promotion. His task was somewhat complex, as the product strategy for Academic-Zone was still evolving.

PRODUCT DEVELOPMENT

In the fall of 2008, in response to Brock University's increasing enrolment and the need to provide timely and appropriate support for its students, Essay-Zone was developed and launched by Academic-Zone Learning Services at the university's Student

Development Centre. Essay-Zone is an online tutorial that teaches students to write properly researched, organized, and cited essays through the use of on-screen pop-ups, virtual quizzes, and flashy graphics. The tutorial is often compared to a virtual book, where users interactively flip through pages and complete quizzes as they finish each chapter. The quizzes give students immediate feedback on their performance, including solutions to the questions they answered incorrectly. Essay-Zone especially targets transitioning students, including first-year students, international students, and mature students who may need to refresh their writing skills.

Jill Brindle created Essay-Zone with co-developers Margaret Groombridge and Philipp Lesmana. Jill completed her B.Ed. at Brock and taught in the public school system for 23 years before returning to work at the university. Her initial appointment was to cover for a sick leave, but she ended up staying. Jill's goal was to raise awareness for Learning Services, as many students were uninformed of the many services it offered. She began thinking of developing a resource that could help students improve their writing skills— and thus Academic-Zone was born.

As Jill continued to develop Academic-Zone, Margaret Groombridge was hired to join the team. Margaret had also completed her B. Ed. at Brock, where she'd been a teaching assistant in the Department of English Language and Literature. Margaret brought a real-world, practical perspective to her work, and she and Jill collaborated closely to further develop Academic-Zone.

As Academic-Zone began growing, they decided to license the resource to other institutions. This shift led them to redo the program's entire software coding, moving from an open-source code (which made it hard to trace the resource's ownership) to a custom-built code that is now Academic-Zone's intellectual property. To make the switch, Learning Services at first hired contract students to work on the coding, but when that didn't work out as planned, Philipp Lesmana joined the team. Philipp too was a Brock graduate, with a background in computer science and an MBA from its business program. Philipp and Margaret were very different: Margaret was extremely practical, while Philipp was very creative and artistic. They complemented each other well.

When developing Essay-Zone, the team wanted to ensure that students would feel comfortable with the academic writing process. With the goal of increasing their confidence in and knowledge of process and terminology, Essay-Zone helped students expand their awareness of the resources available to them, including understanding feedback from assignments, searching through online resources, using student support services, and approaching and speaking with instructors. Academic-Zone also wanted to make sure instructors could implement Essay-Zone quickly and easily so that it didn't create extra workload, as this might reduce its use.

Prior to releasing Essay-Zone across the university, Academic-Zone tested the resource on two student groups: a long-distance education class in 2006 and an international Masters of Accounting class in 2008. Using a program called WebCT, Academic-Zone tracked how much time each student from each group spent on the resource. Analyzing the results, staff realized that international students spent more time on Essay-Zone than others, with some spending as much as three hours on the resource. It appeared that these international students might recognize the need for additional help with writing skills, whereas other students might believe that their skills were already satisfactory.

Within two years of its release, Essay-Zone had approximately 8000 Brock University student registrants and had received a large amount of positive feedback from both students and instructors. The common denominator: they all attested to Essay-Zone's comprehensive approach. Students were able to access Essay-Zone whenever and wherever they wanted, and to assess their own understanding of the different aspects of academic writing. The Essay-Zone feedback clearly indicated what they needed to improve in order to continue developing their writing skills.

FIRST EXTERNAL INTEREST IN ESSAY-ZONE

Essay-Zone's success at Brock University, along with the interest expressed by other academic institutions across Canada, led to the creation of Academic-Zone's website (www.Academic-Zone.com) and to licensing opportunities for the resource. Within a year of its development, Essay-Zone began to stimulate interest across North America, with inquiries coming from as far away as New Zealand. Once an external client licensed use of the product, Academic-Zone began responding to inquiries from places such as Texas State University, City University in Hong Kong, Concordia University in Montreal, and Mount Royal College in Calgary.

Essay-Zone is now licensed to other post-secondary institutions across Canada through the issue of a unique key that allows users to access the Flash workshop material. The main benefit to other institutions is that it saves them the time and money needed for developing their own program in-house. And since Essay-Zone is hosted by Brock University through the online access it provides, it requires no installation and enables support for large numbers of students on the resource at the same time. With their 2011 revenues ranging between $20 000 and $30 000, Jill and Margaret knew that they could do better in the future.

MODULES

As Academic-Zone continued developing Essay-Zone, it began to split the resource into several modules, each having a different focus. The development staff began by creating three main parent modules, any of which could be licensed to other post-secondary institutions.

The first parent module was the original Essay-Zone Post-Secondary, which was created to support students writing academic papers in college and university. This module breaks down the writing process into seven steps: analyzing the assignment, narrowing a topic, organizing and collecting information, developing a thesis, organizing the essay, writing the first draft, and editing the final document. This module offers exercises and quizzes, as well as video and audio multimedia, to make the content interactive for students.

The second parent module developed was Essay-Zone Transition, created to support senior high school students and students transitioning to college and university academic writing. This module encompasses three units: Prep-It, which is the pre-writing stage; Write-It, which is the writing stage; and Polish-It, which is the editing and revision stage. The module was initially crafted to align itself with the Ontario secondary school curriculum.

The third parent module developed was Numeracy-Zone, created to support students who are entering college and university and who might lack confidence in their numeracy skills. This parent module encompasses three Transition Numeracy units, which cover basic calculations such as percentages and decimals, basic statistics, and basic algebra.

In addition to the three parent modules, Academic-Zone has created supplementary modules that serve as add-ons to the parent modules. Four add-on modules have been developed: Business Grammar and Business Formats, both helping students familiarize themselves with standard modes of business communication; Grammar, which helps students bolster their grammar skills; and Aboriginal Focus, which offers additional instruction designed to honour Aboriginal culture while providing models for Aboriginal students. Additional add-on modules are in the process of being developed, including Lab Reports, which will assist students in writing lab reports for science context courses, and Tips for ESL Writers, which will be specifically designed to assist those students for whom English is a second language.

TARGET MARKETS

There were several considerations when selecting a target market. The first decision that needed to be made was whether to target institutions or individuals. So far, only institutional users have accessed Essay-Zone. Academic-Zone charged other institutions a flat licensing fee based on their number of users. This fee provided institutional clients with unlimited access to Essay-Zone for a specified period of time. If Academic-Zone targeted individuals, each user would have to pay a fee to gain access to Essay-Zone and would use it as a replacement for a tutor. There was also a possibility of targeting private-sector businesses, and the same pricing considerations would be relevant.

Post-Secondary Institutions

Targeting post-secondary institutions seemed like an obvious choice, given that when Essay-Zone was first created it was specifically designed to assist these students. Even without active promotional efforts, a number of post-secondary institutions in several Canadian provinces licensed the product. Academic-Zone was still open to targeting individuals at these institutions as well. Exhibits 1 and 2 show post-secondary enrolments by field of study, and the number of institutions by province/territory, respectively.

One major benefit of targeting the post-secondary institutional market is that Academic-Zone had already packaged its resource to target and service this market. Since the modules it offered were ideal for students seeking post-secondary education, no major changes would have to be made. However, the number of Canadian post-secondary institutions is unlikely to change in the near future, which could limit sales, particularly if institutions alone were targeted. With new potential users entering post-secondary studies each year, targeting individuals would have the advantage.

Co-op Offices

A more narrowly defined post-secondary market would be the co-operative education offices in colleges and universities across Canada. Co-op programs have become increasingly important in North America, and enrolling in an academic program that offers a

EXHIBIT 1	Post-Secondary Enrolments by Field of Study, 2009–2010		
Program	Total	University	College
Personal improvement and leisure	22 185	5 451	16 734
Education	102 237	83 742	18 495
Visual and performing arts, and communications technology	81 138	46 746	34 389
Humanities	351 492	211 833	139 656
Social and behavioural sciences and law	243 159	202 227	40 932
Business, management, and public administration	337 836	205 590	132 243
Physical and life sciences and technologies	96 954	92 124	4 830
Mathematics, computer, and information sciences	56 934	35 526	21 408
Architecture, engineering, and related technologies	177 606	98 985	78 618
Agriculture, natural resources, and conservation	26 061	17 598	8 463
Health, parks, recreation, and fitness	209 727	131 052	78 672
Personal, protective, and transportation services	39 192	5 322	33 873
Other instructional programs	161 001	67 692	93 306
Total, instructional programs	1 905 516	1 203 894	701 622

Source: Statistics Canada, CANSIM, table 477-0019.

EXHIBIT 2	Post-Secondary Institutions by Province/Territory		
Province/Territory	Total	University	College
Newfoundland and Labrador	25	5	20
Prince Edward Island	14	2	12
Nova Scotia	42	15	27
New Brunswick	29	10	19
Quebec	350	22	328
Ontario	116	66	50
Manitoba	21	12	9
Saskatchewan	32	14	18
Alberta	35	12	23
British Columbia	33	12	21
Yukon Territory	1	0	1
Northwest Territories	4	0	4
Nunavut	4	0	4
Total, Canada	706	170	536

Source: http://publications.gc.ca/Collection/Statcan/81-582-X/institution.pdf

EXHIBIT 3	Co-op Offices by Province/Territory
Province/Territory	**Number of Offices**
Alberta	7
British Columbia	15
Manitoba	5
New Brunswick	5
Newfoundland and Labrador	2
Nova Scotia	8
Ontario	29
Prince Edward Island	1
Quebec	6
Saskatchewan	2
Yukon	1
Total, Canada	81

Source: Canadian Association for Co-operative Education (CAFCE).

co-op option has become popular among students in post-secondary institutions. And with employers complaining more and more that college and university graduates lack the writing and analytical skills necessary to succeed in the workplace, the Academic-Zone team was seriously considering developing a module that would specifically target students who might wish to improve their résumé writing, cover letter writing, and overall writing skills.

Although co-op education is a subset of the overall post-secondary institutional market, the Academic-Zone staff thought it might be easier to license a unique module to this group rather than sell an institution-wide product. Licensing would likely occur through the initiative of co-op offices, and the licensing fees might be absorbed by the students enrolled in the co-op program. Exhibit 3 shows the number of co-op offices in colleges and universities across Canada, organized by province/territory.

High Schools

There are over 3900 public and private high schools and almost 1.6 million high school students in Canada. The high school market seemed attractive on the basis of size, with many more institutions and individuals than in the post-secondary institution market. Once more, Academic-Zone would have to decide whether to target institutions or students, and a price point would have to be determined. Like the post-secondary institution market, this alternative would result in a low volume of sales and a somewhat limited market.

One major drawback in targeting high schools would be the school boards' involvement in making purchasing decisions. Many wouldn't wish to spend resources, already scarce, on new programs, and price would certainly have a tremendous influence on the success of Essay-Zone in this market. On the other hand, since Academic-Zone would be targeting only about 500 school boards in Canada, the cost of contacting potential clients would be reasonably low. School boards that weren't interested might still be willing to advertise the product to students, and there might be an opportunity to sell to those students who were motivated to improve their writing skills before entering college or university. ESL students in particular might also see a benefit. Major changes to the current modules would be unnecessary; Academic-Zone had already created a module specifically designed to assist students transitioning from high school to college and university.

Home-Schoolers

Lastly, parents who home-school their children was also a target market under consideration. With over 60 000 home-schooled children in Canada and almost 1.4 million in the United States, the opportunity for individually licensing access to Essay-Zone seemed a possibility to the Academic-Zone staff. The majority of parents who choose to home-school their children do so out of a desire to be actively involved in their academic performance. And with research suggesting that more than 90% of Canadian home-educated students score above the national average in both grade equivalency and basic skills; it was evident that parents take their home-schooled children's education seriously. The Academic-Zone staff figured they could license a variation of the current Essay-Zone Transition module that would be specifically targeted to help home-schooled students with their academic writing. Promotions could be carried out by contacting home-schooling associations, such as the Canadian Centre for Home Education or the Home School Legal Defence Association.

Corporate Training and Hiring Departments

Many of Academic-Zone's competitors have targeted the private business, or corporate, market. Targeting corporate human resources and training departments was another option. In this case, the Academic-Zone staff would probably have to create customized resources for each company they serviced and make product modifications. For example, a module that hiring officers could use as a screening test for job applicants' communication and writing skills would be one possibility for development and commercialization. Exhibit 4 shows the number of businesses in Canada by workforce size and province/territory.

The main benefit of targeting the corporate market is that it's much larger than the post-secondary and high school markets and would result in a larger total volume of sales, although each sale's average size could be lower depending on the size of the organization that licenses the product. However, the corporate market might support a higher price point than the education market would.

MARKETING PLAN

Pricing

Academic-Zone's pricing model is based on granting Essay-Zone access to entire institutions rather than individual students. Since each institution has different needs, Academic-Zone has established a flexible pricing scheme. Prices have varied depending on the number of students granted access, with access normally allowed for a one-year period. Exhibit 5 shows Academic-Zone's pricing model.

EXHIBIT 4	Total Number of Businesses by Size and Province/Territory, 2010					
		Number of Business Locations				
Provinces/Territories	Total	Unknown	Employer Businesses	Small (<100)	Medium (100–499)	Large (500+)
Newfoundland and Labrador	26 351	8 494	17 857	17 559	255	43
Prince Edward Island	10 505	4 347	6 158	6 059	86	13
Nova Scotia	55 078	23 490	31 588	30 957	554	77
New Brunswick	42 907	16 190	26 717	26 227	432	58
Quebec	496 463	249 028	247 435	242 710	4 128	597
Ontario	901 190	504 232	396 958	387 986	7 878	1 094
Manitoba	78 400	41 288	37 112	36 275	723	114
Saskatchewan	96 548	56 778	39 770	39 156	547	67
Alberta	344 135	188 815	155 320	152 499	2 481	340
British Columbia	370 262	194 349	175 913	173 170	2 445	298
Yukon Territory	2 985	1 294	1 691	1 656	33	2
Northwest Territories	2 606	981	1 625	1 577	45	3
Nunavut	840	223	617	592	23	2
Total, Canada	2 428 270	1 289 509	1 138 761	1 116 423	19 630	2 708

Source: Statistics Canada, Business Register, December 2010, http://www.ic.gc.ca/eic/site/sbrp-rppe.nsf/eng/rd02601.html

EXHIBIT 5	Essay-Zone Pricing		
Number of Students	Access (Home/On Site)	Duration	Price
Up to 100 students	Unlimited	1 year access	$1250
Up to 500 students	Unlimited	1 year access	$2000
Up to 1000 students	Unlimited	1 year access	$2500
Unlimited	Unlimited	1 year access	$3000

Although this pricing structure has been the only one used in the past, pricing has always been a debated issue within Academic-Zone. After establishing an advisory committee from among various departments within the university to help come to a decision, the issue of pricing remained unresolved. Even in the business plan that a consulting group had prepared several years earlier when Essay-Zone was first launched, pricing was left vague; only a range of potential prices was provided. Some stakeholders argued that

Academic-Zone had seriously underpriced Essay-Zone and should be charging more; others believed that prices should be reduced to reach a greater part of the overall market.

Moreover, as more and more add-on modules have been developed at Academic-Zone, pricing these smaller packages has also become an issue. The current structure encompasses only the pricing of parent modules; it doesn't include any estimates for smaller modules, such as the Grammar Module. These smaller modules could be either sold separately or incorporated into a more comprehensive package. Different clients within each segment would need some customization to meet their specific needs, possibly affecting pricing.

Marketing Promotion

Academic-Zone has established a presence at several Canadian conferences and continues to do so, providing it with a main forum for promoting Essay-Zone to post-secondary institutions and learning centres. This channel gives Academic-Zone the opportunity to communicate face to face with potential customers and to showcase the features Essay-Zone has to offer their institutions. These conferences include those facilitated through the Canadian Association of College and University Student Services and the Association of Universities and Colleges of Canada.

Additionally, Essay-Zone has been promoted through a number of webinars. Interested parties are able to contact Academic-Zone to book a spot and then participate online from remote locations across Canada and the world. These webinars provide a product overview and demonstration, a presentation on the resources behind Academic-Zone, one-on-one meetings and communications for those interested, and even access to Essay-Zone for a limited period for those who wish to try the product.

In order to expand to different markets, Academic-Zone would have to generate ways to target these specific markets, whether through associations and centres or through directly contacting institutions and organizations by email, direct mail, telephone, webinar, or in person.

THE NEXT STEP

As Aaron sat in his office deliberating what he should do next, he reflected on Essay-Zone's roots. He knew that although Academic-Zone had begun by targeting post-secondary institutions, there was a lot of potential to grow the business beyond this market by targeting high schools, home-schooled students, and corporate clients. One thing Aaron was certain about was that Academic-Zone's success would be highly dependent on how quickly the team could make the necessary adjustments to capture any potential market. The team's responsiveness to customizing the modules and responding to clients' service needs would also be critical.

An important meeting was scheduled for the start of his third week. Aaron was expected to present his initial thoughts about a marketing plan, but he also knew that he'd be carefully evaluated on the basis of his recommendations and how he presented them.

"Greener Pastures": The Launch of StaGreen by HydroCan

Anne T. Hale

Stone Age Marketing Consultants was founded five years ago by Cari Clarkstone, Karen Jonestone, and Robert Sommerstone. Their target clients were small startup firms as well as medium-sized firms looking to expand operations. With their newest client, HydroCan, coming in for a meeting the following afternoon, the three founders were discussing the results of their market analysis.

HydroCan was a startup company in the process of obtaining patents in both Canada and the United States for a new type of lawn-care product called StaGreen. Since the company comprised only four agricultural engineers and a financial accountant, it was in need of marketing advice for its new product. StaGreen, when applied to most types of grass, enabled the root system to retain water longer, thus reducing the need for both extra watering and frequent fertilizing. HydroCan was eager to take the product to market but it desperately needed answers to several questions, including which segment to target, how to position its new product, and what type of launch strategy it should use. It had approached Stone-Age Marketing Consultants four weeks ago with its needs, and since then the marketing consultants had analyzed its markets, costs, prices, and communications options. Their last task was to formulate a comprehensive strategy for StaGreen's launch.

INITIAL MEETING WITH HYDROCAN

During the initial meeting between HydroCan and Stone Age, the engineers had outlined the product and its potential benefits. StaGreen was very similar in appearance to most brands of common lawn fertilizer. It was classified as a chemical fertilizer, but with one very important difference: its primary benefit was its effect on the root system of most of the common types of grass used for lawns. The product's small pellets attached to roots and attracted and retained moisture, and extensive laboratory testing had demonstrated that StaGreen reduced the need of manual watering on most types of grass by up to 40%. Such a product would obviously have a high demand.

The first question HydroCan needed addressed was what market to target initially. Gary Gillis, CEO of HydroCan, wanted to target the consumer lawn and garden market. His colleague Carla Humphreys, on the other hand, was more inclined to target the commercial lawn and garden market. Since these two markets required very different launch strategies, selecting the appropriate segment was the primary concern. And given that both Gary and Carla were extremely biased toward their respective positions, the consultants knew they'd have to present strong reasons to support their recommendation. So, to make this task manageable, they divided the research and analysis along the following lines: Cari would investigate the viability of a consumer launch, Karen would investigate the viability of a commercial launch, and Robert would obtain all necessary financial information.

THE CONSUMER MARKET

In 2011 Canadians spent nearly $4.6 billion, at the retail level, on gardening. This figure includes $1.89 billion on grass (both sod and seed), trees, and plants; $1.24 billion on lawn maintenance (with fertilizers accounting for 52% of the total); and $1.47 billion on hand tools, pots, window boxes, books, magazines, landscaping services, and so forth. In other words, gardening is big business in Canada. Lawn care is, however, a highly seasonal enterprise, with 70% of sales occurring in the second and third fiscal quarters (i.e., from April to September).

According to Cari's research, if HydroCan were to target this segment, it would be competing primarily with fertilizers. The consumer fertilizer market is extremely competitive, with the top two firms, Scotts and Ortho Chemicals, controlling approximately 50% of the total consumer market. Both firms are headquartered in the United States (with divisional offices in Canada), and both have extensive international operations. The market-share leader is Scotts, with its two powerful brands, Turf Builder and Miracle-Gro. Turf Builder is a slow-release fertilizer that reduces the number of applications required for a healthy lawn. This slow-release technology is relatively new, having been available to the consumer market for less than two years. "Slow release" simply means that the fertilizing chemicals are released gradually over a number of months; one application could last for a maximum of two years (although most manufacturers recommend applications every year).

Turf Builder is priced slightly lower than most Miracle-Gro products, which are advertised as maximum-growth products and not specifically (i.e., exclusively) aimed at lawn care. Ortho's products are priced competitively with Turf Builder—their added value comes from the inclusion of pesticides in the fertilizer that prevents most common lawn infestations. See Exhibit 1 for pricing information on one main competitive brand of fertilizer products.

EXHIBIT 1	Main Competitors' Estimated Prices for the Consumer Market	
	Size(s)	Retail Price
Scotts Turf Builder	2 × 19.8 kg	$119.99
Scotts Turf Builder EZ Pail	2 × 6.57 kg	$99.99
Scotts Turf Builder EZ Seed	4.5 kg	$39.99
Scotts Turf Builder (various)	6.2 kg	$16.99–$18.99
Scotts Miracle-Gro Liquid	567 g	$9.99

Research has shown that 4 out of 10 consumers in this market have no concrete brand preferences. They rely heavily on in-store advertisements and sales staff for information and recommendations. Many consumers can't recall a fertilizer manufacturer or a brand name. The product with the highest brand-name awareness is Miracle-Gro; however, most associate this name with plant foods rather than lawn fertilizers. So, given these consumer behaviours and attitudes toward this product category, most manufacturers rely on a strong push strategy.

Most lawn-care products are sold by three distinct types of retailers: discount stores, such as Canadian Tire, Walmart, and Sears; specialty stores; and home improvement stores. The discount stores, which buy direct from manufacturers, place strict requirements on their orders and expect price concessions and special support. Accordingly, marketing expenses for both Scotts and Ortho have been increasing, with the bulk of the increase devoted to promotions to discount retailers. This indicates the relative importance of this channel—it's estimated that 60% of all consumer fertilizer sales are made in discount stores, compared with approximately 30% of sales made in specialty stores and 10% of sales made in home improvement stores. Discount stores have, in fact, been spending millions in renovations in order to accommodate larger lawn and garden areas. The same is true with home improvement stores, such as Home Depot Canada, which has approximately 180 locations in Canada.

Specialty stores, the vast majority of which are nurseries, tend to be independently owned and thus much more numerous. While the nine top discount chains across Canada control over 89% of all sales from discount stores, the top 50 specialty garden stores account for less than 28% of all sales from this store type. The most recent research indicates that over 1000 specialty garden stores exist in Canada. Most of these purchase from large horticulture wholesalers and receive little, if any, promotional assistance from the major manufacturers.

Home improvement stores tend to be large, powerful chains, such as Home Depot Canada and Rona. While these stores don't represent a large portion of current sales, they continue to grow in importance. Like discount stores, home improvement stores buy direct from the manufacturers and require price concessions and promotional support.

The large manufacturers of fertilizer products generally spend about 20% of sales on marketing activities. The bulk of this money goes to the sales force, selling in general, and trade promotions. Given the three different channels through which their product is sold, most fertilizer manufacturers recognize the importance of a strong sales force. In terms of trade promotions, they provide in-store literature, displays, and sales training—especially to the large discount and home improvement stores. Less important is advertising. Miracle-Gro is the most heavily advertised brand on the market, and Scotts generally spends 4% of sales on advertising (which probably accounts for the high brand-name awareness). Scotts also advertises Turf Builder, but only during the early spring when demand for lawn fertilizers is at its peak. Most companies run ads for their existing brands and any new brands they may be launching during the spring and early summer months. Thus, advertising expenditures are generally at their highest in March, April, May, and June, and zero at all other times. Only Miracle-Gro is advertised year-round, with different messages at different times of the year. For example, Miracle-Gro advertises its benefits for house plants during the winter months and its benefits for fruits, vegetables, and flowers during the spring and summer months.

THE COMMERCIAL MARKET

The commercial market consists primarily of Canada's 2400 golf courses, but also includes commercial properties, specifically office complexes and apartment buildings. The most lucrative market, however, is golf courses. Currently under fire for being a major source of groundwater pollution owing to the high and frequent levels of fertilizers used to keep courses green, most owners are actively looking for ways to cut both water and fertilizer usage. Course owners spend, on average, $600 000 to maintain their golf courses during the year, of which 42% represents water usage costs and 24% represents fertilizer purchases. For extremely large, complex courses, this figure can run as high as $1.6 million, and for smaller, inner-city public courses, as low as $208 000. Tests have indicated that StaGreen will reduce water usage by one-half and fertilizer usage by one-third. This is the primary reason why Carla Humphreys was so adamant that the company select the commercial market as its primary target market.

The game of golf has been enjoying a renewed popularity after a drastic decrease in participation during the 1980s. The growing number of public courses with reasonable fees, the continued aging of the Canadian population, and the development of better equipment have all contributed to this growth in popularity. It's estimated that the number of golf courses will increase by about 12%, to 2700, within five years. Most golf courses are independently owned and operated, with only 4% of all courses owned by a company that owns more than one course. Courses are dispersed throughout Canada, but British Columbia (Vancouver in particular) boasts the highest number of courses.

Currently, golf courses purchase maintenance supplies from wholesalers that specialize in products uniquely designed for the type of grasses used. Manufacturers of these fertilizers tend to be either small firms or divisions of the larger chemical companies. The market-share leader in golf course fertilizers is Sierra Horticultural Products, a subsidiary of Scotts. Sierra represents only about 2.2% of Scotts total sales. Its biggest competitor in Canada is Nu-Gro Corporation, an Ontario-based horticultural products company. Unlike the firms competing in the consumer lawn-maintenance market, these companies spend only about 9% of sales on marketing activities. They engage in little advertising, preferring to spend their marketing funds on sales calls to golf courses. They provide free samples of their products to non-users and try to build solid, long-lasting relationships with course owners. They know that it takes a tremendous selling effort to get a golf course owner to switch brands. If they're satisfied with their current brand, many course owners are unwilling to risk switching to a new product that may not perform as well. Since the condition of the course is the most important attribute in a consumer's selection of a course to play, course owners tend to be highly brand loyal.

Course owners, however, have two overriding concerns. The first is the growing public debate on the groundwater pollution caused by golf courses. Heavy use of fertilizers and constant manual watering result in a chemical buildup in nearby reservoirs. In fact, according to the U.S. Environmental Protection Agency, golf courses are the major source of groundwater pollution in the United States. More and more negative publicity in the form of newspaper and magazine articles has even resulted in developers being denied permits to construct new courses. Thus, addressing the issue of groundwater pollution is a major priority for course owners.

Their second concern is that of shrinking profits. While golf is growing in popularity and more courses are being built to accommodate demand, the actual number of golfers that can be accommodated on any one course cannot be expanded. And with some courses engaging in green-fees price wars, profit margins for many of the public courses have become strained. So while loyalty may play a role in fertilizer purchases, these difficult problems will also influence purchasing behaviour.

Estimated to be about one-eighth the size of the golf course market is the balance of the commercial lawn-care market: apartment and office complexes. Their needs are much less complex than those of golf courses, resulting in purchasing behaviour that mirrors the consumer market's. Little concrete information is available concerning the number of office complex and apartment buildings, although estimates have put the total figure at around 4400, of which 16.5% represents multiple holdings by one corporation. These commercial real estate property firms spend a disproportionate amount on lawn maintenance, accounting for nearly 26% of the total dollars spent in this sector of the commercial maintenance market. The sector tends to purchase in bulk through wholesalers—generally the same wholesalers that service the specialty stores in the consumer market.

HYDROCAN

HydroCan was incorporated nearly one year ago. It has leased its production facilities and has purchased and/or leased all the equipment and machinery necessary for StaGreen's production. Its facility has the capacity to produce 180 000 kilograms of StaGreen per month. The owners of HydroCan have suggested a quality/value-added pricing strategy. They believe they have a superior product that will save the end user both time and money by reducing the need for fertilizer products and manual watering.

At their initial meeting with Stone Age, HydroCan's founders outlined their ideas about the launch-year marketing strategy for both the consumer and the commercial lawn-care markets. If the company elects to target the consumer market, it will package StaGreen in a 10-kilogram bag, which market research indicates is the most popular size with consumers. It will set its price to trade (i.e., wholesalers and retailers) at $33.50, with variable costs representing 50% of sales. On average, the large discount stores and home improvement stores take a 25% markup on lawn-maintenance products; smaller specialty stores take a larger markup of $35%; and wholesalers (if used) take a 15% markup. Fixed production costs include $900 000 in annual rental (for the site and the equipment), $160 400 in general and administrative expenses, $55 000 in research and development expenses, and $24 700

EXHIBIT 2	Allocation of Marketing Budget for Consumer Market Launch
Marketing Task	**Total Expenditure (Estimates)**
Seasonal discounts	$325 000
In-store displays	$175 000
Magazine advertising	$150 000
Newspaper advertising	$100 000
Sweepstakes	$50 000

in miscellaneous expenses. Distribution costs (including freight, warehousing, and storage) represent a significant yearly expense due to the seasonal nature of demand. Production of StaGreen would be continuous year round; however, sales would be highly concentrated in the months of April through September. This means that the company would have relatively high distribution costs, estimated at $640 000 per year. Not yet included in any of the company's financial statements are the salaries for its four founding partners. They would like to earn $65 000 per year (each), but are willing to forgo their salary in the launch year.

The marketing budget has been set at $800 000, which HydroCan has suggested be allocated to the various tasks, as shown in Exhibit 2. Seasonal discounts are price discounts offered to retailers and wholesalers as an incentive to purchase well in advance of the peak selling season. HydroCan plans to offer these discounts, estimated at 20% off the trade price for each bag purchased, to wholesalers and retailers in the months of November and December as a way to reduce warehouse and storage costs. The displays will cost about $400 each (which includes such promotional materials as brochures), and will be furnished to discount stores, home improvement stores, and as many nurseries as possible. The sweepstakes is used to increase awareness and interest in StaGreen. Consumers will have the chance to win several valuable prizes, including a year of free lawn maintenance, lawn and garden equipment and supplies, and other related prizes.

In terms of the sales force, HydroCan plans on hiring 12 sales reps at an average cost of $70 000 per rep (salary, commission, travel). The sales reps will be responsible for selling the product to the various channels as well as offering sales training seminars.

If HydroCan elects to target the commercial market, then the size of the product will be increased to a 50-kilogram bag, which it will sell to wholesalers or end users at $195. Because it would be charging a slightly higher price under this option, variable costs as a percentage of sales drop to 40%, resulting in a relatively high contribution margin of 60% of sales. Wholesalers, which generally sell directly to commercial users, take a 15% markup. Fixed expenses will remain nearly the same as for the consumer market option, with the exception of marketing and distribution costs. None of the promotional activities, such as displays, seasonal discounts, sweepstakes, or advertising, will be used in the commercial market. Instead, the sales force will be increased to 16 people in order to handle the lengthy sales calls necessary for golf courses. In addition, $150 000 has been set aside so that the sales force can distribute free samples to potential customers. Finally, distribution costs decrease if the commercial market is chosen, given that demand tends to be slightly less seasonal. Thus, costs for freight, warehousing, and storage decrease to $340 000 under this option.

THE DECISION

The three founding partners of Stone Age Marketing Consultants were in the conference room discussing the results of their research and analysis. As Karen Jonestone pointed out, "A strong case can be made for both target markets! Each has its own advantages and limitations." Rob Sommerstone countered with the fact that HydroCan was a startup business. "Its financial resources are extremely limited right now. It can't increase its production capacity for at least two years, and if it hopes to acquire expansion capital to increase its total capacity, it needs to show a profit as early as possible." Cari Clarkstone was considering a more creative solution: targeting selected parts of either or both the consumer and commercial markets.

Before the group could begin to assess the viability of HydroCan and its product, StaGreen, they had to decide on which market to target, how to position StaGreen in that target market, and then how to develop a viable marketing strategy for the launch year. The final pressure for the group was the fact that HydroCan needed to launch in February, just prior to the peak selling season. So the consultants knew there was no time to acquire additional market research; the decision had to be based on the information at hand.

Dillon Controls Ltd.

James E. Nelson and
Mark S. Johnson

"The choices themselves seem simple enough," thought Jac Dillon. "Either we enter the U.S. market in Pennsylvania and New York, we forget about the United States for the time being, or we do some more marketing research." Jac was president of Dillon Controls Ltd., located in Brantford, Ontario. The company was formed in 1980 and, after a slow start, had grown steadily to its present size of 25 employees and annual revenues of about $1.6 million. About 2% of these revenues came from sales to U.S. accounts.

THE AQUAWATCH SYSTEM

Dillon Controls' product line was centred on its AquaWatch System, a computer hardware and software design for the monitoring and control of pressurized water flows. Most often these water flows consisted of either potable water or sewage effluent as the liquids were stored, moved, or treated by municipal water departments.

The system employed an AquaWatch microcomputer installed at individual pumping stations where liquids were stored and moved. Stations were often located many kilometres

This case was written by professor James E. Nelson and doctoral student Mark S. Johnson, University of Colorado. It is intended for use as a basis for class discussion rather than to illustrate either effective or ineffective administrative decision making. Some data are disguised. Copyright © 1990 by the Business Research Division, College of Business and Administration and the Graduate School of Business Administration, University of Colorado, Boulder, Colorado, 80309-0419. Reprinted with permission.

apart, linking geographically dispersed water users (households, businesses, etc.) to water and sewer systems. The microcomputer performed a number of important functions. It governed the starts, stops, and alarms of up to four pumps; monitored levels and available capacities of storage reservoirs; checked pump capacities and power consumptions; and recorded pump flows. It could even measure amounts of rainfall entering reservoirs and adjust pump operations or activate an alarm as needed. Each microcomputer could also be easily connected to a main computer to allow remote control of pumping stations and produce a variety of charts and graphs useful in evaluating pump performance and scheduling needed maintenance.

The AquaWatch System provided a monitoring function that human operators could not match in terms of sophistication, immediacy, and cost. The system permitted each individual substation to control its own pumping operations; collect, analyze, and store data; forecast trends; transmit data and alarms to a central computer; and receive remote commands. Alarms could also be transmitted directly to a pocket-sized receiver carried by one or more operators on call. A supervisor could continually monitor pumping operations in a large system entirely via a computer terminal at a central location and send commands to individual pumps, thereby saving costly service calls and time. The system also reduced the possibility of overflows that could produce disastrous flooding of nearby communities or contamination of potable water.

Dillon Controls personnel would work with water and sewage engineers to design and install the desired AquaWatch System. Personnel would also train engineers and operators to work with the system, and would be available 24 hours a day for consultation. If needed, a company engineer could be physically present to assist engineers and operators whenever major problems arose. Dillon Controls also offered its clients the option of purchasing a complete service contract whereby company personnel would provide periodic testing and maintenance of installed systems. The contract called for clients to pay Dillon for all direct costs of the service plus 15% for overhead.

An AquaWatch System could be configured a number of ways. In its most basic form, the system would be little more than a small "black box" that monitored two or three lift station activities and, when necessary, transmitted an alarm to one or more remote receivers. An intermediate system would monitor additional activities, send data to a central computer via telephone lines, and receive remote commands. An advanced system would provide the same monitoring capabilities but add forecasting features, maintenance management, auxiliary power backup, and data transmission and reception via radio. Prices to customers for the three configurations in early 1991 were about $1500, $2800, and $4800.

AQUAWATCH CUSTOMERS

AquaWatch customers could be divided into two groups—governmental units and industrial companies. The typical application in the first group was a sewage treatment plant having some 4 to 12 pumping stations, each station containing one or more pumps. Pumps would operate intermittently and—unless an AquaWatch or similar system were in place—be monitored by one or more operators who would visit each station once or perhaps twice each day for about half an hour. Operators would take reservoir measurements, record running times of pumps, and sometimes perform limited maintenance and repairs. The sewage plant and stations were typically located in flat or rolling terrain, where gravity could not be used in lieu of pumping. If any monitoring equipment were present at all, it would typically consist of a crude, on-site alarm that would activate whenever fluid levels rose or fell beyond a preset level. Sometimes the alarm would activate a telephone dialing function that alerted an operator some distance from the station.

Numerous industrial companies also stored, moved, and processed large quantities of water or sewage. These applications usually differed little from those in governmental plants, except for their smaller size. On the other hand, a considerably larger number of industrial companies had pumping stations, and so, Jac thought, the two markets offered about identical market potentials.

The two markets desired essentially the same products, although industrial applications often used smaller, simpler equipment. Both markets wanted their monitoring equipment to be accurate and reliable, the two dominant concerns. Equipment should also be easy to use, economical to operate, and require little regular service or maintenance. Purchase price was often not a major consideration—as long as the price was in some appropriate range, customers seemed more interested in actual product performance than in initial outlays.

Jac thought that worldwide demand for these types of systems would continue to be strong for at least the next 10 years. While some demand represented construction of new pumping stations, many applications were replacements of crude monitoring and alarm systems at existing sites. These existing systems depended greatly on regular visits by operators, visits that often continued even after new equipment was installed. Most such trips were probably not necessary. However, many managers found it difficult to dismiss or reassign monitoring personnel who were no longer needed; many were also quite cautious and conservative, desiring some human monitoring of the new equipment "just in case." Once replacements of existing systems was complete, market growth would be limited to new construction and, of course, replacements with more sophisticated systems.

Most customers (as well as non-customers) considered the AquaWatch System to be one of the best on the market. Those knowledgeable in the industry felt that competing products seldom matched AquaWatch's reliability and accuracy. Experts also believed that many competing products lacked the sophistication and flexibility of AquaWatch's design. Beyond these product features, customers also appreciated Dillon Controls' knowledge about water and sanitation engineering. Competing firms often lacked this expertise, offering their products somewhat as a sideline and considering the market too small for an intensive marketing effort.

The market was clearly not too small for Dillon Controls. While Jac had no hard data on market potential for the United States, he thought annual demand there could be as much as $30 million. In Canada, the total market was at least $4 million. Perhaps about 40% of market demand came from new construction while the rest represented replacements of existing systems. Industry sales in the latter category could be increased by more aggressive marketing efforts on the part of competitors in the industry.

DILLON CONTROLS' STRATEGY

Dillon Controls currently marketed its AquaWatch System primarily to sewage treatment plants in Canada as opposed to industrial companies. Approximately 70% of its revenues came from Ontario and Quebec. The company's strategy could be described as providing technologically superior equipment to monitor pumping operations at these plants. The strategy stressed frequent contacts with customers and potential customers to design, supply, and service AquaWatch Systems. The strategy also stressed superior knowledge of water and sanitation engineering along with up-to-date electronics and computer technology. The result was a line of highly specialized sensors, computers, and methods for process controls in water treatment plants.

This was the essence of Dillon Control's strategy: having a special competence that no firm in the market could easily match. The company also prided itself on being a young, creative firm, without an entrenched bureaucracy. Company employees generally worked with enthusiasm and dedication; they talked with each other regularly, openly, and with a great deal of give and take. Most importantly, customers—as well as technology—seemed to drive all areas in the company.

Dillon Controls' strategy in Canada seemed to be fairly well decided. That is, Jac thought that a continuation of present strategies and tactics should continue to produce good results. However, one aspect likely to change would be the establishment of a branch office having both sales and distribution functions somewhere out West, most likely in Vancouver. The plan was to have such an office in operation within the next few years. Having a branch office in Vancouver would greatly simplify sales and service in the western provinces, not to mention increase company sales.

Beyond establishing the branch office, Jac was considering a major strategic decision to enter the U.S. market. The North American Free Trade Agreement, which came into effect in 1989, was prompting many Canadian companies to look southward. Among other things, the agreement eliminated all tariffs on computer products (like the AquaWatch System) traded between Canada and the United States. In addition, Jac's two recent visits to the United States had led him to conclude that the market represented potential far beyond that of Canada, and that the United States seemed perfect for expansion. Industry experts in the United States agreed with Jac that the AquaWatch System outperformed anything used in the U.S. market. Experts thought that many water and sewage engineers would welcome Dillon Controls' products and knowledge. Moreover, Jac thought that U.S. transportation systems and payment arrangements would present few problems.

Entry would most likely be in the form of a sales and service office located in Philadelphia, Pennsylvannia. The Pennsylvania and New York state markets seemed representative of the United States and appeared to offer a good test of the AquaWatch System. While the two states represented only 12% of the U.S. population, they accounted for almost 16% of U.S. manufacturing activity. The office would require an investment of some $200 000 for inventory and other balance sheet items. Annual fixed costs would total upward of $250 000 for salaries and other operating expenses—Jac thought that the office would employ only a general manager, technician, and secretary for at least the first year or two. Each AquaWatch System sold in the United States would be priced to provide a contribution of about 30%. Jac wanted a 35% annual return on any Dillon Controls' investment, to begin no later than the second year. At issue was whether Jac could realistically expect to achieve this goal in the United States.

MARKETING RESEARCH

To estimate the viability of a U.S. sales office, Jac had commissioned the Browning Group in Philadelphia to conduct some limited marketing research with selected personnel in the water and sewage industries in the city and surrounding areas. The research had two purposes: to obtain a sense of market needs and market reactions to Dillon Controls' products and to calculate a rough estimate of market potential in Pennsylvania and New York. Results were intended to help Jac interpret his earlier conversations with industry experts and perhaps allow a decision on market entry.

The research design itself employed two phases of data collection. The first consisted of five one-hour interviews with water and sewage engineers employed by local city and municipal governments. For each interview, an experienced Browning Group interviewer scheduled an appointment with the engineer and then visited his or her office, armed with a set of questions and a tape recorder. Questions included:

1. What procedures do you use to monitor your pumping stations?
2. Is your current monitoring system effective? Costly?
3. What are the costs of a monitoring malfunction?
4. What features would you like to see in a monitoring system?
5. Who decides on the selection of a monitoring system?
6. What is your reaction to the AquaWatch System?

Interviewers were careful to listen closely to the engineers' responses and to probe for additional detail and clarification.

Tapes of the personal interviews were transcribed and then analyzed by the project manager at Browning. The report noted that these results were interesting in that they described typical industry practices and viewpoints. Here is a partial summary from the report:

> The picture that emerges is one of fairly sophisticated personnel making decisions about monitoring equipment that is relatively simple in design. Still, some engineers would appear distrustful of this equipment because they persist in sending operators to pumping stations on a daily basis. The distrust may be justified because potential costs of a malfunction were identified as expensive repairs and cleanups, fines of $10 000 per day of violation, lawsuits, harassment by the Health Department, and public embarrassment. The five engineers identified themselves as key individuals in the decision to purchase new equipment. Without exception, they considered AquaWatch features innovative, highly desirable, and worth the price.

The summary noted also that the primary use of the interview results was to construct a questionnaire that could be administered over the telephone.

The questionnaire was used in the second phase of data collection as part of a telephone survey of 65 utility managers, water and sewage engineers, and pumping station operators in Philadelphia and surrounding areas. All respondents were employed by governmental units. Each interview took about 10 minutes to complete, covering topics identified in questions 1, 2, and 4 above. The Browning Group's research report stated that most interviews found respondents to be quite cooperative, although 15 people refused to participate at all.

The telephone interviews had produced results that could be considered more representative of the market because of the larger sample size. The report had organized these results according to monitoring procedures, system effectiveness and costs, and features desired in a monitoring system:

> All monitoring systems under the responsibility of the 50 respondents were considered to require manual checking. The frequency of operator visits to pumping stations ranged from monthly to

twice daily, depending on flow rates, pumping station history, proximity of nearby communities, monitoring equipment in operation, and other factors. Even the most sophisticated automatic systems were checked because respondents "just don't trust the machine." Each operator was responsible for an average of 15 stations.

Despite the perceived need for double-checking, all respondents considered their current monitoring system to be quite effective. Not one reported a serious pumping malfunction in the past three years that had escaped detection. However, this reliability came at considerable cost—the annual wages and other expenses associated with each monitoring operator averaged about $50 000.

Respondents were about evenly divided between those wishing a simple alarm system and those desiring a sophisticated, versatile microprocessor. Managers and engineers in the former category often said that the only feature they really needed was an emergency signal such as a siren, horn, or light. Sometimes they would add a telephone dialer that would be automatically activated at the same time as the signal. Most agreed that a price of around $2000 would be reasonable for such a system. The latter category of individuals contained engineers desiring many of the AquaWatch System's features, once they knew such equipment was available. A price of $5000 per system seemed acceptable. Some of these respondents were quite knowledgeable about computers and computer programming while others were not. Only four respondents voiced any strong concerns about the cost to purchase and install more sophisticated monitoring equipment. Everyone demanded that the equipment be reliable and accurate.

Jac found the report quite helpful. Much of the information, of course, simply confirmed his own view of the U.S. market. However, it was good to have this knowledge from an independent, objective organization. In addition, to learn that the market consisted of two apparently equally sized segments of simple and sophisticated applications was quite worthwhile. In particular, knowledge of system prices considered acceptable by each segment would make the entry decision easier. Meeting these prices would not be a major problem.

A most important section of the report contained an estimate of market potential for Pennsylvania and New York. The estimate was based on an analysis of discharge permits on file in governmental offices in the two states. These permits were required before any city, municipality, water or sewage district, or industrial company could release sewage or other contaminated water to another system or to a lake or river. Each permit showed the number of pumping stations in operation. Based on a 10% sample of permits, the report had estimated that governmental units in Pennsylvania and New York contained approximately 3000 and 5000 pumping stations for waste water, respectively. Industrial companies in the two states were estimated to add some 3000 and 9000 more pumping stations, respectively. The total number of pumping stations in the two states—20 000—seemed to be growing at about 2% per year.

Finally, a brief section of the report dealt with the study's limitations. Jac agreed that the sample was quite small, that it contained no utility managers or engineers from New York, and that it probably concentrated too heavily on individuals in larger urban areas. In addition, the research told him nothing about competitors and their marketing strategies and tactics. Nor did he learn anything about any state regulations for monitoring equipment, if indeed any existed. However, these shortcomings came as no surprise, representing a consequence of the research design proposed to Jac by the Browning Group some six weeks ago, before the study began.

THE DECISION

Jac's decision seemed a difficult one. The riskiest option was to enter the U.S. market as soon as possible. There was no question about the vast market potential of the United States. However, the company's opportunity for a greatly increased bottom line had to be balanced against the threat of new competitors that were, for the most part, larger and more sophisticated than Dillon Controls. In fact, a friend had jokingly remarked that "a Canadian firm selling microprocessor controls in the United States would be like trying to sell Canadian semiconductors to the Japanese."

The most conservative option was to stay in Canada. Of course, Dillon Controls would continue to respond to the odd inquiry from the United States and would continue to fill orders that the company accepted from U.S. customers. However, it would not seek this sort of business in an aggressive fashion. Nor would it seek representation in the United States through an agent or distributor. The latter option put Dillon Controls out of the picture in terms of controlling sales claims, prices, product installation, service, and other important aspects of customer relations.

Between the two extremes was the option of conducting some additional marketing research. Discussion with the Browning Group had identified the objectives of this research as being to rectify limitations of the first study as well as to provide more accurate estimates of market potential. (The estimates of the numbers of pumping stations in Pennsylvania and New York were accurate to around plus or minus 20%.) This research was estimated to cost $40 000 and take another three months to complete.

Barry Davis: Back on Board?

Barb Gardner

At age 36, the last place Barry Davis expected to find himself was sitting in the front row of a classroom studying accounting with "kids" almost half his age. More than age, however, separated Barry from the other students. A lifetime of experience had been lived in the past six years, owning and working in surf and skate shops throughout Canada, California, Hawaii, Australia, and Puerto Rico. Now within five months of finishing his diploma, Barry Davis was both looking forward and looking back.

Barry had had an entrepreneurial spirit since the age of 12, when he began sharing his love of skateboarding with other kids. He would teach them skills and tricks, and instead of charging money he would accept sports trading cards for payment: he simply wanted to make a difference. Barry often gave away his old skateboards to boys who didn't have one. That was just the way skaters were—they spread the passion and enthusiasm. He also knew back then that it was important to fix a board rather than leave it to gather dust in the garage.

After graduating from high school and then working at skate shops for a few years, Barry, then 22, started a small business with a fellow skater, Jim Russell. They designed and built skateboards and then sold their decks through shops in Banff and Jasper, Alberta, and in Barry's hometown of Brandon, Manitoba. While they shared a love of skateboarding, the friends could not be more different in their approach to business. Barry was goal-oriented, focused, and analytical. Jim was the impetuous, "let's get it done and over with" marketing geek. For six years they built their business to a level of success they hadn't thought possible.

The signs of trouble were easy enough to miss at first. Jim, who lived in Calgary, was usually on the road promoting the business in Vancouver and throughout the B.C. interior; he would visit ski resorts during the winter to build business contacts for summer-time sales. What Barry didn't know was that Jim was also promoting the sale of snowboards, something the business had never produced. The skill involved in building skateboards, Jim thought, would surely transfer over to the production of snowboards, and Barry, he figured, had the technical understanding and the contacts necessary to "deliver the goods." But when Jim delivered the contracts to his partner, Barry was shocked. He couldn't design the snowboards because they had no way to manufacture them: although they were both "boards," the materials and technology were very different. It was an impossible task. And while Jim and Barry scrambled to find a manufacturer, the contracts kept rolling in.

Barry couldn't find any Alberta or B.C. company to which he could subcontract the snowboard manufacturing. Jim tried to account for what he'd done—signed contracts without the consent of his business partner—by explaining that his enthusiasm and marketing hype had gotten away from him when he'd promised what he ultimately knew he couldn't deliver. Fortunately, Barry did eventually find a company in Ontario to undertake the manufacturing. The snowboards were delivered and the contracts were honoured. The Davis-Russell skateboard partnership, however, was over. Barry retained the rights to the skateboard name, business, designs, and technology. Jim walked away with all the client files. Barry took his share of what was left and moved back to Brandon. Jim stayed in Calgary but was never able to successfully build a business.

Barry had always had a desire to travel, so the money that represented his share became both his future business and travel fund. For the next year he visited several countries, eventually landing in Australia, where he managed and then bought a skateboard shop. He remained in Australia for five years before selling the business he'd successfully built there. Barry then took the proceeds and moved back to Calgary.

Looking back at his experience with Jim, Barry recognized that there'd been aspects of management he'd overlooked. The financial side came easily to him, but he didn't have the skills to launch an enterprise. His entrepreneurial spirit was still strong—albeit tempered by the loss of his first business—and he knew he needed to solidify his technical skills to expand any future business. So Barry decided to return to school and get his diploma in accounting, with a minor in marketing.

Although he had money in the bank, Barry worked part-time at a skateboard shop. He also met the woman who would become his fiancé. She'd recently graduated from medical school and received her licence to practise medicine—her dream of building a practice had come true. Barry's dream, meanwhile, was still alive; he wanted to revive his skateboard business. So he had a major life choice to make: either move ahead and become an accounting professional or return to his passion. As he looked back on all he'd achieved, he knew that it was now or never.

ANATOMY OF A SKATEBOARDER

Skateboards are not, of course, an unknown product. They vary from the standard-size skate deck designed for tricks in skateboard parks to the sophisticated high-tech boards used in international competitions. They're used as a means of transportation, as an activity, as an art form, and as a profession. What links these various uses are the boarders themselves.

Barry Davis shared some unique characteristics with other boarders:

- an ability to overcome challenges through sheer persistence
- a sense of control and power
- an appreciation of solitary pursuits
- a sense of freedom and autonomy
- a connection between mind and body
- an intense degree of concentration on a single focus
- self-determination
- self-confidence
- a desire to be "in the groove" or "in the zone"

SKATEBOARD CONSUMERS

Recent research tracking the purchasing practices of those participating in, or influenced by, board sports provides a profile of a "typical" skateboarder: an average to upper-income, 13- to 16-year-old male who skates every day, who has five or more years of skating experience, and who purchases five or more skateboards per year. Favourite brands of skateboards include Girl, Plan B, Chocolate, and Element. Based on online data, the cost of an average board is about $80.

Expenditures on boarding apparel vary according to income level. Based on spring 2011 data, the top four board-sport clothing brands for upper-income teens are Volcom, LRG, Vans, and Hurley. For average-income teens, the top five brands are Fox Racing, Vans, DC, Hurley, and LRG. Teens in the upper-income level also purchase clothing that fits in the broader category of action sports, with the most popular brands produced by Pacific Sunwear, Volcom, Zumiez, and LRG. For average-income teens, American Eagle and Nike are the preferred brands in action-sports clothing. In terms of footwear, upper-income teens prefer Nike, Vans, Steve Madden, and UGG Australia. Vans is the preferred brand for average-income teens.

One department-store trend is the increasing availability of board apparel targeted to lower-income teens. Tony Hawk, a "super star" skateboarder, has a line of clothing in Kohl's, a store similar to Winners in Canada. A key growth area is that of "cross-over" brands, particularly for women. Similar to the growth of yoga wear as street wear, cross-over brands have their roots in board sporting but are widely accepted and worn by those interested in the boarder lifestyle. The attractiveness of this lifestyle has been enhanced through access to media and the growth of national retailers like Zumiez.

Although the average skateboarder is 13 to 16 years old (38% of the consumer base), another 33% is represented by 17- to 24-year-olds who have more disposable income.

These older skaters buy more expensive boards, more apparel, and a greater number of boards per year. Travelling to experience skating in other countries is an emerging trend, as is purchasing sporting goods made from renewable or recycled materials.

THE CHANGING CANADIAN BOARD-SPORT MARKET

A number of major retail giants have announced that they're moving into Canada. Target has confirmed its plans to introduce more than 200 stores in Canada; within six years, it expects to have garnered approximately $6 billion in sales. Express Inc., an American fashion chain, will open 50 stores in the next five years. Large Canadian retailers, therefore, will likely experience declining profit margins, and some may disappear altogether. Foreign retailers are able to enter the market quickly through acquisition of existing Canadian chains with suitable locations and size. Major brands that may enter the Canadian market include Marshall's, J.C. Penney, Norstrom's, Kohl's, and Dick's Sporting Goods. This wave of new American and other foreign retailers will change the competitive retail market and make the fight for market share even more difficult for Canadian specialty board-sport shops.

Two major changes have already impacted the specialty board-sport market. West 49, Canada's premier specialty retailer of fashion and apparel related to the youth action sports lifestyle, was acquired by Billabong, an Australian sportswear and casual clothing manufacturer. West 49 operated more than 130 stores across Canada and was the largest skateboard and snowboard chain. Zumiez Inc., an American specialty retailer with more than 400 action sports and accessories stores, has entered the Canadian marketplace, opening two stores in Vancouver shopping malls as well as three stores in the Toronto area.

Zumiez's entry into Canada may well have a major impact on existing specialty retailers. Some American business writers have drawn a parallel between Zumiez, a mall-based skate-store chain, and Walmart in their impact on independent retailers. Writing in about.com, Bud Stratford expressed his discomfort with the opening of two new Zumiez stores close to two of his city's long-standing "core retailers." The issue, as he saw it, is this: "Are we going to support our infrastructure of independent, core retailers, and everything that they do and represent? Or are we going to support a corporate-owned, mall skate-store chain, and everything that they do and represent?"

Beyond the impact of American chains moving into Canada is the issue of the quality of skateboards being produced. While skateboards from well-known companies were typically made in the United States, blank decks—those without a design—were made in China and were often of lesser quality. More recently the majority of skateboards have been made overseas. In skateboard.about.com, Steve Cave wrote that although some Chinese manufacturers were starting to make better boards, others were still producing the same inferior products: "Some companies, like Almost, just come out and say that they make their boards in China, and people blast 'em for it! So other companies keep it hush hush." This has made it more difficult for skateboarders to tell where their boards are being made. And some companies have made it even more complicated than that: according to Cave, Girl skateboards and Chocolate skateboards (part of the same company), for example, are made in China from wood cut in Canada and then printed in the United States.

Price and competition aren't the only concerns expressed by skateboard enthusiasts. Chris Stevens, founder of Old School Skateboarding.com, argues that the true cost of cheaply produced skateboards isn't found on the price tag but rather the impact of massive overseas factories, which exploit people and harm the environment. And as these skateboards are exported and then sold in huge corporate chains, the exploitation of people and communities continues.

Concerns about price, quality, socioeconomic impact, and the environment aren't restricted to the board-sport industry. All firms, whether they're corporate chains or specialty retailers, have to find a way to compete. Bud Stratford contends that price wars don't work and that skateboard shops must differentiate themselves from their competition. Skategeezer, writing in skateboard.about.com, offers the perspective of an older skateboarder who feels that the focus on the male teenage skater ignores other buyers who have a passion for skateboards; Generation X and the baby boomers are being ignored. Skategeezer's advice is to focus on creating the dream that skateboarding provides, and tap in to the freedom and experience that skateboarding creates:

> Skateboarding needs to shed its myopia. There is a pushback . . . from those who feel that by exposing or marketing other types of skateboards or skaters, we'll somehow lose the core. You won't. You won't simply for the fact that you'll create the process of building brands that appeal to different types of skaters.

The culture of the skateboarder has not, however, been lost. Recent articles in blogs and magazines have identified a new movement where young and old skaters are rediscovering the almost forgotten art form of skateboarding: style over tactics.

Skateboarders' viewpoints and characteristics, then, are undergoing a renewal as more skate parks are developed. Moreover, a challenge is being laid down to consumers: to buy online from skateboarder-owned shops is acceptable, but it's the local shops where people should really buy. The belief is that consumers should move away from the large retailers because it's the skater-owned shops that sponsor contests, invite professional skateboarders to their cities, and provide a place where people can come by and simply hang out.

THE DECISION

In light of all the changes in the Canadian marketplace and within the industry itself, Barry Davis was considering how he might best revive his business.

Calgary, he knew, was the right place to start again. Based on his business experience and his participation in the local skateboarding association, he understood the market. About 20 specialty shops were located in the city, with an estimated 35 000 skaters (about 3.2% of the population). Yet Calgary had only 7311 square metres of outdoor permanent skate parks, whereas Winnipeg, with only 75% of Calgary's population, had almost twice that. According to the City of Calgary's "Skateboarding Amenities Strategy 2011," an additional 22 655 square metres of skateboarding area were required to meet current needs and 25 791 square metres to meet projected needs over the next 10 years. One or more indoor skate parks with an area of 1850 square metres were also needed. The opportunity to participate in the growth of skateboarding in Calgary fit Barry's passion, personality, and commitment to traditional skating.

Barry had an option to lease a retail shop in the Beltine area, located just to the south of Calgary's downtown core. This area was expected to become high density—with a mix of office, retail, multi-unit residential, and public buildings—and to evoke a very urban atmosphere.

Barry had raised some seed money from a group of friends, and was ready to invest $25 000 of his own for his marketing launch campaign. However, he needed to know how to address the needs of the market and how to implement his marketing campaign:

1. Should he reopen his new retail business under the same brand name or should he create a totally new brand? His focus had changed from manufacturing to retailing. Years ago, Barry had built a "cult-like" reputation under the company name Hot Shot Boards, but perhaps that reputation had since been tainted.

2. Given his past business experience, should he also manufacture the boards or should he simply distribute boards made by other firms?

3. If he added a line of apparel or shoes, should he try to sell this line to other retail clothing shops in Calgary or elsewhere in Canada?

4. How could Barry differentiate his business? Was there a niche he could fill?

Tools n' Rules

H. F. (Herb) MacKenzie

In June 2012, Dennis Gaines, owner of Tools n' Rules, was considering what to do next with the Gaines Maxi Brick Rule, his latest invention. When he was first ready to start selling his measuring tapes he'd sent emails to a number of marketing professors at colleges and universities around his region for some advice. Not a single one responded. So Dennis had made some initial marketing decisions on his own, and he was now in a position to rethink them. Should he change his marketing strategy or continue with the one he was currently implementing? He was also in a position to consider one or more opportunities that had recently arisen. During this time he got an email from one of the marketing professors he'd contacted several months before. The two men agreed to meet at Dennis's home to discuss the situation further.

DENNIS GAINES

Dennis Gaines had always been interested in starting things; he was a true entrepreneur at heart. He was born in Edmonton, but at 17 he moved to Brantford, Ontario, where he worked at a manufacturing plant for four years before returning home. Shortly after he arrived in Edmonton Dennis placed an ad in a local newspaper for recording artists interested in joining a band. It wasn't long before he found three interested band hopefuls, and together they formed Nexxt, a light-rock band that seemed to have a shot at succeeding in the very difficult music business. Dennis was the vocalist, but he could play guitar well enough to write his own songs. Nexxt recorded its first album, *Radio Man,* shortly thereafter. Its title song—one of several on the album that Dennis had written—was something of a hit, and Nexxt began playing bars and dance venues around Edmonton. Soon, though, they found that everyone who hired the band just wanted them to play cover songs. Eventually, the band dissolved.

Dennis returned to Brantford, where he decided to apprentice with his brother, who was a bricklayer. The apprenticeship required 5600 hours of labour over four years, but Dennis eventually completed it. He even scored a high enough grade on his exam to qualify for an interprovincial ticket, meaning he was qualified to work in union jobs across Canada. For more than 25 years he practised bricklaying and masonry, but he remained focused on becoming an inventor and starting a business on the side.

THE FIRST INVENTION

Dennis's first invention was Healthy Brush (see Exhibit 1), which he'd devised before electric toothbrushes became popular. It consisted of a plastic container holding six toothbrushes that fit into individual slots filled with mouthwash. Soaking in the antiseptic fluid all day helped reduce germs and gave the toothbrushes a healthy, clean taste that regular-toothbrush users never got to experience. When the mouthwash got contaminated or lost its flavour, the user could simply turn the entire unit upside down over the sink and pour it out. He or she could then loosen a screw at the top of the device to allow its top to rise, letting in fresh mouthwash from the reservoir at the bottom. It was really quite ingenious, and had a lot of potential for success. So for Dennis, its failure was devastating.

Dennis encountered his first problem when he looked for a manufacturer that could make a precision mould. The first company he contacted quoted a price of $30 000, but after spending the first $20 000, Dennis realized that the manufacturer wasn't capable of manufacturing the exact mould he needed. Eventually he did find a company that could do the job, but the cost was $70 000. Another major cost was for a product patent, which involved a $400 one-time application fee as well as an additional $100 annual maintenance fee. What with patent lawyers and other costs, Dennis eventually had to pay about $10 000 to secure a U.S. patent on his product.

When Dennis started to promote Healthy Brush, he was fortunate enough to get an appointment with a senior buyer for one of the world's largest retailers. The buyer expressed much interest, and promised to buy about 30 000 units (10 units for each of the retailer's 3000 locations) in the first order, assuming Dennis could meet the retailer's three requirements. First, he'd need to create a commercial to be shown on prime-time television for three to four months during the product's introduction. Needless to say, that would be extremely costly. Second, he'd need to be able to stock each of the retailer's locations, which meant he'd have to find a third-party firm capable of handling the job. Third, the buyer advised him that "every inch of our store is real estate. We have to make so much money for the space your product needs, or you'll have to send us a cheque for the difference." In the final analysis, Dennis decided not to proceed further with the idea. At this point, the amount he'd invested in Healthy Brush had reached about $200 000.

| EXHIBIT 1 | Healthy Brush Ad |

THE CURRENT INVENTION

In 2011, after years of frustration using the only bricklaying tape on the market, Dennis Gaines had an idea for an improved version—one that bricklayers and masons would find considerably more functional in laying the new maxi-size bricks that were being sold in the Ontario marketplace. (See www.toolsnrules.com for a picture of the tape and a promotional video that explains its use.) Dennis suggested the improvements to the current tape's manufacturer; however, since the manufacturer was "currently selling lots of tapes," it didn't see the need to improve the product. After Dennis talked it over with his wife, Brenda (who earlier in their relationship had spent 10 years in the bricklaying industry), they decided to see if they could perfect the current tape and get their own invention manufactured. Brenda searched www.alibaba.com for manufacturers that could produce a quality product, and found several in China. After reviewing samples, they settled on a manufacturer that quoted $4.50 per tape, with a minimum purchase of 3000 tapes and advance payment of $10 500. A few further fees (including duties and taxes) once the tapes landed in Toronto added about $2000 to the total.

As the next step, Dennis engaged an acquaintance familiar with computer-aided design (CAD) to design the tape with all the markings Dennis wanted. One side of the gauge marked the number of courses (rows) of bricks needed for the required height of the brickwork, with the opposite side showing the number of bricks needed for the required length. The tape also had special gradations to help bricklayers take mortar (the bonding between bricks) into consideration. Dennis's tape was specific to the Ontario market, since the province's two major brick manufacturers supplied a "maxi brick" that was slightly larger than those used in other provinces. At the start of the tape's gauge, Dennis decided to stamp the product's name, "Gaines Maxi Brick Rule," and the company's website; the rule's faceplate also advertised the product and the website. The cost for the CAD designer was $1600. The tape was 26 feet × 1 inch, larger than the standard offered by the competition. The most popular competitor, Bespack (www.bespack.com), offered a 12-foot tape, but its cover was clearly inferior to Gaines's rubberized, shock-absorbing version; moreover, its gauging information was very limited.

When it came time to pay for the finished tapes, Brenda first transferred a small amount of money to the manufacturer in China. When the company contacted her to confirm the exact amount she'd sent, Brenda knew that the banking information was good and that the transfer would work without any difficulty. She then transferred the balance of the money, and she and Dennis awaited the tapes.

INITIAL MARKETING STRATEGY

Before actually marketing the product, Brenda sent about 200 postcards to the retail locations of several major chains (see Exhibit 2). Not a single one replied. She also sent postcards to over 200 Ontario bricklayers at their home addresses. She realized after the fact that the majority of the addresses were taken from an old address list; the postcards didn't reach their recipients and many were returned as undelivered.

About the same time, Dennis sent emails to a fairly large number of college and university marketing professors for advice. When he got no response, and with financing getting more limited, he turned instead to a local brick supplier. Dennis was told that it was

| EXHIBIT 2 | Maxi Brick Rule Postcard |

common to price products on the following basis: one-third for the wholesaler, one-third for manufacturer's margin, and one-third to cover the cost of production (cost of goods sold). With this in mind, Dennis figured his tape should sell to end users for about $20, a price similar to what the competition was charging. A 30% discount to the wholesaler would provide it with its one-third of the selling price; the wholesaler's cost would be $14. Dennis also included freight, making the product F.O.B. the customer's place of business. The pricing strategy seemed to work.

Dennis and Brenda got their first order in November 2011, and within six months they had nine wholesalers selling their product. A few of these wholesalers had multiple locations across the province; one had five locations in its popular regions. Some wholesalers charged the suggested price, while others actually increased the end-user price to $21.95–$22.95, recognizing that the tape was clearly worth the higher price. This also gave the wholesalers closer to a 40% margin, a margin that many wholesalers made on comparable items they sold in their stores.

Dennis and Brenda decided to offer the tapes for sale on the company website as well, but only to end users who were in locations not covered by existing wholesalers. In the first six months Tools n' Rules received only about 10 orders direct, mostly for one or two tapes. In the same period, by contrast, about 1000 tapes were sold to wholesalers, basically all in 50-tape cartons. Exhibit 3 shows the prices Tool n' Rules charged for tapes, with freight and HST included. The shipping charges reflect the approximate actual cost of shipping the tapes to customers within Ontario. (Yes, postage on a single tape is $8.) Dennis and Brenda decided to absorb the freight when wholesalers purchased 50-tape cartons.

EXHIBIT 3	Tools n' Rules Price Schedule				
Quantity	Price per Unit	Total Price	Shipping	13% HST	Total
1	$23.00	$23.00	$8.00	$4.03	$35.03
5	$23.00	$115.00	$15.00	$16.90	$146.90
10	$23.00	$230.00	$20.00	$32.50	$282.50
20	$15.00	$300.00	$25.00	$42.25	$367.25
50	$14.00	$700.00	00.00	$91.00	$791.00

THE JUNE 2012 MEETING

Several months had elapsed since Dennis tried to seek some marketing advice. Then in June 2012 he was contacted out of the blue by a marketing professor who'd just read the email Dennis had sent months earlier. The professor was intrigued by the Gaines Maxi Brick Rule and curious about how the business was doing. As it happened, sales had progressed reasonably well, and a few customers had even started to place repeat orders. Others that had bought tapes still hadn't put them on their shelves because, as one customer remarked, "I want to get rid of your competitor's tapes first—I'm afraid that if my customers see your tapes, I'll get stuck with all the other ones!" Dennis felt that it might be time to review his strategy and to consider several options that had materialized over the past few weeks. He invited the professor to come to his home where they could talk more about his business.

The next weekend, the professor, his wife, and his two dogs went to visit with Dennis, Brenda, and their own two dogs. Following introductions, Brenda happened to notice that one of the professor's dogs had a perfectly white face, with no discoloured tear stains that dogs sometimes get around their eyes. She asked if that was just natural, or if they used something special to keep the dog looking so clean. The professor's wife said, "No, Ceilidh (pronounced "kay lee") always had discoloured streaks around her eyes. We bought lots of very expensive treatments, but nothing really worked. Then one day our groomer mentioned that if we gave the dog a tablespoon of plain yogurt each morning with her food, her eyes would quickly clear up. We started to do that, and it was only a matter of weeks before we really noticed the difference." At this point Dennis spoke up. "While you two are talking about this, I'm sitting here wondering if there's any way to figure out what the active ingredient is in yogurt that does this, and if I can find a way to concentrate it and patent a capsule or pill that I can sell. Oh, well. That's just the way my mind works."

Following some further dog discussions, the topic turned to the Gaines Maxi Brick Rule tape. Dennis outlined three new marketing opportunities that had all arisen within the past few weeks. First, one of the major hardware chains had contacted him, wanting to know whether he'd consider giving it the exclusive right to sell the Gaines tapes in Ontario. If he would, it would ensure complete coverage of the entire province. Dennis would need to do no further marketing; the retailer would manage everything.

Second, one of his Ottawa-area customers had asked whether he'd make it an exclusive supplier of the Gaines Maxi Brick Rule tape in the Ottawa region. It wanted all brick-laying companies in the surrounding area to purchase from it. In exchange, Dennis would need to do no further marketing in that region.

Third, a wholesale customer had inquired whether Dennis would allow it to place its own label on the tape face, thus advertising its company logo, product, and services. It wanted to replace the existing cover label promoting the Gaines Maxi Brick Rule tape and the Tool n' Rules website address.

Of course, Dennis could simply continue operations as he had been doing. He could make some changes to his marketing strategy, or he could choose from among the new opportunities that had recently presented themselves. At this point, Dennis asked the professor if he had any thoughts.

Heat-eze

William A. Preshing and
Denise Walters

Mark Tanner, a successful Canadian entrepreneur, purchased the Canadian rights to manufacture and distribute a reusable chemical heating pad named Heat-eze. The product—a
vinyl bag containing chemicals that produce a constant level of heat—had a variety of
therapeutic uses, including treatment of muscle injuries and relief from arthritic pain. The
task facing management was to develop a strategy for Heat-eze in a market that hadn't
changed in a number of years.

THE COMPANY

Mark owned The Tanner Company, which operated three businesses in western
Canada—a peat-moss company, a mini-warehouse operation, and a landfill site. He
met the inventor of Heat-eze while attending a new-business seminar, and after
considerable investigation, paid $250 000 for the Canadian manufacturing and dis-
tribution rights. Mark also obtained a patent on the product in Canada which would
last 17 years.

THE PRODUCT

Heat-eze consists of a vinyl bag containing a sodium acetate solution and a small stainless steel trigger. Activating the trigger causes the solution to crystallize, producing a predictable and constant level of heat. Since the solution's concentration can be varied, the pad is available in two temperature settings: 117 and 130 degrees Fahrenheit (47 and 54 degrees Celsius). The preset temperature can't be exceeded. The pad gives off heat for about 20 minutes, then starts to cool while still producing enough heat to maintain therapeutic value for up to three hours. Use of the felt cover, which comes with the pad, prevents rapid heat loss. The pad can be prepared for reuse by immersing it in boiling water for 15 minutes or by autoclaving it in a chemical autoclaving unit, which acts in a similar manner to a pressure cooker. The pad can be reused hundreds of times until the vinyl wears out.

The Heat-eze pads could be marketed in various sizes (e.g., 8″ × 18″, 8″ × 8″, 4″ × 4″) and in the shape of a mitt. The vinyl bags, which would be produced by an outside contractor, are stamped from a die and could be made in virtually any size and shape at an average cost per bag of $0.60. Each die costs about $3000 (paid for by the Tanner Company). It could be made in less than three weeks, enabling the company to respond quickly to changing market demand. The sodium acetate solution would be purchased from an Ontario supplier at an average cost per bag of $0.80. Tanner Company obtained an inventory of 200 000 triggers on consignment from the inventor, a sum that didn't have to be paid until the pads were sold. (The triggers are required to "start" the Heat-eze pad the first time it's used.) The inventor had guaranteed to provide a future supply of triggers at a cost of $1.25 per unit. The felt covers and packaging were available from local suppliers at a cost per bag of $0.75.

The filling and sealing process was simple, and neither labour nor capital intensive; it would be done in the mini-warehouse to maintain quality control. One welder and three unskilled workers could produce 150 pads per hour, or 22 000 per month. The combined wages of the welder and three workers would be $75 per hour. The company had purchased two welding machines, one as backup in case of mechanical failure. As production needs increased, new welding machines could be purchased for approximately $7500 each.

THE MARKET

Shortly after obtaining the rights to Heat-eze, Mark Tanner hired Richard McKay as the marketing manager at a salary of $75 000 per year. Richard had extensive sales experience, including the introduction of a number of new products to the Canadian market. His first assignment was to conduct an analysis of Heat-eze's market potential.

Because of Heat-eze's versatility, it could be sold in three broad segments: (1) the medical treatment market, (2) personal warmth (e.g., seat cushions, survival clothing, hand warmers), and (3) heating of inanimate objects (e.g., food service, industrial equipment). After evaluating these market segments, Richard felt the medical treatment segment had the greatest potential for the immediate future, and so he collected further information on this segment.

The Medical Treatment Market

The application of heat is a well-known treatment for relief from pain; and for those who have arthritis and traumatic joint or muscle injury, it increases mobility. This market can be divided into two segments: the institutional and the home market.

Within the institutional market are a number of market sub-segments, including active treatment hospitals, auxiliary hospitals, nursing homes, and physiotherapy and chiropractic clinics. Richard estimated that these facilities' total annual usage would be 45 600 units. He arrived at this estimate by phoning 20 hospitals in the Calgary and Edmonton areas and asking how many of these types of pads would be ordered each year. On average, 40 pads were used by each hospital. Using Statistics Canada data, he found that there were 1520 hospitals in Canada and then projected the annual usage rate at 45 600.

Richard felt that the home use market could be reached primarily through retail pharmacies and secondarily through medical and surgical supply stores. With about 3800 such outlets in Canada, he estimated demand through them at 304 000. This estimate was based on a telephone survey of 30 retail pharmacies and 12 medical supply stores. He explained the product to each respondent and asked how many he or she might sell in one year. On average, the respondents said they would sell 80 units each year. Based on this information, Richard estimated that the total home-use market was 304 000 pads annually.

As well, Richard felt that three market trends indicated a positive future for Heat-eze. First, heat had been underutilized as a means of treatment because of the problems with burns, electrical shocks from heating pads, inconvenience, and high cost. The Heat-eze, with its unique design and features, could surmount these problems. Second, the mean age of the Canadian population was rising and the baby boom generation was now approaching retirement. As people got older, the incidence of arthritis and other associated disorders would increase, leading to a more extensive personal use of the Heat-eze. Third, as more people became fitness-conscious and participated in physical activities, athletic injuries that could be treated with heat would also increase.

THE COMPETITION

No new products had been introduced in the industry in recent years and market shares were stable among competing firms. Heat-eze would compete with four existing products: electric heating pads, hot water bottles, instant hot packs, and reusable hot packs. Richard prepared a competitive analysis for these products (Exhibit 1). The companies producing them were divisions of large multi-product firms, such as 3M and Johnson & Johnson; fabricated rubber manufacturers; and electrical goods manufacturers.

Electric heating pads apply controlled heat over large areas of the body. The pads can cause burns, especially in older patients with decreased skin sensitivity. Pads also carry a slight electric-shock hazard, and because they require electricity to operate, they aren't truly portable.

Hot water bottles are portable and inexpensive but less convenient to use. The temperature is hard to regulate and heat is lost quickly, requiring frequent refilling. As with electric heating pads, there is some danger of burns or scalding from hot water.

Instant hot packs work on an exothermic chemical reaction principle. A larger bag contains water as well as a smaller bag full of chemicals. When the entire bag is crushed the chemicals are released and combine with water to produce heat. These packs are easy

| EXHIBIT 1 | Competitive Analysis | | | | | |

Product Type	Safety	Temperature Control	Selling Price	Heat Retention	Portability, Convenience	Weight, Pliability
Electric heat pad	Burn and shock possible	Controlled, even	$15+	Indefinite	Fair, needs electricity	Fair
Hot water bottle	Burn possible	Uneven	$6+	15-25 min.	Fair, needs refilling	Poor
Instant hot pack	Burns, toxic	Uneven	$3+	10-20 min.	Good	Poor
Reusable hot pack	Good	Good	$40	35-40 min.	Fair, needs reheating	Fair
Home pack	Good	Low heat	$2.50	15-25 min.	Good	Fair
Heat-eze	Good	Good	$20	2 hours	Good	Very Good

to use and inexpensive. However, they give off uneven heat that can cause burns, and the chemicals are often toxic. They are not reusable.

Reusable hot packs are of two types: institutional and home use. The institutional market leader is the Hydropack, a canvas pack filled with gel that's heated in a steam or hot-water autoclave. The pack is wrapped in towels and applied to the patient. The main advantages of the pack are control (it's available in different sizes and the temperature can be regulated by proper heating) and long equipment life (in excess of 20 years). The disadvantages are the high initial cost, the specialized heating equipment required, the higher laundry bills (due to use of towels), and the inability to produce "dry" rather than "moist" heat.

The home-use packs contain chemicals that are activated by hot water or steam. They're portable and provide a controlled temperature, but the heat output is lower and lasts a shorter time than Heat-eze's.

Heat-eze has features that make it superior to all these products. It's truly portable, easy to use, and doesn't require specialized equipment. The temperature is absolutely controlled to reduce the possibility of burns, there are no toxic chemicals involved, and the pad produces therapeutic heat levels for two or more hours.

Based on his assessment of the competitive products, Richard felt that with a good marketing program Heat-eze could achieve a market share of up to 50%. However, he knew that this was a guesstimate at best, and that the actual market share obtained might be quite different. In particular, he was concerned about the need to change traditional patterns of use.

FOCUS GROUPS

To initiate some ideas as to how to market the product, Richard conducted five focus group sessions. These sessions consisted of three groups of consumers who were likely users (e.g., people suffering from arthritis, people in extended care facilities, and physiotherapists). In each session people were shown a sample of the product and asked about its uses, important features, suggested selling price, and where it should be sold. Selected results from the focus groups are provided in Exhibit 2.

EXHIBIT 2	Summary of Focus Group Discussions

The summary is grouped into three categories: (1) consumers as users (particularly the arthritic and home market); (2) the institutional market (extended care facilities and hospitals); and (3) the physiotherapy group (personal and sports-related use).

1. Consumer Market

Key Uses
   a. Substitution for other sources of heat.
   b. Apply heat to ease the pain.
   c. Arthritic users indicate that the pain is so substantial they will try anything on the market to seek relief.
   d. Arthritic users tend to be sensitive to the word *arthritic*, thus anything that indicates relief will catch their attention. This is true with respect to advertisements, packages, discussions on talk shows, meetings with other arthritics, word-of-mouth, etc.
   e. Major use occurs at any time, but there was substantial interest in the fact that the product could be used during the night without significant preparation.

Key Product Features
   a. Portability and controlled heat.
   b. Variable temperature at purchase time (product line question).
   c. Flat product—very useful when user is lying down.
   d. Product durability.
   e. Reusable, therefore only pennies per use.
   f. Length of time heat lasts, particularly when covered in a towel, was viewed to be very positive.
   g. Product could be packed in a suitcase or purse and used when travelling (in a car, plane, etc.).
   h. Product is safe to use (unlike the hot wax treatment for arthritis).
   i. Product is flexible and can be shaped to meet the user's needs.
   j. The product does not leak (unlike a water bottle).

Price
   a. Arthritics were prepared to spend $20 retail for the product, and many indicated they would consider more than one product.
   b. The group indicated that a warranty would be critical to initial purchase decision.
   c. Some felt a towel cover could be provided for an additional sum.

Outlet
   a. The majority of the group felt the product would be best suited to availability in a drugstore or a department store. The great advantage of the department store was the implicit guarantee provided by the store as a part of its retail policy.

2. Institutional Market

The discussion with people in the extended care facilities indicated that they received treatment from the central physiotherapy units. In addition, many were arthritic and indicated they would like to have such a product in their room for use during the night. A major factor in the new product is safety and reliability with respect to temperature control. This is particularly significant for older people because of a reduction in sensitivity to temperature on their skin (they tend to like heat that is too strong and thus harmful to the skin).

The major entry would be through the purchasing activity of the institutions. Individual pads may be acquired but payment would be personal. Price is thus a major factor for older people on restricted incomes.

| EXHIBIT 2 | Summary of Focus Group Discussions   (continued) |

Product acquisition varied greatly depending on whether the individual worked in a private clinic or in a hospital. The distinctions were also made by nurses who attended a focus group earlier. That is, the staff who use the product are important to the decision, but the central purchasing group also assumes a key role. It was indicated that the *major* factor in the minds of central purchasing people in the institutions was the ability to show cost effectiveness, and advice was given to use this part of the presentation for individual buyers for institutions. The private clinics indicated that they also consider cost effectiveness and would look at the new product as the supply of existing heating pads was used up.

3. Physiotherapists

The focus group with physiotherapists indicated that they spend substantial amounts of money on heating pads and are looking for cost-effective products.

Use
  a. Useful where heat is the treatment medium.
  b. Use in emergency cases of hypothermia.
  c. Do not use in cases of inflammation or where internal bleeding may be present. Use in cases of inflammation after an initial treatment period where ice was used as the treatment medium.
  d. Good potential for treatment of seniors because of temperature control, which is essential due to poor circulation.
  e. Good potential for in-home use after physiotherapy treatment program.

Benefits
  a. Convenient.
  b. Cost effective.
  c. Safety due to constant temperature (point made was that heat is damaging; ice will not damage the skin because the person will stop using the ice due to the cold).
  d. Warranty is essential to remove product liability from the user, particularly the user in private clinics. In essence, they indicated a need to guarantee treatment time and product life.

INITIAL MARKETING IDEAS

Based on his analysis of the market, competition, and focus group results, Richard developed a preliminary marketing plan for Heat-eze. He felt that the product could have a retail price of $20, which was in line with the price consumers appeared willing to pay for a reusable pad with Heat-eze's features. Retailers would probably expect a margin of 25% on retail selling price.

Successful marketing of Heat-eze in both the institutional and home markets would probably require acceptance by the medical profession. In the institutional market, a demand for the pads follows only upon the physician's ordering of heat treatments, since home users often buy products on the basis of a doctor's recommendation.

Existing competitive products were marketed through three distributors. Canadian Hospital Products was the only Canadian company that distributed to the institutional market; the company prided itself on carrying Canadian-made products. Northern Medical would distribute the pad to pharmacies and surgical supply stores nationally. In Quebec there was resistance to a product distributed from outside the province, and so a Quebec distributor would be chosen. All three distributors would require margins of 15% on their selling price. Richard considered adding three salespeople to push the distribution of the product; each salesperson would be responsible for servicing either the home, institutional, or Quebec market. Salary and travel expenses for each salesperson were estimated at $60 000 per year.

Richard was uncertain about advertising but knew that the institutional market could be accessed on two levels: through the doctors and other paramedical personnel and through advertising aimed at purchasing agents for hospitals, nursing homes, and clinics. For the home market, promotional considerations would include the type of packaging and the product literature enclosed, as well as the type of advertising that would best reach a market primarily composed of older people.

Based on the information he'd collected, Richard began preparing a marketing plan for Heat-eze. He was optimistic about the success of the venture and looked forward to presenting the plan to Mark Tanner for his approval.

MetroPaint

Monique Finley, Cosimo Girolamo, Allison Carryer, and H. F. (Herb) MacKenzie

It was late December 2010 and Mary Anderson was sitting in her home-based office in St. Catharines, Ontario, where she worked for an international pharmaceutical company. She'd recently decided to leave her sales position and join the management team of MetroPaint, a business venture that her brother-in-law, David, started five years earlier. Her husband, Bruce, David's older brother, had become involved in the business the previous year, and the two men were now planning to expand the business rapidly through franchising operations, first in Ontario and eventually across Canada. Mary would be in charge of sales and the management of franchisor–franchisee relationships. Her first challenge was to make a recommendation concerning the structure of franchisee payments for the right to own and operate independent franchise locations. She'd been discussing a number of alternatives with Bruce and David, who had different views about how pricing should be established, and she was hoping to provide a recommendation that they could all agree on. There was some pressure to decide soon, as David was currently in his least-busy period of the year, and Bruce was planning to launch the promotion campaign to attract potential franchisees at a national franchise trade show at the end of January.

COMPANY BACKGROUND

MetroPaint was an automotive paint-chip restoration business that targeted larger corporate customers, such as rental car agencies and car dealerships, and retail customers. The business was unique, owing to its custom process that required trained, skilled technicians and to its delivery of unparalleled quality within the industry. Car touch-ups were done from a uniquely outfitted van, housing all the equipment and supplies needed to repair vehicles located at dealership lots or, less frequently, in retail customers' driveways. Exhibit 1 lists the services provided by MetroPaint, along with prices for corporate accounts and retail customers. David Anderson also had a small retail location—which he'd begun to rent in mid-2007—where he could accommodate private car owners who wanted the work completed in a shop environment. David had grown the business to include two part-time technicians. The first was hired in 2007 when David started his retail location, and the second was hired in 2008. Corporate accounts, including new and used car dealerships, rental car agencies, and fleet businesses, accounted for nearly 70% of sales, but this percentage was decreasing as more retail customers became aware of the service. Exhibit 2 provides the income statement for the first five years of operations, with a breakdown of revenue from corporate accounts and retail customers. Some retail customers have used the service several times since it began operations. MetroPaint has experienced considerable growth over its first five years, and Bruce took this as an indication that franchise operations would be viable.

EXHIBIT 1	MetroPaint Services and Pricing	
Services	**Description**	**Pricing**
Paint chip repair	Vehicle paint is matched exactly to the damaged vehicle. All chips, scratches, and minor paint damage around the entire vehicle are treated and permanently repaired. No panel painting is involved. All non-damaged paint remains original.	Spot damage: $50 minimum Total vehicle: Corporate $150 Retail $195
Paintless dent repair	Minor dents around the entire vehicle can be popped out. Most are undetectable; some are vastly improved but not perfect. No panel painting is involved. All non-damaged paint remains original.	Small dent: Corporate $75 Retail $95 Multiple dents are priced independently.
Bumper repairs	Scratches, nicks, and more extensive damage to bumpers can be repaired, keeping the undamaged areas of the bumper original. Painting repairs are permanent and colours can be matched exactly.	Bumper blend: Corporate $125 minimum Retail $150 minimum More challenging damage priced independently.

EXHIBIT 2	Income Statement, 2006–2010				
	2006	2007	2008	2009	2010
Revenue: retail	7 667	14 988	29 654	47 671	66 714
Revenue: corporate	74 152	100 721	126 599	131 371	141 897
Revenue: total	81 819	115 709	156 253	179 042	208 611
Expenses:					
Marketing and Sales Promotion	1 050	1 092	1 080	1 155	1 234
General and Administration					
Wages	0	8 190	15 107	20 020	23 135
Garage rental	0	2 700	5 700	5 700	5 700
Supplies	2 801	3 100	3 810	5 107	5 985
Vehicle rental	4 968	4 968	4 968	5 448	5 448
Vehicle operating	2 975	3 090	3 529	3 894	4 014
Utilities	0	622	1 812	1 744	1 926
Telephone	361	374	455	490	642
Postage and supplies	174	155	188	242	262
Insurance	3 300	3 300	3 650	3 650	3 975
Accounting	400	400	600	600	600
Other G&A	1 018	1 233	1 365	1 459	1 666
Total expenses	17 047	29 224	42 264	49 509	54 587
Operating profit	64 772	86 485	113 989	129 533	154 024

It was Bruce who originally suggested the idea of franchising. Although David had created the business, he lacked the vision or the necessary business skills to expand operations beyond his current location. Conversely, although Bruce had no technical expertise in doing this type of automotive paint repair, he did have the operational know-how to build David's business into a franchisable entity. Bruce was a typical over-achiever: he set lofty goals, downplayed obstacles to achieving them, and generally managed to succeed where others frequently failed. He was extremely competitive and loved to be challenged. He had a law degree and an MBA, and was eager to put them to use. Bruce and Mary were financially secure, and Bruce felt he could continue with his law practice, particularly if Mary decided to manage the sales and franchisee relationships for the business. Mary had been successful in sales for many years, and she also had a good knowledge of marketing.

Bruce and Mary found a small office they could rent in downtown St. Catharines that would serve as a head office and provide retail visibility. They didn't want the sales office to be located near David's service location. A friend at the local credit union assured Bruce and Mary that they could get a business line of credit for $600 000 at 1% above prime, owing to both his past relationship with Bruce and the potential he saw in MetroPaint. Unlike David, who was risk averse, Bruce was quite prepared to carry debt, particularly when he saw the opportunity for substantial return.

COMPETITIVE ANALYSIS

Industry Overview

North Americans spend billions of dollars every year to keep their vehicles looking like new. Automotive touch-up services employ skilled technicians to repair common blemishes that commonly accumulate on the surfaces of vehicles. The majority of their revenue is generated through automotive dealerships, and particularly through their used car departments. In the highly competitive business of car sales, vehicles must appear to be in excellent condition in order to sell for the highest prices. Thus, the outward appearance of the vehicle is crucial.

MetroPaint relied on unique methods of repair that had been developed since its inception. David established a systematic process that permitted trained employees to permanently repair stone chips, bumper scuffs, minor rust, and scratches on virtually all domestic and foreign automobiles in only a few hours. MetroPaint filled a unique niche between a car detail shop and a full body shop. The company was premised on a commitment to first-class customer service and utilization of existing state-of-the-art automotive touch-up processes and techniques. One competitor, Minnesota-based Paint Bull, sold repair kits to people who wanted to operate their own businesses repairing paint imperfections on vehicles.

Competitors

MetroPaint offered a more cost-effective alternative to a traditional body shop, as it repaired only the vehicle's damaged areas rather than painting or replacing entire body panels. Some body shops offered minimal touch-up services, but none were able to match the process and techniques, commitment to service, and cost-effective price structure that made MetroPaint the industry leader. The following provides a comparison of competitor alternatives:

MetroPaint

- Independent business with an owner motivated to ensure customer satisfaction
- Fully outfitted mobile van for on-site repairs and a retail service location
- Technicians specifically trained in a unique process for paint repair and precise colour matching
- Faster turnaround time than typical body shop process

Paint Bull

- Business opportunity offering a kit and two weeks' training to technicians who were then on their own to compete for business
- Generally inferior paint matching compared with MetroPaint
- Technicians were free to roam anywhere in search of sales
- Poor reputation for work and customer service
- Work was not guaranteed

Typical Body Shop

- Often unionized workers, not entrepreneurially motivated
- Painters trained to paint body panels; performing touch-up on the side is insufficient to develop the unique skills required to compete with a MetroPaint technician
- Often focused on larger, more expensive repairs to compensate for costly overhead

MARKET ANALYSIS

MetroPaint was part of the multibillion-dollar automotive repair industry. While new car sales were highly cyclical, the demand for MetroPaint's services was relatively stable. In fact, whenever new-vehicle sales declined, people often held onto their vehicles for longer periods of time, which would increase the retail demand for touch-up services.

Market Segments: Corporate Accounts

The market for automobile touch-ups comprised two primary segments: commercial and retail. Commercial accounts were broken down into several significant categories:

Used Car Departments Dealerships' used car departments were MetroPaint's primary customers. Most dealerships had used car lots stocked with later-model vehicles worthy of higher reconditioning costs, and most car dealers wanted their cars on the lot as soon as possible after they were purchased at auction. As MetroPaint generally offered same-day service, dealers wouldn't have vehicles sitting in the back of a body shop for days waiting to be repaired or painted.

New Car Departments The new car department of dealerships was MetroPaint's secondary customer. MetroPaint repaired minor paint blemishes on cars that had been damaged either during transit or while sitting on a dealer's lot. New cars with even a tiny paint chip or scratch were virtually unsellable.

Independent Used Car Dealers Virtually every used car on the market could use MetroPaint's service. The reconditioning dollars from these customers were less reliable. Sometimes they were willing to invest in the look of their vehicles; sometimes they simply sold them "as is."

Rental Car Agencies Prior to returning a vehicle to head office, the local rental car franchisee frequently repaired vehicles to avoid costly damage penalties.

Fleet Companies Prior to sending a vehicle to auction, fleet companies repaired their vehicles to avoid damage penalties.

Insurance Companies MetroPaint was only beginning to explore doing business with insurance companies. It had recently been awarded several large insurance contracts to remove over-spray damage on insured vehicles. As David continued to grow his business, he planned to aggressively target these companies.

Market Segments: Retail Accounts

Retail customers had accounted for an increasing percentage of revenue over the five years MetroPaint was in business, and Mary was convinced that sales to this segment would continue to increase more rapidly than sales to corporate accounts. Retail sales had grown largely through word-of-mouth, but with franchising, Mary planned some advertising and promotion campaigns. Of course, as more franchise locations opened across the province, more people would get to know MetroPaint and new locations would have an easier time establishing their business. Mary thought it would be possible for the two segments to eventually contribute equally to sales revenue. Retail customers were attracted to MetroPaint services for several reasons:

- People who leased vehicles (roughly one-third of all new cars) were often responsible for expensive damage penalties for minor paint scuffs or chips when their lease was up. MetroPaint was able to cost-effectively help people avoid these penalties.

- For those people trying to sell their car privately (or wishing to trade in their vehicle for a newer model), MetroPaint could help convert their vehicle to "like new" condition, allowing them to sell the vehicle for substantially more money.

- For those people who take pride in the appearance of their vehicle, MetroPaint could help preserve the original finish in a cost-effective way. No matter how carefully a person cares for a vehicle, minor paint blemishes are sure to occur. MetroPaint could quickly and cost-effectively remove these blemishes.

METROPAINT FRANCHISE AND EXPANSION OPPORTUNITIES

Businesses generally franchise their operations so that they can grow quickly without needing to raise money through either debt or equity. The franchisee buys the brand equity of the franchisor, and benefits from the franchisor's knowledge and assistance. The franchisor allows the franchisee to operate one or more locations under the franchisor's name, in exchange for a fee. The franchisor benefits when franchisees are motivated to develop their particular locations, and franchisees are usually much more highly motivated than managers employed to operate company-owned locations. The challenge for the franchisor is to come up with the right fee structure for the business: a combination of an upfront franchise fee and ongoing royalties that are usually based on sales revenue.

THE NEW YEAR'S DAY MEETING

David and his family visited Mary and Bruce for New Year's Day dinner, along with Tom and Angela, Bruce and David's parents. After the traditional plum pudding was served, Mary, Bruce, and David gathered in the basement games room to discuss the issue of franchise fees and royalties. Mary started the conversation by explaining what she'd discovered about fees and royalties. Upfront fees for a franchise location for businesses similar to MetroPaint could range from $1000 or less to $20 000 or more. Royalty fees could be as low as 1 or 2%, but could be as high as 7 or 8%. In some operations, the franchisor makes additional profit by requiring the franchisee to buy supplies through the franchisor.

"I think a higher rather than a lower initial franchise fee will ensure that only serious franchisees are attracted," David remarked. "Those who pay a $1000 upfront fee can simply walk away without much financial loss. If they have to pay $20 000, they'll be more committed to ensuring that their location is a success."

"True," said Bruce, "but we could lose a lot of potentially good franchisees if we want too much upfront money."

David was quick to respond. "Don't forget, though, that franchisees require little capital to start a franchise location. The fee they pay will likely be their largest single expense. They can lease a vehicle and a small garage."

"Well," Mary added, "the upfront fees often vary depending on the royalty fees. High upfront fees usually mean lower royalty fees, and when upfront fees are low, franchisors generally make their money from higher royalty fees. Royalty fees have the advantage of providing an ongoing revenue stream for the franchisor."

The three continued to discuss fees and royalties for some time before Tom entered the room. "Are you all going to be antisocial or are you going to help celebrate the new year with the rest of us?"

"Tom, we're having an important discussion here. You're experienced in business, and we'd welcome your opinion." Mary placed her notepad and pen on the table in front of her.

Tom smiled. "I hate it when a conversation starts that way. What are you discussing?"

"If you were considering buying a franchise location, would you rather a higher upfront fee and lower royalties or a lower upfront fee and higher royalties? We're trying to decide how to structure MetroPaint's fees and royalties when we start to franchise locations. Bruce and David have different opinions, and I'm not sure what I think yet."

"Well," Tom began, "I haven't had any first-hand experience with franchises, but I'd certainly be uncomfortable with high upfront fees and lower royalties. That would make me wonder whether the franchisor was serious about the business or just wanted to get as much money as possible before abandoning the franchisees. If the franchisor wanted higher royalties, that would convince me he or she was thinking long term."

David leaned forward in his chair. "Higher royalty fees might also encourage franchisees to cheat the franchisor. Worse, they might even abandon the operation once they understood the business and the repair processes, and then they'd become a competitor."

"That's why we need to create some brand equity quickly. It would also help if we had some branded supplies. Bruce, maybe you could work on finding a manufacturer or two that would make the supplies we need and brand them with the MetroPaint name."

"I'm still thinking about the royalty fees issue," said Bruce. "It seems to me that the higher the royalty fee, the less likely the franchisee would be to report any cash sales to the franchisor."

"I don't see that as a big issue," responded David. The majority of sales are to commercial accounts, and they need receipts. It's only retail customers who'd pay cash."

"Retail customers are becoming increasingly important, though. They initially accounted for less than 10% of sales, but now they account for more than 30%—and I suspect there's still more growth opportunity with this segment."

"I noticed that," Mary put in. "I also think that as new locations open, the development of retail customers will increase more rapidly as the service becomes increasingly known among consumers." Mary picked up her notepad and began to make further notes.

Tom moved toward the door, but before he left the room he turned face to Mary. "You know, if you're really concerned about having franchisees cheat when your royalty payments are high, have you considered low royalty payments supplemented with an annual franchise fee? You could charge an upfront fee, a smaller annual fee, and lower royalty payments."

"Thanks a lot, Tom," Mary responded. "Things are complicated now, and you just made them more complicated. I think we need a break. New Year's Day isn't the best time to think about this. We'll join you upstairs and we can all have a coffee."

MARY'S DECISION

Several days later, Mary sat in her office and considered the discussion. She had almost decided the franchise pricing strategy she'd recommend, and she knew Bruce and David would accept her recommendation. Just as she began to put it in writing, though, some additional considerations came to mind. Mary wondered whether every franchisee should be charged the same fees. Certainly some locations had considerably more opportunity for development than others. (Exhibit 3 provides a breakdown of Ontario regions according to the number of new and used car dealerships by sales revenue.) Of course, royalty fees would increase with volume, but maybe she should consider charging different upfront fees depending on each location's potential. She further wondered whether royalty fees should gradually decrease as volume increased as a way to motivate franchisees to expand their business. Mary wasn't aware of any other franchisor that did this, although of course that didn't preclude considering it.

EXHIBIT 3	Number of Car Dealerships (New and Used) by Territory					
Sales (Millions)	$20-50	$10-20	$5-10	$2.5-5	$1-2.5	$.5-1
Algonquin	4	3	5	5		
Belleville & Vicinity	5	6	1	4	3	
Brampton		2	8	6	4	
Brantford/Paris	4	1	3	4	3	
Burlington		4		9	6	
Cambridge	1		3	4	2	
Carleton & Vicinity	3		4	9		
Chatham	1	2	4	6		
Cornwall	3		5	8		
Embrun & Area		2	5	5		
Gloucester			2	8	4	
Goderich	1	2	3	6		
Guelph	5	3	5	9	1	
Hamilton	1	8	9	6	10	
Kingston/Brockville	5	4	6	5	1	2
Kitchener	7		2	6	4	
Leamington	1	1	4	8		
Lindsay/Peterborough	3	6	14	11	2	
London	1	1	2	6	7	1

EXHIBIT 3	Number of Car Dealerships (New and Used) by Territory (continued)					
Sales (Millions)	$20-50	$10-20	$5-10	$2.5-5	$1-2.5	$.5-1
London North	1	1	9	5	2	1
Markham	2	2	2	6	5	1
Milton/Georgetown	1	2	4	6		
Mississauga	8	6	10	9	5	7
Newmarket/Aurora	7		2	7	4	1
Oakville	3		1	9	2	2
Oshawa/Whitby	3		2	5	6	
Ottawa East	1	4		4	6	3
Ottawa West	2	2	2	6	6	2
Pickering/Ajax	3		2	8	2	
Port Perry/Uxbridge	1		6	2	3	
Richmond Hill	2	1	2	7	4	
Sarnia	2	3	4	3	2	
Scarborough	6	4	11	3	3	4
Simcoe & Area	3	6	2	5		
St. Catharines	2	3	3	2	1	
Stratford	1	3	2	6	1	
Strathroy	2	2	6	3		
Thornhill	2		4	7	2	2
Toronto Central	7	5		2	4	1
Toronto Central West	12		1		1	1
Toronto East York	7	1	2	2	5	
Toronto Etobicoke	6		2	5	2	
Toronto Humber Bay	9			5	4	
Toronto Metro	9	1	1	3	1	2
Toronto North East	2		2	4	3	
Toronto North East	9		1	2	3	2
Toronto North York	9			2	5	1
Toronto West	3	1	2	2	8	4
Toronto York	10	1	2	2	1	1
Wallaceburg & Area		6	4		1	
Waterloo		2	8	3	1	
Welland & Vicinity	3	2	4	8		
Windsor	2	2	3	2	6	2
Woodbridge		1	3	6	2	2
Woodstock	2	2	8	8		

As Mary went to the kitchen to pour herself a coffee, she was struck with yet another thought. Why did she have to recommend one franchisee per territory? The retail and corporate segments were very different. Retail customers would take their vehicles to a service centre where a franchisee would repair their car. But to serve corporate customers, a franchisee needed a mobile van and equipment to go to dealerships and repair vehicles on site. Perhaps they could offer a franchise opportunity to two franchisees in each location. Or maybe they could leverage this by charging a higher franchise fee to a franchisee who wanted to sell to both segments.

Mary sat down with her coffee and mentally prepared herself for the challenge. She was beginning to feel the pressure as the need for her decision loomed closer.

Harrison Measurement Devices Ltd.

Philip Rosson

Harrison Measurement Devices Ltd. (HMD) is a British firm that operates as a manufacturer and an importer/distributor. Its field is electronic instruments, and its imported products account for about 75% of sales. One of the companies HMD represents in the United Kingdom is Measurement Devices of Canada (MDC), a precision instrument firm. HMD and MDC have been working together for about 10 years. The relationship between the two companies had been good until a year ago, when an accident robbed MDC of its top two executives and things started to go wrong. William "Bill" Harrison feels strong ties to MDC, but has been increasingly worried about the Canadian company's seeming indifference to its international operations in general and to the relationship with HMD in particular.

Bill locked his car door and walked across the parking lot toward the station entrance. Although it was a sunny spring morning and the daffodils and tulips provided welcome colour after the greyness of winter, Bill hardly noticed. In a few minutes the train from London would be arriving with Bryan Wright, the export sales manager for Measurement Devices of Canada. Bill was about to spend the day with Bryan, and he wondered what the outcome of their discussions would be.

This case was prepared by Philip Rosson, professor of marketing, Dalhousie University, as a basis for class discussion. Reprinted with permission.

HARRISON MEASUREMENT DEVICES LTD.

Bill was managing director of Harrison Measurement Devices Ltd., part of a small, family-owned U.K. group of companies. The company gained its first sales agency in 1923 from an American manufacturer, making it one of the most well established international trading firms in electronic instruments. HMD sales were the equivalent of about $4 million, with 75% coming from imported distributed items and 25% from sales of its own manufactured items. The company had a total of 12 employees.

HMD was the British distributor for 15 manufacturers located in the United States, Canada, Switzerland, and Japan. Like many firms, it found that the 80/20 rule held true: about 80% of its import sales of $3 million were generated by 20% of the distributorships it held. With current sales of MDC products near $660 000 (at 50% margin), the Measurement Devices of Canada product line was an important one to HMD.

MEASUREMENT DEVICES OF CANADA

Measurement Devices of Canada was a younger and larger organization than its U.K. distributor. Located in southern Ontario and founded in the mid-1950s, it had current sales of $20 million and a workforce of 60 employees. MDC had developed a strong reputation over the years for its high-precision instrumentation and testing equipment, and this led to considerable market expansion. The company had moved in a number of new-product directions. Its original products were very precise devices for use in standards laboratories, and from this base it had more recently established a presence in the oceanographic and electric power fields.

As a result of this expansion, 80% of its sales were now made outside Canada, split evenly between the United States and offshore markets. In the United States the company had its own direct-sales organization, whereas indirect methods were used elsewhere. In the "best" 15 offshore markets, MDC had exclusive distributors; in 30 other markets, it relied on commission agents.

WORKING TOGETHER

HMD and MDC first made contact in New York City. Bill Harrison was on a business trip there when he received an email from his brother saying that a representative of MDC wanted to get in touch with him. Bill and his wife met the senior executive in their hotel room, and after initial introductions, settled down to exchange information. At some point, Bill, who'd had a hectic day, fell asleep. He awoke to find that HMD was now more or less MDC's U.K. distributor, his wife having kept the discussion rolling while he slept.

The two firms soon began to prosper together. The distributorship gave HMD a product line to complement those it already carried. Furthermore, MDC instruments were regarded as the "Cadillacs" of the industry. This ensured entry to a potential customer's premises and an interest in the rest of the HMD product line. As far as MDC was concerned, it could hardly have chosen a more suitable partner: HMD's staff was technically competent, facilities existed for product servicing, and customer contacts were good. Moreover, as time passed, Bill Harrison's long experience and international connections proved invaluable to MDC. He was often asked for an opinion prior to some new move by the Canadian producer. Bill preferred to have a close working relationship with the firms he represented, so he was happy to provide advice. In this way, HMD did an effective job of representing MDC in the United Kingdom and helped with market expansion elsewhere.

As might be expected, the companies' senior executives got along well together. The president and vice-president of marketing—MDC's "international ambassadors"—and Bill Harrison progressed from being business partners to becoming close personal friends. Then, after nine successful years, a tragedy occurred: the two MDC executives were killed in an airplane crash on their way home from a sales trip.

The tragic accident created a management succession crisis within MDC. During this period, international operations were left dangling while other priorities were attended to. No one was able to take charge of the exporting activities that had generated such good sales for the company. Although there was an export sales manager, Bryan Wright, he was a relative newcomer, having been in training at the time of the accident. He was also a middle-level executive, whereas his international predecessors were the company's most senior personnel.

From Bill's point of view, things were still not right a year later. The void in MDC's international operations hadn't been properly filled. Bryan Wright had proved to be a competent manager, but he lacked support because a new vice-president of marketing had yet to be appointed. A new president headed the company, but he'd been the vice-president of engineering and preferred to deal with technical rather than business issues. So despite the fact that Bryan had a lot of ideas about what should be done internationally (most of which were similar to Bill's), he lacked both the position and the support of a superior to bring about the necessary changes.

While the airplane accident precipitated the current problems in the two companies' relationship, Bill realized that things had been going sour for a couple of years. At the outset of the relationship, MDC executives had welcomed the close association with HMD. Over time, however, as the manufacturer grew in size and new personnel came along, it seemed to Bill that his input was increasingly resented. This was unfortunate, because he believed that MDC could become a more sophisticated international competitor if it considered advice given by informed distributors. In the past, MDC had been open to advice and had benefited considerably from it. Yet there were still areas where MDC could effect improvements. For example, its product literature was poor quality and was often inaccurate or outdated. Prices were also worrisome. MDC seemed unable to hold its costs, and its competitors now offered better value-for-money alternatives. Other marketing practices needed attention, too.

THE OCEANOGRAPHIC MARKET

One area where MDC and HMD were in disagreement was the move into the oceanographic field. Bill Harrison was pleased to see MDC moving into new fields, but wondered if it truly appreciated just how new the oceanographic field was. In a way, he believed the company had been led into this field by the technology rather than having considered the fit between its capabilities and the field's success criteria. For example, the customer fit didn't seem even close. The traditional buyers of MDC products for use in standards laboratories were scientists, some of whom were employed by government, some by industry, and some by universities. By and large, they were academic types, used to getting their equipment when the budget permitted. As a result, selling was "gentlemanly," and follow-up visits were required to maintain contacts. Patience was often required, since purchasing cycles could be relatively long. Service needs weren't extensive, for the instruments were used very carefully.

In contrast, oceanographic products were used in the very demanding sea environment. Service needs were acute, owing not just to the harsh operating environment but also to the cost associated with having inoperable equipment. For example, ocean research costs were already high but became even higher if faults in shipboard equipment prevented taking sea measurements. In such a situation the customer demanded service today or tomorrow, wherever the faulty equipment was located. The oceanographic customer was also a difficult type—technically trained but concerned about getting the job done as quickly as possible. Purchasing budgets were much less of a worry; if the equipment was good, reliable, and with proven backup, chances were it could be sold. But selling required more of a push than did the laboratory equipment.

When MDC entered the oceanographic field, a separate distributor was appointed in the United Kingdom. However, the arrangement didn't work out. MDC then asked Bill Harrison to carry the line, and with great reluctance he agreed. Bill's lack of enthusiasm stemmed from his perception that his company wasn't capable of functioning well in this new arena. And if HMD was ill equipped to service the oceanographic customer, that may have repercussions for its more traditional field. Bill was unwilling to risk the company's established reputation in this way, although his concerns about MDC's "one market, one distributor" mentality overrode his unwillingness.

THE CURRENT VISIT

Bill Harrison had strong personal sentiments for MDC as a company. In his opinion, however, some concrete action was required if the business relationship was to survive, let alone prosper.

Bill recognized the good sales of MDC products, but also took note of shrinking profit margins over the last few years due to the increased costs HMD had incurred with the MDC product line. Since MDC was slow to respond to service and other problems, HMD had been putting things right and absorbing the associated costs more and more frequently. These costs could not be absorbed forever. Bill had been willing to help tide MDC over the last difficult year, but he expected a more positive response in the future.

Bill hoped Bryan Wright would bring good news from Canada. Ideally, he hoped to drop the oceanographic line and rebuild the bridges that used to exist between his firm and the manufacturer. A return to the close and helpful relationship that once existed would be welcomed. Still, he wondered if MDC's management wanted to operate in a more formal and distant "buy and sell" manner. If this were the case, Bill Harrison would have to give more serious thought to the MDC distributorship.

Kingston Frontenacs

H. F. (Herb) MacKenzie

It was early August 2010, and Jeff Stilwell had just started his summer vacation. Jeff was the director of marketing and communications for the Kingston Frontenacs, one of the Ontario Hockey League's Eastern Conference teams. The team was seriously considering ways to increase revenue, particularly from ticket sales. Its administration had met several times, and everyone had provided a number of suggestions. It was now up to Jeff to put together a plan for the group's consideration and (hopefully) approval.

Jeff knew that ticket revenue could be increased in only two ways: sell more tickets or increase the tickets' average price. Of course, some combination of the two alternatives would also work. Jeff was equally concerned with long-term growth of fan support. He was pleased with what he'd accomplished with advertising and sponsorship sales, and wanted to make sure that whatever suggestions he made for increasing ticket revenue would be supported by senior administration.

As he relaxed on the patio, Jeff scanned the suggestions that had come up during previous meetings and informal discussions relating to ticket pricing. He was thankful to have several relaxing weeks of "noodle" time, but once his vacation was over, everyone would be expecting to see a plan that could be easily implemented and that would ultimately be successful.

ONTARIO HOCKEY LEAGUE

There are 20 teams in the Ontario Hockey League (OHL), with 10 in the Eastern Conference and 10 in the Western Conference. Each team plays a regular season of 68 games: 34 home games and 34 away games. (The 2009–2010 standings are shown in Exhibit 1.) The OHL, the Quebec Major Junior Hockey League, and the Western Hockey League make up the Canadian Hockey League (CHL), which has a total of 60 teams in nine provinces and five U.S. states. In the 2009–2010 season, attendance at CHL games exceeded 9 million spectators. The CHL might not match the NHL for quality of hockey, but many loyal junior hockey fans believe the excitement is often as great; plus, they get to see future NHL stars as they begin their professional hockey careers. In fact, more NHL players come from the CHL than from any other hockey league. In the NHL's 2010 entry draft, the top three first-round draft choices all came from the OHL. With the first pick, the Edmonton Oilers chose Taylor Hall (40 goals and 66 assists in 57 games) from the Windsor Spitfires. The Boston Bruins, with the second pick, chose Tyler Seguin (48 goals and 58 assists in 63 games) from the Plymouth Whalers. The Florida Panthers chose Erik Gudbranson (2 goals and 21 assists in 41 games), a 201-pound, 6′3″ defenceman from the Kingston Frontenacs, as the third pick. Erik was only the seventh Ottawa-area player to be a top 10 NHL draft pick in the last 30 years.

EXHIBIT 1	OHL Standings, 2009-2010							
Eastern Conference	Wins	Losses	Overtime Losses	Shootout Losses	Points	Goals For	Goals Against	Penalties in Minutes
Barrie Colts	57	9	0	2	116	327	186	1384
Ottawa 67's	37	23	5	3	82	246	219	1014
Mississauga St. Michael's Majors	42	20	4	2	90	222	175	1172
Kingston Frontenacs	33	30	2	3	71	229	251	1316
Brampton Battalion	25	29	7	7	64	167	181	1039
Peterborough Petes	29	35	1	3	62	231	277	1179
Niagara Ice Dogs	26	34	2	6	60	191	233	1184
Sudbury Wolves	26	35	4	3	59	193	267	1297
Oshawa Generals	24	39	3	2	53	216	299	1276
Belleville Bulls	20	40	2	6	48	189	263	1099

EXHIBIT 1	OHL Standings, 2009-2010			(continued)				
Western Conference	Wins	Losses	Overtime Losses	Shootout Losses	Points	Goals For	Goals Against	Penalties in Minutes
Windsor Spitfires	50	12	1	5	106	331	203	1333
London Knights	49	16	1	2	101	273	208	1197
Kitchener Rangers	42	19	4	3	91	286	236	1096
Plymouth Whalers	38	27	1	2	79	245	201	1222
Sault Ste. Marie Greyhounds	36	27	1	4	77	237	213	1318
Saginaw Spirit	34	27	4	3	75	240	230	1344
Guelph Storm	35	29	3	1	74	242	255	1252
Erie Otters	33	28	5	2	73	257	259	1013
Owen Sound Attack	27	33	4	4	62	221	276	1135
Sarnia Sting	17	46	3	2	39	184	295	1293

KINGSTON FRONTENACS

Kingston has had a junior hockey team since 1973, when the Kingston Canadians first entered the OHL; the team played out of the 3300-seat Memorial Centre. In its second season it took the Toronto Marlboros—favoured for the CHL's Memorial Cup—to eight games in the first round of the OHL playoffs, and lost on what has become a Kingston legend: the famous phantom goal. In the 1985–86 season, Kingston goalie Chris Clifford became the first OHL goalie to score a goal. In the 1987–88 season, the team lost 28 consecutive games, the longest losing streak in league history. That was the end for the Kingston Canadians. A new owner renamed the team Kingston Raiders, but after only one season the team changed ownership again. It became the Kingston Frontenacs, named in honour of Louis de Buade de Frontenac, the governor of New France who established Fort Frontenac, where the city of Kingston now stands. With its new name and colours, the team ended its first season one point out of first place. Unfortunately, it lost in the first round of playoffs against its arch rival, the Belleville Bulls. That seventh game, played in Belleville, stands as the longest game ever played in OHL history. The game finished at 1:46 a.m.—after six hours and 16 minutes—in the fourth overtime period.

On February 22, 2008, the Frontenacs played for the first time at the new 5380-seat, state-of-the-art K-Rock Centre. Fan attendance increased immediately, but unfortunately the team had a very disappointing year. That was followed in 2008–09 by an even more disappointing year; however, the team greatly improved its overall performance in 2009–2010 and made the playoffs. (Exhibit 2 lists its win-loss records and other statistics in recent years.)

EXHIBIT 2	Kingston Frontenacs' Win-Loss Records, 2000–2010				
Year	Wins	Losses	Overtime Losses	Shootout Losses	Points
2009-10	33	30	2	3	71
2008-09	18	40	6	4	46
2007-08	25	41	0	2	52
2006-07	31	30	5	2	69
2005-06	37	24	4	3	81
2004-05	28	33	4	3	63
2003-04	30	28	7	3	70
2002-03	25	37	2	4	56
2001-02	18	37	9	4	49
2000-01	28	28	11	1	68

The team has contributed a number of exciting players to the NHL. Chris Stewart was a 2006 first-round draft pick by the Colorado Avalanche. Ethan Werek, a Frontenacs rookie in 2008–09, became the 11th overall rookie points leader, scoring 64 points in his first season. He was selected in the second round of the 2009 NHL draft by the New York Rangers. In the 2009–2010 season, Werek was second in overall scoring among Frontenac players, even though he lost part of the season through injury; he returned to the team lineup for 2010–11. Erik Gudbranson, a star defenceman with the Frontenacs, was the Florida Panthers' first-round 2010 NHL draft pick; it was uncertain whether he'll stay with the Panthers this coming year or return to Kingston for another season. To help strengthen the Frontenacs' defence, younger brother Alex Gudbranson, a 190-pound, 6'2", right-shooting defenceman, has signed as a rookie for the 2010–11 season. When Larry Mavety, Kingston Frontenac Hockey Club's director of hockey operations and general manager, announced the signing of the team's 2010 first-round OHL priority selection, he said, "Alex will make a great addition to our hockey club. He has great size, a good shot, plays with an edge, and isn't afraid to mix it up if necessary."

The team was looking forward to a good 2010–11 season, hoping to improve further on its previous year's performance. (See Exhibit 3 for a list of the Frontenacs' 34 scheduled home games.)

The 2010–11 schedule was very similar to the previous year's, although there were a few "rogue" games. The Monday and Saturday games were something new. Jeff thought the change was unlikely to have much of an impact on overall fan attendance. (Attendance in recent years is shown in Exhibit 4.)

When Jeff thought about the attendance, a number of things concerned him—and might provide some opportunity for growth. He recalled seeing lots of young children at NHL games. While there were certainly many children at Frontenacs games, their percentage seemed much lower—usually about 15%. Jeff also thought about the number of women attending the games: in the previous year they had accounted for only about one-third of fan support, and he wondered what could be done to make the game more attractive to them. Finally, Jeff wondered if something could be done to attract more students. Kingston certainly

EXHIBIT 3	Kingston Frontenacs' 2010-11 Home Schedule	
Fri., Sep. 24	7:30 p.m.	Mississauga St. Michael's Majors
Fri., Oct. 01	7:30 p.m.	Belleville Bulls
Fri., Oct. 08	7:30 p.m.	Oshawa Generals
Sun., Oct. 10	1:00 p.m.	Plymouth Whalers*
Fri., Oct. 15	7:30 p.m.	Belleville Bulls
Wed., Oct. 20	7:00 p.m.	Ottawa 67's
Fri., Oct. 22	7:30 p.m.	Peterborough Petes
Fri., Nov. 05	7:30 p.m.	Barrie Colts
Fri., Nov. 12	7:30 p.m.	Sault Ste. Marie Greyhounds*
Sun., Nov. 14	2:00 p.m.	Sarnia Sting*
Fri., Nov. 26	7:30 p.m.	Brampton Battalion
Sun., Nov. 28	2:00 p.m.	Ottawa 67's
Fri., Dec. 03	7:30 p.m.	Peterborough Petes
Fri., Dec. 17	7:30 p.m.	Belleville Bulls
Sat., Jan. 01	2:00 p.m.	Mississauga St. Michael's Majors
Fri., Jan. 07	7:30 p.m.	Owen Sound Attack*
Fri., Jan. 14	7:30 p.m.	Oshawa Generals
Sun., Jan. 16	2:00 p.m.	Windsor Spitfires*
Fri., Jan. 21	7:30 p.m.	Guelph Storm*
Sun., Jan. 23	2:00 p.m.	Saginaw Spirit*
Fri., Jan. 28	7:30 p.m.	Peterborough Petes
Fri., Feb. 04	7:30 p.m.	London Knights*
Wed., Feb. 09	7:00 p.m.	Niagara Ice Dogs
Fri., Feb. 11	7:30 p.m.	Belleville Bulls
Sun., Feb. 13	2:00 p.m.	Erie Otters*
Fri., Feb. 18	7:30 p.m.	Brampton Battalion
Mon., Feb. 21	2:00 p.m.	Ottawa 67's
Fri., Feb. 25	7:30 p.m.	Oshawa Generals
Fri., Mar. 04	7:30 p.m.	Kitchener Rangers*
Sun., Mar. 06	2:00 p.m.	Barrie Colts
Wed., Mar. 09	7:00 p.m.	Ottawa 67's
Fri., Mar. 11	7:30 p.m.	Oshawa Generals
Sun., Mar. 13	2:00 p.m.	Niagara Ice Dogs
Fri., Mar. 18	7:30 p.m.	Sudbury Wolves

*Teams from the Western Conference (one game at home against each).

EXHIBIT 4	Attendance Figures	
2009–2010 Season	Games	Attendance
Regular season	34	94 735
Playoffs	4	13 991
Friday games	23	64 923
Sunday games	9	23 876
Wednesday games	2	5 937
Season	Attendance	
2008–09	105 174	
2007–08	86 711	
2006–07	76 397	
2005–06	74 731	
2004–05	71 232	
2003–04	67 270	
2002–03	65 518	
2001–02	74 017	
2000–01	80 818	

had considerable potential here. There were about 25 000 students at Queen's University, and St. Lawrence College and Royal Military College contributed about 10 000 and 1500 students, respectively.

TICKET PRICES

Historically, OHL teams have shown little creativity in establishing their ticket prices. Kingston Frontenacs tickets were priced at $18 for adults, $16 for students and seniors, and $12 for children aged 13 and younger. Season tickets provided attendance at all home games, and should the team get into the playoffs, season-ticket holders would be guaranteed seats if they wished to purchase them. Season tickets were $510 for adults, $480 for seniors and students, and $440 for children.

For the 2010–11 season, the team was planning to add "flex packs" of 6 or 12 tickets. These were priced at $192 for a 12-ticket pack and $96 for a 6-ticket pack. With a 12-ticket flex pack, for example, one person could attend 12 games, four people could attend three games, or 12 people could attend one game.

As Jeff began to ponder the notes he'd taken at the pricing strategy meetings, he saw a number of suggestions that stemmed from recent strategies employed by major professional sports teams. Someone had talked about the Toronto Blue Jays, a team that in a recent year had increased its average season ticket prices by 10%, but its average single-game prices by only 1%. At the same time some prices increased, some remained the same, and some decreased, depending on their location in the stadium. During that season the franchise had also explored a varied pricing strategy for particular games. A small number of early-season Tuesday games were designated as "value" games, with ticket prices discounted considerably. About 30 games were designated "premium" games, including seven games against the Boston Red Sox and nine games against the New York Yankees, the two toughest teams in the Jays' division. Someone else had talked about the Toronto Raptors, a team that was much more dependent on single-game ticket sales. The Raptors were charging higher prices for visiting teams that attracted larger crowds. Finally, the New York Yankees baseball team charged higher prices for premium-seat tickets purchased on game day, but lower prices for fans who purchased advance tickets.

When he flipped to the next page of his notes, Jeff saw a number of comments about the strategies NHL teams used. Almost every team in the NHL, it was noted, used some form of variable pricing; they'd been experimenting with it for several years. The Vancouver Canucks, Edmonton Oilers, Calgary Flames, Ottawa Senators, and Montreal Canadiens all charged ticket prices that varied depending on seat location, visiting team, day of the week, and time of season. Only the Toronto Maple Leafs had elected not to use variable pricing for its single-game tickets. It didn't have to. Season tickets accounted for more than 90% of ticket sales, and only about 1000 seats were available for each game for single-game ticket holders. There were seldom any nights with an empty seat—even at the highest ticket prices in the NHL.

But among NHL teams, perhaps the Ottawa Senators were the most creative. Early in its pricing experiments the team had designated a number of games for which it offered discounts as high as 40%, and a small number of additional games for which only children received a 40% discount. At the same time, it charged a 10% premium when the Montreal Canadiens were the visiting team, and a 40% premium when the Toronto Maple Leafs came to Ottawa. The rivalry was such that the Montreal and Toronto teams always drew a large crowd. After trying this strategy, Ottawa became even bolder. In the 2008–09 season it tried "bundling" games. The Senators advertised a special promotion to see the Toronto Maple Leafs ($236.05), or the Montreal Canadiens ($208.05), or the Pittsburgh Penguins, with scoring star Sydney Crosby ($188.05). However, customers who read the fine print found that they could buy one of these tickets only if they also purchased a ticket to see the Buffalo Sabres or the Florida Panthers for an additional $142.05. And the total price didn't include food, drinks, or parking, so a night—or two—could be very costly. Fans weren't pleased, but the team defended its strategy: it would sell out more games and would discourage ticket scalpers, who tended to buy tickets only for high-demand games.

THE DECISION

Jeff had a lot to consider. He wondered whether the team had been too hasty when it implemented the flex-pack price strategy. Could he design a better strategy while maintaining the flex packs, or should he consider revising or dropping the flex packs for future years? Should he recommend some form of flexible pricing, and if so, what should it be? How could he attract more children, women, and students—and could a new price strategy help him do this, or would he need to consider other promotional events to grow these important fan segments? While he was thinking about all this, Jeff was very aware that his goals had to take into account both the short and the long term. He wanted to improve attendance for the 2010–11 season, but he also wanted to create a solid base for long-term fan support.

SPARK Marketing: Responding to Market Opportunities and an Industry Shakeup

Susan Myrden and
Donna Stapleton

It was the middle of August 2010, and significant changes were occurring in Atlantic Canada's communications industry. SPARK Marketing had been making its mark on the communications sector since its inception just one year before and had succeeded in making a name for itself. In fact, times had never been better for this full-service marketing and advertising agency. However, with the industry in flux, companies had to be in tune with ongoing changes in the communications landscape. The past 10 years had seen the introduction of many small marketing and communications companies in the Atlantic Canadian market; plus, the communications industry had experienced a technological revolution. Another change was the recent announcement that a major player, Bristol Group, was shutting down operations.

According to Andrew Best, co-founder of SPARK and responsible for its strategic planning and business development, "The barriers to entry in this business are low. Competitors come and go. I'm certain that many of our competitors thought we didn't stand a chance to survive as a newcomer when we entered this market just over a year ago, but we've had a great year and our goal is to grow our revenue by 10% in our second year." Andrew had identified several opportunities to grow the business. He wondered if he should expand SPARK's online capabilities, focus on market segments that didn't tradition-ally use agencies, or win clients from his closest competitors. Given the competitive nature of the industry, timing was important; therefore, he'd need to make a final decision on the approach SPARK would take by the middle of September.

THE COMMUNICATIONS INDUSTRY

The communications industry, rife as it was with hyper-competition and non-stop innova-tion, was experiencing turbulent times. Large traditional agencies were struggling to re-define themselves, shift their culture, add new services, and restructure. For these firms times had been particularly challenging, as their ways of doing things were ingrained and their traditional business models made it difficult for them to change fast enough. The revolution in the industry had been fuelled by a shift from analogue to digital media and the concomitant decline in traditional media audiences. Some agencies and companies failed to understand that simply shifting traditional content online was not an effective strategy.

The movement into the digital age had changed the face of the industry. According to the Society for Digital Agencies, in the past, industry leaders were known for their strengths in content development, packaging, and distribution. However, the new era was characterized by unprecedented levels of consumer choice, ubiquity, and interactivity. As a result, it was predicted that future industry growth would require agencies that had substantially different competencies. Technology was driving this movement, with businesses having access to significantly more data about, and insight into, consumer interest and behaviours than ever before. Search traffic, social networking and blogs, along with other elements of daily inter-net activity, provided a continuous, real-time window into what audiences deemed impor-tant. Agencies therefore needed to acquire and build new skills, develop deeper audience insights, and build closer relationships with clients and players within the value chain.

The industry saw a number of trends affecting agencies within the market. One high-growth area was the global emergence of mobile phones; the rapid adoption of smartphone devices and the growth of applications had changed the way audiences were reached. This trend was even more prominent for younger generations. In fact, four out of five teens now carried a wireless device, up from 40% in 2004.

The mobile content and advertising market was large and growing. Combined, it was estimated to be close to $1 billion, nearly 10 times the size of the desktop internet market. Mobile internet usage had grown faster than desktop internet adoption, with 40% of iPod/iTouch users accessing the internet more on their mobile devices than on their desktops. For lower-income segments, marketers were seeing many people abandoning computers and obtaining smartphones in order to stay connected at a lower cost. This dominating trend had further forced marketing agencies to provide increased innovation and high-quality content. Marketers had to build digital relationships with consumers, deliver winning experiences, and grab a position of greater influence within this rapidly evolving industry.

Another trend driving results in this highly competitive market was the increasing prevalence of social media outlets. Given consumers' propensity to share information, links, and networks, these outlets had become major distribution hubs for content. For marketing agencies, social media outlets represented potential opportunities to increase traffic to clients' digital sites; consequently, many marketers placed extra emphasis on "social media optimization" to increase audience size. The challenge associated with this was the difficulty in targeting specific user groups whose social networks were the most powerful, influential, and effective. The direct result was a demand for increased cooperation between marketing and information technology—and if technology wasn't core to a marketing agency's operations, it wouldn't be able to compete.

Despite the opportunities that existed for agencies, there was also downward pressure on industry growth. The worldwide recession saw many clients shift to smaller budgets and more digital, targeted approaches. Company spending was shifting in order to maximize success. Marketing was identified as the primary driver of this success; although advertising was still a critical part of the marketing mix, it played a less significant role than it once did. Companies weren't expected to invest large amounts of money in the 30-second spot or flashy billboards; instead, spending would comprise a number of different facets from many different parts of the marketing mix, the majority of them being digital.

Coupled with the transition in spending, clients, who once used traditional agencies, were looking for more flexible and creative companies. Therefore, the larger agencies were experiencing layoffs or massive exits of talented employees who, like clients, were looking for something new and different. In fact, the entire industry was experiencing a shakeup.

Additional industry challenges included increasing pressure to lower prices and rising customer expectations that went beyond service levels and most agencies' capabilities. Consequently, keen players in the communications industry had to start searching for the right combinations of responses among unprecedented uncertainties about existing business models and prospects for future growth.

COMPANY BACKGROUND

SPARK launched itself as a full-service advertising agency on May 1, 2009 (see Exhibit 1 for the company's launch ad), equally owned by Andrew Best and Christa Steeves. Although the company began in St. John's, within a few months it had expanded into other Atlantic provinces. Most of its business initially came from the Newfoundland market: the province had escaped the difficult economic times that had been felt globally, and in fact, the Newfoundland economy was surprisingly strong and growing. But Andrew saw opportunities to service clients in other provinces. "While we began in St. John's," he explained, "we never intended to focus on the provincial market. Bigger is better, and we knew there were opportunities in Atlantic Canada." Servicing the Atlantic Canadian market was facilitated by opening a second office in Halifax.

SPARK's philosophy was to marry strategy with creativity and technology. As a full-service agency, it offered a variety of strategic and creative services, including strategic marketing planning, corporate identity and brand development, internet marketing strategy development, and marketing research. To carry out its clients' strategic initiatives, it combined online and offline tools to create consistent communication and conversation across mediums. The offline tools used included, but weren't limited to, such traditional mediums as television, radio, print, and outdoor advertising, as well as approaches that have gained in popularity, such as ambient and guerrilla marketing. The online mix of offerings included web design and development, website analytics, social network marketing, search engine optimization, email marketing, online advertising and buying, viral marketing, and mobile marketing. Despite the range of offerings SPARK provided, it remained committed to staying on top of emerging trends and technologies in order to evolve with the market. As

EXHIBIT 1	SPARK's Launch Advertisement

Andrew explained, "The tools we use will continue to change, so we look beyond what's working today. But the approach to strategy and the need for creative, cost-effective, audience-focused marketing that drives the client's business forward will remain the same."

SPARK's business model differed from that of its competitors in the St. John's market. Many of these other agencies differentiated themselves within their offline capabilities; very few focused on emerging trends in the online platform. SPARK planned to fill this gap. Given how the industry was changing through technological developments, coupled with recessionary times, SPARK positioned itself as a cutting-edge agency with an extensive offering of online capabilities at a competitive price. Andrew felt that this was what clients were looking for in the Newfoundland market. SPARK achieved this positioning strategy by setting a low fixed overhead and establishing a senior, seasoned in-house team with strong industry knowledge and great industry contacts that gave it access to research, production, and media services external to the company. This allowed SPARK to be creative, technologically savvy, and cost-effective, providing high-priced quality service at a mid-range price.

SPARK tried to foster a corporate culture that kept employees motivated and costs low. "We have a young team with no one close to retirement," Andrew noted. "We have fun and take a youthful approach to work. We're a small company and everyone has a role to play in how we build the business. We're collaborative, focused, and we work to deadlines. We don't have financial perks to motivate our team. The incentive for employees to work hard is pride in their work, the company atmosphere and corporate culture, and being part of a startup business. Our mantra for employees is 'Grow with us and you'll share in our success.'"

SPARK gained recognition almost immediately upon its launch. In fact, just four months after the company started, *Marketing* magazine ran a story on the creation and launch of the new agency. This, of course, helped establish SPARK's credibility in the Atlantic market.

The Team

Having the right team, one that worked well together and with clients, was key to SPARK's success. The leadership team was composed of Andrew and Christa, who brought a combined 18 years of industry experience, and two key players in the creative department (see Exhibit 2 for an organizational chart). In total, 12 people worked at SPARK.

Andrew, as CEO, had a business mind. His experience was diverse, with a base in many industries, including banking, communications, and online marketing. He played multiple roles within the company, including managing the online and interactive marketing initiatives, staying on top of industry and technological changes, and running the day-to-day operations. However, with his history of growing sales for startup and established businesses, his primary role at SPARK was developing the business and propelling the company's strategic direction. Under his leadership and management, SPARK was able to drive sales and profitability for clients.

Christa, director of client services and planning, had a knack for creativity. Her primary role in the agency was spearheading innovation and creative thinking for clients. She was a skilled and experienced marketing professional, with competencies in strategic marketing planning and account management. She characterized herself as a big thinker and she believed in digging deep for consumer insights. She attributed this to her success during more than a decade as a marketing professional with some of Atlantic Canada's best agencies.

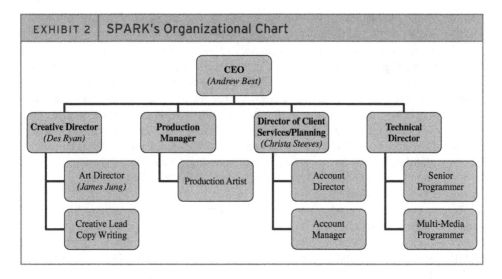

EXHIBIT 2 | SPARK's Organizational Chart

Des Ryan was the creative director. He'd worked throughout Atlantic Canada, and had spent 15 years with Bristol Group, a strong competitor of SPARK's until its recent closing. Andrew and Christa felt blessed to have acquired someone with Des's experience and talent—not to mention his knowledge of Bristol's clients and staff—when he joined the company in November 2009. According to Andrew, "When Des joined our team, Bristol took note. They had already lost client work to us and now they'd lost a key employee."

James Jung was the veteran art director. He played the role of illustrator and designer at SPARK, bringing with him over 20 years of advertising industry experience. He'd worked at award-winning agencies in both Toronto and St. John's, combining solid business and strategic thinking with unparalleled insight and creativity. As Christa explained, "He just plain gets it. His work has made the cash registers ring, changed attitudes, and stirred the soul." James had won a number of awards from across the globe, including Cannes, Advertising and Design Club of Canada, and *Marketing,* among others.

COMPETITION

SPARK was operating in a market with many agency players. To date, 80% of its business was in Newfoundland, with 20% generated from Nova Scotia. Therefore, SPARK needed to monitor its competition in both of these regions.

In Newfoundland, SPARK directly competed with some of the major players in the St. John's market, notably Idea Factory and m5, which were included in the main consideration set for a client looking for a full-service agency. Although Target Marketing and Communications was another full-service agency in the St. John's market, it didn't focus on local clients and so wasn't in direct competition with SPARK, but was certainly an agency that Andrew needed to monitor closely.

Idea Factory, a relatively new player in the communications industry, was closest to SPARK in terms of its positioning and size, and Andrew considered this company SPARK's closest competitor. In business for about a decade and focusing on the Newfoundland and Labrador market, it offered services in marketing and interactive communications, public relations, and marketing research. With fewer than 20 employees, Idea Factory was known for its strong ideas and interactive strategy.

m5, another of SPARK's close competitors, had been in business for 30 years, employing more than 200 people across Atlantic Canada and in its one U.S. office in New Hampshire. This fully integrated agency provided market research, public relations, creative development, web building, printing, audio/video production, and online, direct, and small business marketing. It operated different profit centres within its business, including m5interactive, m5public relations, and other core services. With some of its clients having been loyal for more than 20 years, m5 had some of the highest retention rates among major agencies in Atlantic Canada. In the past it had been known as a retail shop, servicing a large number of retail clients; however, it had expanded its client base to include companies from a variety of industries.

Target, known for its creativity, had been in business for more than 30 years. It employed approximately 50 people, operating from one office in downtown St. John's. *Strategy* magazine had rated Target among the top 10 creative agencies in Canada for the past decade. The agency had won numerous client awards, including Gold at Cannes and the London Internationals. In addition, Target was the only agency east of Quebec to win Gold at the CASSIES (Canadian Advertising Success Stories), which rewards creative based on proven business effectiveness. Target focused on larger national clients, bidding on more expensive work than some of the local agencies.

When the Bristol Group, a major player in the Atlantic Canada market, entered voluntary receivership in July 2010 it created a major opportunity for those agencies left in the market. Bristol had been a leading marketing communications company for more than 30 years, with offices in St. John's, Halifax, Moncton, and Doha, Qatar. Its services included advertising, public relations, marketing research, event management, online marketing, and consulting. Bristol was an experienced agency that serviced large, traditional clients. In an agreement made before its exit, nearly 80 of Bristol's employees, including senior executives, were offered jobs by m5 in a number of its offices. With the move, m5 also acquired many of Bristol's clients, making the company the market leader in volume and number of employees in Atlantic Canada.

On a secondary level, SPARK competed with Applecore, DRAY Media, Colour, and Pilot; these agencies had all carved out specific niches in the St. John's market, but none had the full offering of the main competitive group. Finally, from a tertiary perspective, a number of small shops, production houses, and independent freelancers, such as Waterwerks, Upstream, and Total, were competing for clients' marketing dollars in this market.

In the Halifax market, SPARK was competing with the same agencies as in the St. John's market. Direct competitors also included the Extreme Group, Cossette, Revolve, and Trampoline. Secondary competitors included Chester + Company, Rapport, and Urban Orange; and the over 50 tertiary competitors consisted of small boutique shops that specialized in specific areas or were seen as design shops. Like St. John's, Halifax also had a number of independent freelancers.

SELECTING A STRATEGY

To make the best use of the company's limited resources, Andrew knew SPARK needed a growth strategy that would help it move forward in light of both the changes in the industry and the collapse of Bristol Group. Because Andrew was pleased with the company's performance in the first year, he seriously considered maintaining the status quo. Since its inception, SPARK had been growing at a slow but steady pace, staying under the radar of most competitors. He wondered if that approach was preferred in order to minimize competitive retaliation, or if he should take a more aggressive approach to growth. If the latter, Andrew felt that there were three reasonable alternatives:

1. *Expand online capabilities.* Although SPARK had extensive online capabilities, the industry was moving toward social media as well as mobile and location-based marketing. To help serve existing clients and attract new ones, this option would involve hiring someone who had a strong background in these areas.

2. *Focus on a different segment.* Many small businesses in the local market had the in-house capabilities to conduct ad hoc marketing activities. However, this option would involve targeting those clients that didn't normally use agency firms and didn't understand the benefits an agency could offer.

3. *Target competitors' clients.* With the exit of Bristol Group from the market, many of its clients were in transition. This option would involve SPARK's aggressively targeting clients that had moved to m5 but had yet to develop loyalties to the company.

Andrew pondered the decision. He explained:

If we're going to increase our sales in the Newfoundland and Nova Scotia markets, we'll have to steal business from the competition. I don't consider Target to be a competitor from which we can take business, as it does a different type of work, much bigger in size and scope. It has bigger clients and strong client relationships. We'll have to look to other competitors to take work, especially those that don't give full attention to both online and offline. There are many small players where we should be able to steal business. Plus, m5 is a major competitor and has picked up many of Bristol's clients. The interesting thing about m5 is that it has a silo mentality, with each of its operations separated: m5I, m5PR, and Research. This may help us to attract some of its clients. It's my gut instinct that the Newfoundland market is worth about $25 million in agency work, and the Nova Scotia market is about three times that size. With so many large and small competitors in Atlantic Canada, how can we differentiate our business from the competition and gain a reasonable share of this business? There are a number of strategic directions we can take, but with limited human and financial resources, we need to prioritize our options to establish a clear, strategic approach to growth. Plus, we need to attract clients from competitors without stirring up competitive retaliation.

Andrew knew this decision was important. He decided to weigh out the pros and cons of each alternative so that he'd be prepared to operationalize the plan in the next few weeks.

The Road to the Beaches

*Megan Denty and
Donna Stapleton*

It was July 3, 2010, and Leon Phillips was going through the old promotional pamphlets and small-business stats that littered his desk. He'd just moved into his new office and his new position as marketing coordinator for the Road to the Beaches Tourism Association. His four-month contract, supported by a government grant, was the association's only paid position. Leon hadn't studied marketing in school, so he knew the position would be difficult. But he hadn't wanted to move away from home for work, and, considering himself a quick learner, he'd been willing to take on the challenge.

The Road to the Beaches Tourism Association was a not-for-profit social enterprise that represented the interests of many small businesses in part of Newfoundland and Labrador. The association had very little money. Leon thought about what the chair of the association, Gina Byrne, had said the previous day while she was showing him around: "We represent many small businesses that compete in an industry worth nearly $800 million. We have $1000 in the bank. We certainly don't want to waste money developing flyers and sending them to people who won't read them. We have to find a way to make creative use of our limited resources. How much do you know about the region, by the way?"

Leon could remember his confident reply: "I just finished an accounting diploma at college. I'm brand new to the marketing field and to the organization. Luckily I'm *not* brand new to the region. It's my home, and I know the region has a lot to offer visitors. My whole life I've seen families flocking to the area when the school year ends in June. I enjoy spending time outdoors as well . . . not so much in the hot summer months, more so in the fall. But I guess different people have different preferences."

"Right," Gina had said. "Not everyone likes the same travel experience. But we do have a location here that's worth visiting, and it's our job to communicate that message on behalf of these tourism operators."

Leon now eyed the collection of relevant flyers on his desk. Among them were provincial collaboration projects, several of which contained a section on the Road to the Beaches region. The association focused much of its time on a pamphlet that it published itself: a small, two-colour annual flyer that featured business ads on its out-side and a small map on the inside. (See Exhibit 1.) Also on Leon's desk was a large box of full-colour "lure cards" the association had printed. These cards, which fea-tured Terra Nova National Park, represented the entire region and had no ads. (See Exhibit 2.) In addition, the association had placed an attractive ad titled "Road to the

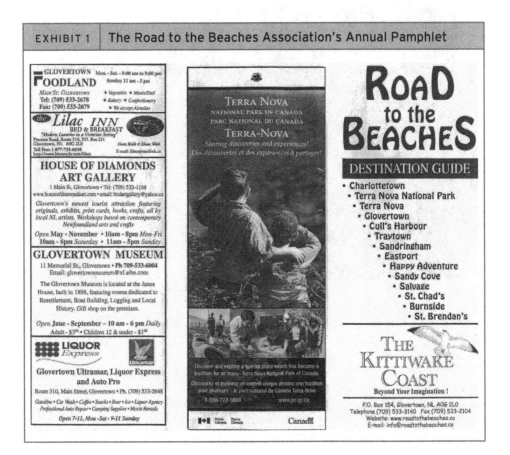

| EXHIBIT 1 | The Road to the Beaches Association's Annual Pamphlet |

EXHIBIT 2	The Road to the Beaches' Lure Card

WELCOME TO THE ROAD TO THE BEACHES

Nestled amongst the many islands and inlets of Bonavista Bay, the Road to the Beaches is the ideal place to enrich your Newfoundland vacation experience. Discover some of Newfoundland's oldest communities, experience nature on one of our many fabulous trails, or enjoy a relaxing day on our beautiful beaches.

HOW TO GET THERE
The Road to the Beaches is located in Central Newfoundland, along the border of Terra Nova National Park.

PARKS & BEACHES
• Eastport Beach
• Sandy Cove Beach
• Wild Cove Park (Salvage)
• Crooked Tree Park (Sandy Cove)

HERITAGE SITES
• Glovertown Museum
• Burnside Archaeology Museum
• Salvage Fishermen Museum
• The Beaches Heritage Centre (Theatre & Art Gallery, Eastport)

ATTRACTIONS
• Splash-n-Putt Resort (Traytown)
• Family Funland (Eastport)
• Terra Nova Golf Resort (Port Blandford)

HIKING & LOOK-OUTS
• Ken Diamond Memorial Park (Glovertown)
• Eastport Beaches Trail
• Sandy Cove Look-Out & Hiking Trail
• Caplin Gulch Walkway (Sandy Cove)
• The Old Trails (Sandy Cove or Salvage)
• Long Chute Trail & Look-Out (Burnside)
• Bloody Bay Cove Aboriginal Quarry (Burnside)

FOR MORE INFORMATION
For more information on events, community attractions and things to do in the area, visit www.roadtothebeaches.ca

Beaches: Experiences . . . Beyond Your Imagination" in the Adventure Central Travel Guide that promoted central Newfoundland to tourists. (The travel guide is available at www.centralnewfoundland.com.)

After he looked over the material, Leon leaned back in his chair. "There are so many small businesses in the area," he thought to himself, "and many of them are competitors. The Road to the Beaches Association represents all of them at once, so how would a business get a competitive advantage? Maybe businesses should do their own marketing individually instead of working with the association." He really wasn't sure what would be best.

Leon had a lot to consider. Association members were pressuring him to get a pamphlet printed immediately, and he also needed to decide on the association's marketing plans for the summer. Since it was the beginning of July, the peak season was already in full gear. How should his time and the association's monetary resources be allocated to meet everyone's needs?

THE REGION AND THE ASSOCIATION

Location

The Road to the Beaches region is a small section of the province of Newfoundland and Labrador. The province, composed of both an island (with 94% of the province's population) and a portion of mainland Canada, is divided for tourism purposes into five regions: Tales of Avalon, Way Out East, Adventure Central, West by Nature, and Labrador Skies. The Adventure Central region is further divided into four sub-regions, one of which, The Kittiwake Coast, is divided still further into a number of smaller regions—one of which is known as the Road to the Beaches region. It's bound by Terra Nova National Park to the south and Square Pond Family and Friends RV Park, just past Gambo, to the northwest. (Maps can be viewed in the travel guide at www.centralnewfoundland.com.)

The island of Newfoundland can be accessed by a ferry that arrives at Port aux Basque on the western end of the province (a seven-hour drive from the Road to the Beaches region) or by a ferry that arrives at Argentia near the eastern end of the province (a two and a half–hour drive from the region). Alternatively, visitors can arrive by plane at one of several provincial airports. The Adventure Central Travel Guide promotes three arrival points for visitors to the central region: St. John's International Airport (a three-hour drive from the region), Deer Lake Regional Airport (a five-hour drive), and Gander International Airport (a 30-minute drive). Bus tours and, occasionally, cruise ships stop at the Visitor Centre in Terra Nova National Park. These visitors rarely leave the park because of the long walking distance to the nearby communities. A marina was currently being constructed in Glovertown that would allow large ships to directly visit the region.

Communities

The region contains 13 communities. The largest is Glovertown, with a population of about 2100. Other communities include Eastport, Traytown, Happy Adventure, Sandringham, Salvage, Charlottetown, Burnside, Sandy Cove, St. Chad's, the town of Terra Nova, and the island of St. Brendan's. All the communities in the region are represented by the Road to the Beaches Tourism Association.

The Association

The Road to the Beaches Tourism Association was formed in October 1997 with the help of funds from a provincial initiative developed to strengthen the rural Newfoundland and Labrador economy. The association is a not-for-profit organization that operates year-round. Its mandate and primary goals are "to raise the profile of the region," "to increase its tourism potential," and "to strengthen the economy of its residents."

At the beginning of each year the association's members elect individuals to accept voluntary positions on the association's board. In July 2010 the association had 48 members (including board members), who represented a variety of small businesses and municipalities. At that time, the association's only paid position was that of marketing coordinator. This four-month position was funded by a provincial project called a Job Creation Partnership (JCP). JCP's funding required that the person filling the position be labelled "unemployed," as defined by the government of Newfoundland and Labrador, and be in a position to gain valuable work experience from the job. Because of this restriction, and because of the area's limited labour market, recruitment for the position was often challenging.

Climate

The peak season for tourism in the Road to the Beaches region is July and August. The summer months have an average temperature of 18 degrees Celsius, and in the shoulder seasons, from May to June and from September to November, temperatures are more in the range of 10 degrees Celsius. The rest of the year, when the land is often covered in snow and the sea is often covered in ice, is considered the off-season.

Geography

A large portion of Road to the Beaches' coastal land is composed of long sandy beaches, uncharacteristic of much of the rest of the province. There are also many wooded areas and cliffs on the land. One community in the region (Salvage) is located in very open water and, as such, is a place where whales and icebergs can be viewed. Many of the other communities have more sheltered bays that allow for swimming and calm-water boating, including sea kayaking and canoeing.

The Bigger Picture

The government of Newfoundland and Labrador does a substantial amount of tourism promotion, not only in Canada but all around the world. It has set ambitious goals for increasing tourism in the province, and in fact has been nationally recognized for a number of its tourism promotion initiatives. The Road to the Beaches region, however, is only a small portion of the province and hence receives only a small portion of provincial visits. The entire Adventure Central region, for example, is visited by only 13% of travellers bound for Newfoundland and Labrador. So, while the provincial government supports the goal of overall tourism growth, the Road to the Beaches region is not specifically promoted.

PROVINCIAL MARKETING AND PROVINCIAL ATTRACTIONS

Newfoundland and Labrador is Canada's youngest and most easterly province. Its economy, which once relied very much on the fishery, has increasingly come to rely on the service industry sectors. Demonstrating its commitment to the tourism industry in particular, in 2010 the provincial government initiated a plan, called Vision 2020, to double annual tourism revenue by that year; it made a $12 million investment in provincial, national, and some international marketing to support this vision. The government estimated that 45% of total tourism revenue was generated by out-of-province and out-of-country visitors, with the remaining 55% generated by residents.

Most provincial tourism ads have focused on history, culture, and nature. Indeed, these were the motivations behind many people's visit to Newfoundland and Labrador. Some of the most cited reasons for coming to the province included whale watching, iceberg viewing, birding (especially puffin viewing), and hiking. The province described visitors to Newfoundland as "sophisticated travellers looking for a natural and exotic experience 'off the beaten path.'" Some very popular attractions include St. John's (the oldest city in North America), Gros Morne National Park (a UNESCO World Heritage site), the community of Twillingate (self-proclaimed iceberg capital of the world), and the Witless Bay Ecological Reserve, where whales, puffins, and icebergs can be viewed from a number of different boat tours.

With a population of about half a million and a population density of about 1.4 people per square kilometre, Newfoundland and Labrador caters to those tourists who come to escape city life and experience nature. Many of these visitors, however, expect a variety of amenities at the locations they visit, such as wireless internet access and entertainment facilities. The provincial government seems to recognize this desired mix of old and new, given the traditional focus of its ads combined with its initiatives to integrate technology into trip planning. After all, the government has found that fully 80% of travellers conduct their trip planning online.

REGIONAL MARKETING

Over the past few years the Road to the Beaches Association has undertaken a number of different marketing efforts on behalf of its members. One of these efforts was the design of a website (www.roadtothebeaches.ca) that features photographs of the region, descriptions of community history, information on regional attractions, and links to local business websites. The Road to the Beaches did not have a social media presence, although a number of unofficial Facebook groups represent communities of the region.

Another marketing project, done in conjunction with Terra Nova National Park, was the design and printing of a lure card for the region. This full-colour card, made of thick, 4" × 9" paper, was conveniently sized and shaped to fit into most pamphlet holders. A quantity of these cards (as well as a lure card featuring only the park) remained at Terra Nova National Park, available for inquiring visitors. (See Exhibit 2.)

Terra Nova National Park, in conjunction with the Heritage Foundation for Terra Nova National Park, published a 40-page Visitor Guide called *Terra Nova Sounds*. The guide, typically republished each July, was sent to anyone seeking information; the park usually received three to seven information package requests by email and phone each week. The *Sounds* contains a wealth of information on things to see and do in the park, other attractions in the Road to the Beaches region, and ads for businesses in the area. The revenue from these ads went to the Heritage Foundation, a not-for-profit organization that provides many of the park's services.

Information on the Road to the Beaches region also made up fairly lengthy sections in the Adventure Central Travel Guide (also available online) and the Kittiwake Coast Travel Guide. The website featuring the guide (www.adventurecentralnewfoundland.com) was promoted at tourism conferences in Canada and the United States in the spring of 2010. Promotion of the central region focused on iceberg viewing, whale watching, and hiking.

The Adventure Central Guide, The Kittiwake Coast Tourism Association Guide, and the Newfoundland and Labrador Travel Guide all offered free listings for all tourism businesses in their respective regions.

The final aspect of the association's communication (and perhaps the most time-consuming for Leon) was the annual two-colour pamphlet. Its printing was organized by the marketing coordinator at the start of his or her contract each July. The coordinator was responsible for contacting each business in the area to obtain its most up-to-date information and to sell advertising space. The design of the 16.5″ × 11″ pamphlet stayed the same each year. The inside contained a map of the region along with some description; it folded up to about the same convenient size as the lure card. The front cover bore a photograph and a list of the region's communities, and the remaining panels were sold as advertising space. The pamphlet was available at the businesses of the association's members and at nearby provincially operated tourist chalets. (See Exhibit 1.)

REGIONAL ATTRACTIONS

Like the rest of Newfoundland and Labrador, the Road to the Beaches region draws people who have an interest in exploring the outdoors. The region has a number of natural features and appealing communities that make it attractive to those with an interest in nature.

Terra Nova National Park

This park contains 14 hiking trails and some shorter fishing trails. Two of the most popular trails are Sandy Pond, a three-kilometre loop around a swimming pond; and the Coastal Trail, a five-kilometre connection between the Visitor Centre and Newman Sound Campground. The park also contains eight day-use areas featuring open fields and picnic tables.

Glovertown

The town of Glovertown boasts Ken Diamond Memorial Park, a four-kilometre trail around a bog adjacent to the Glovertown ball field, Glovertown playground, and Glovertown Gardens (the local arena). Ken Diamond is very popular with locals and is promoted as a main attraction. Also located in the town is the Terra Nova River, which runs right by Glovertown's most popular landmark, the Old Mill, a closed operation that dates back to the 1920s. The river is popular among local salmon fishermen and sea-kayaking enthusiasts from around the province.

Eastport

The town of Eastport is home to the popular Eastport Beach, which is located just off the main road and is sufficiently large to be only rarely crowded. The beach, maintained by the town, has little seaweed and is kept clean; it has change rooms, a volleyball net, and ample parking. A trail leads to the more secluded Northside Beach, which is usually more popular in the evening than during the day.

Traytown

The town of Traytown is walking distance from Malady Head, the smaller of Terra Nova National Park's two campgrounds. A rugged walking trail enters the forest from near the community's outdoor rink. One of the trail's features is "The Rolling Stone," a large boulder that can be easily moved, but not tipped over, in the rock where it lies. Whales can sometimes be seen from Cull's Harbour at the north end of Traytown.

Happy Adventure

Whales can often be seen from this town—a few summers ago, a baby beluga whale swam right into Happy Adventure's wharf.

Salvage

This community is located at the end of the Eastport Peninsula, in much less sheltered waters than the other communities. The land here is also much rockier than the rest of the region; in fact, its buildings and its rocks are often featured in provincial tourism ads. The nine-kilometre Salvage Trails lead to rocky cliffs and great views overlooking the town and the ocean; icebergs and whales can often be seen. And, like others in the region, these trails encompass a lot of berry-picking land. A separate, 24-kilometre system of trails called "The Old Trails" also leaves from Salvage; these wind through the forest to Sandy Cove. Information on both trail systems is available from the Salvage Fishermen's Museum.

Sandy Cove

The town of Sandy Cove boasts the immensely popular Sandy Cove Beach, which is longer and wider than Eastport Beach and farther from the road (and has change rooms, although more limited parking). A one-kilometre trail leads to a lookout at Sandy Cove Beach. Not far from the beach is Crooked Tree Park with its playground, a large swimming area (including a dock), and a picnic area.

Burnside

This is the home of the Long Chute Lookout as well as a small hiking trail; both are centrally located near the Interpretation Centre and focused on the Aboriginal history of the region. Other attractions in this area are accessible only by boat. A hiking trail leads to the top of Bloody Bay Point, and The Beaches area features a model of a teepee.

The Town of Terra Nova

Primarily composed of summer homes, this town is isolated, without any tourism businesses, although it is frequented by locals. There's a nice swimming pond here, as well as two gravel pits that are popular with dirt bike and ATV enthusiasts.

St. Brendan's

This island is just offshore from the Road to the Beaches area; a ferry transports people and cars between St. Brendan's and Burnside several times each day. This inexpensive ferry is sometimes used by tourists who want to experience the region first-hand—the ride is scenic and whales and icebergs can be seen in season.

Other Communities

All these communities are located at least partially on the water and provide easy access to the shore for canoes and sea kayaks. Many of the local waters are popular with kayakers from across the province. Most towns are considered scenic driving routes, and most of the area (especially the trails and parks) provides good venues for bird watching (including puffins, which can sometimes be seen on boating trips).

TOURISM OPERATORS

The Road to the Beaches region encompasses a number of businesses frequented by tourists to the area. Many of these businesses are built around the natural and cultural environment. Whimsicals Café, for example, is in a heritage building that's directly on the water in Glovertown, and the Ocean Breeze Pub is on the scenic rocky coast of the historic town of Salvage. The physical landscape plays a large role in the way businesses are set up and the way visitors spend their time in the Road to the Beaches region.

A complete list of tourism operators in the region can be found in Exhibit 3. The "Canada Select" scores are based on a national system of unbiased professional accommodation ratings. One star indicates that an accommodation is "clean and comfortable and . . . met or exceeded nationally accepted criteria in the areas of facilities, services, amenities and quality of the accommodation." Additional stars indicate additional amenities, while half stars indicate a superior quality of facilities.

Although the only operations listed in Exhibit 3 are tourism-driven, the region contains many other businesses that provide goods and services to visitors: grocery stores, churches, gas stations, post offices, liquor stores, hardware stores, libraries, an organic farm, a dollar store, a florist, a liquidation store, a "good will" centre (a donation-based second-hand clothing store), and an indoor stadium. Some notable absences from infrastructure in the region included a cinema, a retail clothing store, an indoor swimming pool, and a late-night store. Respondents to a 2009 visitor survey commented on these infrastructure gaps as well as the region's confusing directional signage. Many also commented that the region is not well known among tourists and is under-promoted.

Exhibit 4 lists occupancy rates for accommodations in the Kittiwake Coast, which contains the Road to the Beaches region. The average occupancy rate for the peak season was around 63%, and 41% for the shoulder season (these rates reflect the fact that fewer rooms were available in times other than the peak season). Occupancy rates at campgrounds showed a wider range between seasons: Newman Sound Campground at Terra Nova National Park, for example, showed an average electrical-site peak-season occupancy rate of 83% and a shoulder-season rate of 18%. Rates were much lower for unserviced sites, including those at Malady Head Campground. Occupancy rates at

EXHIBIT 3	Tourism Operations in the Road to the Beaches Region		
Operation	Location	Canada Select Rating	Description
	Highway		
Splash 'n' Putt Resort		N/A	**Amusement Park** contains water slide, pools, mini golf, bumper boats, cars, go-carts, playground
Mary Brown's and Moo Moo's Ice Cream		N/A	**Restaurant** (franchise)
Splash 'n' Putt Cabins & Conference Centre		****	**Cabins**
Square Pond Friends and Family RV Park		N/A	**Campground** with electrical sites, fire pits, swimming area, store, playground
	Terra Nova National Park		
Visitor Informational Centre (VIC)		N/A	**Interpretation Centre** contains touch tank, movies, gift shop, displays
Coastal Connections		N/A	Educational **Boat Tour** (from VIC)
Ocean Quest		N/A	**Zodiac Tour, Diving Classes, Kayak Rentals, Bike Rentals** (from VIC)
Starfish Eatery		N/A	**Restaurant** (located in VIC)
Newman Sound Campground		N/A	**Campground** with serviced sites, outdoor theatre, store, kids' activity centre, playground, about 350 campsites, very large, family-oriented, majority stay here, far from communities
Malady Head Campground		N/A	**Campground** with unserviced sites, fire pits, swimming area, playground, about 100 campsites, small, quiet, less busy, secluded, near communities
	Glovertown (population ~ 2100)		
House of Diamonds Art Gallery		N/A	**Art studio and gallery**
Glovertown Museum		N/A	**Museum**
Whimsicals and Cove Rock Café		N/A	**Restaurant and gift shop**
The Old Mill Café		N/A	**Restaurant** (lunch menu)

EXHIBIT 3	Tourism Operations in the Road to the Beaches Region (continued)		

Operation	Location	Canada Select Rating	Description
Steve's Service Centre and Pizzeria		N/A	**Gas bar, restaurant**
My Sister's Place		N/A	**Restaurant and pub**
Alexander Bay Mug Up		N/A	**Snack wagon**
Noah's on the Point		****	**Cabins**
Penney Brook Cottage		***	**Cabins**
Beverly Hillside Suites Bed and Breakfast		****	**B&B**
Cuddle Inn		*** ½	**B&B**
Lilac Inn		****	**B&B**
	Eastport (population ~ 600)		
The Beaches Heritage Centre		N/A	**Theatre and gift shop**
Pinsent Art Studio		N/A	**Art studio**
Rosie's Restaurant		N/A	**Restaurant**
The Little Denier		N/A	**Restaurant**
Vicky's Internet Café		N/A	**Restaurant**
Eastport Chicken Bar		N/A	**Chicken bar**
Salvage Bay Motel		** ½	**Motel**
Seaview Cottages		** ½	**Cabins**
Stay-N-Play Cottages		***	**Cabins**
White Sails Cabins		** ½	**Cabins**
Doctor's Inn Bed & Breakfast		****	**B&B**
Inn by the Sea Bed and Breakfast		****	**B&B**
Shriners RV Park		N/A	**Campground** with electrical sites
	Traytown (population ~ 375)		
Traytown Fisheries		N/A	**Lobster shop**
Bluewater Cabins		** ½	**Cabins and gift shop**
Pinetree Lodge and Cabins		****	**Cabins**
Traytown Cabins		***	**Cabins**

EXHIBIT 3	Tourism Operations in the Road to the Beaches Region (continued)		

Operation	Location	Canada Select Rating	Description
	Happy Adventure (population ~ 325)		
Boson's Whistle		N/A	**Craft shop**
Aunt May's Bed & Breakfast		***½	**B&B**
Inn at Happy Adventure		****½	**B&B and restaurant**
	Sandringham (population ~ 300)		
First Choice Inn Bed and Breakfast		****	**B&B**
	Salvage (population ~ 250)		
Salvage Fisherman's Museum		N/A	**Museum**
Ocean Breeze Pub		N/A	**Pub and restaurant**
Killick Restaurant		N/A	**Restaurant**
	Charlottetown		
Clode Sound Motel & Restaurant		**½	**Motel and restaurant**
Your Place in Terra Nova National Park		***	**Cabin**
	Burnside		
Burnside Interpretation Centre		N/A	**Interpretation Centre, boat tour**
	Sandy Cove		
Sandy Cove Pony Rides		N/A	**Pony rides**
Terra Nova Photo		N/A	**Photo shop**
Sandy Cove Beach Housekeeping Cabins		**½	**Cabins**

Square Pond Family and Friends RV Park and Shriners RV Park were around 97% during the peak season. Accommodation operators knew that it could be difficult for tourists to find any room at all in the region during a busy summer weekend, especially if a customer was willing to stay only at a particular type of location. Indeed, different types of accommodations offered vastly different experiences. A small bed and breakfast, for example, may appeal to one visitor for the same reason that it may deter another.

EXHIBIT 4	Occupancy Rates for the Kittiwake Coast					
Season	Month	Rooms Available		Rooms Sold		Occupancy Rate	
		2008	2009	2008	2009	2008	2009
Off season	January	20 445	20 695	4 826	5 307	23.60%	25.64%
	February	19 507	19 407	6 317	5 969	32.38%	30.76%
	March	21 836	22 072	8 856	8 283	40.56%	37.53%
	April	20 770	21 885	8 254	7 643	39.74%	34.92%
Shoulder season	May	24 567	25 817	8 915	9 534	36.29%	36.93%
	June	27 803	28 160	11 461	12 245	41.22%	43.48%
Peak season	July	30 391	30 746	18 197	19 178	59.88%	62.38%
	August	30 506	30 622	21 210	19 595	69.53%	63.99%
Shoulder season	September	27 368	27 771	12 787	13 959	46.72%	50.26%
	October	23 337	23 948	9 395	9 648	40.26%	40.29%
	November	20 678	20 917	7 293	6 798	35.27%	32.50%
Off season	December	20 336	20 634	4 044	3 998	19.89%	19.38%
Overall		**287 544**	**292 674**	**121 555**	**122 157**	**42.27%**	**41.74%**

Source: Department of Tourism, Culture and Recreation, Government of Newfoundland and Labrador.

MARKET SEGMENTS

A 2008 random survey of park visitors indicated that 77% of the visitors to Terra Nova National Park were from Newfoundland and Labrador; 14% were from other parts of Canada (Maritimes: 2%, Quebec: 3%, Ontario: 7%, and the western provinces: 2%); 4% were from the United States; and the remaining 4% were from other parts of the world. This survey was distributed during the peak season: 55% of respondents indicated that they were travelling with children; and 82% said that they travelled outside of the park. This group was considered as reasonably representing visitors to the Road to the Beaches region.

According to a 2010 survey of regular in-province visitors, the primary reason for visiting Terra Nova National Park was "to spend time with family" (24%), "to experience nature" (19%), "to hike" (15%), "to relax" (14%), "it's a tradition" (7%), "to see the local sights" (7%), "to seek excitement" (3%), "to go boating" (1%), and "other" (10%). This survey question was specific to Terra Nova National Park and didn't necessarily apply to the entire region.

Most local tourism businesses lacked a defined target market and didn't really know which motivations applied specifically to visitors to the Road to the Beaches region. However, the association had come across a tool that the board thought might be useful for these businesses.

The Canadian Tourism Commission (CTC) has an Explorer Quotient (EQ) quiz on its website; it's available for free and takes only about 10 minutes to complete. The quiz asks questions about travel preferences and ideals, then profiles each responder as one of nine "Explorer Types." These types, based on motivation for travel, are meant to describe the market segments for Canadian tourism offerings, and thus serve as a reference to help small tourism businesses segment their markets. Exhibit 5 lists these

EXHIBIT 5	Profile of Canadian Travellers

- *Gentle Explorer* travellers comprise about 17% of Canadians. Seeking comfort and avoiding the unknown, these travellers like organized travel packages and guided tours that offer luxury, exclusivity, and pampering. They enjoy the security of familiar surroundings and often return to past destinations. Desiring structured, well-organized travel that's fun and not a lot of work, they often leave the decision making to others to get all the details right.

- *Cultural Explorer* travellers comprise approximately 13% of Canadians. Preferring to travel with like-minded people, these travellers are not content to just visit historic sites and watch from the sidelines; they want to learn everything they can about the history and culture of a place. When visiting a place they converse with locals, attend festivals, and go off the beaten path to discover how people truly live.

- *Authentic Experiencer* travellers make up about 12% of Canadians. These travellers love the understated beauty of natural and cultural environments. Preferring to integrate with local culture and be fully immersed in the travel experience, they avoid group tours and detailed plans. They use travel as a form of personal development and easily figure out how to get the most from every travel situation and experience.

- *Free Spirit* travellers comprise about 11% of Canadians. Motivated to see and experience as much as possible, these travellers seek exciting and exotic travel destinations that provide a thrill and emotional charge. Often travelling with others who feel the same way, these high-energy travellers seek indulgence and the best of everything they can afford as they see as much as possible. These young and young-at-heart travellers just can't stay at home and are always planning their next trip.

- *Personal History Explorer* travellers are about 11% of Canadians. These travellers seek a deeper understanding of their ancestry, heritage, and roots. Engaging in carefully planned travel, often as part of a group tour, these travellers want to visit all the important landmarks and share their experiences, both during and after travel, with close family and friends. These travellers like to travel in style, comfort, and security and seek hotels that are well recognized and offer amenities for self-indulgence.

- *Cultural History Buff* travellers make up 9% of Canadians. These travellers engage in learning and want to understand the history and culture of others and their present context. They travel alone or in small groups and do not want to be driven by rigid schedules or hurried by others. These travellers move at their own pace, often pursuing personal interests and hobbies as they travel to make their experience more meaningful.

- *No-Hassle Travellers* are about 11% of Canadians. Worry-free travel is important to these people as they seek to escape everyday responsibilities and search for relaxation and simplicity. They enjoy nature and like the purity and serenity of open spaces. They like the safety of familiar places and spending time with family and friends. They often engage in group travel where they can socialize with others. Desiring short breaks and getaways, these travellers minimize planning and just go when they want to visit family and friends.

- *Rejuvenator* travellers comprise about 10% of Canadians. These travellers want to "get away from it all." When travelling, they desire rest and renewal and enjoy short trips to familiar places where they can share experiences with family and friends. These travellers want to be pampered and don't want a hectic schedule of things to do. They can enjoy places with some interesting things to see and experience but they don't want it to become work. For these travellers, it's all about relaxing!

- *Virtual Travellers,* at 6% of Canadians, is the smallest group. These travellers take trips infrequently and do not go far. Most trips are centred on family events and are closer to home. These travellers enjoy simple, understated pleasures and want flexibility when they travel. They like to follow their own schedules and don't want the restrictions of planned tours. They are often active in their communities and satisfy their needs for exploration close to home, where they can enjoy familiar surroundings rather than the uncertainties of new places.

Explorer Types (a more complete description is found at www.eqcaen.canada.travel/allExplorerTypes.php).

According to the CTC, the "Free Spirit," the "Cultural Explorer," the "Authentic Experiencer," the "Personal History Explorer," and the "Cultural History Buff'" represent Canada's strongest prospects. These travellers are said to be "high-yield customers with a keen interest in the unique experience that Canada offers."

THE DECISION

The Adventure Central region of the province had low visitation rates in relation to its size. The region was just starting to be marketed nationally, but the Road to the Beaches region wouldn't be the direct focus. And although the Kittiwake Coast would get exposure from the national promotion, even within the coast area there was competition for visitors' tourism dollars. The Twillingate area, for example, had a more developed tourism sector than did the Road to the Beaches area, and already had an established name—The Iceberg Capital of the World—with global appeal. Knowledge of the Road to the Beaches region was relatively low among visitors to Newfoundland and Labrador.

Leon needed to determine what the Road to the Beaches had to offer the world that was unique; in other words, what the association should focus on as the region's primary appeal. Gina had said that not everyone looked for the same travel experience. That gave Leon an idea: he'd need to determine what sort of person looks for this experience. That way he'd know who the association should be focusing its marketing efforts on. As Gina said, they couldn't afford to spend money sending materials to people who'd never come to the place. He'd have to get them to the people who would actually enjoy the region, the only people who'd even care to look at the pamphlet.

The government of Newfoundland and Labrador had an idea of the type of person who would enjoy visiting the province. Leon wondered if the same person would enjoy the Road to the Beaches region, and, if so, how this person could be convinced to visit and spend time there. He wasn't sure if the region had everything in place that it would need to attract more visitors, especially during the slower shoulder season. Leon also wasn't sure what he could do if the region was actually lacking the amenities desired by the target market.

As well, Leon was considering the motivations for visiting Terra Nova National Park. He knew that many park visitors used the facilities in the local region, but he also knew that much of the park was physically secluded from the rest of the region and that a portion of the visitors were regulars who never participated in any of the attractions that the rest of the region had to offer.

Leon had looked at the Canadian Tourism Commission's Explorer Types. He liked the idea of the model, and some of the descriptions seemed to represent people who visited the area. He asked himself, "How might this information help marketing efforts to attract additional visitors to the region? And could it be used to revise the pamphlet I need to put together?" If he were to continue use of the pamphlet, or some other joint promotion effort, he needed to determine how best to design and distribute it to fulfill its purpose.

Leon had a lot of responsibility for the association's marketing efforts, and many tasks that required his attention. The board of directors and the other association members would want to hear about the proposed marketing ideas at next week's meeting.

Wilderness Newfoundland Adventures

Cori-Jane Radford and
H. F. (Herb) MacKenzie

It was a beautiful January morning in St. John's as Stan Cook, Jr. gazed out his office window, contemplating the 1999 promotional strategy for his family's ecotourism business, Wilderness Newfoundland Adventures (WNA). He was scheduled to meet with his father on Friday to discuss it. It was already Tuesday, and time was short; a number of advertising and promotional items should have been in place by now. Stan Cook, Sr. would be expecting a progress report. Stan, Jr. decided to review the 1998 promotional strategy to see which items should be continued and which should be changed or dropped for 1999.

WNA'S PRODUCT

WNA offers single and multi-day tours, including eight-hour kayak day, half-day, and sunset trips. It also offers weekend tours, multi-day single-activity tours, multi-day combination-activity tours, and on-site and off-site equipment rentals. Tours include instruction on sea kayaking, mountain biking, hiking, canoeing, orienteering, outdoor camping, and wilderness survival skills. WNA offers a comprehensive program for beginner, intermediate, and expert paddlers, and adventurers of all ages.

WNA tours are all-inclusive. The adventurer is supplied with food, camping and sporting equipment, and safety gear; participants bring only appropriate clothing and a backpack. WNA covers all sections of non-consumptive adventure tourism and caters to the traveller who is attracted to these activities. WNA also specializes in outdoor excursions that are modified for its clients.

WNA has recently been focusing on "market-ready" products that are thought to have national and international potential. Sea kayaking is one of these products. According to the Canadian Recreation Canoe Association, sea kayaking is the fastest growing paddling activity, with an annual growth rate of 20%. Many areas of Newfoundland are ideal for this activity: the island boasts over 10 000 miles of fascinating coastline dotted with caves, waterfalls, sea stacks, and arches. Icebergs are abundant from May through July, and thousands of humpback and minke whales visit from late June to mid-August.

WNA mainly uses two-person ocean-going kayaks, which are very stable and seaworthy, and use rudders to steer. And since the Cooks run their day trips in calm Cape Broyle, rarely has anyone ever fallen out of a kayak (although it has happened in knee-deep water when participants were pulling the kayak up on the beach). The guide-to-participant ratio is one to six, with a one-guide (single-person) kayak to every three participant kayaks. WNA's guides are all trained in safety, rescue, and first-aid techniques. Sea kayaking in these circumstances isn't difficult, so people of all ages and fitness levels can participate. WNA has even taken an 84-year-old grandmother on one of its day trips!

HEADQUARTERS

WNA decided to locate its operations in Cape Broyle after a three-year search. The area—located one hour south of St. John's on the Avalon Peninsula—has natural beauty (soaring cliffs, caves, waterfalls, varied topography), nature attractions (icebergs, bird sanctuaries, caribou herd), protection from the wind (a seven-kilometre fjord), an abundance of marine life (whales, seals, otters), proximity to a large urban population (St. John's), a historic property (the 85-year-old community general store), and cultural distinction (it's the "Irish Heart of Newfoundland"). WNA believed this to be a world-class area for sea kayaking, mountain biking, and hiking, and an ideal location for its site.

WNA is the first adventure travel and ecotourism operator to engage the province's unique culture and history. For $150 per month it's leased a Cape Broyle heritage building suitable for barbecues and dinners for groups of up to 30 people. WNA's adventure tours and facilities both provide a unique, memorable experience and highlight the cultural and historical identity that most tourists and visitors welcome.

SHORT SEASON

Newfoundland has a relatively short (late June to mid-September) summer, meaning WNA has a short season in which to generate revenue: kayaking in May and early June is beautiful, but it can be cold and uncomfortable; and although late September is a great time to paddle, the tourist trade usually drops off. As well, once children are back in school, local people lose interest in summer activities. To counter this seasonal disinterest, WNA has encouraged biology and physical-education teachers at local high schools to take their students on kayaking field trips. Biology students were invited to take a close-up look at the marine life in Newfoundland's waters, and phys. ed. students were invited to participate simply for the exercise. This promotion was relatively successful, with 4 out of 12 schools participating in 1998. On average, schools have the potential to take at least two classes of students. WNA currently has 12 two-person kayaks, but is considering purchasing four more for the 1999 season.

TRIP BREAKDOWN

WNA's day trips run from May until early October; an equal number of tourists and local adventurers participate in these shorter trips. People can book any day they wish, although a trip is cancelled if fewer than four people book in advance. During the peak whale and iceberg period WNA runs a five-day kayak trip; a seven-day kayak and mountain bike trip; a 14-day kayak, mountain bike, and canoe youth trip; and several "kayak weekends." In 1998, participants in each type of trip numbered 12, 10, 12, and 16, respectively. Extended trips are made up entirely of tourists who come from all over the world, including Japan, Germany, the United Kingdom, the United States, and other parts of Canada. These trips often involve other areas of the province, such as Trinity Bay, Notre Dame Bay, and Terra Nova National Park. The trips begin when participants arrive at the St. John's airport, where they're met and then taken to the appropriate trailhead.

Tourists book reservations for these excursions months in advance, often by calling the WNA toll-free number. The provincial travel guide, WNA's website, *The Great Outdoorsman* TV program, and the Outdoor Adventure Trade Show seem to be international tourists' primary routes to discovering WNA. As well, wholesalers in both Ontario and the United States represent WNA to their markets, marking up WNA's price by 10 to 15% before advertising it to their customers. This requires limited marketing by WNA, and is a relatively stress-free option, although unpredictable. These wholesalers usually market trips to different locations each year.

WNA markets sea-kayaking packages to both potential tourists and visitors who come to the province. This forward strategy provided WNA with an early introduction in the industry, allowing it to become the province's premier adventure travel and ecotourism company.

COMPANY BACKGROUND

In 1970 Stan Cook, Sr. introduced commercial canoeing to Newfoundland by providing all-inclusive canoeing trips averaging 5 to 10 days in length. These trips included instructions on canoeing operations, trout fishing, camping skills, and orientation with maps and compass instruction. The acquisition of life skills indigenous to outdoor experience, cooperation, self-reliance, and appreciation of the great outdoors were Mr. Cook's main priorities. He guided and instructed both children and adults at all skill levels throughout the 1970s and early 1980s.

During the 1980s Mr. Cook received numerous international inquiries about his ability to coordinate and handle groups interested in canoeing and camping in Newfoundland. Moreover, after joining the Marine Adventures Association of Newfoundland and Labrador in the late 1980s and becoming its secretary/treasurer, he noticed the interest that the province was generating for adventure travel. Consequently, he believed it was economically feasible to expand his canoeing school to encompass an international market interested in adventure travel and ecotourism. In addition to offering the usual training in canoeing and portaging skills, he would take advantage of the province's world-class sea-kayaking and mountain biking opportunities that hadn't yet been properly marketed.

In 1995 Mr. Cook changed the company name from Stan Cook Enterprises to Wilderness Newfoundland Adventures, symbolizing the new focus on international business. The expanded product line was promoted to new target markets, and both the business and Mr. Cook's reputation soon enhanced the Newfoundland and Labrador tourism industry.

Besides Mr. Cook, the company involved two other members of his family and a number of seasonal workers. Stan, Jr. was responsible for daily operations. He had an undergraduate business degree, and was available to manage the business during the earlier and later parts of the season when his father was still teaching phys. ed. at one of the St. John's high schools. Much of the success of WNA can be attributed to its first marketing plan, developed and implemented by Stan, Jr.

Mr. Cook's daughter, Cori-Jane Radford, started working with WNA in 1996, when she assumed responsibility for marketing. This allowed Stan, Jr. to get more involved with daily operations, and to address issues that had previously been ignored. Many of the marketing ideas implemented during 1997 and 1998 were Cori-Jane's creation. But in 1998 she decided to get her MBA, and her involvement with the business diminished.

During the summer of 1998, WNA employed five seasonal employees: three full-time guides (40 hours per week), one part-time guide (15 hours per week at $10 per hour), and a junior guide (30 hours per week at $7 per hour). Guides were hired based on their outdoor qualifications, personality, and knowledge of the history and culture of Newfoundland; and before they could lead trips they underwent a one-week training program followed by a weekend expedition with Mr. Cook and Stan, Jr. See Exhibit 2 for a complete description of a guide's duties on a typical day trip and an overnight.

WNA plans to increase its number of seasonal employees, and the length of the 1999 season, in an attempt to boost revenues and to market itself as a destination in the shoulder seasons. However, this strategy directly hinges on its ability to attract larger volumes of out-of-province travellers. In order to expand further into the international adventure market, the company needs a larger workforce, and perhaps a full-time marketing and salesperson.

This person would be expected to take the marketing responsibilities from Stan, Jr. so that he can concentrate on other important matters. He or she would also be responsible for generating individual sales, both locally and internationally. Currently, the two-day sea-kayak trip sells for $250, the five-day trip is $625, the seven-day combo trip (sea kayak and mountain bike) is $875, and the 14-day youth combo is $980.

ADVENTURE TRAVEL AND ECOTOURISM IN NEWFOUNDLAND AND LABRADOR

The tourism industry in Newfoundland and Labrador has evolved to the point where traditional markets are being segmented into such highly specific niche markets as soft and hard adventure, and ecotourism. Ecotourism is particularly beneficial to the province, owing not only to its careful use of the environment but also to the tendency of nature-oriented travellers to spend more money during their vacations than recreational travellers. The province's ecotourism segment is still in its developmental stages, however, with few quality operators.

Adventure travel is defined as a leisure activity that takes place in an unusual, exotic, remote, or wilderness destination, and is associated with high or low levels of participant activity. These travellers expect to experience varying degrees of risk, excitement, or tranquility, and to be personally tested or stretched in some way. Adventure travel is participatory, informative, interesting, and unique, and as well as excitement, it offers a wide range of challenges in an outdoor setting. A trip might be devoted to one activity or a combination of activities. The duration can be from several hours to several weeks.

Whereas "consumptive" tourism (e.g., hunting or fishing) removes resources, non-consumptive tourism engages the natural habitat without exploiting it. Non-consumptive adventure tourism can be subdivided into three areas: hard adventure, soft adventure, and ecotourism. WNA is most concerned with the latter two, but can offer participants hard adventure if they so desire. All three types of adventure tourism involve travel to a particular natural attraction, some level of physical activity, and activities that offer new or unusual experiences. And although they differ in the degree of physical exertion, it's possible to combine the three into a single tour package.

- *Soft adventure travel* focuses on providing a unique outdoors experience, or "adventure." It involves only a minor element of risk, little physical exertion (with less physically demanding activities), and no skill. All ages and fitness levels can participate.

- *Hard adventure travel* combines a unique experience in an outdoor setting with excitement and a degree of risk. It frequently demands physical exertion, a particular skill level, and preparation and training on the part of the participant.

- *Ecotourism* is purposeful travel that cultivates an understanding of the region's culture and natural history while safeguarding the ecosystem's integrity and producing economic benefits that encourage conservation. An ecotour can be either soft adventure or hard adventure, but not both.

The Appeal of Adventure Travel and Ecotourism

Adventure travel and ecotourism form one of the world's fastest growing tourism sectors. It holds appeal for travellers who are no longer happy with traditional vacations and are looking for excitement, risk, unique experiences, education, and fun.

Analysts believe that worldwide demand for adventure and ecotourism vacations will continue to grow well into the next century, with increasing demand each year. Growth in this sector is currently leading the whole Canadian tourism industry—and is in fact outperforming the Canadian economy as a whole.

Newfoundland and Labrador are in a good position to profit from the increased demand for adventure travel and ecotourism. The province offers pristine environments, wildlife, unique flora and fauna, and exotic, challenging experiences. Almost every region of the province is trying to develop a variety of activities or products to draw visitors. However, the adventure travel and ecotourism business is highly seasonal, with few operators open all year. And despite its potential, Newfoundland and Labrador attracts a small fraction of the North American market. Clearly, there are opportunities for growth in this business. This task isn't easy, though: international competition has kept pace with the growth in demand, and consumers can now choose from the wide variety of appealing activities and experiences available in many countries.

WNA believes its success in the international marketplace depends on both the quality of the experience it provides and on how that experience is marketed and managed. The future success of the province's adventure travel and ecotourism will depend on how well operators are provided with tools to address challenges with informed, effective action.

Target Markets for Adventure Tourism

The target market includes travellers interested in visiting a specific place to engage in a new or unusual participative experience. This group has different product needs that change on a seasonal basis. Many market researchers believe that aging baby boomers will be the single most significant group to determine the nature of demand: they are wealthier, not as interested in the hard, "roughing-it" adventure, have less time, and yet still seek new experiences.

Here are a few statistics about adventure travellers:

- In the United States, an estimated 30 to 40 million people are potential candidates for an adventure trip of some kind.

- In the United Kingdom, an estimated 787 000 people are potential adventure tourism clients. Thirty-five percent of British vacationers seek adventure and are looking for an active holiday where they can get in touch with their daring, adventurous side.

- The outdoor sports segments, totalling 1.3 million people, represent potential for adventure travel.

These travellers fit the following three main profiles:

- *Casual adventure travellers* are the entry-level adventurers, experimenting with newer and challenging outdoor activities. They take short trips (one or two days) to get a "taste of adventure." This market affords the greatest growth potential in the short term. And since there is little difference between these travellers and urban-based tourists, their closely related desires offer an opportunity to attract city-touring visitors for short excursions.

- *Committed adventure travellers* form the most affluent segment. They are fitness-conscious, in the middle- to upper-income brackets, 30 to 55 years old, well educated, and live in urban centres. They demand and are willing to pay for quality accommodations.

- *Expert adventure travellers* are those who are on their way to mastering a sports-related skill or knowledge about a topic (e.g., wildlife), and whose motivation for a trip has shifted from general growth and exploration to the fine-tuning of a particular skill. This market tends to be younger, with less disposable income and a greater inclination to "rough it."

COMPETITION

Since Newfoundland and Labrador has very few quality operators, WNA's major competition for all adventure travel and ecotourism customers comes from outside Canada. Worldwide consumer demand for unique experiences and intriguing packages is fuelling international competition; however, current market opportunities support WNA's products. And by monitoring its larger international competitors, WNA has been trying to improve its products further, providing better value. It remains highly competitive with its current pricing strategy, service quality, product uniqueness (i.e., sea kayaking with whales and icebergs), wilderness environmental appeal, and currency exchange rates.

1998 PROMOTIONAL ACTIVITIES

Stan, Jr. and Cori-Jane generated all the ad concepts and material and decided the 1998 media plan (see Exhibit 1). Cori-Jane created the physical displays and then had films produced by the printer—an approach that's inexpensive compared with hiring a marketing firm, although it is a time-consuming one. With Cori-Jane moving away from the business, Stan, Jr.'s involvement has been increasing.

EXHIBIT 1	WNA Media Budget 1998			
Media	Date	Company	Form of Ad	Cost
TV	07/28/98	The Great Outdoorsman	Half-hour television show	$ 7 500.00
Radio	06/30/98	OZ-FM	60 × 30 sec. spots (2 weeks)	$ 1 750.00
	07/31/98	OZ-FM	60 × 30 sec. spots (2 weeks)	$ 1 750.00
	08/31/98	OZ-FM	60 × 30 sec. spots (2 weeks)	$ 1 750.00
Print	12/29/97	St. John's Visitor's Guide	1/4-page ad–full colour	$ 575.00
	01/15/98	NewTel Communications	Yellow Pages–1/8-page ad–1 colour	$ 1 200.00
	04/30/98	NFLD Sportsman	1/6-page ad–full colour	$ 400.00
	05/03/98	NFLD Sportsman	1/6-page ad–full colour	$ 400.00
	06/07/98	NFLD Sportsman	Full-page ad–full colour–accompanying story	$ 1 300.00
	12/29/97	Provincial Travel Guide	1/4-page ad–full colour	$ 1 500.00
	04/30/98	St. John's Board of Trade	Front cover	$ 1 200.00
	03/31/98	Sterling Press Printers	Small brochure–full colour	$ 1 350.00
Sales promo	06/04/98	Gift certificates	25 half-day trips for 2	$ 2 500.00
Signage	05/02/98	Highway signage	Three 3.6 m × 2.4 m	$ 500.00
	04/26/98	WNA van signage	Full-colour, 4 sides	$ 500.00
Trade show	06/01/98	Kinetic Marketing	NFLD Sportsman Show, St. John's–Booth	$ 600.00
	02/14/98	National Event Management	Outdoor Adventure Show, Toronto–Booth	$ 2 000.00
				$ 26 775.00

Print Advertising

Newfoundland Sportsman Magazine

This 70-page, full-colour, glossy magazine comes out every two months. Twenty thousand copies are printed, and with approximately 5000 subscribers, the remaining copies are distributed to retailers and newsstands all across the province. The magazine is published in Newfoundland and marketed to adults interested in the outdoors. Most readers are between the ages of 18 and 55, and include both men and women in approximately equal numbers. Both consumptive and non-consumptive approaches are represented in *Newfoundland Sportsman*. In 1998 WNA placed three ads in the magazine: two were 1/6-page ads, placed for recognition, and the third was a full-page, full-colour ad that appeared facing an article written by the magazine on sea kayaking and in particular on WNA.

The Newfoundland Travel Guide

This 200-page colour brochure is created by the provincial Department of Tourism. Interested potential tourists from all over the world contact the Department to request information. The guide is then delivered free of charge to anyone expressing an interest in visiting the province. A new guide is published each year, listing accommodations, events, attractions, tours, and services.

All businesses relating to the tourist industry receive a free 100-word listing under their appropriate heading. As well, the Department provides pages in the publication for business that wish to purchase ad space. Rates for 1999 were double the 1998 rates.

Brochures

WNA has produced two brochures. Targeted at both the local population and tourists visiting the St. John's area, a small brochure (see Exhibit 2) was created to advertise WNA's sea-kayaking cruises (although WNA was planning to change its 1999 prices to $100 per person for full-day cruises and $65 per person for half-day and sunset trip). These high-quality brochures are placed throughout the city, in tourist chalets, hotels, motels, restaurants, and any stores that will accept them. They are two-sided, full-colour, and printed on cardboard-type paper cut to 9 cm × 20 cm.

WNA's larger brochure (created and printed in 1996) is mailed to people interested in extended trips. In order to keep the brochure up to date, a pocket inside the back cover allows WNA to insert current prices and information. The brochure was expensive to produce, but most adventurers have been impressed by it.

Radio Advertising

OZ-FM (94.7), a St. John's radio station, reaches approximately 182 000 people over 12 years of age each week. Its target market is 18- to 49-year-old adults with active lifestyles and from all socioeconomic classes.

WNA ran three two-week sets of 30-second ads on OZ-FM throughout the summer. In conjunction with the ads, WNA arranged to have six pairs of free gift certificates given away during *Dawn Patrol,* the station's Friday "morning drive" time slot. *Dawn Patrol* has three radio personalities, and WNA invited all three to participate in a free day trip. This

proved to be a great idea, as when they gave away the passes they were able to make first-hand, favourable comments about sea kayaking. In fact, they continued to promote WNA and sea kayaking with personal comments throughout all the radio advertising campaigns.

Television Advertising

In *The Great Outdoorsman* (TGO), a half-hour Sunday night TV program on the Life Network (carried all over North America), the program host, John Summerfield, and his two-man crew travel all over the world seeking different types of adventure. John, who was interested in sea kayaking with whales and icebergs, contacted Stan, Jr. after meeting him at a trade show—and in July 1997 TGO came to St. John's and filmed an episode. The shooting went extremely well, and both John and WNA received considerable praise. In fact, John enjoyed Newfoundland so much that he decided to return to film another episode with WNA (never before had he done two episodes with the same company and the same product). *The Great Outdoorsman* and its crew returned in July 1998 to film the second episode, which aired in October 1998 (and was scheduled for two repeats during 1999).

WNA has received many benefits and much recognition from these shows, although they were very expensive: WNA paid the TGO team's air travel, accommodations, and meals for four days and three nights, for a total of approximately $2500; as well, a $5000 fee was payable to TGO to participate in its show.

Internet

WNA first created its website (www.wildnfld.ca) in the spring of 1997 after it enlisted a small local webpage design firm to help it develop its online personality. The site gets updated about twice a year (before and after the regular season). WNA is currently investigating e-commerce, hoping to take both bookings and payments over the web.

Signage

St. John's is the end of the line when driving east on the Trans-Canada Highway (TCH), as it's the most easterly city in North America. The TCH is the most-used route into the city; many local businesses have erected signs alongside it to advertise to incoming motor tourists.

WNA decided to strategically place three signs: along the TCH with all the other signs; on a much-used arterial within the city; and along the Southern Shore Highway. This highway follows the coast south from St. John's past Cape Broyle, and then loops back along St. Mary's Bay to the city, a route called the Irish Loop. The signs were designed by Stan, Jr. and Cori-Jane, and were painted by an art student at Stan, Sr.'s high school.

Additional signage was placed on a company van. WNA leased a forest-green Ford AeroStar in April 1998 ($500 per month) to pick up and deliver clients, shuttle equipment, and transport guides to and from the various sites. The WNA van, which is used for only 16 weeks during the summer, requires gas about twice a week, at $60 per fill-up. Cori-Jane thought WNA should take advantage of the vehicle's visibility around St. John's, and so incorporated it into the promotion strategy, hiring a local business that specializes in auto advertising to put WNA's logo and other information on all four sides of the vehicle. The final product was quite impressive, and a number of people remarked on having seen the "Green WNA Machine" around town.

Sales Promotions

In 1998 WNA gave away 25 pairs of "Half-Day Sea Kayak Adventures for Two" gift certificates. Some people won them on the radio, while other tickets were given to local celebrities or other prominent people. WNA wanted to get people to try sea kayaking and thought this might be a good approach, although only 11 pairs were redeemed over the summer.

Trade Shows

The Newfoundland Sportsman Show, sponsored by *Newfoundland Sportsman* magazine, is the largest show of its type in the province. This consumer retail trade fair focuses primarily on the outdoor industry. Many types of land, air, and marine activities are represented, and 8000 to 14 000 interested consumers are drawn to it every year.

A new trade show, the Outdoor Adventure Sports Show (OASS), has been held in February in Toronto for the past two years. Attendees can climb a pyramid wall, test-ride mountain bikes on a demo track, and canoe or kayak in an indoor pool. As well, outfitters from all over North America show what their province/company/activity has to offer the willing adventurer.

Attendance at the 1998 OASS totalled 23 320 people, with 62% either making an adventure purchase there or expressing an intention to make such a purchase. This attendance figure marked a 20% increase over the 1997 figure, and numbers are expected to continue to grow for some time. WNA has participated both years; the show provides it with a venue for reaching potential clients who will come to Newfoundland specifically for WNA's longer-duration adventures. The cost for two people to attend OASS, including travel, accommodation, and meal expenses, amounts to about $2000.

Other Methods

Excluding trade shows, the majority of WNA's personal selling has been informal. Mr. Cook and Stan, Jr. attend many local events, sporting rallies, and other activities that attract adventure-minded people. As well, WNA encourages its summer employees to promote sea kayaking on their own time by giving them a $10 bonus for every customer they take on a full-day kayak trip and a $5 bonus for every customer they take on half-day or sunset trips. This encourages the guides to get a group of friends together to go out kayaking. (At the beginning of the summer, each staff member also receives three free day passes for family and friends.)

In its first two years of operation, WNA had a difficult time attracting local customers. Many people were unfamiliar with sea kayaking; perhaps associating it with the dangerous sport of river kayaking, they were nervous about the prospect. But river and sea kayaking are completely different sports, with very differently shaped vessels and different objectives. Now that people have heard of sea kayaking, though, they're beginning to differentiate WNA from other local outfitters by both reputation and value.

St. John's is becoming a popular tourist destination. Moreover, an increasing number of businesses and associations are holding annual conferences in the oldest city in North America (Exhibit 3 presents a list of conferences planned for the summer of 1999 in St. John's).

EXHIBIT 3	Upcoming Conventions and Events, St. John's, 1999	
Date	Convention	Delegates
May 10-13	Canadian Association of Principals	550
June 1-5	Co-operative Housing Federation of Canada	700
June 11-14	Canadian Council for the Advancement of Education	250
June 13-20	Canadian Corps of Commissioners AGM '99	400
June 17-20	Air Cadet League of Canada	150
June 23-27	CAMRT/CSDMU Joint Meeting	500
July 5-9	Canadian Orthopedic Association	700
July 11-16	Offshore Mechanics and Arctic Engineering	400
August 21-26	Canada Employment & Immigration Union	325
September 19-22	Risk & Insurance Management Society	500
September 27-30	Workers' Compensation Commission	100
October 1-3	International Association of Business Communicators	300

Source: Department of Economic Development and Tourism.

Finally, WNA is considering the possibility of hiring a salesperson. So far, little thought has been given to what this person would do, how he or she would be compensated, and exactly what criteria would be important in selecting an appropriate candidate.

Public Relations

WNA has attempted to take advantage of free publicity. Stan, Jr. has invited several local reporters to participate in a free day trip in return for writing articles on WNA. So far, two reporters have participated, and both have written very positive articles on their experiences. The first was a full-page article, accompanied by five full-colour photos, in *The Evening Telegram* (St. John's); the second (also full-page with full-colour photos) appeared in *Mount Pearl Pride*. (Mount Pearl is a smaller city that borders St. John's.) WNA received many phone calls after these articles appeared.

CONCLUSION

Before making any decisions with respect to the 1999 promotional strategy, Stan, Jr. decided to review the summary of responses to the customer satisfaction surveys collected in 1998. Each person who participated in a day, half-day, or sunset trip between May 24 and September 6, 1998, filled one out. The summary of responses is provided in Exhibit 4.

Stan, Jr. has a tremendous amount of planning to do and decisions to make over the next few days. How successful has the 1998 promotional campaign been? What items should be retained for 1999, and what items should be changed or deleted? How should WNA set its promotional budget? Stan, Jr. knew his father will want answers to all these questions at their Friday meeting.

EXHIBIT 4	WNA Customer Satisfaction Survey Results

Age	Total	Sex	Total	Trip	Total
10-19	48	Male	332	Full day	360
20-29	309	Female	388	Half day	180
30-39	239	**Total**	**720**	Sunset	180
40-49	76			**Total**	**720**
50-59	28				
60+	20				
Total	**720**				

How Did You Like Our Staff and Service?

			Guides		
Friendly	Ratings	Total	Knowledgeable	Ratings	Total
Dissatisfied	1	0	Dissatisfied	1	0
	2	0		2	0
	3	0		3	0
Satisfied	4	11	Satisfied	4	15
	5	33		5	28
	6	73		6	55
100% satisfied	7	603	100% satisfied	7	622
Total		**720**	**Total**		**720**

			Physical Product		
Food	Ratings	Total	Equipment	Ratings	Total
Dissatisfied	1	0	Dissatisfied	1	0
	2	0		2	0
	3	4		3	9
Satisfied	4	14	Satisfied	4	12
	5	32		5	33
	6	68		6	70
100% satisfied	7	602	100% satisfied	7	596
Total		**720**	**Total**		**720**

EXHIBIT 4	WNA Customer Satisfaction Survey Results (continued)

How Do You Feel?

Would You Return?	Ratings	No. of People	Recommend Us to Others?	No. of Ratings	People
No	1	0	No	1	0
	2	0		2	0
Maybe	3	38	Maybe	3	30
	4	66		4	69
Definitely	5	616	Definitely	5	621
Total		**720**	**Total**		**720**

Where Did You Hear About Us?	No. of People	What Influenced You to Try Sea Kayaking?	No. of People
Brochure (large)	10	Advertising:	148
Brochure (small)	99	Brochure	45
Gift certificate	11	Travel guide ad	8
Other	7	Sign on road	8
Phone book (Yellow Pages)	32	OZ-FM ad	44
Radio	66	Television show	24
Referral (word of mouth)	175	*Mount Pearl Pride*	19
Repeat customer	53	Alpine Country Lodge recommendation	15
Television:			
The Great Outdoorsman	19	Always wanted to try sea kayaking	33
Travel Agency	5	Dept. of Tourism recommendation	13
Website	23	Familiarization tour	20
Magazine:		Family recommendation	26
Newfoundland Sportsman	35	For the adventure	15
Provincial Travel Guide	68	Free invitation	10
St. John's Visitor's Guide	12	Friend of the Cooks	22

EXHIBIT 4	WNA Customer Satisfaction Survey Results (continued)

Road sign:		Friend recommendation/	
Harbour arterial	31	going with friends	112
Trans-Canada Highway	19	Good reputation	44
Southern Shore Highway	17	Group from work going	55
Trade show:		Guide recommendation	35
Newfoundland Sportsman	33	Hotel recommendation	22
Outdoor Adventure Show	5	New experience	10
Total	**720**	OZ-FM *Dawn Patrol* recommendation	55
		Received gift certificate	16
		Repeat customer	53
		Wedding day activity	10
		Won on the radio	6
		Total	**720**

Overall Satisfaction with Your Excursion

Overall	Ratings	Total
Dissatisfied	1	0
	2	0
	3	0
Satisfied	4	8
	5	24
	6	96
100% satisfied	7	592
Total		**720**

Wilson's Family Restaurant

*Massine Bouzerar and
H. F. (Herb) MacKenzie*

In June 2012, John Wilson, owner-manager of Wilson's Family Restaurant in Struan, Ontario, was facing a major issue. His sales had been declining for some time, although very gradually, and he'd just heard that Swiss Chalet was about to open a franchise location two blocks from his restaurant. John was of course aware of Swiss Chalet; he often ate there when he travelled to Mississauga, Toronto, and other Ontario cities he sometimes visited. The food was consistently good, the premises unfailingly clean, and the prices reasonable. In short, his experience at Swiss Chalet had always been positive, and he knew that he shouldn't underestimate it as a competitor. John sat in his office, trying to brainstorm some ideas, hoping he could at least mitigate the impact that a new Swiss Chalet would have on his business.

BACKGROUND

Wilson's Family Restaurant

Wilson's Family Restaurant was founded in 1992 by Mark Wilson, a local entrepreneur in Struan. Mark had worked in the hospitality industry for over 30 years when he finally decided to follow his passion: cooking. He'd reached his mid-fifties when he saw a need in Struan for authentic traditional cuisine.

When he opened his restaurant, Mark received a lot of positive feedback from the community: people would describe Wilson's as "the best local and homemade food in town." Many people became regular customers; Mark would see the Friday night crowd, the Sunday lunch crowd, a number of regular local businesspeople who'd come in for lunch throughout the week, and a reasonably large breakfast group. Some of the breakfast customers stopped at Wilson's every morning. As his business continued to grow, Mark invested both time and money to create the best dining experience in town for his customers.

Wilson's, a dine-in restaurant with a 56-person seating capacity, was a place where locals and tourists alike would go to have a pleasant lunch or dinner. Although Struan itself had a population of just over 3200 people, the region around Struan had another 10 000 people, and each year an estimated 1.5 million visitors passed through the town. Furthermore, three cities within 30 to 45 minutes of Struan had a combined population of 412 000 people.

Wilson's offered classic North American dishes, including salads and soups, grilled hamburgers, sandwiches and wraps, fish and chips, and its famous pulled-pork sandwich and rolled-rib dinners. All the desserts were fresh-baked on the premises and varied each week. The menu was designed to showcase a variety of western dishes that appealed to the general population of Struan and offered tourists a taste of local cuisine. Wines were all Ontario wines; beer was all Ontario beer.

Change of Ownership

In December 2009, after managing his restaurant for over 17 years, Mark felt ready to let go of the business and slowly transition his eldest son, John, into being Wilson's new owner-manager. Mark thought that John would best be able to carry on the family business while he retired and moved to the countryside just outside of Struan.

John had recently received his diploma in culinary arts from a local community college. He enjoyed working in food preparation, and was recognized for his creativity in the kitchen. Although he hadn't been involved much with the restaurant beyond working in the kitchen, John knew the importance of customer service. Mark was confident that he'd be customer-oriented and that he'd be able to engage customers and quickly gain their confidence.

After taking over Wilson's, John soon began to feel comfortable in his role as owner-manager. Although many customers missed Mark's humour and his warm greetings whenever they entered the restaurant, John felt that the community was happy to see that the restaurant remained a family business—and, of course, Mark regularly appeared for a "free" meal. John was excited about his new responsibilities, and felt motivated to continue improving operations and increasing the value provided to its customers.

CHALLENGES

Declining Sales

Within the first couple years of managing Wilson's, John noticed that the restaurant was beginning to lose the reputation it once had as "the best local and homemade cuisine around," an image that had been carefully cultivated for two decades. Sales were starting to drop, and the restaurant wasn't as busy during the lunch hour and on Friday nights or for Sunday lunch. It wasn't that a great loss had occurred for any particular time or group of customers; there just seemed to be a general reduction in the number of customers at all times of the day and days of the week.

John believed that his customers needed a change—and the fact that the menu had remained basically the same didn't help. So, in a bid to woo back his lost customers, John decided to add such items as salmon, various cuts of steak, perogies, and gourmet pizzas to the menu. But to his disappointment, he saw no increase in sales.

Competition

John had recently received a phone call from a close friend with more bad news: "Apparently a permit's been issued to build a Swiss Chalet just down the road from you on the old Brighton property . . ." The words echoed in his head as he sat in his office trying to figure out what to do next. Although the new Swiss Chalet's completion date was unknown, John knew that his sales would decrease more quickly once it opened its doors.

Swiss Chalet, a multimillion-dollar Canadian chain, has over 200 locations across the country. It also has several signature dishes that set it apart from its competitors, including its rotisserie chicken, which is made fresh daily. John feared that instead of Wilson's Family Restaurant, tourists to Struan would choose a familiar brand like Swiss Chalet. The new kid in town would be a strong competitor.

OPPORTUNITIES

John began brainstorming possible routes he could take to save his business from complete extinction.

Menu

The first thing he did was visit Swiss Chalet's website and review its online menu (see www.swisschalet.ca), taking careful note of the items where Wilson's might be at a disadvantage, and where there might be opportunities to compete. He also made it a point to visit a Swiss Chalet location and evaluate its menu. John was surprised to see that a number of changes had been made to it since he last ate there. The popular chain had added ribs and, more recently, fish and chips. He also noted flatbreads, and four "new" pasta and rice dishes. John didn't notice many differences between the online and in-store menus, except that in-store, Swiss Chalet also offered beer and wine—a limited selection of popular brands at reasonable prices. One key difference between Wilson's and Swiss Chalet's menu was that the latter included a lot more menu options; however, John felt that Wilson's had more variety. (See Exhibit 1 for the most recent Wilson's Family Restaurant menu.) Still, worried that Swiss Chalet's more numerous options would attract his current customers, John thought about adding more menu items that differed slightly from the ones he currently offered; for example, he considered adding a multigrain option for all his sandwiches, wraps, burgers, and wings, and more pie and cheesecake flavours on the dessert menu.

EXHIBIT 1	Wilson's Family Restaurant Menu

Appetizers

Garlic Bread (Add cheese for $0.99)	$3.99
Garden Salad (Upgrade to Caesar for $0.99)	$2.99
Soup of the Day	$3.49
Chowder of the Day	$3.99
Spinach Dip	
Individual	$4.99
Large	$7.99

Burgers

All burgers are served with your choice of a garden salad, fries, or coleslaw.

Bacon Double Cheese Burger	$14.99
Chicken Burger	$13.49
Mushroom & Swiss Burger	$13.99
Barbecue Burger	$14.49
Meatless Burger	$12.99

Sandwiches and Wraps

All sandwiches and wraps are served with your choice of a garden salad, fries, or coleslaw.

Club Sandwich	$10.49
Smoked Turkey Sandwich	$11.99
Extreme Grilled Cheese Sandwich	$9.99
Egg Salad Sandwich	$8.99
Grilled Chicken Wrap	$11.99
Greek Wrap	$9.99
Chicken Teriyaki Wrap	$12.99

Pizzas

All pizzas come in an individual or a large size.

Margherita	
Individual	$10.99
Large	$22.99
Italian Sausage	
Individual	$13.99
Large	$24.99
Philly Style	
Individual	$14.99
Large	$25.49

EXHIBIT 1	Wilson's Family Restaurant Menu (continued)	
Mediterranean		
Individual		$12.49
Large		$23.99
Hawaiian		
Individual		$12.99
Large		$24.49
Wilson's Specials		
Fish 'n Chips Galore		$9.99
Perogie Madness		$8.99
Meat-lover's Steak		$11.99
Desserts		
Apple Pie		$3.99
Cake of the day		$3.99
Cheesecake of the day		$4.99
Milkshake *(vanilla, chocolate, or strawberry)*		$4.99
Beverages		
Soft Drinks/Bottled Water		$1.49
Freshly Squeezed Juices/Milk		$1.99
Coffee/Tea (bottomless cups)		$1.79

When John examined the pricing, he saw that the two menus were somewhat similar. Wilson's entrees were slightly lower; Swiss Chalet had much lower dessert prices. John was satisfied with Wilson's current prices and felt that he wouldn't have to reduce any of them in anticipation of Swiss Chalet's opening. If anything, John considered including add-ons to Wilson's entrees, such as adding the Soup of the Day to a meal.

As John continued his research on Swiss Chalet, he began to wonder how its takeout and delivery service would affect Wilson's. He'd never considered this kind of service. Swiss Chalet also allowed customers to place their orders online through the company's website, making the ordering process even more convenient. Nonetheless, John was determined to find a way to compete effectively against the large corporate chain.

Promotions

To differentiate itself from its competitors, Wilson's had focused its advertising in specific channels. Promotion included a sign outside the restaurant that was updated weekly, a half-page ad each week in the local newspaper, and flyers included in the local newspaper about every four months. The flyers always had one or more coupons promoting special items through a discount of 15 to 50%, depending on the item's anticipated popularity. John had

EXHIBIT 2	Promotional Expenses, 2012
Newspaper ads	$ 4 500
Flyer inserts	$ 3 600
Radio ads	$ 7 800
TOTAL	$ 15 900

also recently run commercials on the local radio station four to five times a week. Exhibit 2 shows John's current budgeted expenses for promoting Wilson's Family Restaurant.

John was aware that Swiss Chalet could easily match Wilson's local promotion expenses, even on top of the chain's national television commercials. He'd be challenged all right, but with a little creativity he felt sure he could be more effective than Swiss Chalet. He was a good cook and he knew his patrons. He was committed to offering a superior dining experience in a family-restaurant environment. John had never been forced to think about how to really promote his business, but now was the time to focus.

THE DECISION

As John sat in his office at the end of one of his busier days, he began to organize his thoughts concerning his business's future. "With a solid plan, I think Wilson's has what it takes to succeed, even with Swiss Chalet's opening," he thought to himself. The fact remained that Swiss Chalet would be hard to fend off; he'd have to do his best to not let it greatly affect Wilson's sales. Trying to brainstorm ideas on how to set Wilson's apart from the rest of the market, John closed his eyes in the hope that something would come to mind quickly enough to prepare for Swiss Chalet's arrival.

ECCO Shoes

Sherry Finney and Kyle Gillis

Mette Scherrebeck-Hansen, junior project manager of interactive marketing at ECCO Shoes Ltd., had just stepped out the doors of the digital marketing agency's head office into a cool autumn breeze blowing through Copenhagen's narrow streets. She was in a rush to make her train back to ECCO headquarters in Tønder. Once she made it on the train, she'd have some time to absorb all the new information swimming around her brain. As she pressed through the crowd, Mette thought about how she was now beginning to experience first-hand so much of what she'd studied as a marketing student at Cape Breton University in Nova Scotia.

As the city of Copenhagen blurred by Mette's window, she thought of the monumental task she had before her. It was November 11, 2008, and she had about two months until the 2009 spring/summer online campaign was set to launch. The work her team had done over the past six months was now irrelevant; alternative campaign objectives had been settled upon based on new market research. Mette supported the new objectives, and thought they were a step forward. The question now was how to implement them effectively. Her team was working on the campaign with the digital marketing agency, and a lot of creative online solutions would have to be developed and evaluated over the coming weeks. The most effective online strategy to convey the newly minted category engagement platform—"The Comfort to Express Your Style"—had to be established, and it had to be done quickly.

COMPANY BACKGROUND

ECCO was founded in 1963 by Birte and Karl Toosbuy. The pair settled in the rural village of Bredebro, Denmark, to establish their footwear empire. Karl Toosbuy played a major role in the business until his death in 2004; however, his spirit and values were still the cornerstone of ECCO today. While building the business in the early years, he travelled extensively throughout Europe promoting the brand. The Scandinavian countries were particularly receptive to the Danish-designed footwear, and Germany too proved to be a profitable market. By the late 1960s the company had grown significantly from its humble beginnings, and a new factory was being built in Bredebro to accommodate the increased demand.

From the beginning, Karl Toosbuy's emphasis on high quality and advanced design led the company into backward vertical integration: ECCO opened its own tannery and invested heavily in the research and development of design initiatives. Later in the 1980s, the company pursued forward vertical integration by establishing its own retail outlets. The first store was opened in Denmark in 1983.

ECCO's first big-hit shoe, known as the Joker, was launched in 1978. The shoe put the company on the map as a top producer of quality comfort footwear. A year after the Joker's success another successful shoe design, called Free, was launched. By the end of the 1970s ECCO had become a globally recognized brand, with over 50% of its sales coming from outside of Denmark.

The success of these two shoes enabled ECCO to expand into more international markets. In the early 1980s it entered the Japanese marketplace, which proved to be highly receptive to ECCO's footwear. By the end of the decade the company had sold over 10 million pairs in this lucrative market. The company had also identified the United States as a promising market during this time. That move came much more slowly, however, with ECCO carefully preparing for a full-scale entry in an effort to overcome the issues that many other European shoemakers before it had failed to anticipate. One of these was the importance of building a good relationship with independent retailers. ECCO also recognized U.S. consumers' preference for sportier shoe styles, and tailored its designs accordingly. It began testing designs in the United States in 1988 and by 1990 it had opened its first U.S. subsidiary in Salem, Massachusetts. ECCO chose to launch only in particular regions—mainly California and the Northeast—which it perceived would be receptive to its brands. The success was immediate, and a year after its initial strategic launch, it commenced a full-scale entry into the U.S. market.

Throughout all this expansion, production capacities had to be increased as well. ECCO opened its first offshore production facility in Brazil in 1974. Other facilities in Portugal, Slovakia, Indonesia, Thailand, and China also opened to meet the increased demand for ECCO shoes as it continued its global expansion. To ensure that the quality remained consistent in these new factories, ECCO adopted automated production techniques. In fact, it was one of the first shoe designers to use CAD systems and direct injection machinery in its factories—systems most commonly used in automobile design and manufacturing at the time.

Today, ECCO Shoes Ltd. is a world leader in the shoe industry. Toosbuy's vision back in 1963 was to create a comfortable, high-quality shoe. It was that vision that has remained with the company over the years, and has enabled its massive growth and success.

BRAND IMAGE

For the 2008 campaign, ECCO defined its brand image, or essence—as it's referred to in-house—in the slogan "The Most Comfortable Place on Earth." This maxim was at the pinnacle of the ECCO brand architecture and flowed through every strategic plan developed by the company. ECCO believed this type of thinking would give it a competitive advantage: most shoe brands cared only about shoes, but ECCO put the foot first, and was therefore able to create a unique combination of comfort technology and beautiful design. Its shoes made feet look good *and* feel good. ECCO, believing that its consumers would recognize this value unique to the company, came to this conclusion: "Comfortable feet are the foundation for a comfortable me."

But consumers' perception of ECCO's brand image appeared to differ according to region. While the idea of comfort seemed to resonate in ECCO's worldwide marketplaces, the brand's perception beyond that differed drastically depending on location. For instance, in Japan ECCO was seen as a high-fashion line, comparable to Prada or Gucci, whereas in western Europe it was viewed as less fashionable. In that region, the brand struggled with a "granny shoe" image, although research showed that this was changing. Such inconsistency presented a unique challenge to ECCO's global marketing efforts, in that it didn't want to cater too much to one demographic while alienating others. A fine line had to be drawn in order to appeal to all parties.

ECCO had five main brand values. These were geared mainly to the company's products, but they also stood for the company's values as a whole:

- The Foot (It all starts with the foot.)
- Perfection
- Craftsmanship & Technology
- Design & Comfort
- Ensuring Quality & Ethics

Mette knew that in developing the new online campaign, each of these values must be met.

CAMPAIGN STRATEGY

The new global online campaign strategy followed closely in line with the brand image and Toosbuy's founding vision of the company. With comfort as the essence of the campaign, its central ideology was captured in the motto "The Comfort to Express Your Style." Mette realized that a lot could be derived from a simple sentence. ECCO's top management wanted to convey to the consumer the following communication imperatives:

- Inspiration, not dictation (style vs. fashion)
- Authentic, honest, human

- Real people living real lives (storytelling)
- Make it aspirational, admirable, and UNIQUE

ECCO's Engagement Platform—"The Comfort to Express Your Style"—was what it wanted the consumer to think, feel, or do as a result of its communications. The four communication imperatives were the different things it needed to do or say to get that desired response.

It was clear that ECCO didn't want to position itself as dictator in the sense that it was deciding for its target audience what was fashionable. It wanted its customers to be comfortable to express their own style, as its campaign motto put forth. The previous campaign motto, "Comfort and Style," didn't define as clearly the company's position on this issue. ECCO viewed fashion and style as two distinctly different concepts. Style was the unique personal perception and projection of identity, based more on inner values than on outside dictates. It would usually require inner confidence to trust one's own perception rather than the mainstream fashion norms. Style can, therefore, easily differ from person to person, as it was a result of individual personality. Fashion, for ECCO, was the other side of the equation: it was the given norm for how one *should* look at any given time and in any given situation, dictated by the outside fashion world and not based on the individual's own personal beliefs. See Exhibit 1 for ECCO's desired market positioning.

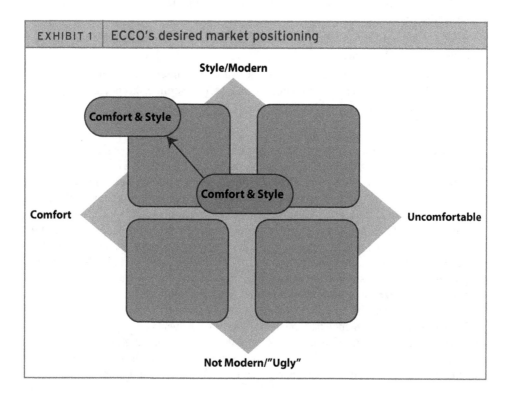

| EXHIBIT 1 | ECCO's desired market positioning |

Axes: Style/Modern (top), Not Modern/"Ugly" (bottom), Comfort (left), Uncomfortable (right). Labels: "Comfort & Style" (upper left) with arrow from "Comfort & Style" (center).

TARGET MARKET

As an online campaign, the target market could be more specifically segmented than a print or billboard campaign. ECCO, having spent extensive time researching its target market, had segmented it into nine distinct types of consumers. It was believed that four of these groups could be influenced by an online campaign. The four still had very different views of what they wanted in a shoe, but the online campaign could be tailored to attract and engage each one. "The Adventurers" was the name of one of these market segments; see Exhibit 2 for a description of this group.

ONLINE DIRECTION

Mette's meeting with the marketing agency had outlined the overall direction in which ECCO hoped to take the online campaign. Based on the new engagement platform, "The Comfort to Express Your Style," ECCO had come up with the following objectives:

- Leverage the design of the offline campaign material in the pursuit of offline/online synergy.
- Support and enhance the campaign message, "The Comfort to Express Your Style."
- Create a bridge between the campaign message and the brand message—"The Most Comfortable Place on Earth"—in order to influence and direct the consumer's perception of ECCO.
- Focus on real people and authenticity to make an eye-to-eye emotional connection with consumers.
- Ensure that the users' primary missions are resolved with minimum effort; e.g., fewest clicks from the front page.
- Continue the dialogue with visitors to the Autumn/Winter 2008 campaign site and establish a dialogue with new visitors to the Spring/Summer 2009 campaign site.
- Gather email permissions from visitors.

As Mette perused the digital marketing agency's report on her train ride back to company headquarters, other campaign principles mentioned in the meeting came rushing back into her mind. The report indicated some of the challenges that must be overcome. Particularly, the target audience was expected to demand authenticity and commitment rather than just another free-floating brand statement. ECCO would have to convince the target audience that the company truly believed in personal style and comfort over the dictatorship of fashion. ECCO had to create an interaction with the target audience that left individuals with the feeling that ECCO had given them an experience of great value, one they would share with and recommend to others. There was also the issue of budget cutbacks; the global economic crisis was swinging into full gear, and ECCO wasn't immune to its effects. Mette realized that more must be done with less. With these principles in mind, Mette knew that it was time to move on to the creative process.

In their meeting, the agency had touched on some of the ways these principles could be achieved. Creating blogging areas and using real people as campaign models were two approaches. One advantage ECCO had was an extensive database of its customers. Information had been compiled on consumers, with their permission, and Mette had access to

EXHIBIT 2 | ECCO's "Adventurers" Market Segment

GfK

Consumer Styles - Global Lifestyle Typology

Adventurers

Values

- Life is a challenge
- Experience of living: adventure, excitement, pleasure, sex, having fun, enjoying life
- With focus on the own person: self-interest, individuality, looking good
- Materialistic demonstration of status, power, wealth
- A varied life from ambitious, youthful, enterprising, curious and creative people
- Sometimes full of romance

Demographics

- Full-time students and young singles under 30 years
- Middle to high education level
- Medium to high income

Marketing / Communication / Media

- Like hip/trendy brands with prestigious names
- Always on the lookout for new products
- Show-off (Owning nice things tell the world "I have made it")
- Like to have fun now
- Trust in all kind of advertisement

	-	Ø	+
Media:			
Print (magazines) (frequency)	○	●	○
TV (weekly time)	●	○	○
Radio (weekly time)	○	●	○
Internet (weekly time)	○	○	●

Lifestyle

- Visit a disco/night club or karaoke bar
- Play electronic, video, or computer games
- Electronics, computers, technology
- Go to a concert, stage performance, show
- Go to sporting events, go to the movies
- Internet or World Wide Web
- Participating in sports

Source: GfK Roper Consumer Styles, Target Group Report World, Global Survey 25 countries
©GfK SE | Lifestyle Research | Germany 2013

Source: Courtesy Gfk.

this database. So, any costs associated with using real people in the campaign were relatively low, as ECCO could access, and contact, the category of consumer it desired through its database and the website.

CONCLUSION

Mette realized she had an advantage in creating online solutions to ECCO's campaign objectives: she basically fell into one of the consumer categories ECCO had segmented. She could ask herself, "What would attract me to this website?" Having grown up in the digital age, Mette was aware of all the latest online trends and the technology's current potential. The recent surge of social-networking sites wasn't lost on her, either; she knew that most people who spend time on the internet are searching for some sort of community. How to create a community within ECCO's online campaign was really at the heart of the matter. She knew that she was perhaps the best-suited individual to come up with the creative online concepts to best reflect the established objectives. Thinking outside the box was something she was an expert in, and she'd have to put her innovative thinking skills to work. Imaginative and original thought was necessary in order to come up with the concepts that would meet the campaign strategy and follow the online direction. Mette rested her head on the back of her seat as she reflected on the monumental task before her. She had a busy two months ahead.

Tyndale Treasures Community Store

Dave McKenzie and
Christopher A. Ross

In September 2007, the Tyndale St-Georges Community Centre (TSGCC) management team was wondering what should be done about the Tyndale Treasures Community Store in Little Burgundy, Montreal. The store, which sold used clothing, small appliances, and other household items, was part of the Retail Sales and Warehouse Training Project, one of the many initiatives of TSGCC's Adult Development and Education program. Management was concerned about the store's low financial contribution to the project and the inordinate amount of time the project's manager had to devote to the store's day-to-day operations. According to the TSGCC's director, the situation was becoming urgent.

BACKGROUND

Late in the year 1926, industrialist Charles Johnson sat in his Ville St. Pierre office. He was thinking of his employees, many of whom lived in the Montreal area now known as Little Burgundy. Johnson had a strong social conscience, and was concerned about the workers' material, social, moral, and spiritual welfare. A man of action, he approached Montreal's

Dave McKenzie, Coordinator, Institute for Community Entrepreneurship and Development, and Professor Christopher A. Ross, marketing department, Concordia University, wrote this case. It is to be used for discussion purposes only, and is not designed to illustrate either effective or ineffective handling of an administrative or commercial situation. Some of the information in this case may have been disguised but essential relationships have been retained. Copyright © 2008. Reprinted with permission.

Presbyterian community with his plan for a settlement house to keep children off the street. Johnson was persuasive, and came away with a $100 grant from his colleagues to cover the first year's operation. With this money and the support of the Johnson family, Tyndale House came into being in early 1927 in the area of des Seigneurs and Notre Dame streets. In the 1970s the Anglican Diocese of Montreal joined the Presbyterian Church of Canada in support of Tyndale, which then became known as Tyndale St-Georges Community Centre.

From the outset, TSGCC focused on services for youth, even when broadening its sphere of activities to meet the needs of the surrounding community. It was instrumental in the creation of such offshoot services as Le Garde-Manger Pour Tous, Youth in Motion, the Little Burgundy Council, the Little Burgundy Coalition, the Little Burgundy Festival, Action Refugee Montreal, and most recently the CPE (Centre de la petite enfance) Tyndale St-Georges, a subsidized daycare centre.

In keeping with its past, TSGCC continued to work as a not-for-profit charitable organization, providing services to more than 2000 members of the Little Burgundy community without regard to race or religious affiliation. Its programs ranged from preschool to adult development. The organization aspired to help individuals and families attain greater self-reliance and fulfillment. It provided encouragement, tools, opportunities, and support through educational, cultural, social, and recreational programs.[1] According to TSGCC's 2005–2010 Strategic Plan, "Our first priority will continue to be to serve the underprivileged and economically disadvantaged population of Little Burgundy. When our resources permit and when our expertise can fill a particular need which cannot be met by other agencies, we may extend our activity beyond Little Burgundy as we have in the past."[2]

TSGCC PROGRAMS

Tyndale St-Georges Community Centre had good links with the Little Burgundy Coalition, the St. Henri CLSC,[3] and the two Montreal English-language universities: Concordia and McGill. In 2006–2007 it operated with a budget of $1.4 million and approximately 30 full-time and 16 part-time employees as well as 300 volunteers. It offered a number of different programs aimed at community development. These were as follows:

1. *The Early Childhood Educational Program.* This program offered a variety of services aimed at preparing children, five years old and younger, and their parents for the school system. The objective was to stimulate the child's cognitive, social, and emotional development in an enhanced learning environment. As well, the program sought to break the isolation felt by many parents in the community. Activities were held between 9:30 a.m. and 3:00 p.m., Monday to Thursday. The local CLSC and a women's centre partnered in some of these activities.

2. *The School-Age Children, Youth, and Families Program.* This after-school program was offered to 70 children in grades 1 to 6 (6 to 12 years old) who were bussed to the centre each weekday. The children received one hour of special tutoring and homework assistance from a competent team, and one hour of recreation; the program ended at 6:00 p.m. An evening program, from 6:30 to 8:30 p.m. for children aged 9 to 15, focused

[1]Tyndale St-Georges Community Centre 75th Anniversary Appeal: A Tradition to Maintain, A Future to Build. (No date.)
[2]Tyndale St-Georges Community Centre, *Strategic Plan: 2005–2010*, adopted June 13, 2005, p. 3.
[3]CLSC stands for Centre Locale de Santé Communautaire/Local Community Health Centre.

on mentoring and leadership, and a Saturday program, for 6- to 15-year-olds, focused on tutoring and teaching different musical instruments. Finally, a seven-week summer day camp, running from the last week in June to the end of the first week in August, accommodated about 80 children. There was also a parent resource worker who helped liaise between the child, parent, teacher, and school.

3. *Language Program.* English was taught in conjunction with Concordia University's TESL (Teaching English as a Second Language) Department. Most of the teachers in the program were from Concordia, and Tyndale was a recognized TESL internship placement centre. About 550 to 600 students from about 90 different countries were enrolled in the program.

4. *Adult Development and Education.* Training was provided to adults aged 16 and over who were trying to either (1) enter the job market, (2) make a transition, or (3) further their education. Resources included an employment centre, vocational counsellors, a community employment assistant, and both French and English language training. The Tyndale Treasures Retailing and Warehousing Professional Development Project was a major initiative in this program; it was designed to train participants for the retail sector. The Tyndale Treasures Community Store provided participants with hands-on retail experience through supervised, in-store training for 12 hours over two days. Participants acquired the skills needed to work effectively as cashiers, sales clerks, and warehouse clerks. Among its priorities, the Adult Development and Education program wanted to "maintain and enhance Tyndale Treasures as a job training site and if possible as a fundraising activity."

For TSGCC as a whole, it was expected that for the 2006–07 fiscal year the operating deficit for all its programs would be $70 431, with the Adult Development and Education program contributing $29 409. For the 2007–08 fiscal year, TSGCC's overall deficit was projected to be $123 997, while the Adult Development and Education's deficit was forecasted to be $36 835.

THE MANAGEMENT TEAM

TSGCC's director, Patricia Rossi, had been employed at the centre for the past six years. Prior to her arrival she had travelled extensively and had worked with abused women in the not-for-profit sector for 17 years. She'd been the director of a shelter for abused women and children in Lachine, Quebec, and president of the Federation of Women's Shelters.

The Development and Education program director, Cynthia Homan, had begun her 20-year career as an entrepreneur in the pastry-making business. She then went into the corporate world for about six years, and subsequently founded another business that retailed sport collectibles. When the market fell out of that business, she retrained and for five years worked in customer service for a large manufacturer. She subsequently went on to be a sales manager and an office manager.

Tyndale Treasures Retail and Warehouse Training Project's manager, Beverly Trought, had a B.A. in Human Relations and a Graduate Diploma in Community Economic Development from Concordia University, and had been involved in community development for several years. With a group of five other women she'd founded a not-for-profit organization at Place Benoit. This organization was supported by Centraide (Montreal's United Way) and the City of Montreal. It included a youth club, a parents' workshop, and a collective

EXHIBIT 1	Partial Organizational Chart of Tyndale St. Georges Community Centre

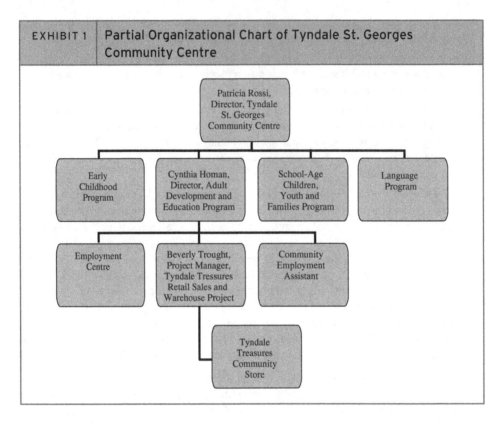

kitchen. She had been involved with this organization for about 11 years, though for the past two and a half years she'd been with TSGCC. (See Exhibit 1 for a partial organization chart.)

TYNDALE TREASURES COMMUNITY STORE

The Retail Sales and Warehouse Training Project was partially funded through its program fees and by the Zellers Foundation, Imperial Tobacco, and the Quebec government. Long-term relationships had also been established with such retailers as Zellers and Winners. Training sessions were held in TSGCC's Little Burgundy Employment Centre, located in the same building as the community store at 731 des Seigneurs (corner of St. Antoine Street); the building was owned by L'Office Municipale d'Habitation, and other community groups had access to space in it. The store occupied about 600 square feet on the main floor of the Employment Centre along with over 2000 square feet of storage room in its basement.

The Training Project's objective was to build personal and professional skills and broaden opportunities for gainful, permanent employment. In general, participants were taught leadership skills, interpersonal communication, and basic workplace French. More specifically, they were taught selling techniques, visual merchandising, point-of-sale procedures, inventory management, loss prevention, and fashion coordinating. For the warehouse, they learned about receiving procedures, quality control, stocking, and preparation of goods for sale.

The community store began almost by accident. TSGCC used to receive donated clothing and then give it away in the community; some people in the Employment Centre also began to sell clothing to their friends. Over time the idea of opening a retail outlet developed, so a project proposal was written and funding was sought from the provincial government. From that proposal came the idea of using the store to train participants for the retail sector.

By the fall of 2007 a decision had to be made about the store's future. The TSGCC's board of directors felt that the store could generate enough income to be self-sustaining. The management team also felt that, ideally, the store could at least fund the training program. Beverly agreed that the store had the potential to increase sales; however, a manager and a store assistant (who would help promote the store) would need to be hired. Thus, the immediate goal was to generate enough revenue to cover the direct expenses as well as the manager's and employees' salaries. The store was now in its third year of operation. In the first year sales were about $5000, second-year sales were $8000, and third-year sales were $9433 (Exhibit 2 shows the monthly sales for the first, second, and third years).

Operations

The store sold clothing, household articles, dishes, pots, pans, jewellery, baby items, and shoes. Food wasn't sold (although the store's management had been approached). The store's stock was donated by community members and churches. People heard about the store and donated their items; in addition, clothing manufacturers' employees sometimes donated stock. With well-established connections to clothing manufacturers, the churches donated new clothing and brought surplus clothing from their bazaars. Because of the randomness with which stock was donated, the Adult Education Centre's employees and participants often had to sort through it, removing whatever was unlikely to sell and trying to select the best quality and the cleanest. The donated clothing was largely for women and children, with the vast majority being adult clothing. Management was always surprised at the sizable quantity of donated stock, but the question remained as to whether the flow would continue over time. The more immediate problem, however, was keeping up with the volume of incoming stock.

Beverly, whose salary was paid by the provincial government agency Emploi Quebec to manage the retail and warehouse training project, spent about half her weekly hours managing the Tyndale Treasures Community Store. Emploi Quebec also paid minimum wage ($8 per hour) for a period of six months to a part-time employee. Every six months a new employee started, and it took about three months for that person to be fully comfortable with store operations. It was believed that a full-time manager would be able to relieve Beverly, who could then devote more time to the training project and to training the new store employees while spending less time replacing employees at lunchtime or when they were otherwise unavailable. Often when the employees were at lunch, the store had to be closed.

Current and projected monthly expenses for the store are shown in Exhibit 3. Hours were from 10:00 a.m. to 5:00 p.m., Monday to Friday. (The store wasn't open on Saturday because of lack of personnel.)

The Market and Customer Profile

The Montreal district of Little Burgundy was bounded by the Ville Marie Highway to the north, the Lachine Canal to the south, Atwater Street to the west, and Guy Street to the east. St. Henri was on its western border.

Historically, Little Burgundy had been home to a large proportion of the city's English-speaking black community, most of whom were Canadian-born of Caribbean origin. The past 15 years, however, had seen an influx of new immigrants into the community's subsidized housing. Since 2002, yuppies had also been moving into several relatively

EXHIBIT 2	Monthly Sales ($) of Tyndale Treasures											
Year	Sept.	Oct.	Nov.	Dec.	Jan.	Feb.	Mar.	Apr.	May	June	July	Aug.	Total
2004–2005	58.86	202	502.25	738.98	387.50	278.75	151.25	459.35	330.35	1008.77	683.93	755.14	5557.13
2005–2006	840	875	629	285	541	280	571	520	1405	823	461	842	8070
2006–2007	714	581	918	682	831	787	607	846	1141	1265	728	333	9433
												Closed for 2 weeks summer vacation	

EXHIBIT 3	Current Monthly Expenses for Tyndale Treasures Store	
Rent		$ 174.00
Maintenance		$ 90.00
Telephone		$ 60.00
Internet		$ 25.00
Municipal taxes		$ 65.00
Supplies (bags, cash tapes)		$ 150.00
Advertising		$ 125.00
Subtotal		**$ 689.00**
*Store Assistant salary		$ 1120.00
Benefits[1]		$ 179.20
*Coordination by Project Manager (14hrs/wk. @$18.00)		$ 1008.00
Total		**$2996.20**
Projected Monthly Labour Costs for Store		
Store Manager: (35hrs/wk @ $13.00 per hr)		$ 1820.00
Benefits		$ 291.20
Store Assistant: (35hrs/wk @ $8.00 per hr)		$ 1120.00
Benefits[1]		$ 179.20
Total		**$ 3410.40**

*Paid by Emploi Quebec Subsidy.
[1]Benefits calculated at 16% of wages.

expensive condominiums built on the southern edge of the community near the Lachine Canal. Their presence increased the district's average salaries and resulted in Little Burgundy's losing the statistical appearance of a disadvantaged community.

The 2001 census separated Little Burgundy into four census tracts (67, 68, 77, and 78). (See Appendix 1 for a portrait of all four tracts.) Tyndale Treasures Community Store was located in census tract 68. Little Burgundy's total population was 9459, of which 36% (3405) were immigrants and 21.5% (2034) were members of the black community. The median age of those living in Little Burgundy was 39 to 44, and 43% of the community comprised single-person households.[4] The census tracts' population breakdown and unemployment rates were as follows:

Census Tracts	Population	Unemployment Rate Male	Unemployment Rate Female
67	1765	8%	8%
68	2088	35%	26%
77	2289	11%	11%
78	3317	10%	9%

---

[4]2001 Canadian Census, Statistics Canada.

The changing demographics of Little Burgundy had a positive impact on the community store. In its first year, the majority of customers were from the black community. Subsequently, customers came from the English-speaking Asian communities in the area, with a small number from the adjacent districts of St. Henri and Point St. Charles.

The store's customers fell primarily into four categories. The first was those who were "down and out" and who really needed good clothing and household items at a cheap price. This category included street people, mostly men, shopping for jackets and shoes. They accounted for about 10% of sales. The second category was newly arrived immigrant women, aged 35 to 45 with two or three children, from Pakistan, India, or Bangladesh, and long-time black residents who accounted for 80% of sales. The third category was affluent persons, who lived in the condos near the Lachine Canal and who represented about 5% of sales. Finally, 5% of sales were bought by students at Concordia, which was located 1.2 kilometres from the store. Customers in the last two categories were motivated to visit the store after receiving advertising flyers.

With about 205 customer transactions in an average month, the average customer spent an estimated $3 to $4 per store visit, with the average transaction being $3.83. The management team was hoping to increase this average to about $5 per visit. Management also estimated that, in general, customers tended to visit about once per month, although some customers came in more often.

Competition

The Salvation Army had been operating thrift stores in Canada for over 100 years. One of its stores, located within .5 kilometre on 1620 Notre Dame St. West, was a major competitor. It occupied several thousand square feet of space and, in contrast to the rather cramped community store, it was laid out much like a regular department store, with items clearly labelled and displayed. Its lower floor was devoted almost entirely to clothing, its upper floor to furniture. The staff constantly replenished, rehung, and reorganized stock. The Salvation Army offered "excellent value at an affordable price" and had brighter, cleaner, more user-friendly stores. It also sold items on eBay through its "Sally Store."[5]

Other competitors within walking distance included the Welcome Hall Mission at 1490 St. Antoine Street West (about half a kilometre away). Through its Family Services it conducted food distribution on Tuesdays and Fridays, with clothing and household items distributed on Wednesdays by appointment. La Gaillarde, a co-operative, was located at 4019 Rue Notre-Dame West (corner of St. Henri), about two kilometres away; it operated a boutique with lines that included second-hand clothing, a showcase for local eco-designers, and a selection of retro clothes.

Competitors farther afield included Renaissance, a nonprofit organization founded in 1994. Its mission was (1) the professional and social integration of people who were having difficulties joining the labour market, and (2) the promotion of a commitment by each individual to protect the environment. It sold used goods through a network of nine stores across Montreal under the banner "Frippe-Prix Renaissance." Its slogan was "Everything for everyone at everyday low prices!" Items offered for sale included furniture,

---

[5]http://thrifstore.ca/history. Accessed September 6, 2007.

toys, small household appliances, and electronic components, along with a few new products such as underwear, T-shirts, and diapers, all at low prices. It also operated Simpli-cité, a new branch of high-end clothing and accessories on consignment. It was believed that Renaissance's prices were much higher than those at the Tyndale Treasures Community Store. Its two closest locations were four and six and a half kilometres away. Le Chainon Inc., a women's shelter, operated Le Coffre aux Tresors du Chainon about five kilometres away on St. Laurent Blvd. This nonprofit store carried used clothing, books, CDs, and accessories for the house. The store's annual sales were believed to total more than $500 000.

A host of other second-hand clothing stores were located in other parts of Montreal. Some, such as Value Village, operated on a commercial basis and had about six stores across the city, with 200 across Canada. Value Village bought clothing from not-for-profit organizations based on the number of boxes and bags delivered. It also bought directly from individual customers and then paid designated charities. Items sold included clothing, books, toys, and electronics.[6]

Pricing

The project manager wanted the store's products to be relatively inexpensive, in keeping with Tyndale's policy of serving the underprivileged and economically disadvantaged. There was some price variation among the different items, but rarely was an item more than $5. Men's suits, ladies' jackets, and skirts for the office were all priced at $5. Other items were frequently priced lower. For new clothing, prices were occasionally as high as $6.99. Pricing was based on an item's feel, newness, and judgment of quality. The maximum price at which an item was sold was $8 and the lowest price was $0.50.

Sometimes customers bargained, and the price was lowered as a result. Since the store was there to support the community, it was felt that it made no sense to keep any particular item. But Beverly realized that if the store was to support the salary of a manager and an assistant, a more systematic approach to pricing would have to be adopted. "Nice, good quality clothing may have to be priced at $7.99," she noted.

In setting prices, she sometimes compared prices with those at the nearby Salvation Army store. If the Salvation Army sold an item for $9.99, Tyndale sold it for $4. Although Tyndale Treasures compared itself with Renaissance and Value Village, the most frequent comparison was with the Salvation Army simply because clients also made that comparison.

Promotion

The store's promotional activities were fairly simple and straightforward. Personal selling was provided by the store assistant, as well as participants in the retail and warehousing program when they worked in the store. Flyers were the most common form of advertising, most often used to promote special sales or events at the store. They were distributed door to door in the neighbourhood, on the street, and in customers' shopping bags. (Exhibits 4 and 5 are examples of the store's promotional flyers.) Promotional tables with household items and

---

[6]www.valuevillage.com/whoweare/about_us.php. Accessed July 8, 2007.

EXHIBIT 4	Advertising Flyer

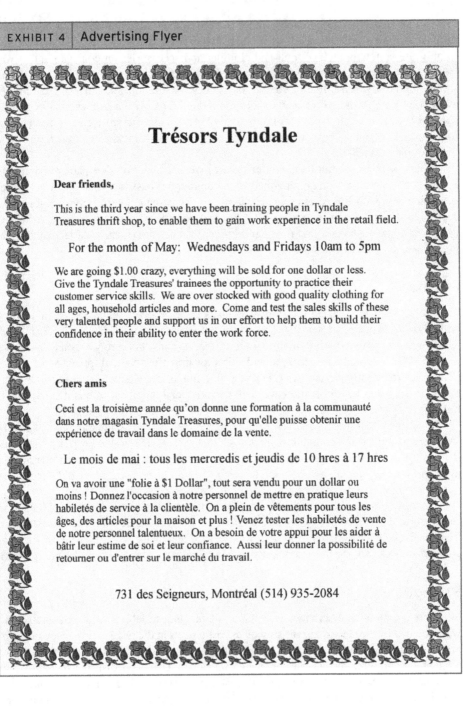

Trésors Tyndale

Dear friends,

This is the third year since we have been training people in Tyndale Treasures thrift shop, to enable them to gain work experience in the retail field.

For the month of May: Wednesdays and Fridays 10am to 5pm

We are going $1.00 crazy, everything will be sold for one dollar or less. Give the Tyndale Treasures' trainees the opportunity to practice their customer service skills. We are over stocked with good quality clothing for all ages, household articles and more. Come and test the sales skills of these very talented people and support us in our effort to help them to build their confidence in their ability to enter the work force.

Chers amis

Ceci est la troisième année qu'on donne une formation à la communauté dans notre magasin Tyndale Treasures, pour qu'elle puisse obtenir une expérience de travail dans le domaine de la vente.

Le mois de mai : tous les mercredis et jeudis de 10 hres à 17 hres

On va avoir une "folie à $1 Dollar", tout sera vendu pour un dollar ou moins ! Donnez l'occasion à notre personnel de mettre en pratique leurs habiletés de service à la clientèle. On a plein de vêtements pour tous les âges, des articles pour la maison et plus ! Venez tester les habiletés de vente de notre personnel talentueux. On a besoin de votre appui pour les aider à bâtir leur estime de soi et leur confiance. Aussi leur donner la possibilité de retourner ou d'entrer sur le marché du travail.

731 des Seigneurs, Montréal (514) 935-2084

EXHIBIT 5	Advertising Flyer

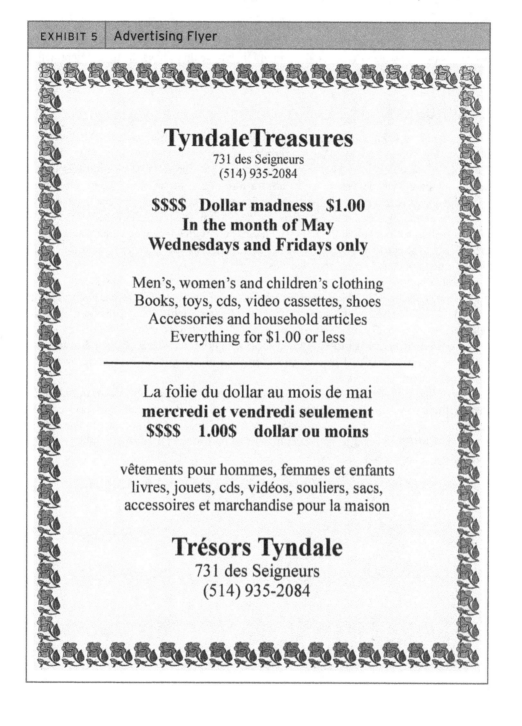

TyndaleTreasures
731 des Seigneurs
(514) 935-2084

$$$$ Dollar madness $1.00
In the month of May
Wednesdays and Fridays only

Men's, women's and children's clothing
Books, toys, cds, video cassettes, shoes
Accessories and household articles
Everything for $1.00 or less

La folie du dollar au mois de mai
mercredi et vendredi seulement
$$$$ 1.00$ dollar ou moins

vêtements pour hommes, femmes et enfants
livres, jouets, cds, vidéos, souliers, sacs,
accessoires et marchandise pour la maison

Trésors Tyndale
731 des Seigneurs
(514) 935-2084

clothing were also set up just outside the store. In addition, it was assumed that word-of-mouth played a very important role in the store's promotion. As Beverley explained, "Someone needs to sit down and work on the promotion, but we don't have the time. My principal activity is running the training project."

CONCLUSION

The management team considered various options for the community store. They thought of expanding their current location, but didn't have the room. There was an empty space in the building once occupied by a restaurant, but competition for that location was fierce, and in any case Tyndale Treasures couldn't afford to pay the monthly $2000 rent. They considered a move to a space on Notre Dame Street, but the rent was also deemed too high.

Management also examined options for increasing sales. These included selling in bulk as well as selling valuable items—including an original Brownie camera and a 19th-century photo album—on eBay. According to Beverly, however, their problem was insufficient time to plan and organize such sales.

Another option, suggested by Cynthia, was Dress for Success, whereby the store could put the nicest pieces of clothing together as a suit or ensemble and try to market it. Cynthia said she'd also like to see the store moving into higher quality second-hand clothes; she felt there was a niche for that. She wanted to sell clothes that were in really good condition because she believed that those moving into the district, as well as Concordia students, would be a good market. "I want to push for more clothing that's been outgrown," she said, "rather than worn to death."

According to Patricia, the store had almost complete freedom to do what had to be done without constraint from the board of directors. She felt, however, that service to the community needed to remain an important objective. Whatever the solution to these problems, the TSGCC wanted to have a complete and reasonable plan that could be implemented by January 2008.

Appendix 1

Portrait of Census Tracts

TRACT 67: ATWATER-GEORGES VANIER/ ST. ANTOINE-ST. JACQUES

- Decrease in population (–3%) between 1996 and 2001, explained by the decrease in families with children (–21%).
- Highest augmentation of the gross average rent between 1996 and 2001; decrease in the number of tenants and increase in the number of owners.
- Lowest unemployment rate in Little Burgundy.
- Largest proportion of allophones (i.e., people who speak neither French nor English).
- Largest proportion of people between 15 and 24.

TRACT 68: GEORGES VANIER-GUY/ ST. ANTOINE-ST. JACQUES

- Increase in population (6%) between 1996 and 2001. Most are families with children; 34% of households have four or more people.
- Most people aged between 0 and 19.
- Biggest concentration of HLM (Habitation à Loyer Modéré, or low-income housing) for families in Montreal (1441 units). This sector is constituted almost entirely of social housing.
- High rate of unemployment, low rate of job market activity, low incomes; 40% of incomes are from government transfers (social welfare, unemployment insurance, etc.).
- Most youth between 15 and 24 (85%) are attending school, and a few of them are active on the job market.
- Most are immigrants (in terms of percentage of tract population).

TRACT 77: ATWATER-GEORGES VANIER/ ST. JACQUES-CANAL DE LACHINE

- Most senior citizens live in this area; a seniors residence is situated here (145).
- Almost half of the households are composed of one person.
- Most single parents (53%).
- Of the population aged 20 and over, 39% have a university degree.
- Work income of residents is close to the Montreal average, but the income of single mothers is half the size of single mothers in Montreal.

Source: Little Burgundy: Forum on the Profile of the Neighbourhood, Participants' Guidebook presented by Convercite in collaboration with the organisms and partners of the Little Burgundy Coalition/Healthy Neighbourhood, April 8, 2004.

- Tenants make up 70% of the population.
- Almost 50% of the residential real estate was built between 1981 and 1990.
- Average gross rent is $415 (compared with $570 for Montreal).

TRACT 78: GEORGES VANIER–GUY/ ST. JACQUES–CANAL DE LACHINE

- Population increased by 8% between 1996 and 2001.
- Families with children decreased by 9%.
- Almost half of the households were composed of one person in 2001.
- Population largely composed of persons over 40 years of age.
- Higher work income than the average Montrealer.
- Lower unemployment rate than the average Montrealer.
- Most homogenous sector of Little Burgundy; large proportion of people born in Quebec, francophone and Catholic.
- Number of house owners increased by 53% between 1991 and 2001.
- One-fifth (20%) of residential real estate was built between 1991 and 2001.

The Medicine Chest

*Tashia Batstone and
Donna Stapleton*

It was October 25, 2006, and Michelle Janes, owner and head pharmacist of the Medicine Chest Pharmacy, had just returned from a meeting with Jeff Hill, a sales representative for McKesson Drugs. Jeff had presented Michelle with an interesting business opportunity. He knew that the Medicine Chest provided pharmaceutical services to several local nursing homes and that the company's current process of blister-packaging the drugs was labour intensive. He also knew that Michelle was always interested in new technology, and so he'd given her information about the PACMED Server +.

The literature explained that the PACKMED Server + was an integrated, computerized dispensing system that allows pharmacies to use an automated process for order processing and medication packaging.[1] Michelle immediately recognized its potential, but also saw that implementing such a system would involve significant costs, not the least of which was the $200 000 price tag of the equipment itself. She knew that in order to gain a competitive advantage she'd have to be the first pharmacy in the area to operate the system. She'd have to make a decision quickly.

[1]McKesson Drugs, Product Information Brochure. PACMED Server +.

As she sat back looking out at the pharmacy, Michelle realized that she didn't want to work forever. In fact, she was considering scaling back her hours over the next five years; and in 10 years wanted to retire completely. She wondered whether integrating the new system into her existing operations would improve the services she could provide to her customers while at the same time increasing the pharmacy's profitability.

BACKGROUND

Michelle Janes incorporated Riverview Pharmacy Ltd. in October 1996, and since that time the company had been operating under the trade name The Medicine Chest. Before its launch Michelle had been a pharmacist for many years. She realized very early in the life of the business that there was no way her small pharmacy could hope to compete on price with such corporate pharmacies as Lawton's Drugs, Shoppers Drug Mart, and more recently, discounters like Walmart and Loblaws. And so Michelle sought to create a niche for herself in the local market by offering superior customer service. Consequently, the Medicine Chest offered very little storefront and focused primarily on the prescription business.

As part of this focus, Michelle and her staff became well known for providing customers with personalized advice, including strict monitoring of drug interactions and the provision of such services as blood-pressure monitoring. As well, unlike the large pharmacies, the Medicine Chest allowed people to buy prescriptions on credit. Customers appreciated this service, as many people in the area were employed in seasonal industries. Michelle's philosophy had always been that the staff must do whatever it takes to keep the customer happy.

In addition to its walk-in operations, the Medicine Chest provided prescriptions to four local nursing homes. Although these homes paid a lower dispensing fee than that charged to walk-in clients, the number of their prescriptions more than compensated for the lower cost. Nursing home prescriptions accounted for more than 20% of all prescriptions filled.

LOCATION

The Medicine Chest operated in Witless Bay, a small community located on the Southern Avalon Peninsula, about a half-hour drive from St. John's. Its residents thus had the convenience of urban living within the traditional rural Newfoundland setting. While many commuted to the city on a regular basis, a strong sense of community prevailed. The population was about 1200; however, the proximity of other communities resulted in a potential customer base of over 7000 people. The Medicine Chest was located on the main road into the community; the building also housed the office of one of the three family physicians operating in the area. Many people still turned to local businesses with a trust that had been built up over the years.

In short, people in the community of Witless Bay all knew Michelle Janes; she'd been a pharmacist in the area for over 25 years and they respected her opinion. Michelle felt that this was one of the reasons she'd been able to successfully operate her business despite increasing competition from lower-priced pharmacies.

SERVICES AND OPERATIONS

The Medicine Chest serviced two main client bases in Witless Bay and the surrounding area: walk-in prescriptions and nursing home clients.

Ever since starting operations in 1996, the business had had a walk-in storefront with a pharmacist on duty six days a week (it was closed on Sunday). Customers were charged a dispensing fee of $9.25 per prescription. Due to space limitations the pharmacy carried only limited storefront inventory: basic health care and beauty products and a small supply of greeting cards. Michelle felt she needed to carry these products to meet her customers' requests, even though the items were adding very little to her bottom line.

The Medicine Chest began servicing nursing homes in the Witless Bay area in 1998. Given the age and health of these patients, each resident was often required to take a number of different prescriptions. Several years ago the Medicine Chest introduced a blister packaging system to facilitate the tracking and distribution of these prescriptions. Prescription cards, prepared for each resident on a monthly basis, contained all the drugs the patient would need for a seven-day period in individually packaged dosages. Four cards were prepared per patient, one for each week. Each card contained 28 individual plastic-covered pockets, called "blister packs," that allowed the pharmacy to place all the medications the patient required for a seven-day period into four individual daily doses. For example, if a patient was prescribed three medications, each requiring four doses per day, each blister pack contained three pills. The pharmacy was also responsible for providing each patient with a personalized tracking sheet. This sheet ensured that the nursing home staff was held accountable for dispensing the prescriptions by having to record and monitor which drugs were daily administered to the patients. Each card was individually labelled with the patient's name, the prescriptions contained in the card, and the dosing requirements.

Up to this point, pharmacy technicians had manually prepared the blister-pack cards for distribution to the nursing homes at the end of each month. Since the technicians had to individually place each medication into the individual blister pocket for each daily dose over the seven-day period, the process was very time consuming. After the card was filled, the blister packs were then labelled and heat-sealed. Prior to being sent to the nursing homes, each individual card was thoroughly checked by a pharmacist. Exhibit 1 shows an example of the blister-pack cards, along with additional information about the associated costs.

Providing the blister packing for the four nursing homes took about 75 hours of technician time per month. The pharmacist time required to check each card was about 40 hours per month. As well, during the month the patient's physician would often change the prescription, making it necessary to redo the cards with the revised prescriptions.

FINANCIAL SITUATION

Over the past several years the Medicine Chest had enjoyed a sustained level of profitability and provided a good living for Michelle and her family. Michelle's husband, Dan, was also employed by the business. Dan was responsible for the daily bookkeeping and helped Michelle manage the pharmacy operations. The Medicine Cabinet was mostly debt free, with only a few trade payables. The business rented its premises for about $1000 per month. Other than rent and related operating costs, the business's main costs were the purchase of drugs and wages. The company's most recent income statement is presented in Exhibit 2.

Jeff had told Michelle that McKesson would be willing to finance the PACMED system's $200 000 purchase cost by entering into a leasing arrangement with the Medicine Chest. The lease term would be over 10 years and require monthly payments of $2600. Michelle felt that this was a very good offer, and that the Medicine Chest could comfortably afford the monthly cost.

EXHIBIT 1	Blister-Pack Cards

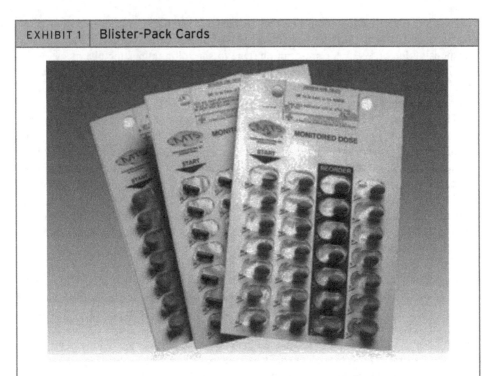

Selected cost information for the blister-packaging operation:

- Little capital was invested in the operation.
- The average hourly wage of a pharmacy technician was $8.50. The blister-packaging operation required about 75 hours per month of technician time.
- Pharmacists were paid an annual fixed salary of about $75 000 per year, equating to about $35 per hour. Checking the prescriptions required about 40 hours per month.
- The materials cost of each blister card was about $2.
- The cost of printing labels and preparing the tracking sheets was estimated at $0.10 per prescription.
- On average, each patient using the packing system was prescribed four medications.

THE PHARMACY BUSINESS

In the pharmacy business, revenue was generated from two main sources: the customer's dispensing fee and markups on the prescription drugs. In recent years, increasing competition from major discount chains such as Walmart and Loblaws has put pressure on small operators' ability to charge high dispensing fees. As well, many insurance companies are no longer covering these fees, requiring that the patient absorb these costs. Michelle recognized early on that she couldn't afford to lower her dispensing fees to compete, and so had kept her dispensing fee at $9.25. The main discount competition was from Loblaws (Dominion), located about 20 minutes from the Medicine Chest. Dominion was charging a

EXHIBIT 2	The Medicine Chest	

Income Statement

Year Ended January 31, 2006

January 31	2006	2005
Sales	$2 153 240	$2 132 698
Less: Cost of sales	1 576 799	1 479 006
Gross profit	576 441	653 692
Expenses:		
Wages and employee benefits	276 799	270 243
Advertising and promotion	7 022	5 267
Amortization	10 200	14 188
Automobiles	7 291	6 850
Bad debts	5 500	4 000
Rent	12 012	14 196
Municipal taxes	2 171	2 100
Utilities and telephone	8 462	7 048
Insurance	11 208	11 946
Professional fees	3 894	5 911
Repairs and maintenance	2 150	732
Bank charges and interest	5 620	3 478
Office supplies and postage	7 270	5 791
Sundry	2 845	1 408
	362 444	354 158
Income before tax	213 997	299 534
Less income tax expense	36 552	63 342
Net income	**$177 445**	**$236 192**

dispensing fee of $4.25 per prescription. While the decision not to lower the dispensing fee had resulted in some loss in business, the superior customer service offered at the Medicine Chest ensured that the store maintained a loyal customer base. The Government of Newfoundland and Labrador paid dispensing fees for the prescriptions of nursing home patients, senior citizens, and recipients of social services. It currently caps the fee for these prescriptions at $6.50.

Pharmacies also earn revenue not only from the markups but also the rebates on drugs. Although the markups vary, generic drugs can typically be sold for an average of 33%

markup on cost; markups on brand-name drugs are typically lower but can be as high as 25%. Many drug companies, particularly the large generic companies like Apotex Inc. and Novopharm Limited, also offer promotional rebates to pharmacies, which can receive reimbursements of up to 60% of the dollar value of the drugs sold. According to the Ontario Pharmacy Association, these rebates are designed to help pharmacists cover the cost of educating patients about the new drugs and investing in infrastructure upgrades.[2]

In planning for the future of the Medicine Chest, Michelle saw considerable potential. As with other health care–related industries, the pharmacy business is expected to continue to grow owing to the demographic shifts associated with an aging population.[3] In a report prepared for the Eastern Health Care Board, which is responsible for the administration of nursing homes in Eastern Newfoundland, Graham Worral estimated that seniors would make up one-quarter of the Newfoundland population by 2026.[4] There was no doubt that an aging population meant an increased need for prescription medication. And with adult working children needing to find long-term care facilities for their aging parents, Michelle expected significant growth particularly in the nursing home business. In fact, in recent years two more nursing homes had opened in the Witless Bay area alone.

But Michelle also saw that small pharmacies in Canada were facing two very real problems. First, increasing competition from discount pharmacies was placing downward pressure on the ability to earn revenue from dispensing fees. Two discount pharmacies that had recently opened within 30 kilometres of the Medicine Chest were charging fees of under $5 per prescription, and Michelle knew that despite her efforts the Medicine Chest had lost some customers.

Second, proposed legislative changes had many independent pharmacists in Newfoundland worrying about the future of the industry. In 2006 the Ontario government introduced controversial new legislation, *The Transparent Drug System for Patients Act 2006,* or *Bill 102*, to increase the transparency and accountability of drug companies and pharmacies in their dealings with Ontario Drug Benefit Program. If passed, the legislation would significantly affect Ontario pharmacies' profitability by (1) eliminating promotional allowances paid by generic drug companies, (2) restricting the government's reimbursement for generic medications to 50% of the cost of related brand-name drugs, and (3) limiting pharmacies to an 8% markup on drug sales, capping profit at a maximum of $25 per prescription.[5] Michelle realized that if similar legislation were passed in Newfoundland it could reduce her bottom-line profit by as much as 25%.

THE PACMED SYSTEM

Michelle had always tried to operate the Medicine Chest using leading-edge technologies. In fact, her pharmacy had been one of the first in Newfoundland to integrate computerized billing and patient files. At their meeting Jeff had given her a data sheet outlining the

[2]Silversides, Anne. (2006, August 15). "Pharmacies Receiving Massive Rebates from Generic Drug Manufacturers," *Canadian Medical Association Journal,* 175 (4).

[3]A Strategic Health Plan for Newfoundland and Labrador. (2001). www.health.gov.nl.ca/health/strategichealthplan/pdf /HealthyTogetherdocument.pdf. Accessed November 12, 2006.

[4]Worrall, Graham, and Knight, John. (2003). Short Report: Care for People Aged 75 and Older. *Canadian Family Physician.* 49:623-629.

[5]Ontario Ministry of Health, Media Debrief - April 13, 2006. www.health.gov.on.ca/english/public/legislation/drugs/hu _drugsact.html. Accessed November 25, 2006.

PACMED system's selling features, chief of which was its automated packaging and labelling capabilities. Based on supplier claims, the PACMED system could produce up to 60 doses per minute. Instead of blister cards, each daily drug dose was packaged automatically in tamper-resistant wrapping, with dosing and patient information automatically printed on each individually prepared package. The system's unique software stored patient information, eliminating the need to re-enter the prescription information each month. And because the system was automated, Michelle felt that one of its most significant benefits was the ease with which prescriptions could be modified and new drug packages prepared when prescriptions changed during the month. (A photo of the PACMED system can be seen in Exhibit 3, along with additional information.)

The information indicated that the PACMED system could be expected to reduce labour costs by 70%. Michelle felt that the system would reduce technician time by 70% to

---

EXHIBIT 3 | The PACMED Packaging System

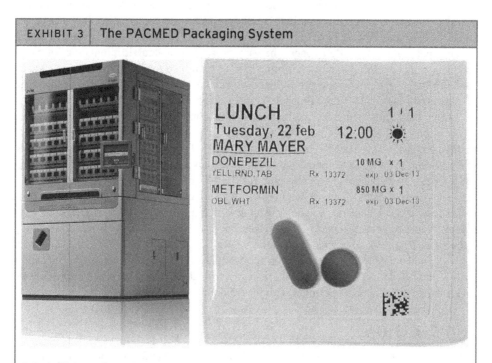

Selected information related to the PACMED system:

- Capital cost of the system was $200 000.

- Lease cost of $2600 per month was based on an 8% interest rate.

- The cost of packaging was $0.0297 per pouch, including the labelling.

- Estimated life of the system was 10 years.

- The system accommodated 500 different drugs in individual canisters; additional drugs could be added manually through a special tablet tray system.

Source: Courtesy McKesson Canada.

80% per month, given that the manual work of filling the blister cards would be eliminated. She also felt that since the system's individual packages were larger, it would be much easier for the pharmacist to check each prescription. Michelle estimated that this could result in up to 50% savings of pharmacist time.

In addition to improved packaging capabilities, the PACMED system was expected to optimize inventory management. The machine stored up to 500 different medications and could track lot numbers and expiration dates automatically, allowing for increased accuracy in restocking and reordering.

PRELIMINARY MARKET RESEARCH

Michelle was very interested in the PACMED system, as she felt it could save the business considerable time and cost. The Medicine Chest currently provided its blister-packing service only to its nursing home patients and a few elderly clients who found the prepackaged dosing convenient. Given the time involved in preparing the packs, Michelle hadn't marketed the service to her general clientele. Yet she was fairly certain that many of her patients, particularly the elderly ones who were prescribed several different types of medications, would be willing to pay a premium to have their medication individually packaged by dose. She'd performed some preliminary informal market research and determined that, in addition to the $9.25 dispensing fee, many customers would be willing to pay about $2.75 per prescription for the packing service. Along with its 12 000 nursing home prescriptions, the Medicine Chest was filling upwards of 30 000 non–nursing home prescriptions annually, and Michelle believed that about 50 of these non-nursing home customers, with an average of four prescriptions per month, would avail themselves of the service.

Michelle also considered not charging for the service but instead using it as a marketing tool to further enhance her philosophy of superior customer service. She estimated that in this case about 100 of her existing customers (again averaging four prescriptions each month) would avail themselves of the service. Moreover, the Medicine Chest could enjoy as much as 10 to 15% growth in the number of walk-in prescriptions it filled, and without having to add any staff. Michelle was unsure whether she'd be able to obtain contracts for the other nursing homes in the area. Still, she'd gain considerable time savings for servicing the four homes currently under contract with the Medicine Chest.

THE DECISION

Michelle had been seriously considering the future of the Medicine Chest. She'd hoped that her children would one day take over the family business, but both her sons had decided to pursue other careers. Michelle was currently in her late forties and intended to work full time for the next five years; after that she wanted to reduce her hours and, when the time was right, to sell the business. The $200 000 purchase price for the PACMED machine would require a considerable investment in both money and effort, and Michelle wondered if now was the time to be taking on such an ambitious project.

Scheff Rotary Cutting Tools

H. F. (Herb) MacKenzie

In early September 2011, Hamilton Milner, president and owner of Scheff Rotary Cutting Tools, was informed by the company salesperson for British Columbia, Winston Tung, that he'd be leaving the company at the end of the year to start his own tourist-related business on Vancouver Island. At first, Hamilton considered it a regular employee turnover problem, and was thinking of simply hiring a replacement salesperson. After some reflection, however, he started to wonder whether this might be an opportunity to make a more strategic channel decision. He gathered the information he thought would help him with his decision. After reviewing it for a few weeks, Hamilton decided to email it all to his son, Carson, who was enrolled in one of Canada's best-known MBA programs. Then he phoned Carson to explain his preliminary plans and ask him for his thoughts. While there was some urgency to make a decision, Hamilton knew he had at least a month or so to decide his course of action.

COMPANY BACKGROUND

Scheff Rotary Cutting Tools is a Canadian distributor of such rotary cutting tools as drills, taps, dies, milling cutters, reamers, and a number of less common miscellaneous cutting tools. These tools are used by manufacturers to remove material during the manufacturing process. For example, drills are used to drill holes through wood, metal, cement, or other materials. Taps are used to thread holes, and dies are used to thread bars, bolts, and other fasteners. Cutting tools must be harder than the materials they cut or shape. Hardness is an important characteristic because, during the cutting process, high heat is generated. This means that cutting tools can be made of different materials depending on what they're intended to cut (see Exhibit 1). Toughness and wear resistance are other important characteristics, and these also vary depending on the materials used to manufacture the cutting tools.

Scheff was started by Hamilton's father, John Milner, more than 30 years ago. John's first experience selling cutting tools began in the 1940s when he moved to Canada from the United Kingdom to open a branch office representing a steel and tool manufacturer from Sheffield, England. Montreal was chosen for the location because it was a major eastern Canadian seaport that could easily handle large shipments of heavy tool steel bars as well as crates of cutting tools. John sold the company's products throughout Quebec, and found two distributors—one in Alberta and one in Nova Scotia—to sell the company's products outside Quebec. By the 1970s the plant in England discontinued production of tool steel bars, and the company's only remaining product line was rotary cutting tools (and a few linear cutting tools, such as hacksaw and bandsaw blades). With the loss of tool steel sales, the Canadian operation's sales were almost halved. Its two distributors had also reduced sales, making them less reliant on John for supplies. They began to source some of their cutting tools elsewhere.

John Milner realized that his Canadian operation would soon be closed, so he approached the manufacturer and asked if it would appoint him as the exclusive Canadian distributor for its cutting tool products. John had married a Canadian woman shortly after he arrived in Canada; they were raising three children in Montreal and didn't want to leave. Fortunately the U.K. manufacturer agreed, and John started his own business. He

EXHIBIT 1	Tool Materials, Properties, and Uses
Materials	**Properties and Uses**
Carbon steel	Very inexpensive. These tools are very sensitive to heat and so are generally used only as hand-operated tools. Sales have been steadily declining since the 1950s.
High-speed steel (HSS)	Inexpensive. Sales have been growing steadily since the 1950s, and today they're the most commonly used cutting tools. High-speed steel retains hardness at moderate heat; able to retain sharp cutting edges.
Cobalt	More expensive. As the percentage of cobalt increases, these tools become very resistant to heat. Commonly used for machining abrasive or work-hardened materials such as stainless steel and titanium. Greater wear resistance; able to retain sharp cutting edges.

chose the name Scheff Rotary Cutting Tools because Scheff reminded him of Sheffield, where all his cutting tools were manufactured. Shortly after he started his business, the U.K. manufacturer dropped its carbon steel tools line (it had not yet begun to manufacture cobalt tools), and John had to look for an alternative supplier. In a decision he would later describe as "a good accident," he elected to import a line of carbon steel cutting tools branded with the Scheff name. Shortly afterward he found a U.S. manufacturer of cobalt tools, which he also had manufactured under the Scheff brand. Eventually, Scheff bought a small tool and die shop in Ontario and began manufacturing some specialty items under its own brand, expanding its product line to include a number of cutting tools with carbide inserts for very demanding applications. These were considerably more expensive than cobalt cutting tools. As his business grew, John moved his head office from Montreal to Toronto and opened a smaller, secondary location in Edmonton. He realized that while his least and most expensive tools were branded with the Scheff name, his most popular line of cutting tools, those made of high-speed steel, was still branded by the U.K. manufacturer. As he began to source additional products, John purchased from manufacturers in Germany, Poland, Sweden, the United Kingdom, Japan, Taiwan, and the United States.

By the 1990s, Hamilton, John's eldest son, took over management of the business. The company had grown considerably, with sales approaching $120 million. There were three salespeople who worked out of the Mississauga office: one covered Toronto and the immediate surrounding areas, another covered the rest of Ontario, and the third covered Quebec and the four Atlantic provinces. The Edmonton office also included three salespeople, with a similar arrangement: one covered most of Alberta, another British Columbia and a small portion of Alberta, and the third Saskatchewan and Manitoba. One of the first things Hamilton did once he had control of the company was to sell the manufacturing operations, outsourcing the production of specialty tools as they were needed. "This gives us much greater flexibility," he remarked. "We can look for the manufacturer with the best capability to manufacture whatever specialty item we need, and we're not tied to the production capabilities of a single operation."

The company that started as a distributor had returned to its roots: by the late 1990s, it was simply a distributor again. The difference was that it now sold a complete line of products, all branded with the Scheff name. Hamilton's goal now was to establish a network of industrial distributors across Canada. But first he had to establish a pricing strategy, and to determine which products Scheff would continue to sell direct to end-user accounts and which it would sell through its distributors. To make things easy for both Scheff and its distributors, Hamilton determined list prices for all products by simply increasing the company's estimated landed costs by 150%. That is, a product estimated to cost $4 would have a list price of $10. The company's margin at list price would thus be 60% ($10.00 – $4/$10).

However, nothing was ever sold at list price. Exhibit 2 shows the discount structure for end-user accounts and distributor accounts. Salespeople were paid a base salary and given a commission on all sales. When they sold to end-user accounts they received a commission of 5% of sales when the end-user paid list less 30%, with their commission decreasing as the discount to the customer increased beyond this level. For each 1% increase in the discount to the customer, the salesperson lost 0.5% commission. That is, the discount was shared equally between the salesperson and Scheff. For all distributor sales, the salesperson received 1% commission. This didn't vary with the discount the distributor received, since this discount was determined by order size and was largely beyond the salesperson's control.

EXHIBIT 2	Scheff Rotary Cutting Tools' Price List,[1] July 1, 2011
Direct to End-User Sales	**Distributor Sales**
Less 30%	Less 30/10% (multiplier = 0.63)
Salespeople could negotiate lower prices: from 30/1% (multiplier = 0.693) to 30/5% (multiplier = 0.665) maximum, at their discretion.	Orders over $2000 Less 30/10/10% (multiplier = 0.567)
	Orders over $5000 Less 30/10/10/10% (multiplier = 0.51)

[1]The discount schedule hasn't changed in more than 15 years. The list price has averaged a 3% increase since 2000, with very little variance.

Hamilton thought this discount structure would help keep conflict with the company's distributors at a minimum. Even at the lowest dollar value of an order, a distributor would buy at a lower price than an end-user account, and larger distributors could certainly compete directly with Scheff, since the Scheff salespeople were instructed that under no circumstance could they offer an end-user account a discount greater than less 30/5%. However, conflict was sometimes still an issue. In the earlier years, several distributors dropped the Scheff brand because they didn't want to sell the same brand that end-users could buy direct from what they saw as the "manufacturer." However, in recent years conflict seemed to have been mostly eliminated, and distributor sales continued to grow as new distributors were signed at the rate of approximately 5 to 10 accounts per year. (In 2010, for example, Sam Brooks opened six new distributor accounts as the number of suppliers to the Alberta oil fields was constantly increasing; Jake Cormier added two new distributors, both in New Brunswick; Tom Arkell added one new distributor, but lost two distributors; and distributors remained unchanged in the other three territories.)

CURRENT SITUATION

Hamilton had been watching the company's performance for several years. He was satisfied with its profitability, but there were a few things that increasingly concerned him. His first concern was that gross margin, particularly on direct sales to end-user accounts, had been decreasing over the past decade, in 2010 reaching its lowest level ever: 41.1% (see Exhibit 3). Second, he was concerned about the variability of gross margin by salesperson. Tom Arkell, for example, had the lowest gross margin on sales to end-user accounts (40.2%), but he also had the highest gross margin on sales to distributor accounts (29.1%). Tom also, however, had the highest overall gross margin across all of his sales: 30.9% (see Exhibit 4). Third, Hamilton was concerned that sales calls per account, particularly to distributor accounts, had been increasing. Although he didn't have the actual data to support this belief, he did notice considerable variability in how many sales calls salespeople made to their distributor accounts (see Exhibit 5).

Hamilton sent the information that he had to Carson, who was in his final year of a Canadian MBA program. In a phone conversation, he provided Carson with his

EXHIBIT 3	Sales and Gross Margin by Channel				
Year Ending	Direct Sales (End-user Accounts) ($000)	Gross Margin (%)	Distributor Sales ($000)	Gross Margin (%)	Total Sales ($000)
2010	$ 2 183	41.1	$ 10 737	27.1	$ 12 920
2009	$ 2 150	41.4	$ 10 239	27.0	$ 12 389
2008	$ 2 107	41.4	$ 9 962	27.1	$ 12 069
2007	$ 2 023	41.7	$ 9 613	27.3	$ 11 636
2006	$ 2 004	41.6	$ 8 944	27.2	$ 10 948
2005	$ 1 969	42.0	$ 8 577	27.4	$ 10 546

EXHIBIT 4	2010 Direct Selling Expenses, Sales, and Gross Margin by Salesperson						
Salesperson	Direct Selling Expenses	Direct Sales ($000)	Gross Margin (%)	Distributor Sales ($000)	Gross Margin (%)	Total Sales ($000)	Gross Margin (%)
Tom Arkell (Mississauga)	$ 116 277	$ 411	40.2	$ 2 151	29.1	$ 2 562	30.9
Timothy Hoover (ON)	$ 125 599	$ 370	41.6	$ 1 602	27.2	$ 1 972	29.9
Jake Cormier (PQ and ATL)	$ 129 402	$ 333	41.8	$ 1 744	27.1	$ 2 077	29.5
Sam Brooks (AB)	$ 120 980	$ 374	41.4	$ 2 018	24.6	$ 2 392	27.2
Adam Meagher (MB and SK)	$ 128 422	$ 401	40.5	$ 1 798	26.8	$ 2 199	29.3
Winston Tung (BC)	$ 130 389	$ 294	41.1	$ 1 424	25.9	$ 1 718	28.5

EXHIBIT 5	2010 Salesperson Activity				
Salesperson	End-user Accounts	End-user Sales Calls	Distributor Accounts	Distributor Sales Calls	Total Sales Calls (Accounts and Prospects)
Tom Arkell (Mississauga)	38	133	32	143	299
Timothy Hoover (ON)	35	120	25	88	342
Jake Cormier (PQ and ATL)	29	108	26	86	362
Sam Brooks (AB)	26	75	28	82	232
Adam Meagher (MB and SK)	27	84	26	92	306
Winston Tung (BC)	26	101	20	65	242

thoughts: "I'm thinking of discontinuing direct sales to end-user accounts and focusing completely on distributor accounts. We'd still target major end-user accounts, but through our distributors. It would give us an opportunity to solidify our relationships with our distributors, and I believe we could gain some additional ones as well. I also think we can cut our sales calls per distributor to a single visit per year, supported by telephone calls and email communications, and possibly some additional sales support from the office. I think I can get the sales force down to two salespeople. I'd have one salesperson as distributor accounts manager for the entire country, and I'd like that person to be an expert at product applications as well. I see this salesperson supporting the sales of specialty products through our distributors; that is, some of the products we're now selling direct to end users. Our two best product applications experts are Tom Arkell and Sam Brooks. Tom's already working out of the Mississauga office, and I suspect it wouldn't take much to get Sam to move here if I were to ask him. I know his grandchildren are all located somewhere near here, Oakville and Waterloo, I believe. I'd have the second salesperson as a market development manager whose role would be to open new accounts and take some of the pressure off the distributor accounts manager by servicing accounts in the Mississauga area. The more I think about this, the more sense it makes, but I still feel that maybe I should leave things the way they are and simply find a replacement for Winston Tung in British Columbia. I'd like your thoughts. Keep your mind open because there might be other things I should consider, and I'm perfectly willing to do that as I don't have to rush my decision for a month or two."

Carson responded, "No pressure, eh! I'm just getting ready for my midterm exams in three weeks . . . Just kidding. I'll noodle this while I'm studying and you can call me next weekend. I certainly don't know the business as well as you do, but maybe that's a good thing. We'll see." With that, Carson and Hamilton agreed to talk further the following weekend. As he continued to think about his situation over the following week, Hamilton grew increasingly comfortable with making a change to eliminate completely direct sales to end-user accounts, but he needed to give it some more thought, and he still wanted to hear what Carson had to say.

Homes of Distinction

*Massine Bouzerar and
H. F. (Herb) MacKenzie*

In May 2012, Sheryl Bruggeling sat in her office as she attempted to plan for the Homes of Distinction Christmas Home Tour in November. Having just been hired as chair of the tour's organizing committee, she was assigned the task of increasing the organization's bottom line so that it could make a greater contribution to the Niagara Life Centre. Sheryl had been involved with the home tour from the very beginning, starting out as a volunteer, becoming a home captain the following year, and sitting as the co-chair of the organizing committee in 2011. She'd come up with several ideas to raise more money for this year's event, but she was unsure which ideas were viable and ultimately which route she should take. With the fundraiser approaching, decisions had to be made.

BACKGROUND

Niagara Life Centre

The Niagara Life Centre (NLC) is a not-for-profit, Christian-based counselling ministry founded by Donna Beckett in 1985 in Beamsville, Ontario, to help young women with unplanned pregnancies. It began by providing hope and support to young mothers as well as mothers and fathers in need of parenting help and emotional support. The NLC has since expanded its services to all women, men, teens, children, and families who find themselves in need of any form of counselling. NLC counsellors address such issues as depression, abuse, relationship problems, and anger. Within a few years the centre realized the growing demand for counselling, which encouraged it to expand across the Niagara region; it now serves almost every community in the region. More than 10 000 people have sought the NLC's services over the past 20 years, and demand for counselling continues to grow. Although the centre initially provided its services free, the Turning Point Ministries' board felt it was necessary to begin charging a $30 fee per individual session and $10 per group session, although it's still heavily subsidized by the NLC. The NLC strives for constant growth and is committed to meeting the needs of the Niagara community.

The NLC hosts several events throughout the year to raise money to cover its counselling services. Its three largest annual fundraising events are the Walk/Run for Life, the Banquet and Silent Auction, and the Homes of Distinction Christmas Home Tour. At the Walk/Run for Life, which takes place in late April, youth and adults participate in the five-kilometre walk or compete in the one- or five-kilometre timed runs. Over 25 prizes are awarded each year. The event offers such family-friendly activities as balloon creations, face painting, and a barbecue lunch. On average, the Walk/Run for Life has raised about $20 000 annually, with all proceeds going to the NLC. At the annual end-of-year Banquet and Silent Auction, guests bid on donated items; the event also features testimonies from individuals involved with the NLC as well as a full-course dinner. Each year about 300 people attend the banquet, and over $20 000 is raised through tickets sales and the silent auction.

Homes of Distinction Christmas Home Tour

Founded in 2009, the Homes of Distinction Christmas Home Tour takes place every year in mid-November. The tour features about six homes and churches in the Niagara region, with new locations chosen each year. At $25 per person, or $30 at the door, guests are able to visit the homes any time between 10 a.m. and 5 p.m. and in whichever order they choose. The tour offers a $12.50 gourmet lunch, which includes a selection of soups, artisan breads, dessert, and coffee, tea, or water. Tickets for the event are sold at several local retailers and on the organization's website.

Homeowners open their houses for the entirety of the tour; some choose to stay in while others vacate for the day, leaving their homes in the hands of their home captain, whose responsibility it is to supervise the tour volunteers. The team in charge of finding the homes each year usually do so through either personal contacts or word-of-mouth. Homeowners tend to enjoy having their houses on the tour, as it gives them the chance to proudly show the home that they've worked hard to renovate and decorate.

Decorators and designers in the region also donate their time to decorate the houses, filling them with some of their own furniture and decorations. Although all work is done at their expense, the tour gives decorators/designers free exposure. The homeowners themselves sometimes purchase their wares after the tour, and guests often visit the decorators' and designers' venues to buy items they've seen. As sponsors, decorators and designers are given ad space in the tour's program and their logos are included on rack cards and posters. They're also given the opportunity to place a representative in the home along with brochures and other promotional materials.

NIAGARA MARKET

With the tour taking place in Jordan and Vineland, Homes of Distinction targets individuals residing throughout the Niagara region. Sheryl estimated that 98% of participants are women; she described a typical attendee as someone who wants to renovate, completely revamp, or simply redecorate her home and is seeking fresh ideas from the tour. The few men who do attend are usually more interested in the houses' architecture and historical background. Based on turnout in the first three years of her involvement, Sheryl has split the target market into three segments: primary, secondary, and tertiary.

The primary market comprises women aged 35 to 50, who Sheryl believes are typically the ones looking to refurnish their homes. After having owned a home for a few years, these women now have the disposable income to attend the tour for ideas on where to start with renovations or redecorating. This market typically pays closer attention to the way the house is decorated and by which vendors and suppliers rather than look at the structure of the home itself.

The secondary market is women aged 20 to 35 who are soon-to-be home buyers. These women attend the tour to get a sense of what they'd like in their future home. They tend to look at the size of the property, the number of bedrooms, and any special features they take a liking to. These women enjoy the decorating aspect of the tour; however, not being home-owners yet, they don't typically purchase any of the items on display by the decorators and designers.

The tertiary market consists of women aged 50 and older, long-time homeowners who've already renovated and decorated their homes to their liking. These women usually attend the tour with friends, considering it more of an outing than an opportunity for renovating ideas. They usually tend to look for small items to add to a room. Although this market tends to be the smallest, Sheryl sees a huge opportunity to specifically target these women as a way to grow the tour.

Market Research

The only form of primary market research Homes of Distinction has conducted is a yearly survey included in the Home Tour Guide. To encourage guests to fill it out, a completed survey must be submitted for the chance to win one of the many door prizes available, including free tickets for the following year's tour, gift certificates from decorators and designers, and gift baskets and floral arrangements from the many sponsors. Exhibit 1 lists the questions asked in the 2011 survey.

Most questions were designed to identify where individuals heard about the tour and what recommendations they would make for the organizing team. Although the current survey has served this purpose, Sheryl felt it could capture more demographic information.

EXHIBIT 1	Survey, 2011

**Homes of Distinction 2011 Christmas Home Tour
Evaluation and Door Prize Entry**

Please take a moment to help us make the Homes of Distinction Christmas Home Tour better by filling out this evaluation and placing it in the box provided. Your evaluation is also your entry form for door prizes.

Why did you attend the Home Tour?

- Christmas decorating ideas
- Support Niagara Life Centre
- Other _____

- A fun day out with friends
- Building a home

How did your hear about the Homes of Distinction Tour?

- Newspaper
- Radio
- Friend

- Retailer
- Facebook
- Other _____

Would you like to receive more information from Niagara Life Centre?

- Subscribe to newsletter
- Email updates

- Event news
- Prayer calendar

The best part of the tour was _____

To make this tour even better _____

I am interested in

- Decorating a home
- Sponsorship opportunities

- Having my home on the tour
- Volunteering

Contact Information

Name _____
Phone _____
Email _____
Address _____

Source: Niagara Life Centre.

Major home tours in the region include the Niagara-on-the-Lake Holiday House Tour, which takes place in early December, and the Hamilton Holiday House Tour of Distinctive Homes, which takes place in early November. Both are priced similarly to the NLC's Homes of Distinction, although the Hamilton tour includes do-it-yourself classes where guests are taught how to create and design holiday arrangements. Sheryl hopes that, with sponsors' help, Homes of Distinction could eventually offer similar classes. Other tours include the Fonthill Home for the Holidays, which usually happens the same weekend as Homes of Distinction, and the Canadian Federation of University Women Spring Tour.

CHALLENGES

In 2011, over 350 people attended the home tour, and over 225 tickets were sold for the gourmet lunch. Event sponsors were given complimentary admission to the tour, while volunteers were given a discounted rate. The hope was to increase attendance at the event so that retailers and decorators would see the value in continuing as event sponsors. However, the 2011 figures indicated a drop in attendance from 2010, when over 550 attended. Exhibit 2 shows detailed income statements comparing the 2011 and 2010 results.

EXHIBIT 2	Homes of Distinction Income Statement, 2010–2011			
	2011		**2010**	
Expenses	**Budgeted**	**Actual**	**Budgeted**	**Actual**
Pretour Expenses				
Room and hall fees	$113.00	$0.00	–	$0.00
Pretour	$113.00	$0.00	–	$152.29
Advertising				
Newspaper	$1 695.00	$1 200.00	–	$243.41
Radio	$5 650.00	$0.00	–	$0.00
Kijiji	$0.00	$0.00	–	$13.99
Printing				
Rack card	$1 299.50	$669.00	–	$1 275.77
Tickets	$339.00	$174.00	–	$286.18
Posters	$113.00	$85.00	–	$100.00
Signs	$339.00	$2 870.10	–	$321.88
Booklets	$1 695.00	$2 436.00	–	$1 731.90
Postage	$0.00	$0.00	–	$330.25
Lunch Expenses				
Supplies	$200.00	$415.79	–	$674.59
Ice	$250.00	$8.97	–	$0.00
Church rental	$682.50	$200.00	–	$100.00
Miscellaneous				
Thank-you gifts	$56.50	$0.00	–	$167.00
Balloons, napkins	$339.00	$69.95	–	$0.00
Website development	$565.00	$0.00	–	$593.25
Taxes	$113.00	$319.61	–	$0.00
Aprons	$0.00	$0.00	–	$494.37
Miscellaneous	$0.00	$0.00	–	$586.78
Total Expenses	**$13 562.50**	**$8 448.42**	**$3 000.00**	**$7 071.66**

EXHIBIT 2	Homes of Distinction Income Statement, 2010–2011 (continued)			
	2011		**2010**	
Income	**Budgeted**	**Actual**	**Budgeted**	**Actual**
Admissions				
Ticket sales	$10 000.00	$8 648.16	–	$8 477.00
Lunch	$3 437.50	$2 826.25	–	$2 176.00
Ads in Program				
Full-page	$200.00	$200.00	–	$0.00
Half-page	$225.00	$90.00	–	$0.00
Quarter-page	$175.00	$0.00	–	$0.00
Upgrades	$500.00	$100.00	–	$0.00
Sponsorships				
Total sponsorship	–	$6 532.00	–	$4 835.00
Total Income	**$14 537.50**	**$18 396.41**	–	**$15 588.00**
Profit/Loss	**$1 994.26**	**$9 947.99**	–	**$8 416.34**

Source: Niagara Life Centre.

With the other NLC fundraising events each contributing about $20 000 to the organization, Sheryl's goal was to increase Homes of Distinction's revenues to match these events. Given how difficult it was to get sponsorships, Sheryl felt that either increasing the tour's ticket price or improving turnout would be instrumental in achieving this goal.

Sheryl was considering a number of ticket-pricing options. She could increase prices for the tour or create ticket packages: a tour and lunch package, or a tour and lunch package that included free do-it-yourself classes or even a limousine ride. She also considered a six-ticket package with free lunches, which real estate agents could give their clients.

To help increase the number of tour attendees, Sheryl felt she should focus on either boosting the primary market or targeting the secondary or tertiary market. She was also considering moving the tour closer to St. Catharines, which is the Niagara region's largest community.

PROMOTIONAL PLAN

Regardless of which revenue path she would take, Sheryl organized a promotional plan that included different channels the organization could use.

Direct Mail and Email

Sheryl looked at different direct mail and email methods to contact possible attendees prior to the tour. Direct mail might be used to send rack cards to past attendees who hadn't provided an email address. Volunteer lists and email addresses collected from previous home tours could be used to contact potential participants for the 2012 tour. Sheryl planned to send email notices two days after Labour Day, on October 1, about two days after Thanksgiving (mid-October), on November 1, and on November 15. She believed that giving people ample notice and keeping in constant communication would be vital for retaining the current customer base and growing it further. She also hoped to use this method to target different decorators and designers after getting possible contacts from a real estate agent.

Print and Radio Ads

Sheryl planned to place a quarter-page print ad in two local newspapers, *Niagara This Week* and *The Standard,* three weeks before the tour. Although she was unsure of pricing, she knew that, on average, a quarter-page ad costs anywhere from $300 to $500 per insertion. She also planned to place a quarter-page colour ad in local Niagara magazines, including *Niagara Magazine, Niagara Magazine Interiors, Niagara Weddings, Niagara Seasons,* and *Key to Niagara.* Given the high anticipated cost, she would consider a trade for sponsorship of the tour.

Radio advertising had been used for the 2010 tour, but in light of its high cost and its ineffectiveness (at least as indicated by the survey results), Sheryl wasn't interested in using this channel.

Telemarketing

Sheryl also considered using telemarketing as a method of increasing ticket sales. Not being able to add phone lines, she would use two volunteers at a time to make calls to local businesses, institutions, and individuals in an attempt to sell tour tickets. By emphasizing the fact that all proceeds went to the NLC, Sheryl felt this could be a viable way of increasing ticket sales.

Publicity

Sheryl had several ideas about how to get positive publicity in the local community. She considered contacting local television stations—including TV Cogeco (the local cable station) and CHCH Morning Live—to feature Homes of Distinction, but figured she'd be unlikely to get free airtime. She could also post information on local newspapers' event calendars to raise awareness for the tour. Lastly, she could send local newspapers a series of press releases: as soon as she secured houses for the 2012 tour, when new photos of houses became available, when designers and decorators were secured, and again just a few weeks prior to the event.

Website and Social Media

Sheryl planned to add a link to Facebook and Twitter on the tour's website. She also planned to add to the site the new Official Tour Guide; a link to Google Maps, which would have all the home addresses on it; a listing of the home addresses, which had appeared only in the Guide; and a link for sponsorship opportunities.

SHERYL'S DECISION

As Sheryl sat down to review what she had to accomplish, she began to consider her options. She could raise prices for either the tickets or the luncheon. In either case she'd need to provide greater value, possibly by adding another component to the tour, although she wasn't sure what that could be. Maybe she could devise some sort of contest to spark interest among potential participants. Aside from raising prices or changing events, Sheryl knew she should consider whether she was targeting the right market, or if there were additional opportunities targeting other markets. She needed to bring a budget of some sort to the committee for their review and approval, and to do that she'd need to consider what types of expenses would be necessary in order to implement whatever strategy she proposed. Sheryl closed her eyes for a moment to help focus her thinking. She knew that Homes of Distinction would ultimately have to raise $20 000 or more if it were to be successful and bring in the support needed by the centre. As she sorted through her notes once more, she knew that she had to present a coherent plan to the committee at its next meeting just a few weeks away.

Trinity University: The Annual Fund Campaign

H. F. (Herb) MacKenzie and
Mariya Yurukova

In February 2012, Mariya Yurukova was preparing for the pre-launch of the Trinity University Annual Fund Campaign. She'd just received a visit from Ben Adamson, associate vice-president of Development, who'd said they needed more revenue for the coming year as the university was committed to offering 20 new entrance scholarships for students from foreign universities. It was Trinity's first attempt to target foreign students; in previous years, not many of these students had chosen the university. "Mariya, the president has set a new target of $600 000 for next year's annual campaign. It's not that much more than last year, but it is an increase. I need you to think how we can reach that target, and I need suggestions for specific promotions or events we can use. My personal goal for capital fundraising has been increased from $4 million to $5 million, and I don't think I'll have much time to get involved with the campaign this coming year. So I'll have to put all the responsibility on you. Fortunately, I think you're capable and I'm glad I have you to manage this for us."

"Do I get any more resources?" Mariya asked.

"I wish I could say yes, but we have serious resource constraints, as you know. Every other area in the university has had to reduce their budget for next year. We escaped any cuts because the president recognizes how important it is for us to bring in revenue. In fact, he commented in our last meeting that it was time we focused more on the long term. We need to begin now to put things in place so that the university gets more self-funding for scholarships, student activities, and to support the research activities of our younger scholars. Our needs continually grow, and our funds are continually cut."

There was a pause. "Oh well," Mariya said finally. "Even if we could get more money, the real issue is finding and training quality telefundraisers—and managing our current space and hardware is already a challenge. There just isn't space for expansion, and our phones and computers are used pretty much to capacity."

Undaunted, Ben continued. "I have to present a plan at the next senior administration meeting a week from today, so I'm hoping you can give this some serious thought and pass on your recommendations so that I can make a solid presentation. We need to either show how it can be done or have a very compelling story outlining why it's impossible. As I see it, there are only two things to consider. First, we need to look more closely at who we're contacting, and maybe be a bit more strategic about it. Second, we need to think about other channels through which we can contact prospects. Maybe we can improve our efficiency by using alternatives to telefundraising. You're a lot closer to the data than I am, and I trust your judgment and respect your creativity. Can we meet late Thursday to discuss what we should do next? That'll give me Friday and the weekend to prepare my final presentation."

"I'll certainly have something for you on Thursday," Mariya promised, "assuming I don't get too many interruptions over the next three days." Ben assured Mariya that she wouldn't, and the meeting ended as Ben retreated from Mariya's office.

THE FUNDRAISING INDUSTRY

Canada had more than 85 000 registered charities in 2011. They varied in focus (health care, education, religious organizations, etc.) and in scope (local, national, international). Most charities in Canada use a variety of fundraising channels: telemarketing, direct marketing, e-solicitation, events (e.g., walk-a-thons, golf tournaments), lotteries, text-message solicitation, canvassing (door to door), and grocery store checkout campaigns. Some charities use revenue from donations to offset administrative costs, while others receive government funding or funding from organizations for which they fundraise. For example, a hospital foundation could be subsidized by the hospital, with all donations going to the cause at hand, while an anti-poverty agency, such as World Vision, could withhold a percentage of every dollar received for administrative and fundraising costs. While there is no set standard, given the large variety of charities and fundraising channels, it's generally agreed that no more than 40% percent of donation dollars gets allocated to administrative costs.

Most charities rely on basic demographic information to conduct their solicitations—address, phone number/email address, age, and, in some cases, gender. Education-based charities like colleges and universities can frequently paint a more comprehensive picture of their potential donors, including the aforementioned demographics along with education (degree program, class, and graduation year), employment, and marital status. All this information is frequently available for segmenting their alumni base, although usually not for every prospect in their database.

TRINITY UNIVERSITY

Trinity University is one of Canada's newest universities. Originally a college, it was granted university status within the past decade. Since then it has grown rapidly, adding many new undergraduate programs. It remains an undergraduate university, but there is now talk of starting one or more master's programs. About 60% of its students have graduated since the institution got its university status. The first graduating class with over 500 students was in 2003, the first with over 750 students was in 2008, and the first with over 1000 students was in 2011. Trinity has expanded its degrees and programs, and now 6602 of its 11 011 students have graduated since it was granted university status (Exhibit 1). Within the last three years 26% of total students have graduated, representing 43.5% of those who hold a Trinity University degree.

EXHIBIT 1	Alumni by Graduation Year and Faculty						
Class	Total Alumni	Applied Health Sciences	Business	Education	Humanities	Math and Science	Social Sciences
Trinity University	4 409						
2003	502	81	163	0	0	181	77
2004	519	88	158	0	12	178	83
2005	559	93	145	24	34	164	99
2006	658	112	172	46	60	176	92
2007	709	120	179	50	66	190	104
2008	782	134	194	58	68	208	120
2009	901	156	230	59	78	242	136
2010	968	166	241	68	75	263	155
2011	1004	172	252	79	84	259	158
Total	**11 011**	**1 122**	**1 734**	**384**	**477**	**1 861**	**1 024**

THE ANNUAL FUND CAMPAIGN

The Annual Fund campaign was established in 2009 as an outbound call centre, formerly known as CallGrad. In its first year it solicited parents of current Trinity students, and after 2010 it took over the entire "family campaign" (faculty, staff, and retirees). However, the primary target market for the Annual Fund was the university's alumni. In 2011 a concerted effort was made to improve the information in the alumni database and to maintain contact with alumni through a number of communications vehicles. The Annual Fund's mission statement remains focused on generating revenue for Trinity University, creating and maintaining a positive image among Trinity alumni, and serving as the primary connection between the university and its alumni. The fund is part of the Alumni Relations' portfolio, which in turn is part of University Advancement, along with Development and Donor Relations and Marketing Communications.

The Annual Fund employs one full-time employee, Mariya, and about six part-time student employees (callers). In 2010–2011 the fund received $427 000 in donations, about a 23% increase over the previous year. Telefundraising (gifts under $200 solicited by phone) brought in $135 400; direct marketing brought in $8900; online soliciting raised an additional $7700; the leadership gifts officer (who focused on gifts between $200 and $500) brought in $192 600; and the balance was contributed by faculty, staff, and un-solicited donations. Telefundraising contacted a total of 1800 prospects—approximately 80% of whom were alumni and 20% parents of Trinity students. Because direct marketing had been unable to demonstrate an acceptable ROI, resources had earlier shifted to tele-fundraising; however, with telefundraising resources at a fixed level, Mariya felt that she should still consider direct mail as a channel. Low-cost online solicitation had been con-ducted for the first time in 2011, but with modest success and mainly among previous donors ($7700).

Historically, the Annual Fund had segmented the alumni base in two basic ways: by faculty and by giving history. The resulting segments could include, for example, Faculty of Business donors (those who contributed the previous year), lapsed donors (those who contributed in the past but not during the previous year), and non-donors (those who have never contributed). Similar donor profiles were created for all other faculties. This seg-mentation allowed targeted solicitation based on affinity (e.g., Faculty of Business alumni would be asked to donate to the Faculty of Business Scholarship Fund). But in recent years the Annual Fund had been mandated to raise unrestricted funds for the area of greatest need. In other words, these funds could be used for any given faculty, or for such non-faculty uses as student entrance scholarships or the Trinity University library. Therefore, in 2010, the target markets were determined based on previous giving history and by grad-uation year (e.g., milestone anniversaries marking 5 or 10 years since graduation, etc.). The Annual Fund telesolicitors had not yet contacted any graduates within three years of their graduation. Unfortunately, this three-year gap allowed contact information to become outdated, making it more difficult to reach individuals when their three-year anniversary arrived. It also meant a lost opportunity to engage with potential donors for a considerable time after their graduation.

SEGMENTATION

Mariya Yurukova began contemplating the segmentation of the alumni base. Her main issue was the more than 3000 young alumni who'd never been solicited by the Annual Fund. Contacting them through telesoliciting wouldn't be possible, given her constraints, but even if she could contact them she wasn't sure the results would be encouraging. Based on historical attempts to contact recent graduates, she was able to find the following statis-tics: 30% would have moved, 30% wouldn't pick up the phone, 5% would still be attend-ing school (post-graduate or second degree), 3.5% would donate an average $69 regardless of the channel, and the rest would simply say no. The key to success would be to get to the coveted 3.5% without wasting too much of her limited resources. Mariya started thinking about how she could narrow down the focus on these would-be donors.

Segmentation by Graduation Year

One possibility was to segment by graduation year, which would split the database into equal sets of between 500 and 1000 students. Mariya could zero in on those most likely to donate based on how long it had been since they graduated, since of course those who'd graduated in more recent years may still be looking for long-term job placements and career paths. This method would be easy to execute and would allow for easy comparison among graduation classes. But although it would provide equal coverage of all alumni within each targeted segment, it would also require some general assumptions about demographics and common interests, which may not be totally valid. Still, focusing on students within particular graduation years would help achieve one of the longer-term goals of the Annual Fund: to update contact information and keep alumni involved. But, Mariya realized, not everyone within a graduation year has an equal likelihood of donating; therefore, considerable resources could be spent on individuals with a lower likelihood of donating. This would decrease overall revenue.

Segmentation by Faculty

Upon careful examination of her donor pool, Mariya noticed that the likelihood of donating differed greatly among alumni from the six faculties (see Exhibit 2). Graduates from different programs follow different career paths, and their desire and ability to donate seems related to the type of degree they have. For example, science graduates take longer to find jobs immediately after graduation; many choose to pursue more education (e.g., medical school), or at least continue in a post-graduate program. But once they get established in their careers, they're more likely to contribute back to their alma mater, often with larger than average donations.

EXHIBIT 2	Donations by Faculty					
All Donors	Applied Health Science	Business	Education	Humanities	Math and Science	Social Sciences
Contact rate	23%	36%	29%	41%	37%	44%
Promise rate	21%	26%	21%	23%	26%	21%
Average donation	$83.00	$104.00	$84.00	$101.00	$101.00	$84.00
First-time Donors	17%	23%	22%	10%	7%	21%
Contact rate	16%	22%	21%	40%	30%	35%
Promise rate	8%	6%	7%	6%	8%	5%
Average donation	$61.22	$73.79	$66.94	$40.12	$69.00	$59.43

Segmentation by Extra-Curricular Involvement

Mariya also thought about using more creative ways to segment the pool. Based on university mandate and studies from other universities, it was generally understood that students who were involved with the school would be most likely to give back after graduation. Therefore, she could establish a pool of those who'd been part of a club, had an on-campus job, or were part of the Residence Action Council (RAC), and prioritize this group to be contacted first. But after analyzing the database, results showed that the university hadn't been keeping an accurate record of student involvement; it had data for only 500 alumni from the 2008–2010 classes who'd been actively involved as students. Nevertheless, the Annual Fund coordinator favoured this segment to outperform any others.

Segmentation Based on Trinity University Involvement

Based on previous results and studies, Mariya considered as her next priority segment those alumni who had proactively provided Trinity with email addresses and employment information. Alumni who remembered to update Trinity in this way would be presumably more likely to have remained involved with the university and to donate to it. But since many of the young alumni pool (graduating classes 2009–2011) had been out of touch with the university, information on involvement was scarce. Moreover, by not contacting a fair representation of each graduation year, the Annual Fund would miss out on acquiring new contact and employment information for future years.

FUNDRAISING CHANNELS

Mariya realized that contacting alumni had to be done strategically, using a combination of solicitation channels to ensure coverage yet minimize expenses. She considered these various channels.

Direct Mail

Direct marketing (mail) is one of the oldest, most established fundraising strategies. It involves writing a letter, usually from a highly recognized and respected individual, which outlines the case for supporting a particular cause and includes a response device that can be used to mail in a donation. Mariya estimated the average cost of a direct-mail piece at about $0.88 each, based on outgoing postage, a printed letter on Trinity letterhead, a response card that could be returned with a donation, and an addressed return envelope. Data available from non-university samples indicated that response rates varied based on the segment targeted. Direct mail had been highly effective with older people who aren't tech-savvy and who allocate a great deal of time to sorting mail. It's also popular with regular small donors ($25–$50) who tend to donate to several charities. Even with a highly responsive segment, direct-mail responses rarely exceed 5%, and the average donation is slightly lower than that of other solicitation channels, like online giving and telefundraising.

Mariya considered using this channel to target specific alumni. For example, she could send direct-mail packages to previous donors, inviting them to donate to the fund as they previously had. She'd have to develop both a subject line and a cover solicitation letter and calculate both the cost and the expected return. Mariya believed that if she could strategically use direct mail, she might be able to get larger donations and a reasonable response rate.

Telefundraising

Next, Mariya considered her favourite method of solicitation: telefundraising. It was highly personalized, effective, but also costly. The first university campaign of this kind was conducted in the United States in 1985. Telefundraising, just like telemarketing, relies on sales techniques such as persuasion to generate revenue. It's a costly endeavour, as it involves paid time for numerous employees, and it can be volatile in its outcomes and timing (e.g., the Stanley Cup playoff games are guaranteed to create a lack of engagement by—and even adverse reaction from—fans when their game is interrupted). Depending on the efficiency of the program, it could cost $5.20 to contact one person. Response rates vary greatly based on segment: between 5 and 10% for low-likelihood segments and 60 to 80% for high-likelihood segments. The average donation is much greater than received from direct mail, though; it can reach $100 or more. This channel is suited for younger people, especially those who have a family and own their own home. It can serve many purposes at once (solicit donations, promote events, sell tickets, update contact and employment information, etc.).

The effectiveness of telesoliciting depends very much on having an up-to-date list of phone numbers. With young alumni, this is especially challenging, as this segment is highly mobile and prefers using cell phones, which of course aren't included in regular phone listings. Many calls are bound to be unanswered, or answered by someone other than their intended recipient. At $5.20 per call Mariya had to use this approach very strategically, as the cost could really snowball if calls were left unanswered or the telesolicitor wasn't sufficiently persuasive. She'd need to create a specific promotion to encourage alumni to contribute to the Annual Fund. For example, she could entice individuals to donate a sum of money corresponding with their final year as a way of honouring their graduation (e.g., an alumnus who graduated in 2011 would be asked to donate $20.11).

Online Solicitation

Finally, Mariya considered the least expensive option of all: online solicitation. The percentage of online donation revenues varies greatly depending on the purpose, or industry, of the soliciting organization (see Exhibit 3). Online fundraising is a fairly recent phenomenon, coinciding with the popularity of social networks like Facebook. It's quickly gaining popularity, as it's inexpensive and therefore demonstrates a high return on resources employed. It's successful with 25- to 34-year-olds, and recent studies show that it can have tremendous impact on revenue. Event planners have recently concluded that a "like" on a Facebook fan page could translate into $1.84 in ticket sales revenue. However, it's also non-invasive and a less engaging tool, which makes it easy to ignore. Given that the average time spent reading a solicitation email is under 30 seconds, a tremendous marketing effort is needed to ensure that information is communicated in a concise yet persuasive manner. Response rates to online solicitation are similar to those for direct mail, yet average donations tend to be much higher. Much like direct mail and telefundraising, online fundraising is restricted in its reach primarily to those who want to be involved (i.e., those who are your fans on Facebook). Going forward with this channel, Mariya realized, meant she'd have to come up with an effective subject line and message to include in the emails sent out to alumni and parents.

The Annual Fund had about 2000 available email addresses for all alumni and 400 Facebook fans (many of whom could also be part of the 2000 email addresses). About 50% of the email addresses belonged to young alumni, and 35% of the Facebook fans were 25 to 34 years old. As a way of capitalizing on these fans, Mariya also considered sending them a Facebook message, which would be similar to a solicitation email, asking them to donate to the Annual Fund. Mariya felt that she'd have to craft this message carefully, as she'd be targeting a predominantly younger market.

EXHIBIT 3	Percentage of Total Fundraising Revenue from Online Giving
Sector	Percentage
Education	3%
Arts, Culture, and Humanities	5%
Environment and Animals	10%
Public/Social Benefit	12%
Entertainment	14%
Health	15%
International Affairs	16%
Human Services	25%

THE DECISION

Mariya knew she had a considerable challenge. She was working with only a fraction of the information she wished she had concerning potential donors. Because fundraising was a new initiative for Trinity University, the graduate database was far from complete, and information was frequently missing even for those who were in the database. While Mariya had been trying to improve the database for the past few years, she realized that going forward, this would be important: she'd have to address the issue and present a strategy for improving it in the future. In fact, she thought, this might be the most important contribution she could make—and Ben would likely be pleased if she had a plan he could present to senior administration. Still, the short term required that she create a plan to raise funds in the coming year, as the Annual Fund Campaign would soon have to be rolled out. Ben would expect her to be as explicit and detailed as possible about the promotional ideas she'd recommend and the messages she'd send through each contact medium she chose.

Canadian Defence Production Ltd.

H. F. (Herb) MacKenzie

Stewart MacIsaac was excited when he got the unexpected phone call from Jim Greeley, a senior buyer for Canadian Defence Production Ltd. in Halifax.

"I know it's been a year since we bought that prototype reel from you," Jim began, "but we just got a contract from the Canadian government to build 10 more bear traps and we desperately need to hold our price on these units. Could you possibly sell us 10 new reels at the same price you charged last year?"

"I'll see what I can do and call you back today," Stewart replied.

Once he'd retrieved the previous year's file, he saw that he'd supplied the reel for $10 863 F.O.B. the customer's warehouse. Exhibit 1 shows a breakdown of the pricing in Stewart's file.

Then Stewart reviewed his notes in the file. The reel was designed as part of a "bear trap" on Canadian navy ships. These bear traps would hook onto helicopters in rough weather and haul them safely onto landing pads on the ship decks. The reel was really a model SM heavy-duty steel mill reel, except that some of the exposed parts were made of stainless steel to provide a longer life in the salt-water atmosphere. A special engineering charge was added to the cost of the reel, as it was a nonstandard item that had to be specially engineered. The

EXHIBIT 1	Pricing for the Special Gleason Heavy Duty SM Reel
Manufacturer's list price	$5 000.00
Special engineering charge (25%)	1 250.00
Total list price	6 250.00
Distributor discount (20%)	1 250.00
Distributor net cost	5 000.00
Estimated currency exchange (36.5%)	1 825.00
Estimated duty (22.5%)	1 535.63
Estimated freight	255.00
Estimated brokerage	75.00
Estimated distributor cost, F.O.B. Halifax	8 690.63
Markup (25%)	2 172.66
Selling price, F.O.B. destination	$10 863.29

manufacturer—Gleason Reel (www.hubbell-gleason.com)—had suggested at the time it quoted that Stewart could keep the full 20% discount, since it thought that only one other manufacturer was capable of building the unit, and that its price would likely be much higher.

Stewart contacted the manufacturer about the 10 new units, and was surprised when it quoted a price of only $4000 each, less 40/10%. When he asked for the price to be verified, the order desk clarified: first, there'd been a 20% reduction on all SM series reels, accounting for the $4000; and second, given the large quantity, the distributor discount was increased to less 40/10% instead of the 20% given on the original reel.

As Stewart estimated his cost, things got even better. The original reel was imported from the United States at 22.5% duty, as "not otherwise provided for manufacturers of iron or steel, tariff item 44603-1." But in the interim, the company Stewart worked for got a duty remission on series SM steel mill reels as "machinery of a class or kind not manufactured in Canada, tariff item 42700-1," with the savings supposedly passed on to the end customer. The currency exchange rate had also improved in Stewart's favour, and the estimated freight and brokerage charges per unit had dropped considerably because of the increased shipment size. Stewart estimated his new cost as shown in Exhibit 2.

Now that he had all the figures, Stewart had to decide what selling price he would quote to Jim Greeley.

EXHIBIT 2	Updated Pricing for the Gleason Special Heavy Duty SM Reel
Manufacturer's list price	$4 000.00
Distributor discount (40/10%)	1 840.00
Distributor net cost	2 160.00
Estimated currency exchange (1.5%)	32.40
Estimated duty (remitted)	00.00
Estimated freight	90.00
Estimated brokerage	15.00
Estimated distributor cost, F.O.B. Halifax	$2 297.40

Seeing Clearly: Lucentis and Avastin

Eric Dolansky

Dr. Clyde Reed finished reading the newspaper article his friend had sent him. His mother had recently been diagnosed with wet age-related macular degeneration (AMD). Clyde was an anesthesiologist, not an eye doctor, but he always tried to help his family with their medical concerns. His mother's doctor had recommended a drug called Lucentis, which was fully covered by government health care. He trusted his mother's doctor, but wanted to double-check her options himself, so he contacted an old friend from medical school who was now an ophthalmologist and asked about the diagnosis. Apparently there was some controversy around treatment for wet AMD, and the eye doctor had sent Dr. Reed the newspaper article to fill him in on what had been going on.

The *Globe and Mail* article his friend sent, "Why Is a $1575-a-Month Drug Approved and a $7 One Isn't?," [1] alerted Clyde to the idea that there may be more to his mother's treatment decision than he'd originally thought. The article was about Genentech, a pharmaceutical company that sold two very similar drugs for very different

---

[1]Picard, A. (2011, September 26). Why is a $1575-a-month drug approved and a $7 one isn't? *The Globe and Mail.*

prices (through its parent company, Roche, and its international subsidiaries, e.g., Novartis in Canada).[2] One of these drugs, Lucentis, was designed to treat wet AMD; the other, Avastin, was approved for use as a cancer-fighting drug but was often used to combat AMD as well. The problem arose from the difference in price, alluded to in the title of the article. Avastin, which wasn't covered by government health plans nor officially approved for use in the eye, was about $7 per monthly dose. Lucentis was $1575 per month, a cost covered by government health care. In April 2011 a report commissioned by the National Institutes of Health in the United States presented results of a year-long study indicating that the two drugs were equally effective in fighting AMD.

Clyde contemplated what might be his best course of action. He dealt with pharmaceutical companies all the time, so the high pricing didn't really surprise him. These companies invested a great deal of money in the research and development of new drugs, many of which never see the light of day. Those drugs that do make it to market had to earn huge profits in order to fund all the new development. Clyde had also seen first-hand the strain Canada's health care system was under, so he figured $7 per month wasn't too much to pay for his mother's treatment if it meant more than 200 times as much could be used for other patients and problems. But was Avastin the right choice? Was it truly as safe as Lucentis, or was the price indicating otherwise? Clyde began researching this disease and its treatment on the web, trying to get as much information as possible to make an informed, logical decision.

AGE-RELATED MACULAR DEGENERATION

AMD is a relatively common eye disease that tends to emerge late in life. It reduces the ability to see detail, and left untreated leads to blindness. The disease affects the macula, the part of the eye responsible for seeing fine details in one's central vision. It affects about 30% of people over the age of 75 (and about 2% of middle-aged people),[3] with approximately 200 000 new cases each year.[4] There are two forms of AMD, wet and dry. Dry AMD accounts for 85 to 90% of all AMD cases,[5] and tends to advance gradually. It's caused by yellowish deposits called drusen growing under the retina, which in turn causes vision to blur. A greater number of drusen, or larger drusen, lead to a breakdown of the light-sensitive cells of the retina, which causes blindness.

Wet AMD advances much more quickly. Instead of deposits, extra blood vessels grow behind the macula. These blood vessels break easily, resulting in blood leaking behind the eye, which displaces and damages the macula.[6] Swift treatment is necessary to prevent total vision loss. Wet AMD occurs more often among those who are overweight or obese, those who smoke, and those who have a family history of the disease.[7] Women are more

---

[2]Novartis declined the opportunity to participate in the writing of this business case.
[3]National Eye Institute (2009, September). Facts about age-related macular degeneration. www.nei.nih.gov/health /maculardegen/armd_facts.asp
[4]Haddrill, M. (2011, May). Lucentis vs. Avastin: A macular degeneration treatment controversy. www.allaboutvision.com
[5]National Eye Institute (2009, September). Facts about age-related macular degeneration. www.nei.nih.gov/health /maculardegen/armd_facts.asp
[6]Ibid.
[7]Ibid.

likely to develop AMD, as are Caucasians.[8] The disease is detected through a dilated eye exam, a visual acuity test, and/or a tonometric test (which measures the pressure in the eye), and can be diagnosed through the results of these tests.[9]

There are three basic treatment options for wet or dry AMD: laser surgery, photo-dynamic therapy, and drug injections. Laser treatment, also called photocoagulation, involves firing a laser into the eye to destroy the leaky blood vessels behind the macula. This treatment is rarely used because it doesn't prevent further development of the disease and the treatment itself causes damage to the eye.[10] During the surgery the laser needs to pass through the retina, damaging it and creating a blind spot in the patient's central vision.[11]

Photodynamic therapy also involves the use of a laser into the eye, but it uses a "cool" laser and therefore doesn't damage the retina. Light-activated drugs are injected into the patient's bloodstream and collect in the new blood vessels behind the macula. When exposed to the cool laser, the drugs activate and destroy those blood vessels.[12] This treatment can stabilize vision, but it often destroys only the existing blood vessels and doesn't prevent the growth of new ones.

The third treatment available for wet AMD is the injection of drugs into the eye. Earlier drugs, such as Macugen (manufactured and sold by Eyetech Inc., an independent pharmaceutical company), had been effective in inhibiting further blood vessel growth and slowing vision loss. Macugen, however, didn't destroy the existing vessels, nor did it restore lost vision. A more recent drug, Lucentis, did just that: 40% of patients reported improved vision after using Lucentis. It also prevented further vision loss in 95% of patients.[13]

GENENTECH AND LUCENTIS

Lucentis (which is the brand name—the generic name is Ranibizumab) was introduced in 2006 by Genentech, a San Francisco–based subsidiary of the global Roche Group of pharmaceutical companies. According to Genentech's website,[14] its positioning and role is as follows:

> Considered the founder of the biotechnology industry, Genentech has been delivering on the promise of biotechnology for more than 30 years, using human genetic information to discover, develop, manufacture and commercialize medicines to treat patients with serious or life-threatening medical conditions. Today, Genentech is among the world's leading biotech companies, with multiple products on the market and a promising development pipeline.

Genentech defines its corporate mission in this way:

> Our aim as a leading healthcare company is to create, produce and market innovative solutions of high quality for unmet medical needs. Our products and services help to prevent, diagnose and

---

[8]Ibid.
[9]Ibid.
[10]Canadian National Institute for the Blind (2009). Treatments for wet AMD. www.cnib.ca/en/your-eyes/eye-conditions/amd/treatment/treatment-wet
[11]Ibid.
[12]Ibid.
[13]Ibid.
[14]Genentech (current as of 2012). Company mission and goals. www.gene.com

treat diseases, thus enhancing people's health and quality of life. We do this in a responsible and ethical manner and with a commitment to sustainable development, respecting the needs of the individual, the society and the environment.

Genentech claims three core values: integrity (defined as "being consistently open, honest, ethical and genuine"), courage (to be "entrepreneurial, and thus take risks, reach beyond boundaries and experiment"), and passion ("using drive and commitment to energize and inspire others"). Lucentis was one of a string of successful drugs that Genentech had introduced.

One benefit of Lucentis was the low incidence of side effects. Treatment using Lucentis involved injections of the drug through the white of the eye into the central cavity. Over 100 000 people in North America had been treated using Lucentis in its first five years on the market, and according to the Lucentis website,[15] over 90% of these patients had their vision stabilize or improve. The drug cost $1575 per month (in Canada—reported costs in the United States are as high as $2000 per month), with a typical treatment period lasting two years.[16] In Canada the drug is fully covered through government-funded health care programs in every province,[17] and in the United States the drug is covered by Medicare (with a 20% co-payment by the patient).[18]

AVASTIN

Another drug introduced by Genentech was Avastin (generic name Bevacizumab). The drug was initially approved for use for metastatic cancers (cancers that spread from one organ to another). The initial approval in 2004 was for treatment of colon cancer, with later approvals in 2006 (lung cancer) and 2008 (breast cancer). Like Lucentis, Avastin was developed from a genetically engineered mouse antibody. Also like Lucentis, it was designed to prevent the growth of abnormal blood vessels, in this case the vessels that grew to feed blood to tumours.[19]

Avastin was not without controversy. Its approval for use as a breast cancer drug was revoked in 2010 in both the United States and Canada. According to the Food and Drug Administration (FDA), although the drug was effective in fighting the tumours, there was no evidence that it extended or improved life.[20] Because of the possibility of such side effects as hypertension (high blood pressure), hemorrhaging, and bowel perforation, the lack of clear benefits caused the drug to lose its approval. This didn't mean the drug couldn't be sold; it could be prescribed "off-label," meaning not for its initial intended use. Without an FDA approval, however, neither insurance companies nor Medicare would reimburse use of the drug in the United States.[21] In Canada the cost of the drug was no longer reimbursed for use in fighting breast cancer.[22] Avastin was, however, still considered

---

[15]Genentech (2012). About Lucentis. www.lucentis.com
[16]Picard, 2011.
[17]Ibid.
[18]Haddrill, 2011.
[19]Genentech (2012). How Avastin is designed to work. www.avastin.com
[20]Pollack, A. (2011, November 18). FDA revokes approval of Avastin for use as a breast cancer drug. *New York Times.*
[21]Ibid.
[22]The Canadian Press (2011, November 18). Avastin approval for breast cancer pulled.

useful for treatment of other forms of cancer, though it had fallen from a leadership position among cancer drugs, losing 15% market share in the United States and 8% worldwide in 2010. The drug that overtook Avastin as market leader was Rituxan, also produced and distributed internationally by the Roche Group.

AVASTIN AS TREATMENT FOR WET AMD

Because of the molecular similarity between Avastin and Lucentis (the molecules were nearly identical, with those of Avastin a bit larger than those of Lucentis), some eye doctors began using Avastin to treat wet AMD as early as 2006.[23] Not only was Avastin believed to be effective in treating wet AMD, it was far less expensive. One eye injection of Avastin cost $150 in the U.S. (with a $50 reimbursement from Medicare, though this was suspended briefly in 2010 and then reinstated[24]) and $7 in Canada.[25]

Use of Avastin to treat wet AMD is relatively safe. Because of the low dosages involved and because the drug was injected directly into the eye (and not into the bloodstream), chances of side effects such as hypertension and hemorrhaging are low. The biggest potential risk that Avastin poses to patients is in its handling and distribution. Because of its primary and approved use as a cancer drug, Genentech and its distributors (such as Novartis) sold Avastin only in vials of 100 to 400 milligrams, and a typical dose for eye injection was only 1.25 milligrams. This made it difficult for eye doctors to safely use Avastin.[26] When handled by compounding pharmacies, which take large quantities of a drug and parcel out dosages in a safe and sterile way, the risk of infection is sharply reduced. However, it would be unsafe for doctors or non-compounding pharmacies to divide the Avastin themselves or repeatedly inject patients from the same vial, and would increase the probability of infecting the patient's eye.

In 2007, to counter off-label use of Avastin, Genentech stopped selling it to compounding pharmacies. As a result, use of Avastin for AMD dropped, while at the same time eye infections from Avastin use rose. Ophthalmologists (eye doctors) protested this decision, and the American Academy of Ophthalmologists appealed to Genentech to reverse it. The International Academy of Compounding Pharmacists publicly doubted the reasoning behind Genentech's move, claiming that it was profit-motivated[27] and not intended to ensure patients' safety.

Under pressure, Genentech did reverse its decision, and announced that Avastin would be sent to any eye doctors who wanted it as well as to compounding pharmacies. The company stood by its reasoning that safety was a concern, and that Lucentis was the proper drug to treat wet AMD. Genentech has a hardship program to help those who can't afford the drug explore other payment options. According to the company website, it had given away $2.3 billion in free medicine since 1985, offered a co-pay program for insured patients who couldn't afford their co-payments, and provided an access program for the uninsured.

---

[23]Haddrill, 2011.
[24]Ibid.
[25]Picard, 2011.
[26]Ibid.
[27]Haddrill, 2011.

MARKET SITUATION

Off-label use of Avastin for wet AMD had continued since 2006. As of 2010, 220 000 people had wet AMD, requiring approximately 1.64 million dosages of drugs per year to fight it. In 2010, 700 000 of these doses were Lucentis and the rest were Avastin.[28] Avastin was more popular in the United States than in Canada because of the out-of-pocket costs involved (the patient paid about 20% of the cost of Lucentis, or $400, versus $100 net for Avastin, both per month).[29] The health-regulating bodies in Canada and the United States still hadn't approved Avastin for wet AMD use, with the exception of the provincial health agencies in British Columbia and Nova Scotia,[30] so it was still an off-label use.

One reason why Avastin hadn't been approved for use in fighting wet AMD was that Genentech hadn't applied for approval of the drug for this purpose. Genentech maintained that use of Avastin for this disease wasn't the safest option, and continued to package Avastin in the large quantities intended for cancer treatment. While some decried the company's action as profiteering at the expense of patients and taxpayers, others, such as the Canadian Council for the Blind, supported Genentech's position.[31] It was believed that if Avastin were approved and used exclusively (with no use of Lucentis), Medicare in the United States would have saved $1 billion annually (with Canadian provincial governments collectively saving 10% of that amount).[32]

In April 2011 an article published in the *New England Journal of Medicine* (and requested and funded by the National Institutes of Health in the United States) reported the results of a year-long study comparing the safety of Avastin and Lucentis across 1185 patients. The general conclusion was that they were equally safe and effective in treating wet AMD.[33] Incidences of death, heart attacks, and strokes were low and the same regardless of which drug was used. The only difference of note was that 24% of those patients using Avastin were hospitalized during the year, as opposed to only 19% of those given Lucentis.[34] These hospitalizations were for several reasons, not just eye-related concerns. There was no direct evidence that this difference was due to the drug they were given.

Genentech and Roche also funded their own study. This study, which involved examining the archived records of 78 000 Medicare recipients, found that those patients who received Avastin were 11% more likely to die, 57% more likely to suffer a stroke, and 80% more likely to have further eye problems.[35]

Toward the end of 2011, Genentech settled a lawsuit with rival Regeneron. Genentech had previously sued Regeneron for patent infringement over its eye drug Eylea, which was identical to Lucentis. Under the terms of the deal, Regeneron would pay a penalty of $60 million as a licensing fee and royalties of 4.75 to 5.5% (depending on Eylea sales volume).[36]

---

[28]Ibid.
[29]Haddrill, 2011.
[30]Picard, 2011.
[31]Ibid.
[32]Ibid.
[33]*National Institutes of Health News* (2011, April 28). NIH study finds Avastin and Lucentis are equally effective in treating age-related macular degeneration.
[34]Ibid.
[35]Silverman, E. (2011, May 3). All Eyes Are on Roche, Lucentis, and Avastin. www.pharmalot.com
[36]Migliore, L. (2012, January 3). Regeneron Reaches Partial Deal with Roche, Firm to Pay Rival Royalties on U.S. Sales of Eylea. *Toronto Star.*

TREATMENT DECISION

Clyde had now read all the information he could obtain from the internet on the topics of AMD, Genentech and its drugs, and the history of this situation. One comment from one of the articles stood out:

> "Is it fair that Genentech should lose out? What of the patients (or countries) who cannot afford Lucentis? Is it fair that treatment be available only to those who are wealthy?"[37]

These questions were posed by British researchers in an article in a prominent ophthalmology journal. For Clyde, they underscored the two sides of this concern. In a sense, Genentech did what a business is supposed to do—maximize profit. For a pharmaceutical company, this also meant it could have the funds necessary to research new treatments for different problems. On the other hand, there was something about this that didn't seem proper, and Clyde wasn't sure he wanted to support Genentech and its associated companies by making the government pay a much higher price for his mother's treatment.

---

[37]Haddrill, 2011.

Bridge View Custom Cabinets

Michael Madore

Bridge View Custom Cabinets (BVCC) is a family-owned cabinet manufacturer in Lethbridge, Alberta, a small city with a population of about 85 000 in its urban core and an additional 200 000 in the surrounding region. BVCC has been operating for only two years, making it a relatively new competitor in the cabinet-making industry. Its name was chosen because of its connection with the community: the railway bridge that can be seen from the company's property is the largest of its kind in Canada.

In early spring 2012, Fred Ferber, co-owner of BVCC, approached Logan Michaels, owner of Maverick Marketing. "I'd like some advice from you, and I hope I can get it quickly," Fred began. "BVCC is growing considerably slower than I had anticipated, and I'm concerned that we're missing opportunities our competitors are getting. I know you have a good reputation for helping small businesses in the Lethbridge area, and that's why I'm turning to you for help. Can you do something for me in the next few weeks?"

Logan thought about it for a few minutes before committing. "Okay. I'm sure I can help. Let's discuss your current situation and I'll see what I can do from there."

CURRENT SITUATION

Bridge View Custom Cabinets is owned (solely by Fred) and operated by Fred and Wilma Ferber, both of whom are active in the company's day-to-day operations. Fred's main role is building, installing, and finishing custom cabinets. However, when he has extra time between jobs, which is rare, he also fills the role of company salesperson. Wilma is the office manager. She oversees all administrative processes, manages the company website, and develops computer-aided designs (CAD) for the cabinets the company produces. There's also one full-time salaried employee whose job is to assist in building the cabinets in the shop and then to help deliver, install, and finish them on site.

THE MARKET

The real estate market in Lethbridge has remained strong throughout the recession, but there's some concern about a potential residential-home glut. As Fred remarked, "Some of the major builders have a surplus of homes. I did a bit of digging myself and have learned that as many as several hundred homes from five major builders are currently unsold. This supply and demand situation could have some impact on BVCC—we may have to consider rethinking our marketing strategy."

Bridge View Custom Cabinets has been targeting multiple market segments: general contractors, individual homeowners (also known as do-it-yourselfers, or DIY), and commercial renovators (who work with both general contractors and individual homeowners). Starter homes tend to be bought by Generation Y; custom-built homes that usually have higher-end finishes tend to be bought by baby boomers and a small number from Generation X; and home renovators in the DIY market tend to be about equally divided between the baby boomers and Generation X.

In 2010—the last full year for which data are available—Lethbridge and its outlying area (about 20 kilometres around the city) issued 859 permits. The breakdown for these permits is provided in Exhibit 1.

BVCC's sales have so far been concentrated on homeowners and commercial renovators, and mainly in the city core.

EXHIBIT 1	Lethbridge and Area Building Permits, 2011
Type of Building Structure Permit	Number of Permits
City: new detached-home startups	366
City: duplex homes	42
City: residential alterations	289
Outlying area: new detached-home startups	85
Outlying area: duplex homes	12
Outlying area: residential alterations	65

THE COMPETITION

Six competitors, including BVCC, operate in the Lethbridge area. Most have been in business for 10 to 20 years, with the oldest one having been established in 1968. All competitors have a good reputation and a solid core of business. Over the years a few small cabinet manufacturers have tried to compete, but have been unsuccessful and subsequently gone bankrupt. These competitors all have one or more general contractors they work closely with, but they all compete very aggressively in the homeowner (DIY) segment.

Lethbridge has two major home-improvement stores: Home Depot and Totem. Both carry shelving units that they sell mainly to starter-home customers. Most of these customers are do-it-yourselfers.

THE PRODUCT

BVCC manufactures custom cabinets built to specifications for general contractors, home renovators, and DIY homeowners. It also refinishes cabinets, which may be done for any of these segments but is frequently initiated by homeowners as a single renovation project that may not include any additional work.

Generic-grade (low-end) cabinets are frequently made for general contractors who are building starter or lower-priced homes. Once BVCC has completed a computer-aided design, that design can be used multiple times to build identical cabinets for a particular general contractor. General contractors typically have several standard residential-home floor plans so that they can take a cookie-cutter approach to building these lower-end cabinets. Occasionally, general contractors will request a higher-end set of cabinets for what they want to showcase as a model home. These cabinets have the same design, since the home's floor plan is still standard, but the wood, the finish, and the cabinet hardware (hinges, pulls, etc.) are better quality.

Home renovators and do-it-yourselfers almost always need custom cabinets (whether lower or higher end), given that older or custom-designed homes have varying floor plans. Some customers simply want newer cabinets, and some want an upgrade or refinishing of their existing cabinets. Sometimes they get this done through a home renovator, and sometimes they themselves hire a cabinet manufacturer to refinish and repair their existing cabinets. BVCC has also focused somewhat on this business.

The great majority of cabinets have been for kitchens, but they're occasionally made for bathrooms, studies, or formal dining rooms.

LOCATION

Bridge View Custom Cabinets is in Lethbridge's industrial park, where most manufacturers and business-to-business (B2B) resellers are located. The company has only its address number (to the left of the entrance) and a sign with its name (on a small window). Clients come to BVCC for their initial meeting with Fred, or sometimes Fred will go to their location if appropriate. Clients normally meet with Fred and Wilma in the "front stage" of the shop. The store layout is illustrated in Exhibit 2. As shown, BVCC uses a typical servuction system design, whereby the front stage includes a reception area, a cabinet hardware

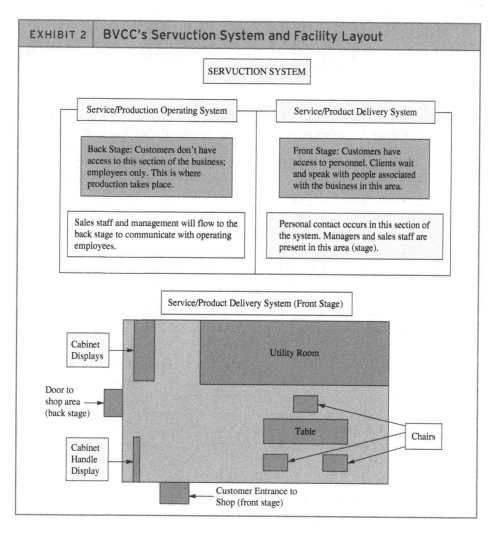

EXHIBIT 2 | BVCC's Servuction System and Facility Layout

SERVUCTION SYSTEM

Service/Production Operating System

Back Stage: Customers don't have access to this section of the business; employees only. This is where production takes place.

Sales staff and management will flow to the back stage to communicate with operating employees.

Service/Product Delivery System

Front Stage: Customers have access to personnel. Clients wait and speak with people associated with the business in this area.

Personal contact occurs in this section of the system. Managers and sales staff are present in this area (stage).

Service/Product Delivery System (Front Stage)

Cabinet Displays

Utility Room

Door to shop area (back stage)

Chairs

Table

Cabinet Handle Display

Customer Entrance to Shop (front stage)

display, and a small display area with some generic (low-end) cabinets. The rest of the floor space (or "back stage) is dedicated to manufacturing cabinets.

When customers enter the store reception area, a desk and chairs are positioned to their right. A computer monitor sits on the desk; this is where Wilma manages her administrative duties, answers the phone, and makes cabinet designs (CAD). Fred and the employee enter this area as well to gain access to the back stage. To the customer's left are the two displays: one of cabinet hardware (near the entrance, extending from floor to ceiling), and the other of generic cabinet models (farther along the wall, on the other side of the entrance to the back stage). The wall next to the desk has a minor-league hockey sweater and a picture of a local minor-league hockey team that BVCC has sponsored for the past two years.

Fred and Wilma try to keep the front-stage area clean and neat, but dust continually enters from the back stage, settling on the floor, the desk, and both displays. Fred also has a habit of leaving boxes of hardware in the area, before they're used in the manufacturing process.

PROMOTION

While Fred and Wilma know that BVCC needs to better manage promotion, they're unsure how to do so. To date, they've dabbled with a number of promotional activities:

- BVCC's website provides contact information, news about current operations and activities, a list of services the company provides, and a gallery of its manufacturing processes and some finished products. No external marketing of the website has been done, beyond including it on the company business cards. The site has never had any search engine optimization (SEO), nor has it been promoted in any other fashion online. And since the company's limited promotional literature was printed prior to getting a website, it's not included in any of this literature.

- Fred currently acts as salesperson for the company, on those rare occasions when he has time. He's been calling mainly on general contractors, hoping to establish a relationship with one or more of them so that he can get some volume production of a select few cabinet designs. But he doesn't like the selling process, and would rather be doing "important" work. Fred finds the overall sales process time-consuming and stressful. Between having to prospect, make appointments, prepare proposals, present, and follow up to see if he's landed the contract, Fred finds it far too tedious. He'd much rather have a hammer in his hand and sawdust on his work trousers.

- Fred sometimes meets with DIY customers, either when they visit the store or at their home if they prefer. He feels these sales meetings are less stressful, largely because DIY customers approach BVCC with a problem they've already identified, and Fred can be somewhat more reactive. He is still, however, uncomfortable in his sales role. Wilma sometimes does the in-store selling when Fred is away or is otherwise busy. While she's sociable and friendly, she too isn't comfortable as a salesperson.

- The company has a picture portfolio of kitchen and bathroom cabinets that it's installed in Lethbridge-area homes. This portfolio is available to prospects who come to BVCC, and is taken to appointments when Fred goes off site.

- Each year BVCC has a booth at the local home-and-garden show. General contractors and home renovators attend this show, as do all of BVCC's competitors.

- For promotional literature, BVCC has a one-page glossy brochure that's given to customers who visit the store or who stop at the company booth at the home-and-garden show. Since the brochure doesn't include BVCC's website, Fred and Wilma attach their business cards to the brochures when they're handed out.

- BVCC has supported a local minor-hockey league team for the past two years. The company pays for the hockey jerseys, and throws an end-of-season pizza party for players and their parents.

BVCC doesn't currently have a promotion budget, nor is there really any plan for ongoing promotional activities. "We sort of wing it," Fred admitted. "We know we should be putting more resources into promotion, but we don't know how much, or where to focus."

PRICE

Cabinet prices can vary, but the basic lower-end models BVCC sells average $10 000 per set, with higher-end custom cabinets averaging $20 000. Cost of goods sold is about 30% for the lower-end cabinets and 40% for the higher-end custom cabinets. A complete breakdown of operational costs is included in Exhibit 3. BVCC's pricing strategy is to match industry pricing standards. Fred believes that BVCC should charge basically what its competitors are charging in order to keep on a level playing field in the industry.

The only method of payment BVCC currently accepts is cheques or cash. It does allow general contractors up to 60 days to pay, but any other customer is expected to pay once the finishing work is complete and signed off. Basically, clients need to have a cheque or cash in hand when they sign off.

EXHIBIT 3	Expenses, 2011
Item	Cost
Rent	$4000 per month
Fred and Wilma's salaries	$5000 per person per month
Employee salary	$2750 per month
Utilities	$300 per month
Interest on bank loan	$600 per month
Professional fees and licences	$3000 per year

MANUFACTURING CAPACITY

All of BVCC's manufacturing and refinishing occurs in the back stage. Its total space allows for a maximum of eight sets of cabinets to be built per month, well beyond the current two sets per month. One-third of these are higher-end custom-built cabinets sold to home renovators and general contractors, while the rest are lower-end generic designs split evenly between general contractors and home renovators, and DIY customers who are renovating homes. During its first two years, BVCC has averaged six sets of cabinets coming in for restoration and refinishing per year, which on average earns $10 000 per set of "average cabinets." Cost of goods sold is 25% of sales. BVCC hasn't done more work in this area owing to its labour intensity, and has consequently lost potential refinishing customers. It's considered purchasing a piece of used equipment for $65 000, which would allow BVCC to refinish an additional 10 units per year and lower its price for refinishing an average set of cabinets to $8000. The cost of goods sold would come down to 15%, but the company would have a bank loan amortized over five years (straight-line method) at a current fixed interest rate of 6.5% (see Exhibit 4).

The company has room for this piece of equipment in the back-stage area, whose second floor (measuring 15 × 15 feet, or 25 square metres) is used to store shop materials; it really has no dedicated use, however, and basically sits empty.

EXHIBIT 4	Interest Table: Proposed Refinishing Equipment Purchase, 2012*
Years	Interest Payment
Year One	$ 3890.17
Year Two	$ 3128.63
Year Three	$ 2316.07
Year Four	$ 1449.06
Year Five	$ 524.01

* Based on a blended payment over five years; assumes an additional $600 interest payment per month for a previous capital commitment (as shown in Exhibit 3).

RECOMMENDATIONS

Logan spent the following week analyzing BVCC's business and gathering his thoughts. He wanted to prepare a comprehensive set of recommendations for Fred and Wilma, but he also wanted to be realistic about what they could accomplish going forward. He knew that Fred and Wilma would take his recommendations seriously. From discussions he'd had with Fred in particular, he knew there was pride in owning the business, and a strong desire to see it succeed. Now it was time to put his thoughts in writing.

Caribou Mathematics Competition

Massine Bouzerar and
H. F. (Herb) MacKenzie

On May 15, 2012, Dr. Thomas Wolf got off the phone with one of his main sponsors for the Caribou Mathematics Competition. The news he'd received was not good. He'd just found out that the sponsor was suddenly unable to contribute a $1500 cheque that was supposed to cover the cost of student prizes. The last contest of the year had been held the previous week, on May 9, which meant Thomas would have to write cheques himself for the year's top participants. Moreover, the competition was beginning to grow and he'd need to find enough sponsorship to help him move forward in the next couple of years. Thomas was also considering expanding the competition to include high school students, and was already in the process of hiring someone to research and write high school–level math questions. If he decided to go forward with that, it would certainly impact the funding he needed. While his goal had never been to make money, as a private individual Thomas also needed to ensure that he didn't have to contribute his own financial resources. He'd already devoted a considerable amount of his free time to organizing and managing the competition.

BACKGROUND

Thomas Wolf taught mathematics at Brock University in St. Catharines, Ontario. He started the Caribou Mathematics Competition in 2009 out of his interest in and commitment to math education. Brock University had never supported the competition, aside from allowing Thomas to use its server to manage communications and the large databases that had been developed over the past few years. So Thomas had been trying to operate the competition on a not-for-profit, breakeven basis.

The competition features online contests held on six days in a school year. These contests are available free of charge to the young competitors and schools that register, and are offered in three different categories: grades 3/4, grades 5/6, and grades 7/8. On some days as many as 6000 students have participated; a total of 12 658 students competed across the three categories for the 2011–2012 Caribou Cup.

Caribou's mission is to provide challenging math activities for Canadian students in grades 3 to 8, to show that mathematical puzzles can be fun, and to create an environment where students find learning and competing in math contests challenging and exciting. Thomas founded the contest as a way to foster the spirit of competition and to improve the critical thinking skills of young Canadians. He strongly believes that it's the students who compete in these contests who will drive the competition and help it succeed.

All contests are offered online through the Caribou website and must be taken on a predetermined date (between 7:30 a.m. and 3:30 p.m. for each respective time zone), and under the supervision of a teacher, librarian, or administrative staff person. To enter a contest, students must first find out whether their school plans to enter students in the contest and whether a teacher at their school would be willing to supervise them. This information is readily available on Caribou's website, where students can check whether their school is registered for a given contest. Thomas has found it difficult to convince teachers to actually administer the testing, despite the fact that it requires very little of their time and effort. Students who are home-schooled may contact their local public library to check whether it would be willing to supervise them. Since Caribou contests are offered online, the organization is able to provide students with feedback on the same day the test is written, which eliminates the long wait students often experience with handwritten tests.

The contests are provided in both English and French. Prizes are awarded for the top competitors of the Caribou Cup, based on a total score tabulated across all six contests conducted in each category over the year. After contest results are posted, students are able to print off a certificate that includes their ranking across Canada, within their province, and within their school district. Cash prizes are awarded to top students until the purse is completely expended and each of the grade categories has a maximum purse of $500. The cash awards have so far been sponsored by Canadian research institutes and learning societies. Exhibit 1 shows how cash prizes are assigned to the top competitors at the end of the year.

A unique feature of the Caribou Mathematics Competition is that schools are also awarded cash prizes for their students who place among the winners. Approximately 30% of the total prize money is distributed to schools as an incentive to encourage their students to participate and to help them prepare.

Another feature Caribou offers is a collection of all previous contests free of charge on its website for students to practise with. Solutions are also provided on the website, with some of the last two years' solutions available in video form. On some days up to 1900 practice tests have been taken online by students who wish to improve their chances of winning the Caribou Cup.

EXHIBIT 1	Cash Prizes	
	Student	School
First prize	$100 × (points/total points)*	$30 × (points/total points)
Second prize	$75 × (points/total points)	$22.50 × (points/total points)
Third prize	$50 × (points/total points)	$15 × (points/total points)
Fourth or more	$30 × (points/total points)	$9 × (points/total points)

Source: Caribou Mathematics Competition.

*Prize determination: A student will accumulate points throughout the year. At the end of the year, the number of points achieved will be divided by the total possible number of points. For example, if a student takes part in six contests and earns 480 points and the total number of points possible was 576, then the ratio is (480/576) = 0.8333. If this was the top student, he or she would receive $83.33 ($100 × 0.8333). The remaining prizes are awarded in this fashion until the $500 purse is empty. The school this student attends would receive $25 ($30 × 0.8333).

Caribou's website also provides logic games as well as a "Puzzle of the Day" to stimulate students' interest in mathematics and to encourage them to develop their critical thinking skills (see Exhibit 2).

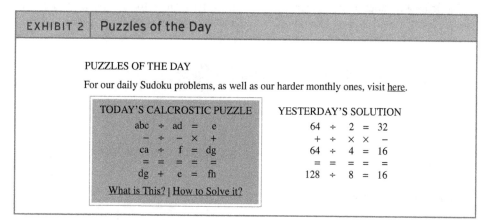

EXHIBIT 2	Puzzles of the Day

PUZZLES OF THE DAY

For our daily Sudoku problems, as well our harder monthly ones, visit here.

TODAY'S CALCROSTIC PUZZLE

abc ÷ ad = e
− ÷ − × +
ca ÷ f = dg
= = = = =
dg + e = fh

What is This? | How to Solve it?

YESTERDAY'S SOLUTION

64 ÷ 2 = 32
+ ÷ × × −
64 ÷ 4 = 16
= = = = =
128 ÷ 8 = 16

Source: Caribou Mathematics Competition.

These contests are not based on any particular provincial school curriculum so that they're fair for students from across Canada. Rather than testing general concepts covered in their respective schools, the questions test the students' logic, common sense, and ability to read carefully. Furthermore, a month prior to every contest, Caribou announces what game it will feature so that students have time to practise it.

MARKET ANALYSIS

Although any Canadian student in grades 3 to 8 may participate in the Caribou Mathematics Competition, some provinces have much higher participation rates and others haven't yet had a single student compete. Exhibit 3 shows the number of grade 7 and 8 participants from the last contest, sorted by province.

EXHIBIT 3	Grades 7 and 8 Contest Participation, May 9, 2012	
Province	Number of Schools	Number of Participants
Alberta	2	58
British Columbia	10	181
Manitoba	1	2
New Brunswick	5	124
Nova Scotia	3	55
Ontario	100	1389
Prince Edward Island	1	13
Quebec	1	18

Source: Caribou Mathematics Competition.

Based on the number of schools across Canada and the number of students in each grade, the participation rate for Caribou has certainly not reached its full potential. Exhibit 4 shows the number of schools, both elementary and secondary, in each province in Canada. Exhibit 5 shows the number of students in each grade across each province.

Participation varies across all six contests offered throughout the year, and yet a pattern was apparent: as the end of the school year approached, fewer students participated. In

EXHIBIT 4	Number of Schools Across Canada, 2012*
Province	Schools
Alberta	2 392
British Columbia	1 779
Manitoba	649
New Brunswick	345
Newfoundland and Labrador	319
Nova Scotia	426
Northwest Territories	48
Nunavut	42
Ontario	4 931
Prince Edward Island	69
Quebec	3 419
Saskatchewan	721
Yukon	31
CANADA	15 171

Source: Canadian Information Centre for International Credentials, Education in Canada, 2012.

*Although elementary and secondary schools aren't listed separately, it's assumed that two-thirds of all Canadian schools are classified as elementary.

EXHIBIT 5 | Number of Students per Grade, 2010

Grade	NL	PE	NS	NB	QC	ON	MB	SK	AB	BC	YT	NT	NU
Province													
1	4 862	1 514	9 965	7 326	72 291	131 089	12 338	11 740	41 839	36 261	346	596	710
2	4 863	1 422	8 542	7 214	72 502	129 637	12 378	11 203	40 507	36 228	348	550	688
3	4 935	1 327	8 846	7 269	71 226	134 463	12 570	11 660	39 719	36 746	334	551	694
4	5 099	1 458	9 117	7 543	71 837	133 015	12 795	11 486	39 867	37 336	364	565	646
5	5 228	1 472	9 444	7 705	70 694	137 475	12 901	11 861	40 863	38 570	356	582	667
6	5 212	1 498	9 544	7 997	71 400	140 805	13 023	12 025	41 535	39 945	351	547	658
7	5 344	1 704	9 817	8 104	73 093	143 015	12 959	12 071	41 371	41 496	377	618	636
8	5 493	1 788	10 482	8 278	77 493	148 841	13 861	12 578	42 711	44 182	399	617	638
9	5 556	1 873	10 664	9 263	82 035	163 035	15 193	13 032	43 768	46 375	373	745	695
10	5 990	1 934	11 290	9 423	69 913	164 332	15 575	14 574	46 438	50 097	456	1143	969
11	5 765	2 006	11 806	9 711	61 405	166 940	14 968	13 220	46 222	52 518	396	826	823
12	6 582	1 959	11 451	9 564	–	223 248	15 854	13 651	58 819	50 420	470	635	525

Source: Statistics Canada, Elementary-Secondary Education Survey, 2010.

EXHIBIT 6	Grade 7/8 Participation in Ontario, 2011–2012 Caribou Cup					
	Oct. 2011	Nov. 2011	Jan. 2012	Feb. 2012	April 2012	May 2012
Number of schools	79	95	103	109	106	100
Number of participants	1743	1576	1945	1846	1656	1390

Source: Caribou Mathematics Competition.

Thomas's view, it was the weaker students who withdrew as the year progressed. Exhibit 6 shows participation in Ontario in the grades 7 and 8 category for the 2011–2012 Caribou Cup.

OTHER MATHEMATICS COMPETITIONS

A number of other mathematics competitions are offered across Canada and internationally. These competitions vary in the number of contest categories they offer per year, how participant categories are organized, and the registration fees they charge. The three most notable competitions servicing the Canadian market are the University of Waterloo's Centre for Education in Mathematics and Computing, Mathematical Kangaroo, and Mathematica.

The Centre for Education in Mathematics and Computing

The Centre for Education in Mathematics and Computing (CEMC), founded in 1995 at the University of Waterloo, is Canada's largest and most recognized outreach organization for creating and promoting activities and materials in mathematics and computer science. CEMC offers contests to students in grades 7 to 12. There is one contest per year, per grade level, with testing dates differing across grades. In 2012, approximately 205 000 participants from 55 different countries participated in a contest facilitated by CEMC. These contests are offered in both English and French, and prizes are awarded mostly in the form of certificates, medals, and plaques. Some categories do offer cash prizes, ranging between $200 and $500 for regional and national achievement.

Unlike Caribou, CEMC's yearly contests are written by hand, and a school or library staff member supervises the testing and returns the tests to CEMC for evaluation. Because the test is handwritten, contest results may not be available for a considerable time; as many as four to six weeks may pass before results are known. CEMC offers numerous publications and practice materials, at $3 for the first item and $1 for each additional item for Canadian sales, and at $10 for the first item and $2 for each additional item for international sales.

CEMC charges a contest registration fee ranging from $3 to $14, depending on the category, with a shipping fee of $5 per Canadian school or 15% of the registration fees for schools outside of Canada. In addition to this revenue, CEMC has numerous sponsors, including a $12.5 million sponsorship from the Bill & Melinda Gates Foundation and sponsorships from Deloitte, Esso, and the University of Waterloo.

Mathematical Kangaroo

Mathematical Kangaroo, founded in 1991 in France, is celebrated as the math competition with the highest participation in the world, with over 5 million students from over 47 countries.

Students from grades 1 to 12 compete in six categories based on grade level (i.e., grades 1 and 2, grades 3 and 4, etc.). The contest is held annually on the third Thursday of March and is offered in both English and French. Cash prizes are not awarded; however, winners do get medals and may get invited, at no cost, to an International Math Kangaroo Camp.

Like the University of Waterloo's CEMC competition, Mathematical Kangaroo's contest is written by hand, and the students require supervision in order to compete. Contest results are available approximately two months after the test date. However, Mathematical Kangaroo also provides practice questions on its website, and free online training classes during the month of the contest.

Mathematical Kangaroo has a registration fee of $15 per student to cover the cost of organizing the event. In Canada, it also receives sponsorships from various Canadian universities and colleges, the Canadian Mathematical Society, and the Institute of Electrical and Electronics Engineers.

Mathematica

Founded in 1990 in Montreal, Mathematica is a Canada-wide mathematics competition, with most competitors coming from Quebec. Mathematica believes that learning mathematics through problem-resolution activities is the most efficient way to develop lasting mathematical skills. Participants in this contest come from grades 3 to 9, with students from each grade participating in their own contest. The competition is held annually in mid-April; since its inception, over 900 000 students across Canada have participated. Students in select categories who receive a perfect score on their test are given a $250 merit scholarship to attend the international MathPath camp, a summer math camp in the United States for highly gifted students.

Like the two preceding competitions, Mathematica's contests are handwritten and require teacher or librarian supervision during testing. Contest winners are typically posted on its website a month after the contest has taken place. One English and one French practice test is available free online for each category as a way to encourage students to prepare for the contest. Previous contest questionnaires with detailed solutions are available at a fee of $6 each, and packages for the Pythagoras contest with detailed solutions are available for $35.95.

Mathematica's fee structure is based on how many contests a school decides to enter. If a school participates in one, two, three, four, five, six, or seven contests, the registration fees are $95, $185, $275, $365, $455, $545, and $635, respectively, and the school may enrol as many as 30 students per contest.

SPONSORSHIPS

Although Caribou's contests don't have any registration fees, Caribou welcomes donations from organizations, teachers, and parents. Since its inception, Caribou has received only two donations, both in 2010 (one from a teacher and one from a parent), for a total of $300.

The competition's main sponsor for the last two years, the Fields Institute for Research in Mathematical Sciences, has just reduced its annual sponsorship from $8000 to $6000, and a new sponsor for the 2012/2013 Caribou Cup, SHARCNET, has provided $5330.67 to cover the cost of specific expenses.

EXHIBIT 7	Expenses, 2011-2012	
Cash prizes		$ 1 500.00
Experience Works		$ 8 274.63
Miscellaneous expenses		$ 2 070.30
TOTAL		**$11 844.93**

Source: Caribou Mathematics Competition.

Exhibit 7 shows Caribou's expenses for 2011–2012. Although the organization comes close to breaking even, Thomas feels an obligation to a former student who donated time to the contest as a computer programmer while he was an undergraduate student at Brock. Thomas has been paying the student when he can, but he estimates that the student deserves about $5000 for unpaid service. Some students who work on the contest questions and administration of test results are hired through the Experience Works program at Brock University. Faculty compete for these students each year, and successful faculty get students whose wages are subsidized by the university. In 2011–2012, Thomas's share of student wages was $8274.63. This figure is unlikely to decrease in subsequent years, but it could be higher if Thomas is unsuccessful at getting students under this program. Finally, Thomas must come up with $1500 for the cash prizes promised by the sponsor that recently decided to back out.

THOMAS'S DILEMMA

Thomas was at a crossroads. The status quo wasn't acceptable, but growth would create another whole set of problems. Thomas wondered if he should continue operations as they are, while sacrificing time he could be focusing on his research, or try to expand the competition to include all grades from 3 through 12. He also wondered whether it would be appropriate to seek better corporate sponsorship, and how he should do so. Attempts in the past to get banks and accounting firms to sponsor the competition have been unsuccessful. He might have to charge a registration fee for students and/or schools, but if so, should the fee vary by grade or by the number of students per school that register? If successful, should he raise the prize monies? Or should he raise the prize monies to attract more participants? Thomas also considered what impact charging a registration fee would have on contest participation rates, but he was sure that if registration fees went up, participation rates would decline—unless he implements an effective marketing strategy. Although he's not interested in making a profit, he does realize that revenue is important if he wishes his contest to survive, and to grow.

Thomas was an acknowledged mathematician, but he knew he was a marketing novice. So he's decided to approach the university's Faculty of Business to see what advice its members might have. Your professor has chosen to involve you in the situation analysis, and has asked you what recommendations you would make.

Bovine Booties

H. F. (Herb) MacKenzie

In the summer of 2012, Ted Henderson was enjoying an evening barbecue at the home of his friend Brett Welch. The two friends had seldom seen each other over the four years since they'd graduated together from university. Their conversation turned to business, what each had been doing over the past year, and what their plans were for the future.

Brett had developed a successful import business that he operated mainly from his home in Oakville, Ontario. He imported rubber boots from China and sold them to retailers across Canada. With three manufacturing sources in China he'd developed a complete line of men's, women's, and children's rubber boots. These included specialty boots with soft tops and drawstrings so that they could be tightened against one's legs, low-profile boots that came barely above the ankles, thigh-high boots, steel-toed safety boots, and boots in various colours and patterns. By 2012 Brett's sales had exceeded $7 million, about 70% of which came from major retail chains. Ted, on the other hand, had spent his first two years after graduation working for a not-for-profit organization, followed by a year at a bank; in the last year he'd been working at an insurance firm. He'd explored a number of potential employment options, but none had particularly satisfied him, and he was now looking for something else.

"You know, Brett, I envy what you've done since graduation. You've become a self-made person. You seem to be doing what you want to do, and you appear successful at it. I wish I could start my own business."

Brett nodded. "There's lots of opportunity for good salespeople who have something worth selling. Being an agent, distributor, or importer are the only careers I'd ever consider. I know you'd be good at any of these jobs, too—you just need to find the right product."

The two men continued to discuss business, and soon they were sharing their second bottle of Cabernet Franc. Suddenly, Brett offered a suggestion. "You know, I might have an idea for you."

Ted waited. Brett continued to think for a minute, then spoke. "Do you remember that startup company that started selling 'Shoes for Moos' back in the 1980s or 1990s?"

"Oh, right, we did a case on it in business school," Ted replied. "Weren't they little boots or something for cows with hoof disease?"

"Yes, right. And I think the company failed. But you know, I'm not convinced that the product was a bad idea. I just think the strategy may have been wrong, and the boots had some issues as well. I always felt that the company should have been a success in Canada."

After they'd discussed the idea further, Ted promised to dig up a copy of the business case they'd studied and do an updated analysis. They agreed that if they could both see the possibilities for success, they'd start a new enterprise focused solely on the product. Ted would manage the business and Brett would help find a manufacturer, provide a modest investment (not to exceed $40 000), and be a sounding board as the business was launched. Brett, of course, expected to maintain some ownership in the business, but was very willing to negotiate that on good terms. Ted said he could get an additional $10 000.

As the evening came to an end, the friends agreed to meet in two weeks, after Brett returned from his sales trip to Vancouver.

SHOES FOR MOOS

Ted was indeed able to find a copy of the case he and Brett had analyzed in their business program. After a quick read and some thought, he began to believe that a similar product could succeed if it was marketed appropriately. As a preliminary step, he began to investigate what had happened based on the case, and to see what updated information he might need.

The product was described on the company's brochure as "specially designed rubber boots" made of fabric-backed rubber with yellow textured soles. These "shoes" were designed to fit a cow's foot. They had two straps: one that fit above and one that fit below the cow's dew claw (a residual toe on the rear of the leg that doesn't come in contact with the ground). When he looked at the photo, Ted thought it would be easy to make a product that wouldn't violate any existing patent, if one was still valid.

The cost to produce Shoes for Moos was originally $19 per shoe, in minimum lots of 100. The company was considering selling the shoes for somewhere between $39.95 and $79.95 per shoe, depending on what distribution strategy would be used and what the promotional expenses might be. Ted wasn't sure what the cost of a "bootie" from China would be, but he did note that Canadian Tire had recently listed children's rubber boots at about $10 per pair in its weekly sales flyer, which suggested to Ted that he could probably get boots from China for well under $5 each.

When Ted looked at what kind of distribution Shoes for Moos was considering, he saw a number of options: direct sales by the owner of the business, manufacturer's agents, wholesalers of veterinarian supplies, veterinarians, and wholesale and retail farm supply outlets, among others. Ted couldn't identify any immediately favourable alternative, but he realized that any one of these would involve a tradeoff. If he chose a channel that was too short, such as selling the product himself to farmers, the costs would be far too high and the selling efficiency far too low. He didn't think he'd be able to generate the response needed to make the product a success. On the other hand, if he chose a channel that was too long, he'd have to provide an acceptable margin for so many intermediaries that the selling price to farmers would have to be high, which would certainly reduce sales. Given these considerations, Ted decided to look specifically at veterinarians as his only channel intermediaries, and possibly at veterinarian wholesalers as well.

After reflecting on the alternatives discussed in the business case, Ted decided to update some data and take another look at the potential market.

CUSTOMER ANALYSIS

Ted found that the owner of Shoes for Moos expected to get 80% of his sales for dairy cows and the remaining 20% for beef cows. The logic seemed reasonable. Beef cows, if they were older, would simply be slaughtered and would end up as hamburgers or steaks. If they were younger, the farmer might try to cure them of their hoof problems, since they'd become more valuable as they grew in size. A small number, however, would simply be slaughtered to become veal: meat from young cattle, mostly males. (Dairy cows were always female.) It was based on this information that Ted decided to explore the dairy cow market; he could simply add a percentage to cover expected sales for beef cows. Exhibit 1 lists the number of dairy farms across Canada, by province, and Exhibit 2 lists the number of dairy cows by province.

On Monday morning, Ted called a friend at the University of Guelph's Small Animal Clinic, Dr. Graham, and asked her whether she was familiar with hoof disease in cows. She referred Ted to an associate, Dr. Rashid, who specialized in large animals. In his phone conversation with Dr. Rashid, Ted said he'd heard that during certain times of the year—notably in the spring when the fields were damp and in the winter when cows were housed together indoors—up to 20% of a herd could have hoof disease. Dr. Rashid said yes, that could be true, but the estimate was likely too high. A normal annual range would be 2 to 20% of cows, but he thought it would more commonly range between 5 and 15%. Dr. Rashid also said that although he seldom treated cows himself, he'd guess that large-animal veterinarians would likely treat less than half of the cows with infected hooves, since farmers were just as likely to treat the cows themselves.

Next, Ted decided to do some research on milk production. From the Shoes for Moos business case, Ted learned that cows produced milk for about 300 days per year, averaging an annual 5450 litres. Ted looked for information on milk prices and discovered that farmers generally sold their milk to dairies for about $0.62 per litre. From information in the business case, Ted discovered that milk production from cows with hoof disease was reduced by 20 to 80%, depending on the severity of the disease. If the cow had to be placed on antibiotics the milk production went to zero, as milk from cows on these powerful drugs couldn't be sold. In fact, not only was the milk unsellable during the three or four days a

EXHIBIT 1	Canadian Dairy Farms by Province, 2007-2011									
	BC	AB	SK	MB	ON	QC	NB	NS	PEI	NL	CANADA
2011	512	592	182	344	4 137	6 281	219	245	200	34	**12 746**
2010	529	598	190	356	4 191	6 375	234	248	209	35	**12 965**
2009	542	615	202	388	4 243	6 492	231	253	213	35	**13 214**
2008	556	638	226	410	4 352	6 661	233	261	212	38	**13 587**
2007	572	660	230	425	4 508	6 869	240	272	222	38	**14 036**

Source: Number of Farms, Dairy Cows and Dairy Heifers, Canadian Dairy Information Centre, http://www.dairyinfo.gc.ca/index_e.php?s1=dff-fcil&s2=farm-ferme&s3=nb

EXHIBIT 2	Canadian Dairy Cows by Province, 2008-2012 ('000)									
	BC	AB	SK	MB	ON	QC	NB	NS	PEI	NL	CANADA
2012	71.5	90.0	29.0	44.5	322.9	368.0	18.7	21.8	13.2	5.7	**985.3**
2011	70.5	90.0	30.0	44.5	322.0	366.0	18.7	22.5	13.0	5.9	**983.1**
2010	71.1	89.0	30.0	46.0	320.5	364.0	19.5	21.5	13.2	6.2	**981.0**
2009	71.1	87.0	29.0	45.0	320.0	365.0	19.0	23.0	12.8	6.6	**978.5**
2008	70.8	83.5	29.0	44.0	320.0	375.0	18.8	23.5	13.0	6.7	**984.3**

Source: Food Statistics 2009, Statistics Canada, http://www.statcan.gc.ca/pub/21-020-x/2009001/t026-eng.htm

cow was on antibiotics, it couldn't be sold for another three to four days after drug treatment stopped. Of course, the cost of the antibiotics and veterinarian services would also be important, but Ted decided not to call Dr. Rashid back. He simply guessed that the cost for treatment would be $6 to $20 per cow for the antibiotics and $20 to $30 on average per cow for a vet visit. Ted felt this was a conservative estimate.

DISTRIBUTION OPTIONS

Ted began to consider distribution, figuring that once he'd settled this he'd be better able to consider promotion options. The Shoes for Moos business case included a number of options, and he wasn't sure what the company finally chose. Still, he almost immediately decided that veterinarians were the obvious choice, and was reasonably certain that this wasn't the strategy Shoes for Moos had chosen. Selling through veterinarians would lend credibility to the product, would get market exposure much more quickly than trying to sell to individual farmers, and would avoid the difficulties involved in finding and then managing a group of manufacturer's agents.

Ted called Dr. Graham again and asked her whether she had any information on veterinarians across Canada. She said she'd recently read a report and would email it to Ted when she could get her hands on it. When Ted received it an hour later, he thought it was exactly what he needed. Among all the facts in the report, he figured the following were the most important:

- Canada had approximately 3000 veterinary practices: 10% of them were large-animal practices; 30% were mixed (large and small) animal practices; 60% were small-animal practices.

- There were just over 12 000 veterinarians in Canada.

- The majority of veterinarians, 36.5%, practised in Ontario; Quebec had 22%; Alberta and British Columbia each had 12.5%; and the remaining provinces each had less than 5%.

- The majority of veterinary practices were small: 35% had four or fewer employees, and nearly 95% had fewer than 20 employees.

Most veterinarians purchased supplies and services from a Canada-wide veterinary wholesaler, CDMV Inc. Ted had little information on this company beyond the fact that its head office was in Quebec, with offices in Nova Scotia and Alberta, and that it had more than 200 employees. Ted assumed that, as a wholesaler, CDMV would want somewhere between 15 and 25% margin on the products it sold, and that it would be interested in handling anything that was in demand by veterinarians. Veterinarians, on the other hand, would most likely require at least 40% for anything they held in inventory, and they might accept less for volume purchases or items that they simply bought and resold (i.e., items that ran through their business without the vets actually carrying inventory).

PROMOTION

When Ted reviewed the many ways Shoes for Moos had considered promoting its product, he realized that he could easily spend a tremendous amount of money. So he quickly decided that he'd promote the product only to veterinarians; a few trade shows and some posters for distribution in veterinary offices would be sufficient. Without doing a lot of research, Ted figured he'd need to attend about four trade shows each year: one in eastern Canada, one in Quebec, one in Ontario (London's Western Fair Farm Show, which draws about 200 000 visitors each year), and one in western Canada (Ag Expo, held annually in Calgary and advertised as the biggest of its kind in Canada). Again without much research, Ted estimated that each show would cost, on average, about $5000, considering registration, booth rental, travel, meals, hotels, etc.

Ted was able to get a preliminary price on 1000 wall posters: $2500. Mailing tubes and postage for these posters was estimated at $3 each. Smaller pre-folded, full-colour flyers could be purchased for $0.15 each, in lots of 10 000. Ted had originally investigated magazine advertising, and discovered that some magazines—in both English and French—targeted veterinarians, and others targeted dairy farmers. A one-third-page colour ad was about $600 to $1000 per insertion, and these were mostly monthly magazines. That sounded pretty steep, so Ted had quickly decided he wouldn't worry about this medium.

THE SUBSEQUENT MEETING

Ted was still organizing his thoughts about "Bovine Booties" when Brett returned from Vancouver. The two friends met to talk about the concept in greater detail. They began by discussing the physical product. After discarding several early ideas, Brett came up with a proposal they both immediately recognized as the winner. "We can get boots with four rubber D-rings vulcanized right onto the sides so that they're an integral part of the boot, two on each side. The flat side of the D would fit against the boot, and then the straps could fit through the ring and be easily tightened. We could even use simple Velcro straps."

"Yes," Ted added, "and we could get the straps in a variety of colours. Farmers could use the different colours to indicate the severity of the disease, or anything else they wanted."

"Good idea, Ted. I'm not sure how important that would be, but it certainly wouldn't affect the product cost. What'll we call the product—surely not 'Bovine Booties'?"

Ted and Brett discussed whether the name was too cute, whether it said anything about the product, and whether it would be easily remembered. At one point they discussed "Hoof Healers," but decided that wouldn't work because the company that originally sold Shoes for Moos had also designed a product called Hoof Healers for horses. Ted and Brett considered "Hoof-Ease," and finally "Bessie Boots." At that point they realized they'd had too much wine, and put off this particular decision until later.

Eventually, Brett said he'd email a sketch of the product they wanted to his manufacturers in China to see what prices they could get. It was only a matter of days before he got his replies. Prices ranged from $3.44 to $3.60 per boot. All prices were F.O.B. Toronto, close enough that Brett or Ted could pick up the boots when they arrived. The company with the lowest price required a minimum order of 6000 boots; the other two required a minimum of 5000 boots. All the companies promised to send samples within the next few weeks, and payment was required with the order. Brett called Ted and gave him the news. Then he said he was about to leave for the East Coast for a few weeks, and asked Ted to put together a marketing plan so that they could make a decision as soon as he returned. "If you can convince me there's potential here, I'll give you that initial financial investment I promised. We can negotiate the terms of the loan then, too."

Enviro-Plumber

Carman Cullen

It was December 20, 2012, and Joe Smit, a naturalized Canadian entrepreneur born in Germany, had just asked the Brock MBA Small Business Consulting Group for their advice. Joe told the consultants that he owned the North American distribution rights to what he referred to as the "best product in the world." He'd purchased the rights in June 2011 for $20 000 at the ACHEMA trade show in Frankfurt. (ACHEMA, organized by Messe Frankfurt GmbH, is the pre-eminent European trade show for "chemical engineering, environmental protection, and biotechnology.") European rights were owned by the multi-national chemical company that actually manufactured the product. The company would make its money by selling the product to Joe, who in turn could sell it in North America.

THE PRODUCT

The product was a drain cleaner that cleared even the worst clogged sinks, toilets, showers, and floor drains. It was in the form of a can, about the same size as a can of Drano (the leading drain-cleaning brand). Joe had been amazed at the demonstrations put on by the chemical company representatives at Frankfurt. Trade-show attendees were asked to clog demonstration sinks and pipes with rags and cork and assorted waste products. Then the can was inverted in the drain, and with a slight push on the bottom of the can, a wave of pressure was created in the sink or toilet, completely cleaning the drain. There was never a need for a second shot, and each 200-gram can provided 10 shots. The active ingredients were certified environmentally friendly in Europe, and the product bore the Blue Angel certification in Germany to substantiate this claim. These active ingredients created a forceful reaction that pushed clogs through the pipes, leaving only a few ice crystals behind that could be washed away with hot water after the clog was gone. Because the product used HFCs (hydrofluorocarbons) and not CFCs (chlorofluorocarbons), German environmentalists endorsed it.

In short, Joe was impressed. Here was an effective, environmentally friendly product with affordable distribution rights that he felt strongly would be popular and successful in Canada and the United States. The product could be named whatever Joe wanted to call it for the North American market, and the chemical company would provide the name and all U.S./Canadian government labelling requirements as part of the landed cost, which was $2.50 per can, F.O.B. Canadian or U.S. destination. After conversations with his wife, Joe decided that the best brand name would be Enviro-Plumber. The distribution rights were for three and a half years, beginning at the signing of the contract—which Joe did on July 1 (Canada Day), 2011, in Frankfurt. In order to keep the rights for a further five years (until 2019), Joe had to meet a minimum sales hurdle of 500 000 units by December 31, 2014. Joe was convinced this could be easily accomplished.

THE ISSUE

Over a cup of coffee at the consultants' office, Joe disclosed that since signing the agreement he'd sold a total of 25 000 units, most of them in the northeastern United States through a contract with a small chain of hardware stores. Joe showed the consultants a video of Enviro-Plumber cleaning drains—and it impressed them, too. "There's nothing like this product for effectiveness," Joe said, "and it's environmentally friendly to boot." But with only 25 000 units sold so far, Joe's dreams of wealth from the world's greatest product were going down the drain. He told the MBA students that he had no idea what to try next. He had expected to get rich from Enviro-Plumber, but was fresh out of ideas as to how to make that happen.

THE CONSULTANTS' QUESTIONS

The consultants had several questions for Joe. First, they asked for more details on the numbers. He told them that the $2.50 landed cost per can was in Canadian dollars, and that the price was firm for the three-year term of the agreement; if the 500 000-unit target was achieved by 2014, the price would be revisited. The minimum order was 30 000 units (each container held 30 000 cans), with payment due one week after receipt of the container from the chemical company. Joe had two warehouses—in Buffalo, New York, and Niagara Falls, Ontario—to accommodate his numerous businesses, each of which specialized in environmentally friendly consumer products. He could accommodate 90 000 units in the Niagara Falls facility and about 300 000 in the Buffalo warehouse. Joe was prepared to invest a further $250 000 in the venture. He had already purchased, and received, 90 000 units (cost to Joe: $225 000), with one-third in Niagara Falls and the remainder (less 20 000 already sold) in the Buffalo warehouse. He'd sold only about 5000 units in Canada.

The MBA student consultants then asked about Joe's fixed costs, and he told them that he had two salespeople dedicated to his businesses, one in Canada and one in the United States. Each rep cost Joe around $65 000, including all expenses. He'd spent $10 000 printing flyers and hiring companies to distribute the flyers in major cities across North America. However, to date, the flyers had been distributed only in Toronto, Ottawa, London, Cleveland, and Pittsburgh. Additional expenses he'd allocated to Enviro-Plumber totalled another $40 000. This was starting to get expensive.

But then Joe hit them with a real problem. He'd been in negotiations with a major hardware chain, whose buyer seemed very impressed with the product's quality. The buyer said he'd order 50 000 units on a trial basis, but with two constraints. First, he demanded a keystone markup on the product. That is, whatever he paid Joe per can would be marked up 100% on cost; in essence, he'd simply double Joe's price. Second, the retailer demanded "significant promotional support" for the product. Joe asked what "significant" meant, and the buyer said, "Whatever it takes to sell 50 000 of these as quickly as possible—it's your company. You tell me."

The consultants asked Joe, an experienced entrepreneur with years of experience selling environmentally relevant products, for his explanation of the poor sales to date. "I think it has to do with consumer behaviour," Joe began. "North Americans are more squeamish than people in other parts of the world—they don't like messes. Enviro-Plumber causes some splashing, and even my wife hated that aspect of the product. But I've got that fixed." Joe had found a company in Pittsburgh that designed and manufactured a handle and splash protector that could be used for clogged toilets. The cost to Joe was $4.95 per unit, based on a minimum order of 1000 units. Joe thought this was expensive, but had concluded that the consumer only ever needed to buy one handle and protector.

The students' final question was about the competition. They knew about Drano and Liquid-Plumr, but not much else. Joe, who'd been ready for that question, handed them a competitive analysis sheet (see Exhibit 1). He explained that Drano was the industry

EXHIBIT 1	Competitive Analysis	
Brand	Size	Price
Drano	500 g (crystals)	$6.59
Liquid Drano (Max Gel)	900 mL	$4.92
Liquid Drano (Max Gel)	2.3 L	$8.48
Drano Foamer	500 mL	$5.84
Liquid-Plumr	909 mL	$4.49
Liquid-Plumr Pro	900 mL	$4.33
Liquid-Plumr Foamy Pipe Snake	503 mL	$4.20
Clear Line Liquid Drain Opener	1 L	$8.99
Plumber's helper	NA	$14.96
Plumber	NA	$100.00 per hour
Enviro-Plumber	200 g (10 shots)	????

leader, and sold at various prices depending on its version and size and the retailer's pricing strategy. Liquid-Plumr generally sold at fairly similar prices. Most products in competition with Enviro-Plumber contained caustic, corrosive chemicals, and most weren't useful for a clogged toilet. For that, people had to use a plunger—a "plumber's helper"—essentially a wooden stick with a rubber attachment on the end. Other than that, people had to call an actual plumber.

Joe expressed his concern and his frustration. He knew his product was excellent, but he was in serious danger of losing the distribution rights in two years.

Page Two

H. F. (Herb) MacKenzie

It was July 2012, and the Struan Downtown Business Association's monthly meeting had just wrapped up when Bob Turner, president of the association and owner of the Argyle Building on Back Street, approached Tim Langille. "Tim. The other day Tammy Smith asked if the Argyle Building would be available for rent soon. I told her that I hoped it would be, but that I'd promised to discuss it with another potential tenant first. I remembered you'd asked more than a year ago whether it would be available once the federal government closed its offices, and, frankly, I'd prefer to have you as a tenant than Tammy and all her junk."

Tim was the owner of Page Two, a downtown "pre-owned" bookstore. He'd been thinking for some time that he had to make some changes, but this took him completely by surprise. "Wow," he said. "I don't know what to say. How soon do you need an answer?"

"The government has paid its $800 rent for next month, but it'll be out of the building by the end of next week. I can let you start moving in as soon as they leave, and you can have next month free, courtesy of the government, but I'll need to start charging you right after that. I can give you the same deal, and it's a good one considering that heat and electricity is included. I really can't afford to do better than that. I guess I need an answer within two weeks or I'll have to offer it to Tammy."

Tim agreed to decide quickly, and the two friends left the meeting and headed home. Tim realized that the new location would solve his parking problems, and he was excited about the possibility of the two large display windows that faced Back Street. Tourists and visitors to the town would immediately see his books, and that could well improve his sales. On the other hand, he might lose much of the walking traffic that went by his current location, and his rent would double. His current rent also included heat and electricity, so his only other business expense was $70 per month for insurance. The decision whether to change location was a significant one for Tim, but he knew he needed to make a number of other important decisions concerning his business. The world was changing, and more rapidly than he liked.

PAGE TWO

Tim Langille began Page Two, a used bookstore, in 1974. When he first graduated from university he'd taken a job at a branch of one of Canada's largest banks, but within six months he knew it wasn't for him. He left to work with a local hardware wholesaler, but six months later he decided that wasn't his calling in life either. So then he switched to a manager-trainee position at a big retail chain. He learned a lot about merchandising—and floor cleaning—but within a few months he knew once more that he wouldn't last long. That was when he came up with the idea for starting his own retail operation: Page Two.

To acquire a stock of books and magazines, Tim ran ads in the classified section of several newspapers in surrounding towns. He offered cash payment of 10% of the cover price for all paperbacks and comic books, and for a select group of magazines. Over the following winter he visited everyone who called him, collecting thousands of books and magazines, which he stored in his parents' basement.

In the spring of 1974 Tim found a location for his store—and after weeks of painting walls, building and painting wooden shelves, and arranging inventory, Page Two was opened. The operation was simple. Tim paid 10% of the original cover price when he purchased a book and then sold it for 50% of the cover price, thus making a gross margin of 80%. The business was practically an overnight success. Word spread around the town and surrounding communities, and a regular clientele soon developed. Many customers would buy books, read them, and return them on their next trip to the store. As one customer remarked, "This is great. I buy the book for half price, sell it back to Tim, and I can get everything I want to read for 40 cents on the dollar."

The original store was quite small, but Tim was able to display about 9000 books and several hundred comic books and magazines. There was only limited walk-by traffic and no parking next to the building. However, there was some parking across the street that belonged to another retailer, whose manager let Tim's customers use it to load and unload books.

Eventually, Tim found a source for new adult magazines and books, and he began to sell them as well. The gross margin, of course, was considerably smaller: for a $10 magazine, Tim would pay $6. Still, he quickly realized the advantages of selling these materials. He could sell a new magazine, plastic wrapped, for $10, make $4 gross margin, buy it back again a week or two later for $1, then reseal it and sell it again as new for $10. After a few cycles it would get bent or torn and have to be sold as used for $5, but in the meantime Tim had made considerable money. He soon developed a sizable higher-priced inventory that had a high turnover rate—in fact it was so high that often someone would bring in a large amount of adult material that he would resell before he even had the chance to put it on display. Sometimes Tim would conveniently forget that he bought the material, or that he sold it. The machine receipts got "lost" and the money went into his pocket. He was a bit uncomfortable selling this sort of thing, but it really wasn't hardcore, and not even as revealing as newsstand magazines like *Playboy* or *Penthouse.* These materials, along with the more common newsstand adult magazines, were a very important part of Tim's early business. As he recalled, "My book customers would come in and spend $4 to $6 per visit, but some of my adult book and magazine customers would spend $40 or $50 per visit—and they'd do it on a weekly basis. It only took a few of these customers to pay the entire rent on my store."

Other important money makers for Tim when he first started his business were scratch cards and punch boards (this was before the government got involved with lottery tickets and instant scratch cards). Various sets of scratch cards could be bought for $200 to $500 per set, and then individual cards were sold to customers for $0.25 to $1. People could win several levels of prizes, but when the complete set was sold, the seller would earn $50 to several hundred dollars. Punch boards worked on the same principle. Customers paid $0.10 or $0.25 per punch, depending on the board, and could win prizes of various amounts. Tim paid $125 for the most popular board. It took in $1000 when all holes were punched, and paid out a total of $500 to winners. Tim's profit per board was $375, and he often sold two boards per week. Of course, these were illegal, although they were commonly sold at many locations at the time. The market for these disappeared once the government got heavily involved in "legalized" gambling.

Soon after Page Two became a success, a local accounting firm bought the building and Tim was forced to move to the other end of town. In retrospect, the move proved to be good for his business. Immediately adjacent to the new location was a lot of town-owned free parking; several restaurants and small retailers were close by; and the size of his merchandising space had nearly doubled, not to mention the large display window overlooking Front Street. Tim was able to remove many of his wooden shelves to his new location, but he put them all against the outer walls, using the interior space for wire paperback display racks where he could put books with the covers facing outward. It didn't take Tim long to realize that the new display strategy had a tremendous impact on sales. Everyone who entered the store walked along the aisles looking at the covers, with very few customers looking at the books along the walls with only their spines displayed. Consequently, Tim moved all his older books to the wall locations and placed his newer and more expensive books in the centre displays.

Sales increased by about 40% the first year—and part of that increase came from a change in price strategy. As the only used bookstore in the area, Tim decided he could increase his prices to 60% of the cover price, rounded to the nearest $0.05. For example, a book that originally sold for $7.95 was sold used by Tim for $4.80. To help ensure that this wouldn't upset his best customers, Tim gave book-exchanging customers a 15% credit instead of 10% cash—and if customers didn't want to use all their credit immediately, he'd keep track of their credit on handwritten recipe cards. Most customers didn't notice the change in selling price, and many were pleased that they now got more for the used books they brought to Page Two. They simply made their selections after looking at the covers, and were happy to get the books they wanted at considerably less than the original cover price. With his expanded business, Tim decided to hire some part-time help. He found a young woman who was willing to work 20 hours per week, and he was happy to get some flexibility in his own working hours. Then, another tragedy struck. The town condemned the building Page Two was in, and Tim was forced, on short notice, to change locations again.

Tim found what turned out to be an almost ideal location. It was inside a downtown mall that spanned Front Street and Back Street. People could enter from either street, walk through a hallway, and exit on the opposite street. Page Two was third from the Back Street entrance, and close to several high-traffic businesses, notably a hair salon next door and a popular coffee shop next to that. The floor display area was about the same as the previous location's, but there was an extremely large basement that made a great storage area for both excess inventory and older books that would only be sold at sacrifice prices.

The location also had a window display area open to the hallway, and this gave Tim the idea to expand his inventory to include cassette music tapes, VHS videotapes, and, eventually, CDs and DVDs. When he moved locations, Tim decided to stop selling his adult material, except for adult magazines available on many local newsstands, but he sealed these in plastic so that customers couldn't browse them in the store. He did add some hard-cover books, but only ones that were of local interest: historical books, local authors, etc. He bought many of these as remainders—books that were discontinued by publishers, which unloaded them for $1 or $2 per copy just to clear inventory. Tim also replaced his part-time worker with a full-time worker. His part-time worker wasn't interested in more hours, and Tim suspected she'd been taking money from the till. His new employee was able to work a full 40-hour week at $10 per hour, and said she'd be happy to work extra hours when and if needed.

By 2002 Tim had added greeting cards, which he placed on six revolving display racks outside his store entrance in the mall hallway each morning. Sales were surprisingly good, maybe because there were few nearby competitors selling greeting cards, and maybe because of the coffee shop traffic. Many of the women who worked in nearby offices and who regularly visited the coffee shop stopped to buy the cards, which ranged in price from $2.95 to $7.95 each. With all the walk-by traffic, Tim soon got the idea to advertise photocopy and fax services as well. Single photocopies were $0.10 each for letter size or smaller, and $0.12 each for legal size. Customers got a 20% discount for 25 copies or more. Faxes were $1 for the first page and $0.50 for additional pages if they were local, $2 per page and $1 for additional pages if they were long distance. Finally, Tim decided to get into selling lottery tickets. Many coffee shop patrons dropped in to buy these tickets on their way to or from the coffee shop, and within a year Tim was selling about $1200 per month of lottery tickets.

Tim's main concern about his location was the lack of parking near the mall. Outside the entrance were four or five parking meters, but customers (assuming they could get a space) would have to carry their used books into the mall and past several stores to get to Page Two. His initial fear—that customers would be unwilling to bring large quantities of books into the mall—proved unfounded, but he still found the parking to be a problem. His own car had to be parked at a considerable distance in order to avoid costly meter fees.

TAMMY'S TREASURES

Tammy Smith had just opened Tammy's Treasures on Struan's Back Street. Many of the townspeople had referred to it as Tammy's Trash, but as the quality and quantity of her inventory began to expand it was evolving into a somewhat respectable business. It was at the opposite end of town from the Argyle Building, in a low-traffic area, saved somewhat by the town library, a taxi stand, and a barber shop. Tammy had previously owned a second-hand clothing store and a diner, both of which failed. Fortunately, she didn't bring any of her used clothing to Tammy's Treasures. Her new store was a combination consignment and used-goods store that carried used furniture, musical instruments, tools, and almost anything else she thought might sell. Tammy would take almost anything on consignment and offer it at the price suggested by the consignee. If sold, Tammy would keep between 20 and 30%, depending on the value of the sale, and give the balance to the consignee. She also included a clause that after 30 days she had the right to reduce the selling price by 10% per week until the item finally sold, or until it was reclaimed by the owner. If the owner was in a hurry for payment, Tammy would purchase the item for cash, but the price paid was a fraction of what the owner might get by consigning the item. For example, she might pay $20 for a pine table that she would then price at $100, recognizing that sometimes she might get her asking price and sometimes she might have to heavily discount the item to get rid of it.

Tammy had recently started adding music cassettes, VHS tapes, CDs, DVDs, and used books for sale, even hardcover books. Her selection of these items was very limited, but she'd begun advertising in area newspapers that she was willing to pay cash for used paperback books, comics, and select magazines. In her store, she priced these items at 50% of their cover price. Customers who were willing to trade rather than sell books were credited with 20% of the cover price of any book she accepted.

THE SITUATION

Initially, Tim wasn't too concerned with competition. He'd seen many threats in the past, including flea markets and garage sales, but they'd had a minimal effect on his sales. These flea markets had offered paperbacks at very low prices, but selections were poor; as some flea market vendors began to focus on used books their selection improved, but their prices also increased. They were never able to carry the selection or quantity of books that Page Two did, and they usually attracted a different group of customers than those who stopped at Tim's store.

When Tammy's Treasures first opened, Tim was pleased to see that she was starting to carry hardcover books. Since she didn't specialize in them, he was certain Tammy would eventually amass a collection of dusty, poorly displayed books that would negatively impact the store atmosphere and reinforce its junky image. He *was* concerned, however, when he heard that she was no longer buying hardcover books and music cassettes, VHS tapes, and CDs. And when she began actively seeking paperbacks—the staple of his business—his concern grew. Her price strategy would likely attract a large number of his customers if she ever achieved a good selection, some better merchandising displays, and a better location. The fact that she was considering the Argyle Building certainly raised a red flag. The building had two very large display windows facing Back Street. Tammy could use one to make an attractive book display and the other to display her furniture and more costly items. Tim had little doubt that if Tammy moved to the Argyle Building, his sales would go down.

THE DECISION

Ultimately, Tim knew his major decision was whether to rent the Argyle Building. Part of him said it would be a great location. It would still be close to the coffee shop; in fact, people in the coffee shop could look out the window and see the Argyle Building across the street. The new location came with eight free-parking spots at the side of the building. Finally, while there was limited storage space, several small offices were at the back that he could use for either storage or his book-sealing operations.

Tim also thought about several other courses of action, most of which he could contemplate regardless of his decision on the building.

1. Tim was considering a customer loyalty program. Customers who joined would get a number of benefits, including a higher credit for books that were brought in for exchange (20% instead of the current 15%), and they could save these credits against future purchases if they wanted to. Members who purchased music cassettes, VHS videos, CDs, and DVDs would get a free item once they purchased five of a similar item; that is, buy five CDs and get one free. Tim could also establish a database of customers, keeping track of special items they might like and letting them know when such items became available.

2. Tim wondered what to do about the selling price differential on paperbacks, comic books, and magazines. He could move now to reduce his price to 50% from 60% of the cover price, which would be less obvious than doing it after Tammy got her book business established. He might do it quietly by simply changing the sign in the store (or he could boldly proclaim it in the store), or he could take this as an opportunity to advertise his business and nearly 40 years of service to the community, promoting not just a new price strategy on books, but also his fax and photocopy services and his new book and greeting card selections.

3. Tim was considering expanding his operations to include selling paperbacks and greeting cards from other locations. He thought about putting wire paperback racks in garages, laundromats, and other locations. He had an opportunity to buy upwards of 70 revolving paperback display racks that each had 28 pockets and held about 112 books. The original price of the racks was $196, but Tim could buy them for $120 each, assuming he would take a minimum of 25 units. He also thought about selling greeting cards at women's hair salons. Being next to a hair salon in his current location, he'd noticed that many women would look at his greeting cards in the hallway while they were getting their hair done, and he thought similar locations could provide a great opportunity. Unfortunately, he couldn't find greeting card racks at a low price and would have to pay either $149 for a 36-pocket floor-model rack or $74 for a 20-pocket counter rack. If he decided on either of these options, he'd have to place his material in the racks on consignment, and he'd need to monitor and replace inventory on a regular basis. He'd also need to pay the business owners where his racks were installed a reasonable commission on sales, although he hadn't yet considered what level of commission would be appropriate.

4. Tim also knew he'd have to make some important product decisions. He should probably liquidate some of his products, and maybe place greater emphasis on others. He was also concerned that his anchor product, used paperbacks, seemed to be increasingly under attack from e-books, but the impact was still very small. Tim had never been concerned much with paperwork. He kept his business accounting as simple as possible: cash in, purchases for inventory out, add starting inventory, subtract closing inventory and operating expenses, and whatever was left was his income. He wished he'd tracked some product categories better, but without real data, the best he could do was estimate his sales breakdown and his gross margins (shown in Exhibit 1) and use his personal experience to help him make decisions. He'd already stopped purchasing used paperbacks that were below a certain cover price. Currently that was $5.95, but he was thinking it was time to raise it again.

EXHIBIT 1	Estimated Sales and Gross Margins per Product Category	
	Estimated Annual Sales	Gross Margin
Used books, magazines, comics	$59 900	83.3%
New books	$32 500	45.0%
DVDs	$2 300	80.0%
CDs	$5 200	80.0%
VHS tapes	$550	80.0%
Music cassettes	$1 260	80.0%
New cards, calendars	$5 800	45.0%
Photocopies	$960	*80.0%
Faxes	$1 800	*95.0%
Lottery tickets	$13 428	5.0%

*Best estimate.

W.H. Plastics Inc.

Christopher A. Ross

It was early February 2008 when William (Bill) Harnad began reviewing the current status of his company, W.H. Plastics Inc. The company designed and produced steel moulds; using injection moulding, it also produced plastic parts and products. It could decorate its plastic products and provide product assembly and packaging services. Having been established in 1989 in Hamilton, Ontario, the company planned to celebrate its 20th anniversary the following year. Bill wanted to make sure that W.H. entered 2009 with enough momentum to celebrate in style, but he was increasingly concerned about storm clouds on the horizon.

First, in the past few years the Canadian dollar had appreciated in value relative to the U.S. dollar, making the company's products more expensive there. Second, Chinese competitors looked as if they'd be a significant force in the next few years. Third, competition was becoming increasingly global. And fourth, the company seemed over-dependent on one major customer, which was responsible for about 74% of its sales. All of these issues prompted Bill's review of the company's operations with the objective of developing a plan of action.

Christopher A. Ross, professor, John Molson School of Business, Concordia University, wrote this case. Used with their permission, it is partly based on a student group report that was submitted in the fall of 2007. It is to be used for discussion purposes only. It is not designed to illustrate either effective or ineffective handling of an administrative or commercial situation. Some of the information in the case may have been disguised but essential relationships have been retained. Copyright © 2008. Reprinted with permission.

THE COMPANY

W.H. Plastics was very much a family business. Bill Harnad was its founder and president, and also its engineering manager. He was 55 years old and had worked in plastics all his life. ("I really love plastics," he said.) His wife, Liz, an accounting graduate, was the administrative controller. Their eldest son, David, was the production manager, and Nathalie, their eldest daughter and middle child, was quality assurance manager. Finally, their youngest child and second daughter, Lynn, was responsible for the purchasing department. While each had a formal position in the company, key decisions were often made as a family. Most production decisions, for example, were made by Bill, David, and Nathalie. They also handled many of the marketing decisions. There was no formal occupant of the sales/marketing position. (See Exhibit 1 for an organizational chart.)

W.H. began operations as a small machine shop, fabricating steel moulds used in the production of plastic products. Demand quickly increased, and after six years of constant and steady growth W.H. moved to a larger manufacturing facility. The company subsequently introduced injection-moulding services for the manufacture of plastic products. Over time, and in order to meet client demands, W.H. expanded its services to include such lateral processes as decorating on plastic and product assembly and packaging. From 1989 to 2007 W.H. grew from three employees to the current 170, with annual sales of over $18 million. (See Exhibit 2.)

W.H. saw itself as an innovative manufacturing solutions provider. It had state-of-the-art injection-moulding machines, equipped with computers and robotic arms for materials handling. It tried to follow a policy of continual improvement, especially since plastic technology was constantly evolving. The company continually researched new materials

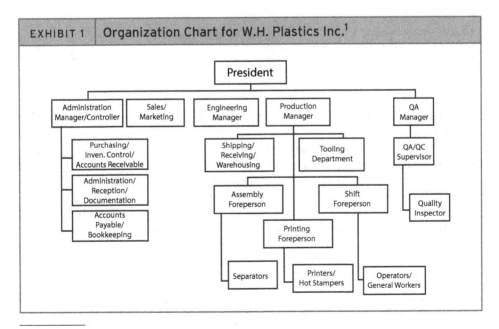

EXHIBIT 1 **Organization Chart for W.H. Plastics Inc.**[1]

---

[1]Source: Company files.

EXHIBIT 2	Statement of Earnings for Years Ending September 30 (In Canadian Dollars)[2]	
	2006	2007
Gross Sales	17 260 350	18 454 258
Less: Discounts and Returns	(209 926)	(210 452)
Net Sales	17 050 424	18 243 806
Less: Purchases and Small Tools	(6 751 248)	(7 213 630)
Less: Manufacturing Expense*	(7 830 894)	(8 152 024)
Gross Income	**2 468 282**	**2 878 152**
Selling Expense	(443 254)	(445 878)
Admin. Expense	(1 513 000)	(1 510 776)
Operating Income	**512 028**	**921 498**
Other Income	23 576	23 342
TOTAL	**535 604**	**944 840**
Financial Expense	(84 032)	(85 748)
Total Income Before Taxes	**451 572**	**859 092**

* Approximately 33% to 40% of manufacturing expenses were fixed.

Manufacturing Expense includes manpower and labour, unemployment, Q.P.P. and Q.H.I.P., electricity, heating, packaging, factory maintenance, repair and maintenance, import and export duties, equipment rental and leasing, and sub-contracting.

Selling Expense includes delivery expense, travelling, and promotion.

Administrative Expense includes administrative salaries, insurance, professional fees, software, telephone, and office expenses. No expenses were reported for marketing.

and processes, and had recently been a recipient of a Canadian Business Excellence award for the development of new products and two R&D awards from a major North American appliance manufacturer. In 2002, W.H. achieved ISO 9002 certification.

The company offered a wide range of design services, which included assisting customers in identifying and resolving issues related to product design. The moulds produced ranged from simple to complex, and were of varying sizes and types. W.H. used state-of-art moulding machines to provide a wide range of plastic parts. Its field of expertise included high-finish and precision-injection moulding[3] as well as the manufacture of products using difficult-to-mould engineering resins, multi-material/multi-colour mouldings, and robotic and automated moulding optimization systems. The company also had

[2]Source: Company files.
[3]Injection moulding is a technological process for introducing a fluid, such as a plastic, under pressure into a mould's cavity. Most plastic raw materials used in injection moulding aren't fluid, but rather come in pellets. The pellets are heated until a melt is obtained.

expertise in decorating and printing on plastic. Services included single to multi-colour printing, hot stamping, paint to silk-screen services, and a full range of colour matching. Finally, W.H. assembled and packaged products according to customer specifications. Altogether, the company produced over 700 different products on 16 injection machines. Yearly quantities ranged from 500 to 10 million pieces.

One of W.H.'s specialties was knobs and dials. It made a wide range of these, from heavy-duty mechanical knobs to heat-resistant, flame-retardant knobs for all types of industries. Other products included ski poles and goggles, tiles, compact discs, optic lenses, mini-circuits, toys, electrical plugs and receptacles, flower pots, ice cube trays, and coin sorters. Examples of these manufactured products are shown in Exhibit 3.

EXHIBIT 3	Examples of Products

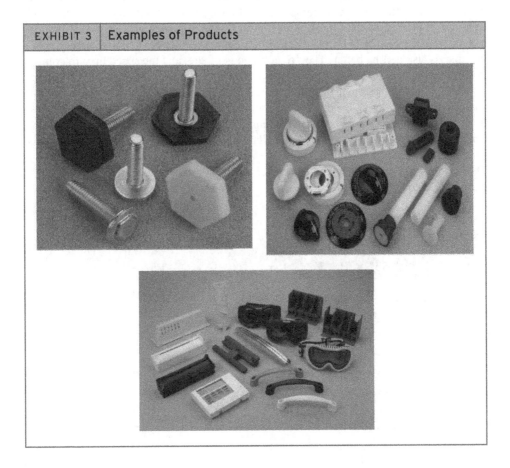

The company saw potential applications for its skills and products in a wide variety of industries. These included the appliance, pharmaceutical, sporting goods, construction, automotive, military, household, communications, and promotional industries. W.H. had sold its products in North America (Canada, the United States, Mexico), South America (Brazil), Europe (Belgium, Italy, Luxembourg, Netherlands, Spain, and the U.K.), Asia (Japan), and Australia.

THE CONCERNS

In recent years, the Canadian dollar had risen from roughly US$0.69 to about US$1.00 (See Exhibit 4). "A big challenge for us is the increase in the value of the dollar," Bill said. "That increase means that our products are more expensive for our clients. About 75 to 80% of our sales are to the United States. About 10% are outside North America (Europe and South America) and the rest is in Canada, mostly to U.S.-owned plants. Outside of North America, we supply the aerospace industry."

The second concern was competition from China. "We're starting to see a change with China," Bill said. "Compared to last year, prices in China have gone up anywhere from 20 to 28% because of transportation and the high cost of fuel. China is sort of stabilizing for us. But if we're to compete, we'll have to cut labour costs. China doesn't have raw materials, so they must be paying the same price we do. But the cost of raw materials is going up because the price of petroleum is going up. Chinese quality, while variable, is also getting better. They're going to get there, and the speed they're going at is pretty impressive."

W.H.'s third concern was that competition was no longer local. "The challenge is to compete globally. Many big corporations are moving out of North America. The big push is for Mexico, so now you have parts coming in from China, being assembled in Mexico, and then shipped back to Canada or the United States. It's now a global economy, and small- and medium-sized companies will have a problem moving offshore in order to compete. They can bring in parts, but to get to the level where they can be manufacturing offshore—that's still a problem."

EXHIBIT 4	Average Monthly Exchange Rates, 1998–2008 (US$1 = CDN$)[4]	
	Year	$Canadian
	January 1998	$0.6941
	January 1999	$0.6582
	January 2000	$0.6902
	January 2001	$0.6653
	January 2002	$0.6249
	January 2003	$0.6489
	January 2004	$0.7716
	January 2005	$0.8161
	January 2006	$0.8641
	January 2007	$0.8504
	January 2008	$0.9890

[4]Source: www.bankofcanada.ca/cgi-bin/famecgi_fdps. Accessed May 20, 2008.

Bill's final concern was that 74% of W.H.'s sales were to one customer, a large appliance manufacturer. "I worry about it all the time. Once you do good work, they want to give you more and more," he said. He was trying to offset this dependence, but the company found it difficult. Bill explained that he was trying to develop the business—W.H. was starting to work for more than one appliance manufacturer and it had started quoting in the automotive industry—but that "meanwhile, back on the farm, there's one customer who wants to give you more and more all the time. So what do you do?" This concern was particularly acute in 2007–2008 because of the housing crisis in the United States and the fear of a U.S. recession.

THE PLASTICS INDUSTRY[5]

Plastic was used in virtually every segment of the economy; it had displaced paper, glass, and metal in many traditional applications. Its popularity was enhanced by its unique attributes, including ease of processing, light weight, and resistance to corrosion. Technical developments in plastic processing, equipment manufacturing, and engineering had also increased the use of plastics in the health care, automotive, telecommunications, and electronic sectors. Some newer plastics were sufficiently heat resistant to replace some metal parts in engines, and strong enough to replace metal beams in buildings.

The North American plastic industry was made up of approximately 16 000 companies producing plastic and rubber products, with combined annual revenues of US$175 billion. Product specialization by manufacturers had resulted in a highly fragmented industry determined by material type, manufacturing processes, and end users. The 50 largest companies—which included Dow Chemical, Sealed Air Corporation, Carlisle Companies, Newell Rubbermaid, and Alcoa[6]—represented only 30% of the market. Membership in NAFTA provided Canada with easy access to this market.

In general, large plastic injection-moulding companies enjoyed economies of scale, both in buying raw materials and in manufacturing commodity products like bottles and plastic film. Smaller companies, by contrast, competed in niches by producing specialized products and offering product development expertise.

Given the nature of the global market, manufacturers were constantly trying to find ways to be as cost effective as possible. Moreover, globalization had motivated many manufacturers to outsource their production, particularly to China. With plastic moulding companies following the same trend, China's mass injection-moulding market had been growing—which meant that Canadian suppliers were forced to cater to the needs of niche markets. They also had to find ways to reduce cost, for example by improving their total quality management and increasing the efficiency of their operations.

A major trend in the industry's favour, however, was the strong demand for recycled plastics. Responding to consumers' desires, major plastic-packaging users had begun

---

[5]This section is drawn from the following documents: 1. Canadian Plastics Products Industry, www.ic.gc.ca/epic/site/plastics-plastiques.nsf/en/p101384e.html. Accessed February 2, 2008. 2. Plastics, www.investicanada.gc.ca/en/industry sectors/plastics.aspx. Accessed March 14, 2008.

[6]Plastic Products in the USA, Euromonitor International, www.portal.euromonitor.com, mercury.concordia.ca/portal/server.pt. Accessed March 17, 2008.

incorporating at least some recycled plastic content in their products as part of the growing interest in recycling. This had forced suppliers to do the same.

The Canadian plastics industry could be categorized into four sub-sectors:

1. Synthetic resins production—the raw materials from which plastic products are produced.
2. Plastic machinery manufacturing.
3. Mould and die making—used to form plastic products.
4. Plastic products.

The Canadian synthetic resins industry had shipments of $10.6 billion in 2006 and employed about 7180 people in 103 establishments. Approximately 68% of these shipments were exported, with 89% going to the United States. Most of the larger firms producing synthetic resins in Canada were U.S. or European owned; Nova Chemicals and Petromont were the largest producers with headquarters in Canada.

Synthetic resins, which are derived from petrochemicals, are the raw material from which plastic products are made. There are two categories of resins: thermoplastics and thermosets. Thermoplastics—including polyethylene, polypropylene, polystyrene, and polyvinyl chloride—are the most commonly used materials in plastics processing. These materials soften on the application of heat and solidify when cooled, an ability that is reversible, making the recycling of thermoplastics relatively straightforward. Thermosets, however, are cured via a chemical reaction that's not generally reversible, meaning that it's difficult to recycle these resins.

Another way to characterize resins was by the price versus performance relationship. Commodity resins were produced in high volumes and commanded a relatively low price per unit volume. Engineering or specialty resins offered higher performance on attributes such as heat resistance, flame retardation, mechanical strength, and electrical properties. They were produced in limited quantities and commanded a higher price. Synthetic resins accounted for 30 to 50% of the final value of a plastic product. W.H. used engineering resins in the fabrication of its products.

The plastic machinery sub-sector consisted of manufacturers of machines and auxiliary equipment used to produce a wide range of plastic products, mainly for the packaging, construction, and automotive sectors, and to a lesser extent for electrical and electronic components, furniture, and a variety of other end uses. In 2006, this sub-sector comprised 59 establishments and employed 4600 people. The value of shipments was $1 billion, 96% of which was exported. The companies in this sub-sector had become highly specialized in order to compete in the domestic and international markets. Canadian manufacturers had gained an international reputation for quality; their main export markets were the United States (62%), China (8%), Luxembourg (7%), and Mexico (3%). The majority of machinery manufacturers were located in Ontario.

Companies in the mould sub-sector generally specialized in this product area. For each plastic product, a unique mould had to be designed and manufactured to meet the customer's needs. Simply by changing the mould, the same machine could be used to produce a variety of plastic products. In 2006, this sub-sector comprised approximately 241 establishments with 8590 employees and shipments of $1.3 billion, of which 79% was exported.

Like the rest of the industry, mould-making companies tended to be small, but there were a few larger companies. Of the top 10 North American mould makers in 2006, six were Canadian firms. In 2006, the main export markets were the United States (87%), Mexico (3%), and Japan (1%).

In 2006, about 1540 establishments had as their principal activity the processing of synthetic resins into plastic products. This generated shipments of $20.4 billion and employed 94 700 people. Approximately 46% of shipments were exported, mainly to the United States. In some industries—for example, shampoo, furniture, toys, and razor manufacturing—plastic production was often a secondary activity whereby the manufacturers produced plastic for their own consumption. The industry was facing a number of challenges: the escalation in the value of the Canadian dollar, high energy prices, high raw material prices, and increasing competition from rapidly developing economies.

THE CANADIAN PLASTICS INDUSTRY

In Canada, three major product lines dominated the use of plastics: packaging (34%), construction products (26%), and automotive components (18%). Electrical and electronic products and furniture each constituted 5% of the end-use market for plastic products. Demand for plastic products was expected to continue growing faster than the economy as a whole, although not as fast as in the past.

The Canadian plastics industry was dominated by small and medium-sized companies, and was almost 95% Canadian owned. Approximately 90% of exports as a whole went to the United States.

According to Industry Canada, the industry faced a number of competitiveness issues:

a. The small size of many Canadian establishments.

b. The fact that relatively few firms were undertaking in-house R&D, despite the accelerating rate of technological change in the industry.

c. The need to increase exports and to encourage more firms to export.

d. The challenge of addressing environmental issues.

e. The ability to meet technology and skill requirements while maintaining competitiveness, primarily with nearby U.S. competitors.

The industry's regional distribution in Canada was as follows: 51% of all establishments were located in Ontario, 25% were in Quebec, 11% were in the Prairie provinces, 9% were in British Columbia, and 4% were in the Atlantic provinces. Approximately 62% of the overall industry and 100% of the automotive-components sub-sector were in Ontario. (Exhibit 5 lists the names of representative companies in each sector.)

W.H. operated in a niche market. Unlike many other companies, it made its own moulds and then used them to produce plastic products. It therefore operated in two of the industry sub-sectors, which insulated it somewhat from the ups and downs of the individual sub-sectors. The company wasn't in the volume business; its niche was complex engineering resin jobs, a special field. Raw materials for these jobs could cost approximately $39 per pound. "We specialize in complex plastic manufacturing," Bill said. "If somebody came and said 'Could you make that bottle cap for me?' we'd probably say no. If it was special,

EXHIBIT 5	Representative Companies in Industry Subsectors[7]			
Synthetic Resins	Plastic Machinery	Moulds	Plastic Products
Alpha/Owens Corning	Alpha Marathon	Husky Injection Moulding Systems	Camoplast
Basell	AR Engineering	Omega Tool	IPL
Dow Chemical	Brampton Engineering	Wentworth Technologies	Jim Pattison Group
Imperial Oil	Macro Engineering	Reko	Plasticor Inc.
Petromont	Engel	Build-A-Mould	Domco
Nova Chemicals	Corma	Active Burgess	IPEX

we'd do it—we're not interested in making spoons and forks. I want the company to go more and more into engineering. We have the expertise, we have the engineering, and our strength is the tool room, where we make the moulds."

CUSTOMERS

Companies that usually bought plastic injection-moulded pieces weren't easily defined. They varied in size, usage frequency, and usage purpose. The evidence suggested, however, that they required a minimum level of income to deal with the substantial initial cost of a mould. Moulds were priced based on size and complexity of manufacture; a small, relatively simple mould could cost in the region of $10 000. Customers for moulds had to be able to sell enough of their products in order to cover the cost of the mould.

Though these companies served different markets, their approach to selecting suppliers was very similar. They were all motivated by a need they couldn't satisfy without outside help. Once they'd determined their need for plastic injection moulding, they began their search for suppliers. First-time users of plastic-injection suppliers relied on internet search engines or network referrals for prospecting potential suppliers. Attributes such as the supplier's physical proximity influenced their decision. Once potential suppliers were identified, users then provided them with a description of their needs.

When all the information about potential suppliers was collected, the customers evaluated each company to find out which was the most capable, at a competitive price. Evaluation was based on a number of key criteria, such as proximity, quality, etc. Customers typically asked the following questions: Does the supplier have the capacity to produce the necessary quantities? If the needed quantities increase, will the supplier be able to meet the new requirements? Can the supplier fabricate the products for a predetermined delivery date? Will the supplier be in a position to help if we run into production problems? How closely can it work with our team? Does it have quality procedures in place to minimize product-defect levels?

---

[7]Source: Canadian Plastic Products Industry, Industry Canada. www.ic.gc.ca/epic/site/plastics-plastiques.nsf/en/p101383e.html. Accessed February 20, 2008.

Over the years, W.H.'s management had observed differences in the way certain customer groups approached the purchasing process. Customers in the appliance sector, for example, expected excellent customer service and decor capabilities, and demanded speed, competitive prices, and quality. They were regular repeat customers, and their purchasers were experienced buyers. They also had a lengthy buying process, from conceptualization to delivery, and bought on the basis of proximity to plant, reputation, and word-of-mouth. Finally, these customers weren't terribly loyal to their suppliers.

Customers from the aerospace and military sectors focused primarily on durability and quality. Suppliers had little room to deviate from specifications. Purchases were sporadic, but high-volume. These customers chose suppliers based on their experience—although the buyers themselves weren't experienced, they were looking for viable solutions and were impatient with defects. They were not price sensitive.

Customers in the automotive sector required timely delivery, competitive prices, high quality, high volume capacity, and good customer service. They would sometimes find customers via the internet, through their reputation, or based on past experience. Their purchasers were often experienced buyers, and purchases were made regularly. They too had a lengthy buying process, from conceptualization to delivery. They required quality standardized suppliers (ISO). Their selection requirements were lengthy, but they tended to be loyal to their suppliers. Repeat purchases needed to be done as smoothly as possible.

Once all the potential suppliers had been identified, the customer's next stage was to select one company that best fit the necessary criteria. The selected supplier had to meet all expectations that had been identified. Production had to be consistent with the proposed criteria. Once the mould was made, customers could still switch suppliers because the mould was their property. The customer's quality department evaluated the supplier's work, its forecast team evaluated delivery time, and all departments appraised the level of customer service.

MARKET SECTORS

W.H. served a number of market sectors, including appliance and household, aerospace and military, sporting, automotive, and electronics. (See Exhibit 6.) This diversity demonstrated the company's flexibility. Its growth, however, had been a direct result of its expertise in the fabrication and decor of knobs and dials. As cited earlier, W.H.'s success was due largely to its sales to one major appliance manufacturer. While other customers ordered sporadically, usually when they needed more stock, the appliance customer had consistently increased purchases throughout the years. The other industries, meanwhile, had been quite stagnant in terms of sales.

The company didn't target any one sector, reasoning that its products were specific to a customer's needs. W.H. targeted "any company needing turnkey solutions to plastic injection moulding using any type of engineered resin in high volumes." These high volumes resulted from the high setup costs that couldn't be justified with fewer than 2000 pieces per day. Thus the target market consisted of large companies that mass-produced products and needed a constant supply of injection-moulded parts. Customers weren't only buying injection-moulded products, they were also buying know-how, expertise, and problem- solving capabilities.

EXHIBIT 6	Sales Distribution among Different Industrial Sectors[8]
Sectors	Sales Percentage
Appliance and household	74%
Aerospace and military	10%
Sporting	8%
Automotive	5%
Electronic	2%
Other	1%

COMPETITION

Competition was based mainly on just-in-time manufacturing capabilities and in-house research and development. W.H. had addressed these criteria and had worked with customers to develop products. It had also set up lean manufacturing.

W.H. had two major competitors, both of which were based in the United States. One competitor, Eagle Industries Inc., was an injection-moulding company of approximately the same size as W.H. Its customers included appliance, housewares, agriculture, and furniture manufacturers. It had capabilities in thermoplastic extrusions, plastic sheet fabrication, short-run, and large parts. The company was located close to its largest client and could easily service other clients that were close by. Its main advantage over W.H. was location, since Eagle Industries lacked W.H.'s decoration capabilities.

W.H.'s other competitor was Johnson Plastics. It was considered the major competitor in the knob business, with plant facilities in Asia, Mexico, and the United States. Johnson offered a broad range of moulding technologies and was a leading supplier of decorative plastic parts for the appliance industry. Its services included parts designing and engineering, mould designing, injection moulding, finishing, and assembling. The company served the appliance, automotive, and plumbing industries, and supplied knobs and dials to many other types of industries. It had recently opened two manufacturing plants in China that allowed the company to price competitively. However, W.H. had successfully won over some of Johnson's customers as a result of its attention to detail and delivery time.

W.H. considered its major competitors to be the other companies that focused on knobs and dials, and didn't view other Canadian companies as competitors since they weren't involved in that area. "We're in a little niche market," Bill said. "A lot of plastic companies go after big, big volumes, and of course that's where they're competing with everybody who has an injection press."

W.H. also faced competition from Chinese imports. With the rising Canadian dollar, U.S. companies had looked to alternative plastic suppliers, specifically in China. Having lost some contracts to low-cost injection-moulding manufacturers there, W.H. had been forced to price at a level that just covered its costs—but even then prices were much higher than those of Chinese-based manufacturers. But these manufacturers were having a number

---

[8]Source: Company files.

of quality issues, and some of the contracts W.H. had lost had since been reinstated. Then there was the issue of delivery time: it took about seven weeks for China to deliver new products to markets, and about three weeks for repeat purchases. This had forced U.S. companies to spend more aggressively on distribution centres and warehousing while losing out on companies with just-in-time delivery systems.

Finally, certain industries, like steel, that had once been a competitive threat to W.H. had become less so. Advances in electronics had put some pressure on W.H.'s knob specialization; for example, some appliance manufacturers had started to experiment with other technologies to replace knobs, one of which was electronic membranes that offered touch displays instead of conventional knobs. This product variation didn't appeal to consumers, however, and much of this change had slowed or even reversed. W.H. had since kept a keen watch on electronic trends in the appliance industry.

COMPETITIVE EDGE

W.H. took pride in its on-time delivery, high-quality products, and competitive pricing. The company also believed that its engineering and technical support, customer service and support, quality systems, and automated system design contributed to its competitive advantage.

Customization and specialization of plastic mouldings was W.H.'s core competence. The firm's ability to manufacture products according to client specifications added to its competitive advantage. It used materials effectively and did some in-house recycling, which not only significantly reduced costs but also contributed to the environment. Moreover, it had its own R&D program and practised just-in-time manufacturing, which it believed gave it a real advantage over the Chinese competition.

From conception to delivery, a typical part passed through many different departments, and before each part could move to the next stage it required approval from the quality department. Both the client and the engineering department would conceptualize a new part before the technical drawings were sketched. Once a functional drawing was complete it was transferred to the tooling department, where fabrication of the mould commenced. Upon completion, the mould was tested in the production department and set up for fabrication of the actual part. Sample parts were tested in accordance with the standards established by the customer and the technical drawings. Once the part was approved, it was ready for mass production, unless it had a decorative component. Since the images on the products had their own technical drawings, the printing department had to follow the guidelines and create the samples. At this stage, the part was approved by both W.H.'s quality department and the customer. Upon approval, packaging specifications were made, again by both W.H. and the customer, and the part was prepared for regular delivery. The assembly department handled the packaging and the final inspection of each part; these frequent inspections lessened the likelihood of defective products being shipped to customers.

MARKETING AT W.H.

The company didn't have an established marketing strategy, and so, although it was excellent at customer retention through superior service and quality practices, it wasn't very successful at attracting new customers. One of the problems was that W.H. was very uncertain as to which markets it should target. In the custom moulding industry, it was the customers that usually sought out manufacturers, not the other way around. Consequently, W.H. had focused more on making it easier for customers to find it than on prospecting for potential customers. In 2005, for example, it revamped its outdated website to make it more visually appealing. The website listed the company's services, showed pictures of products, noted the industries and countries in which it was interested, and gave a bit of company history. As with many other websites, how to contact the company was prominently displayed. One could access the site in English, French, or Spanish.

But W.H. didn't get most of its customers via the internet; in the last two or three years, most of its customers were either known to the company or were referred to it. In short, people who needed these products knew where to go. They were already knowledgeable. Still, as Bill explained, "Customers in our field are OEMs [original equipment manufacturers], but I do a lot of selling. I go to see customers, we try to get new customers, we target. For example, we may look at a certain thing we want to go after, look at the companies that may need it, do some research, know what business they're in. Then we start going after them by getting in touch with their procurement departments, and we start developing a relationship. With the internet it's changed a bit. There are a lot of buyers who go on the internet; they look, identify companies who can do what they want, and then they contact the companies."

W.H.'s distinct advantage was its ability to deliver products quickly: an element not easily achieved by many companies. W.H. had become almost indispensable to its customers because of its ability to adapt to constant line changes. This had lessened the potential business loss from cheaper Chinese alternatives. Whereas most Chinese manufacturers took approximately three months from conceptualization to production, W.H. finished the project in three to six weeks. Moreover, Chinese manufacturers took a minimum of three weeks to deliver the parts to their clients; W.H. could deliver in one to three days.

But again, the rising Canadian dollar meant U.S. companies (about 80% of W.H.'s business) were increasingly turning to China, meaning in turn that W.H. had been forced to cut costs as much as possible. But this wasn't proving to be easy. W.H. was already keeping salaries at a minimum, which had resulted, in part, in high employee absenteeism and turnover, a big concern for some members of the management team. Many of the employees were low-skilled immigrants with little or no education, and the monotony of many of the tasks plus low wages made it difficult for W.H. to keep them motivated. This had put pressure on W.H. to simplify employee processes in order to reduce the cost of training.

The pressure to reduce costs had continued unabated. While W.H. had tried to accommodate its customers, in some cases the company's margins were so thin that it couldn't meet clients' demands. Management had considered importing certain high-cost parts from China, but they lacked experience in dealing directly with a Chinese manufacturer. Knowledge of shipping, logistics, and duties on products from China to W.H.'s warehouse was necessary for successful implementation. In addition, importing parts would run the risk of losing flexibility in its just-in-time competency. Management was also concerned about the amount of planning and organization involved in importing, and didn't think W.H. had the manpower for such a drastic operational move. Some clients, they believed, would also want to share in any cost savings, thereby continuing the pressure on the margins.

All products were distributed directly to customers. In most cases the customer made its own arrangements to pick up goods from W.H.'s warehouse; for example, one major customer usually notified W.H. of its trucks' arrival times and W.H. made all the arrangements for speedy collection. If a customer requested an urgent delivery, W.H. would use Fed-Ex, UPS, Purolator, or any other suitable courier to deliver the goods. With this channel, delivery normally took 24 hours within Canada and three days to the United States.

W.H. used a markup strategy for its pricing, allocating approximately 10% as markup profit, which it included in the list price. The markup percentage varied greatly, however, depending on the job. More labour-intensive parts usually had a higher markup, since these parts involved more difficulty (and more defects were likely, based on employee error).

After Chinese firms entered the industry, W.H. had to continually fight on the basis of both price and quality. It had to provide the highest quality at the asked price in order to create value for its customers. Pricing varied with respect to customers, orders, product, and urgency of the order.

The company relied primarily on word-of-mouth, referrals, and its website to attract customers, and, in fact, had no expense line for marketing activities (See Exhibit 2.)

THE FUTURE

W.H.'s management team was in general agreement that to ensure growth the company needed to enter new segments of the market and attract new customers. But the team also wanted to maintain the company's core values: first, to maintain its reputation for credibility, integrity, and consistency, and, second, to meet or exceed customers' quality requirements. W.H.'s goal was to increase its profit margin to 9% by the end of fiscal 2009.

Bill and his management team felt that the best way to attract new customers was to focus on their area of expertise and "leverage their proficiencies." They wanted to create more awareness for the company, improve its image in the marketplace, and secure maximum contracts in their segment. They recognized that the company lacked an established strategy and hadn't been very successful in attracting new customers. They had attempted networking by joining the local Chamber of Commerce in 2003, and a year later won an Award of Excellence. W.H. had also been a finalist in the exporting category, which had given it free exposure in trade journals. They had attended trade shows in the past but were unimpressed with the results. Bill felt that maybe some public relations would help. He also wondered about Google advertising and the possibility of putting more emphasis on personal selling by enhancing his business cards and having a catalogue. He was wondering what action he should take to ensure the continued success of the company in the face of all the competitive pressures.

Spriware Canada Inc.

Mark Parker

It was early 2012, and Kenneth Weller, CEO of Spriware Canada Inc., was thinking about his company's next strategic direction. It had invested heavily in Canada, and although sales were quite impressive for a new company in a very competitive industry, Kenneth knew that Spriware's current profitability wouldn't allow it to achieve its targeted payback period. He was considering two options: cutting prices to drive an increase in market share (a market penetration strategy), or entering a new international market that appeared to have considerable potential (a market development strategy).

THE COMPANY

Spriware Canada Inc. was a manufacturer of refrigerators for middle-class families. It produced a line of high-quality, functional, extremely energy-efficient refrigerators with no fancy gadgets or features. The company's new $60-million plant, located in Surrey, British Columbia, began production at the beginning of 2011; it had a capacity to produce 100 000 refrigerators per year, and could be expanded to produce another 50 000 units at a capital cost of $10 million. No extra labour or overhead would be required for the additional production. All refrigerators were sold in Canada, where Spriware had a 10% market share after its first year of operation.

Spriware's success was due to several aspects of its marketing strategy. First, it distributed its product exclusively through two large retail groups. The company co-marketed with these groups, developing television and newspaper advertising for their primary target market: young middle-class families with a household income of around $70 000. Second, Spriware priced its products competitively. The average retail price for its refrigerators was $1500, compared with about $1700 for similar competitor models and private brands. Third, the company offered a competitive warranty, which included covering repair costs for the first five years of ownership, provided that repair-service companies subcontracted by Spriware were used.

In 2011 the company had revenue of $90 million, operating costs of $42 million (including variable material and energy costs of $500 per appliance, and fixed labour costs of $12 million), and fixed overhead costs of $42 million (including an annual marketing cost of $10 million). Net income, after 30% corporate income tax, was only $4 million, a profit performance well below Spriware's targeted after-tax return on investment (ROI) of 10%. Kenneth Weller was especially concerned about how this would affect the five-year payback period he'd set. The market for refrigerators in Canada wasn't expected to grow at all over the next two years, and longer-term growth was expected to be about only 3% per year.

KENNETH'S DILEMMA

Price Reduction

Kenneth thought about his first option: reducing the average price of Spriware refrigerators in an attempt to increase market share. His marketing director, a recent graduate of an international business program, advised him that based on her analysis, the firm could increase market share to 15% if he reduced his prices by 10%. This would enable Spriware to take market share away from lower-quality brands by effectively offering its product at the same price but with better performance and warranties. In the longer term, the manager believed that with proper marketing and product-positioning strategies, Spriware could obtain 20 to 25% of the market, as Canadian households were increasingly looking for greater value for their money. But Kenneth's concern was that his current pricing was already competitive for the products Spriware offered, and reflected fair value for what customers received. Why should Spriware undersell itself? As well, he feared that a price reduction strategy could start a price war in the short term. This was, after all, an industry with 10 manufacturers, all of which had excess capacity and were aggressive in maintaining sales volumes.

Overseas Export

Then Kenneth turned to his second option: exporting to an overseas market in an attempt to produce and sell more refrigerators. His highly skilled marketing director, through intelligence gathering, had identified market potential in the island nation of Mabuhailand, located in the Pacific region around Indonesia and the Philippines. In the last 20 years Mabuhailand had emerged into a fairly stable democracy, governed by the pro-business centrist Liberal Democratic Party. This had followed nearly 30 years of corrupt dictatorship and infighting among various extreme political factions, several of which still existed and were reported to be dissatisfied with the distribution of political power formed under the country's new constitution. Extreme groups were considered to be either ultra-nationalistic and anti-foreigner, or left-wing with a desire for complete control of the nation's emerging commercial and industrial system. Some of the groups were reported to have links to the Chinese government, whose past political and economic involvement in the country was still resented by many of its people. Despite its success, the country had been plagued at times with violent protests, resulting in road blockades and disruption of some commercial activities.

The people of Mabuhailand were an interesting mix of Chinese, Malay, and Portuguese, the result of a colonial past in which Portugal had occupied such areas as Formosa (present-day Taiwan). The dialect, known as Latgalog, was unique to the country. Little was known about it, especially its symbolic aspects; it had been described as Brazilian Portuguese with an Asian sound to it. Literacy rates, while improved, were still quite low at only about 70% of the population. However, virtually all young people under the age of 18 (25% of the population) were receiving education; they showed a great interest and were highly motivated to learn. English was compulsory in school as of age five. Mabuhailand had one government-owned television station, though only about 30% of households owned a TV. The country had one privately held national newspaper, *Mabu Express,* in circulation.

The culture was characterized by strong family ties, with two or more generations living in the same household, and a strong sense of obligation to the community, with activities focused around the local Catholic or nontraditional Protestant churches. Informal communication within communities was an important source of information for many people. Traditional authority was shown great respect. However, with the country's growing economic prosperity, many younger families were looking to live on their own.

Mabuhailand was rich in natural resources, including high-value precious metals, copper, cobalt, diamonds, and offshore oil reserves. Following political change, the country's leaders encouraged foreign investment in order to develop these resources and train the population. The ruling party's policy had been to encourage domestic industries through a stable, competitive tax policy. Resources accounted for 40% of the economy, and the government was looking to encourage more value-added manufacturing as part of the economic mix. With an industrious and hard-working population numbering around 10 million, the country had increased its GDP in 10 years from $40 billion to $120 billion in 2011. Over the next five years economic development policies were forecasted to grow the economy by $10 billion each year. Most tax revenues, representing 30% of GDP, were derived from business taxes and import duties, and had enabled the country to build needed infrastructure, including ports, roads, electric power utilities, and social services like hospitals and schools. But more would be needed. Economists at the International Monetary Fund had predicted that over the next five years government spending could rise to at least $50 billion annually, based on the government's infrastructure and social spending plans. The government had previously resisted borrowing to finance spending, and as a matter of policy strove to achieve balanced budgets. Total outstanding government debt was estimated at 40% of GDP.

Because many of the nation's 2.5 million households now had power, and given the country's growing per capita income levels, Kenneth believed that Mabuhailand represented a tremendous opportunity for refrigerator sales. A benchmarking exercise with other developing nations had suggested that, based on Mabuhailand's income levels, annual purchases should be one refrigerator for approximately every 40 households. However, according to government import statistics, in 2011 only 20 000 units had been purchased, representing an estimated retail value of $24 million. Kenneth thought there may be several reasons for this low level of demand. Import statistics showed that virtually all the units were re-exports from Hong Kong, which he suspected were secondary, low-quality units likely made in China. The sale of refrigerators was handled by numerous small-scale retailers, many of which weren't appliance specialists but rather remnants of the old traditional economy. Larger modern retailers had begun to emerge, and their refrigerators tended to be purchased from numerous traders, who in turn had bought them from various manufacturers in China, reselling them to any outfit that would take them. There was no advertising or marketing of any significance.

Kenneth believed that he could capitalize on a first-mover advantage and quickly become the market leader. At the projected economic growth rate, the resulting gains in income would result in 1 in 30 households purchasing refrigerators within the next five years, and 1 in 20 households purchasing refrigerators within 10 years. Spriware's market studies further suggested that, based on neighbouring markets' performance, it could sell refrigerators into Mabuhailand at $1400 per unit, net of distribution costs. The price wouldn't include import duties paid to the government, which would represent 5% of the selling price. This duty was applied to all of the nation's $40 billion of annual imports.

Although Kenneth was excited about the trade opportunity, he knew he had a couple of issues to consider. First, he wondered whether Mabuhailand's economy would grow as strongly as was forecasted. This forecast was based on a doubling of resource production in the next five years and stable prices at current levels—reflecting strong demand in emerging nations like China and India. However, about two-thirds of the resource sector's growth had been due to a doubling in prices over the past 10 years rather than any increase in output, and many observers believed that the nation's commodity prices should have increased by only 3 to 5% per year in the last decade. As a result, there was concern that these commodity prices ran the risk of collapse.

Second, Kenneth knew that to be positioned in this market longer term, he'd eventually have to build a plant in the country, even if it was on a smaller scale than the Canadian operation. He'd had discussions with senior Ministry of Industry and Trade representatives, who'd visited him in Surrey to discuss this trade opportunity. The sense he got from these discussions was that the government would likely accept imported products for a period of time, but eventually its policy would be to encourage domestic industries. No doubt, Kenneth thought, the government would soon use duties as a means to encourage and protect domestic development of the industry.

Still, the longer-term prospects in Mabuhailand were great, and neighbouring countries could hold additional opportunities. Government officials had hinted at these countries' moves to develop a regional trading bloc, with the goal of eliminating import duties and excess customs regulations. But, Kenneth wondered, did he want to commit assets in Mabuhailand? Labour costs would be a mere 20% of what they were in Canada, but what about productivity and training needs? What about marketing and promotion? Kenneth felt it was time to have a discussion with his management team. He wanted to get their input into what would be Spriware's best course of action.

Petridis Vineyard: To Wine or Not to Wine

Mark Parker

In early 2012 Anthony Petridis was considering entering a new venture, one tied to his family heritage and dear to his heart. He'd always wanted to get into the wine industry, and now he had the opportunity. The question he really faced was to what extent he wanted to become involved. He could simply be a grape grower, or he could become a wine producer by outsourcing his production to a local winery. And if he chose the latter, he wasn't sure whether to export to the Chinese market, and what marketing strategy he should implement.

BACKGROUND

Anthony, a successful entrepreneur, had done well in the property market through investments in his holding company, Thikankel Inc. He had significant retained earnings on the company's balance sheet and felt it was time to diversify his investments. Reflecting his family's tradition of owning vineyards and producing wine in Greece, their country of origin, Anthony was looking to acquire a vineyard in Ontario's Niagara region in order to capitalize on the developing wine industry there.

The property was a 45-acre vineyard in Niagara-on-the-Lake; it was run by an independent farmer who was now looking to retire. The cost of acquiring the property was $1.5 million. The vineyard was in many ways managed as a hobby farm. It wasn't involved in wine production, but rather sold its grapes to local wineries on a "spot price" basis at the end of the season. This differed from many established vineyards that had nurtured relationships with local wineries and had annual contracts in place to sell their grapes to specific wineries at agreed prices.

In 2010 the property cultivated about 74 tonnes of grapes on about 30 acres of land. Half of this production was made up of Cabernet Franc and Cabernet Sauvignon grape varieties, which were used solely for table wine production. The remaining varieties were also used for table wine, but with some quality improvement could possibly be used for ice wine. The farm also cultivated 37 tonnes and 9 tonnes of Vidal and Riesling grapes, respectively, on about 10 acres of land. These grapes were sold exclusively for the production of ice wine.

The table-wine grape yield per acre had fallen from 3.0 tonnes in 2008 to 2.5 tonnes in 2010, which to some degree resulted from cyclical weather patterns that affect grape yields and quality. Viniculture experts believed that the farm could potentially yield up to 4.5 tonnes of grapes per acre for table wine. However, such yields could reduce quality further and limit the grapes to production of large-volume, mediocre wines.

Grapes used for table-wine production can produce about 750 litres of juice per tonne of grapes, while grapes used for ice wine can produce only 200 litres. This reflects the grapes' late harvest in November, a time when temperatures reach minus 8 degrees Centigrade: the grapes are both harvested and processed while frozen, therefore yielding considerably less juice.

In 2010, the average price this vineyard received for table-wine grapes was $1890 per tonne, and for ice-wine grapes $780 per tonne. The vineyard's realized price in 2008 for table-wine grapes was in excess of $1900 per tonne. Due to quality issues and the fact that the farm hadn't established proper relationships and contracts with local wineries, prices received for its grapes were estimated to be 30 to 40% below the market average. The full cost of the operation—comprising virtually all fixed costs—was about $300 000 annually. The farm had made a profit in only one of the previous four years.

Although modern cultivating practices could improve yields while maintaining an acceptable level of quality, Anthony still had his heart set on ice-wine production. However, incurring the capital cost to construct facilities for ice wine would be expensive—and risky, too, given his lack of experience in both the local wine sector and the export market. So Anthony looked to outsource production, and discovered that there were wine producers in the area with sufficient surplus production capacity to produce wine on his behalf. Some of these producers were currently exporting both ice and table wine to the Chinese market. The costs of converting grapes to ice wine would include about $200 per tonne of grapes for pressing into juice. Then the costs of preparing the juice, bottling, and storage would be about $6.25 per litre of wine (with bottling and storage costs alone at about $5.50 per litre).

THE CHINESE WINE MARKET

As he considered whether to become a wine producer, Anthony undertook some research into the wine market in China. In 2010 this emerging nation of 1.34 billion people had a per capita income of $7400 (on a purchasing power–parity basis) compared with its 2008 per capita income of $6200. About 10% of the population earned more than the national average, and average Chinese incomes were projected to double between 2010 and 2014.

An estimated 8% of the total population was able to afford wine, and market studies had suggested that 60% of wine drinkers in China prefer imported wine over domestically produced products. Wine drinkers in China were particularly sensitive to pricing, though, and wine costing more than $12 per 750-millilitre bottle was perceived as expensive. However, younger consumers and businesspeople were more open to trying a variety of wines. As well, consumers would pay at least three times more for a 200-millilitre bottle of ice wine. In fact, some ice-wine products in China sold for as much as $100 per bottle.

The dollar value of China's wine market was estimated at $3.8 billion. About 90% of wine consumed was locally made (with five companies accounting for about half of all domestic production), while the remaining 10% was imported. Of the latter, about 72% was bottled, with the remainder brought in as bulk and sold to bottlers, which then distributed the wine under their own label. Of the total imports, France was the leader with 46%, followed by Australia with 20%, Italy with 8%, the United States with 5%, Chile with 5%, and Spain with 4%.

In 2009 Canada exported $6.2 million worth of wine to China, an increase of 25% over 2008 exports. Ice wine accounted for 52% of these exports, standard table wine 32%, and sparkling wine 14%. Canada's other significant ice-wine export markets included South Korea, $2.5 million; United States, $1.2 million; Singapore, $1 million; and Japan, $500 000.

Bottled ice wine from Canada carried the Vintner's Quality Alliance (VQA) symbol, which is designed to maintain integrity of the wine produced by ensuring that its origin is accurate and reliable. The VQA symbol, contrary to popular belief, doesn't represent a superior quality product; nevertheless, it's had some effect in creating a brand image for Ontario wines. Under VQA terms, ice wine imported in bulk isn't considered ice wine, but rather a "late harvest" wine. In any case, consumers in China have tended to purchase wine primarily on the basis of price.

Tariffs on wine imported into China ranged from 10 to 30%. Bottled wine was subject to about a 12 to 14% tariff, while wine in bulk faced tariffs of about 20%. Including the 10% consumption tax and the 17% value-added tax, the overall tariffs on imported wine were 48% for bottled wine and 56% for wine in bulk. There were no quotas in place.

Entry into the Chinese ice-wine market was undertaken through either joint venture or direct exporting. One Canadian firm entered into a joint venture with Changyu Winery for the production of ice wine within China. (Changyu accounts for 20% of total domestic wine production there.) The joint venture was said to be producing 600 000 litres of ice wine—believed to be 50% higher than total Canadian production. In other cases, producers have partnered or sold bulk wine to bottlers in China, which then handle all distribution and marketing of the final product.

The preferred means of entering the market was through a distributor or wholesaler. Most Canadian companies used distributors, and sold their products F.O.B the West Coast. That is, they paid for freight to the port of exit, Vancouver, and the Chinese importer was responsible for freight and insurance beyond that point. Distributors guaranteed market reach and coverage across various regions, but finding a reputable distributor was difficult, since they didn't generally place importance on contracts. Product quality was also unimportant to these distributors; for them, pricing was the key issue—and with no standard prices or markups, they tended to be very aggressive in negotiating deals. While most restricted the distribution of their product to defined regions, many would sell indiscriminately across the country. As one observer commented, the wine market in China was like the "wild west." Many distributors would sell anything they could, wherever they could; they refused to focus on specific geographic markets or customer segments.

Ice-wine producers also distributed directly to large retailers or wholesalers, since in this way they were better able to directly target the final consumer. Supermarkets in China used various promotional strategies for wine products, including tasting events and pricing specials. Licences weren't required to sell wine in China.

Entering the Chinese market held many challenges, one of the main ones being protection of intellectual property. Although government officials were working to help protect patents and avert counterfeiting, there continued to be many incidents of intellectual property theft. For example, one Canadian ice-wine producer had its trademark and label stolen for use in Chinese-produced wine, even though the company hadn't yet sold ice wine into the Chinese market. The company had to spend $60 000 in legal fees in an attempt to protect its trademark before entering the market. Moreover, many producers or bottlers import bulk wine, blend or dilute it, and then resell it as a full-fledged "ice wine" product. In the most egregious instances, Chinese distributors would take ordinary red table wine and add sugar, then label and sell the product as ice wine. Some even included a red maple leaf, suggesting it was a Canadian product.

In response to such issues with the quality and branding of ice wines produced in China, the Chinese government had adjusted import regulations and was making an effort to better define what constitutes "ice wine." New standards were being implemented for the wholesaling and retailing of ice wines, and there were now hygiene standards for distilled wine.

ANTHONY'S DILEMMA

Anthony considered all the facts and issues. Cultivating grapes for sale to existing wineries was the simplest option, yet in recent years the market had faced a surplus of grapes, which was expected to continue in the foreseeable future. This, obviously, would adversely affect grape prices. Maybe moving downstream into actual wine production for the fast-growing Chinese market made more sense: after all, it would offer more value added and a better return on his investment. The question of whether he'd simply produce in bulk or ship bottled product to China depended on more than simply the margins he could obtain. Bottled product would offer higher margins—but could he effectively position and brand his product in a market that seemed to be driven more by price than quality considerations?

The other issue was which distribution channels could offer the best option for market entry while ensuring sufficient margins, given the various risks he would encounter. And, in the back of his mind, Anthony wondered how he should price his product so that he'd gain value—while still ensuring margins in what appeared to be a highly competitive and unstructured market. Anthony now felt it was best to review his options, analyze their financial feasibility, and make his decision based on a careful assessment of the potential risks.

The Investment Proposal

Kenneth Harling

In early January of 2013, Manuel Pena, a venture capitalist, was attending a presentation conducted by two brothers—Dr. Adya Bharat and Dr. Sidhu Bharat—in New York City. Manuel had been invited to the meeting by Sydney Smithers, a friend of his who knew he'd been actively looking for small businesses in which to invest. Sydney, a fellow Canadian, owned two businesses: one was a nursing home and the other, Durable Medical Equipment (DME), sold medical supplies for elderly people, including such items as walkers, canes, and special toilet seats. Sydney and the Bharat brothers were hoping Manuel would agree to invest $100 000 in their business proposition.

Sydney had gotten to know Adya while they were graduate students together at a major Canadian university. Adya had earned a Ph.D. in neuroscience there, and when he subsequently obtained work with a company that developed artificial human organs, he moved to New York, where its research facility was located. He was later joined there by his brother, Sidhu, who'd recently completed a Ph.D. in aeronautical engineering and had gotten a job building mathematical models for a big drug company in the city. His models amalgamated statistics on patient responses to a range of drugs so that doctors could better achieve their clinical intent when prescribing medication.

All three had since come together with the idea of providing an integrated medical service. Their original plan had been to target the U.S. market; given that the United States lacked public health insurance, the business would help individuals determine what medical treatment they could afford. Providing the service required first compiling medical records and personal financial information electronically; an adviser would then use this information to recommend a course of treatment. However, after spending $135 000 developing the programming, the three had concluded that their idea would be too difficult to implement in the United States—government regulations and legal issues there had proved too challenging. So they turned to their birthplace, India, in search of opportunity. The Bharat brothers had since established their business in the city of Pune.

THE PROPOSAL

"This is a great time to expand in India," Sidhu said. There's no such service there, since 75% of health care is private pay. And Pune is the best city to do it in. Plus, by being first with our service, we'll be better able to establish our reputation. Any competition that may come along afterward will simply help sell our service to customers."

"Pune is known as the Oxford of the East because of its educational institutions," Adya put in. "But it also has well established manufacturing industries. We grew up there, but since then it's changed completely. It's grown tremendously as more people have moved to the city to work with companies that have set up operations in information technology and automotive manufacturing. Pune's population is now 9.6 million, and it has the highest per capita income of any city in India—50% higher than India's average income.

"The need for our service stems from the increasing mobility of Indian society," Adya continued. "Young people used to live with their parents and support them. Now they're moving to Pune and other cities for high-paying jobs that have them working 12 hours a day. Since they're no longer living with their parents, the parents have had to become more self-reliant.

"We realized the need for this service because of our own parents' situation. Our father is 80 and has diabetes, and our mother is 76 and has cardiovascular problems. We were paying an agency a monthly fee to send a nurse around once a week, but we got worried when we'd talk to them. They seemed to be becoming ever more depressed. I went home and discovered that we weren't getting the medical care we thought we were paying for—the so-called nurse was just doing housekeeping. This is a common problem in India: you don't get what you think you're paying for.

"Six months ago I started our business in Pune, and began by serving our parents. I hired a registered nurse who visits our parents once a week—she takes them for walks, talks to them, and provides therapy. She also takes them to see their respective doctors every month."

"I used to dread talking to my parents," Sidhu added. "They seemed really unhappy. But now when we talk to them we can tell they're in good spirits, and we know their medical needs are being met."

"When I saw other people in Pune with circumstances similar to ours," Adya resumed, "I knew our business had potential. So I went out and hired a manager, who used to work for a not-for-profit organization that helped young girls escape from prostitution. He's now sold our service to four other families. We're charging $200 per month for it—and given that Pune's average per capita income is $2400 per month, this isn't expensive. Plus, we're in the process of getting government certification, which will guarantee to potential customers the quality of care the company provides. Unfortunately, government services move slowly in India, so getting the certification is taking much longer than we expected."

"Nonetheless," said Sidhu, "our service is meeting with great success. Just the other day our manager told us that one of our customers came in to pay ahead of time because he was so pleased with what we were providing his parents."

Sydney, who'd so far been silent, now spoke up with obvious excitement. "And the great thing is that people will need DME. Right now there's so little awareness of what's available to help patients. We should be able to sell lots of equipment once people become aware of what we can offer. To grow this business in India, we're looking for a total of $300 000 from three interested investors. Do you have any questions?"

THE DECISION

Manuel reflected on what he'd heard. As the presenters spoke, he'd noted various issues. Now he had the opportunity to ask for clarification and further information before he committed to making a decision. He knew, though, that the three men expected a firm answer.